Lecture Notes of the Institute for Computer Sciences, Social Informatics and Telecommunications Engineering 130

T0235647

Gérard Memmi   Ulf Blanke (Eds.)

Mobile Computing, Applications, and Services

5th International Conference, MobiCASE 2013
Paris, France, November 7-8, 2013
Revised Selected Papers

 Springer

Volume Editors

Gérard Memmi
Télécom ParisTech
LTCI, UMR CNRS 5141, Paris, France
E-mail: gerard.memmi@telecom-paristech.fr

Ulf Blanke
ETH Zürich, Zürich, Switzerland
E-mail: blankeu@ethz.ch

ISSN 1867-8211   e-ISSN 1867-822X
ISBN 978-3-319-05451-3   e-ISBN 978-3-319-05452-0
DOI 10.1007/978-3-319-05452-0

Springer Cham Heidelberg New York Dordrecht London

Library of Congress Control Number: 2014933280

Typesetting: Camera-ready by author, data conversion by Scientific Publishing Services, Chennai, India

Printed on acid-free paper

Springer is part of Springer Science+Business Media (www.springer.com)

Preface

This volume contains the papers presented at the 5th International Conference on Mobile Computing, Applications, and Services (MobiCASE), which was held November 7–8, 2013, in Paris, France. MobiCASE brought together leading researchers, developers, and professionals in the field of mobile technologies. The conference was sponsored by ICST and technically co-sponsored by the IEEE Computer Society and Create-Net in association with the European Alliance for Innovation (EAI). MobiCASE was also sponsored by Inria, Institut Mines-Telecom, and CEA-List.

The aim of the MobiCASE conferences is to provide a platform for researchers from academia and industry to advance mobile application and services research, an exciting area that has attracted significant attention from the community in recent years. The first MobiCASE conference, MobiCASE 2009, was held in San Diego, during October 26–29, 2009; the second, MobiCASE 2010, was held in Santa Clara, during October 25–28, 2010; the third, MobiCASE 2011, was held in Los Angeles, during October 24–27, 2011; the fourth, MobiCASE 2012 was held in Seattle, during October 11–12, 2012.

This year MobiCASE 2013 debuted for the first time in Europe and attracted innovators from around the world to share the latest knowledge on mobile applications and services research.

The conference received a total of 64 submissions and the Program Committee selected 13 long papers and five short papers for oral presentation at the conference, following a highly selective review process. An additional nine papers were accepted for poster presentation.

In addition to the mobiCASE main track, a workshop on "Near Field Communication for Mobile Applications" was organized by Pascal Urien and brought together experts to discuss next-generation applications based on NFC. Another highlight of the conference was the industry track. This year, the industry track focused on mobile development for the automotive industry and delivered insights into trends in mobile communication for cars with an invited talk from Otmar Schreiner from Continental.

In addition to the regular papers included in this volume, the conference featured two keynote speeches by Dominique Hazael-Massieux (W3C) with the title "The Web: On Mobile and Beyond" and Tony Wasserman from Carnegie Mellon University-Silicon Valley on "Mobile Application Development and the End of High-Ceremony Processes."

I would like to sincerely thank the members of the Program Committee and the external reviewers for their hard work in reviewing the submissions. Furthermore, I would like to thank Gerard Memmi (general chair) for his support in ramping up a great edition of MobiCASE in 2013 and his tireless efforts in managing all of the local arrangements required for a successful meeting.

We were honored to be part of this year's MobiCASE and look forward to the continued success of the conference in coming years.

December 2013   Ulf Blanke

Organization

Steering Committee

Martin Griss Carnegie Mellon Silicon Valley, USA
Thomas Phan Samsung R&D
Petros Zerfos IBM Research

General Chair

Gerard Memmi Télécom ParisTech, France

Technical Program Chair

Ulf Blanke ETH Zürich, Switzerland

Workshop Chair

Pascal Urien Télécom ParisTech, France

Industry Track Chairs

Bernard Odier Inria, France
Christian Martin Institut Mines-Télécom Silicon Valley

Poster and Demo Chair

Rémi Sharrock Télécom ParisTech, France

Sponsorship Chair

Karine Gosse CEA LIST

Publicity Chair

Rémi Sharrock Télécom ParisTech, France

Web Chair

Marko Borazio   TU Darmstadt, Germany

Local Arrangement Chairs

Christian Martin   Institut Mines-Télécom Silicon Valley
Erika Polini   European Alliance for Innovation

Technical Program Committee

Sasan Adibi   Royal Melbourne Institute of Technology,
                                   Australia
Michael Beigl   Teco, KIT
Oliver Brdiczka   Palo Alto Research Center (PARC), USA
Licia Capra   University College London, UK
Ralf Carbon   Fraunhofer IESE, Germany
Kate Farrahi   Johannes Kepler Universität Linz, Austria
Hassan Ghasemzadeh   UCLA, USA
Jaap Ham   University of Eidhoven, The Netherlands
Amaç Herdağdelen   Facebook Research
Steffen Hess   Fraunhofer IESE, Germany
Paul Holleis   DoComo Euro Labs
Jennifer L. Wong   Stony Brook University, USA
Karin Hummel   ETH Zürich, Switzerland
Tâm Huynh   Deutsche Telekom, Germany
Sibren Isaacman   Loyola University Maryland, USA
Valérie Issarny   Inria, France
Fahim Kawsar   Bell Laboratories
Holger Kenn   Microsoft Research ATL Europe
Andrew Kun   University of New Hampshire, USA
Kai Kunze   Osaka Prefecture University, Japan
Nic Lane   Microsoft Research Asia
Paul Lukowicz   DFKI, Bonn
Kazuya Murao   Kobe University, Japan
Jean-Baptiste Prost   PoleStar
Helena Rodrigues   Universidade do Minho, Portugal
Junehwa Song   KAIST, South Korea
Samuel Tardieu   Télécom ParisTech, France
Kristof Van Laerhoven   TU Darmstadt, Germany
Pablo Vidales   Grupo National Provincial
Djamal Zeghlache   Télécom SudParis, France

External Reviewers

Moustafa Alzantot	Egypt-Japan University for Science and Technology
Oliver Amft	TU Eindhoven - ActLab, The Netherlands
Daniel Ashbrook	Nokia Research
Stephane Beauregard	Qualcomm
Eugen Berlin	TU Darmstadt, Germany
Nadia Berthouze	University College London, UK
Marko Borazio	TU Darmstadt, Germany
Kai Breiner	Fraunhofer IESE, Germany
Duncan Brumby	University College London, UK
Xiang Cao	University of Toronto, Canada
Burcu Cinaz	ETH-Zürich, Switzerland
Gianni Di Caro	The Swiss AI Lab IDSIA
Trinh Minh Tri	Do Idiap
Nicolas Etienne	PoleStar
Friederike Eyssel	University of Bielefeld, Germany
David Fernandez	PoleStar
Victor Fonte	University of Minho, Portugal
Baptiste Godefroy	PoleStar
Dawud Gordon	Karlsruhe University, Germany
Yves Guiard	Télécom ParisTech, France
Anne Hess	Fraunhofer IESE, Germany
Gerold Hoelzl	Johannes Kepler University Linz, Austria
Theus Hossmann	ETH-Zürich, Switzerland
Wijnand Ijsselstein	TU Eindhoven, The Netherlands
Rui Jose	University of Minho, Portugal
Katsuhiko Kaji	Nagoya University, Japan
Borje Karlsson	Microsoft Research
Takuya Katayama	Kobe University, Japan
Andreas Lachenmann	Microsoft Research
Sunghoon Ivan Lee	UCLA, USA
Andreas Maier	Fraunhofer IESE, Germany
Afra Mashhadi	Alcatel-Lucent
Sinziana Mazilu	ETH-Zürich, Switzerland
Florian Michahelles	ETH-Zürich, Switzerland
Darakhshan Mir	Rutgers University, USA
Bobak Mortazavi	UCLA, USA
Syed Agha Muhammad	TU Darmstadt, Germany
Matthias Naab	Fraunhofer IESE, Germany
Long Nguyen	Polestar
Megan Olsen	Loyola University, USA
Eunjeong Park	UCLA, USA
Mashfiqui Rabbi	Cornell University, USA

Carlos Ribeiro	Tecnico Lisbon, Portugal
Till Riedel	Karlsruhe University, Germany
Norman Riegel	Fraunhofer IESE, Germany
Privender Saini	Philips
Johannes Schöning	Hasselt University, Belgium
Julian Schütte	Fraunhofer AISEC, Germany
Hans-Peter Schwefel	The Telecommunications Research Center Vienna FTW, Austria
Ahmed Serhrouchni	Télécom ParisTech, France
Harsimrat Singh	University College London, UK
Ivan Tashev	Microsoft Research
Tim Tijs	Philips
Marcus Trapp	Fraunhofer IESE, Germany
Danilo Valerio	The Telecommunications Research Center Vienna FTW, Austria
Hans Weda	Philips
Wenyao Xu	University at Buffalo, USA

Workshop Committee

Damien Sauveron	Limoges University, France
Didier Donsez	Grenoble University, France
Joachim Posegga	Passau University, Germany
Lu HongQian Karen	Gemalto, Austin, USA
Marc Pasquet	GREYC laboratory, Caen University, France
Maryline Laurent	Télécom SudParis, France
Mohammed Achemlal	Orange Labs, Caen, France
Peter Honeyman	University of Michigan, USA
Samia Bouzefrane	CNAM, Paris, France
Serge Chaumette	LaBRI, Bordeaux Unversity, France
Selwyn Piramuthu	University of Florida, USA

Table of Contents

Papers

Lowering the Barrier for Crowdsensing Application Development 1
  Scott Heggen, Amul Adagale, and Jamie Payton

Towards User Interface Components for Dashboard Applications
on Smartphones 19
  Marcus Homann, Vassilena Banova, Paul Oelbermann,
  Holger Wittges, and Helmut Krcmar

User-Centric Quality of Experience Measurement 33
  Bachir Chihani, Khalil ur Rehman Laghari, Emmanuel Bertin,
  Denis Collange, Noël Crespi, and Tiago H. Falk

Online Reviews as First Class Artifacts in Mobile App Development 47
  Claudia Iacob, Rachel Harrison, and Shamal Faily

SaSYS: A Swipe Gesture-Based System for Exploring Urban
Environments for the Visually Impaired 54
  Jee-Eun Kim, Masahiro Bessho, Noboru Koshizuka, and
  Ken Sakamura

Smartphone Interactions Change for Different Intimacy Contexts 72
  Mattia Gustarini and Katarzyna Wac

Geometric Layout Analysis in a Wearable Reading Device for the Blind
and Visually Impaired 90
  Roman Guilbourd and Raul Rojas

Ring GINA: A Wearable Computer Interaction Device 98
  Joseph Greenspun and Kristofer S.J. Pister

Intelligent Energy-Efficient Triggering of Geolocation Fix Acquisitions
Based on Transitions between Activity Recognition States 104
  Thomas Phan

Fine-Grained Activity Recognition of Pedestrians Travelling
by Subway 122
  Marco Maier and Florian Dorfmeister

Reconciling Cloud and Mobile Computing Using Activity-Based
Predictive Caching 140
  Dawud Gordon, Sven Frauen, and Michael Beigl

Towards Smartphone-Based Assessment of Burnout 158
  Christiana Tsiourti and Katarzyna Wac

An Improvement of NFC-SEC with Signed Exchanges
for an e-Prescription-Based Application 166
  Mohamad Hamze, Fabrice Peyrard, and Emmanuel Conchon

KeySens: Passive User Authentication through Micro-behavior
Modeling of Soft Keyboard Interaction 184
  Benjamin Draffin, Jiang Zhu, and Joy Zhang

A Study of Graphical Password for Mobile Devices 202
  Xiaoyuan Suo

A Cloudlet-Based Proximal Discovery Service for Machine-to-Machine
Applications... 215
  Jonas Michel and Christine Julien

LOX Framework: Designing Human Computation Games to Update
Street Views 233
  Jongin Lee, John Kim, and Kwan Hong Lee

Chill-Out: Relaxation Training through Respiratory Biofeedback
in a Mobile Casual Game 252
  Avinash Parnandi, Beena Ahmed, Eva Shipp, and
  Ricardo Gutierrez-Osuna

Posters

Using Low-Power Sensors to Enhance Interaction on Wristwatches
and Bracelets... 261
  Simon T. Perrault and Eric Lecolinet

Towards Unsupervised Remote Therapy for Individuals with Aphasia ... 265
  Conor Higgins, Áine Kearns, Conor Ryan, Mikael Fernstrom, and
  Sue Franklin

Empowering Mobile Users: Create Your Own Mobile Application
for Data Collection in the Cloud 269
  Arlindo F. da Conceição, Jimmy V. Sánchez,
  Alvaro H. Mamani-Aliaga, Bruno G. dos Santos,
  Matheus F. Mendonça, Dario Vieira, and Vladimir Rocha

Design and Evaluation of a Medication Application for People
with Parkinson's Disease.. 273
  Ana Correia de Barros, João Cevada, Àngels Bayés,
  Sheila Alcaine, and Berta Mestre

A Mobile Environmental Air Quality Information System as a Support
for m-Health 277
  Elena Mitreska, Danco Davcev, and Kosta Mitreski

A Privacy-Preserving Contactless Transport Service for NFC
Smartphones 282
  Ghada Arfaoui, Sébastien Gambs, Patrick Lacharme,
  Jean-Francois Lalande, Roch Lescuyer, and
  Jean-Claude Paillès

iOS Application for Guiding Visually Impaired People at the University
of Alicante 286
  Alejandro Zaragoza, Javier Ortiz, Juan José Galiana-Merino, and
  Irene Sentana

Phone Call Translator System in Real-Time 290
  Yoko Iimura, Yu Kojo, Masahiro Oota, and Shinya Tachimoto

An Approach for Using Mobile Devices in Industrial Safety-Critical
Embedded Systems.. 294
  Ashraf Armoush, Dominik Franke, Igor Kalkov, and
  Stefan Kowalewski

NFC Workshop

Debugging and Rapid Prototyping of NFC Secure Element
Applications... 298
  Michael Roland

Enhancing the Restaurant Dining Experience with an NFC-Enabled
Mobile User Interface.. 314
  Diego Argueta, Yu-Ta Lu, Jing Ma, Diego Rodriguez,
  Yuan-Hung Yang, Thomas Phan, and Won Jeon

Securing NFC Mobile Services with Cloud of Secure
Elements (CoSE) 322
  Pascal Urien and Selwyn Piramuthu

Author Index 333

Best Paper

Reconciling Cloud and Mobile Computing Using Activity-Based Predictive Caching

Gordon, Dawud Dawud.Gordon@kit.edu
Frauen, Sven Frauen@teco.edu
Beigl, Michael Michael.Beigl@kit.edu
Karlsruhe Institute of Technology (KIT), Karlsruhe, Germany

Best Paper Nominees

Intelligent Energy-Efficient Triggering of Geolocation Fix Acquisitions Based on Transitions Between Activity Recognition States

Phan, Thomas thomas.phan@samsung.com
Samsung Research America - Silicon Valley

Fine-Grained Activity Recognition of Pedestrians Travelling by Subway

Marco Maier marco.maier@ifi.lmu.de
Florian Dorfmeister florian.dorfmeister@ifi.lmu.de
Mobile and Distributed Systems Group
Ludwig-Maximilians-University Munich

Lowering the Barrier for Crowdsensing Application Development

Heggen, Scott sheggen@uncc.edu
Adagale, Amul aadagale@uncc.edu
Payton, Jamie payton@uncc.edu
Department of Computer Science
The University of North Carolina at Charlotte

Lowering the Barrier for Crowdsensing Application Development

Scott Heggen, Amul Adagale, and Jamie Payton

Department of Computer Science
The University of North Carolina at Charlotte
{sheggen,aadagale,payton}@uncc.edu

Abstract. Crowdsensing has the potential to support human-driven sensing and data collection at an unprecedented scale. While many organizers of data collection campaigns may have extensive domain knowledge, they do not necessarily have the skills required to develop robust software for crowdsensing. In this paper, we present Mobile Campaign Designer, a tool that simplifies the creation of mobile crowdsensing applications. Using Mobile Campaign Designer, an organizer is able to define parameters about their crowdsensing campaign, and the tool generates the source code and an executable for a tailored mobile application that embodies the current best practices in crowdsensing. An evaluation of the tool shows that users at all levels of technical expertise are capable of creating a crowdsensing application in an average of five minutes, and the generated applications are comparable in quality to existing crowdsensing applications.

Keywords: crowdsensing, participatory sensing, mobile phone sensing, end-user programming.

1   Introduction

Crowdsensing provides an opportunity for a fundamental shift in the way governments, organizations, research institutions, communities, and individuals gather data to make decisions. In this emerging class of software systems, participants use the sensors (e.g., cameras, GPS, accelerometers) and input capabilities of their smartphones to collect digital samples of the surrounding world for a data collection campaign, typically organized to address a scientific question or civic issue. Such an approach can supplement data from special-purpose sensors, or even replace their use, providing data from a fine-grained, human perspective and potentially reducing the costs of large-scale data collection efforts.

Crowdsensing is driven by volunteers who use the sensors embedded in their smartphones to collect data. Crowdsensing applications have been developed for a variety of domains, including environmental monitoring [21,25,18], wildlife and habitat monitoring [4,20,29], health and well-being [33,6,15], social networking [22], road traffic monitoring [37], and fuel-efficient driving [7]. Given the

G. Memmi and U. Blanke (Eds.): MobiCASE 2013, LNICST 130, pp. 1–18, 2014.

success of these initial deployments and the commercial success of crowdsourcing (e.g., [2]), it is reasonable to expect a significant increase in demand for
crowdsensing systems.

Campaign organizers (i.e., individuals interested in distributing a crowdsensing application as a data collection tool) may include scientists, community organizers, interested citizens, and hobbyists. Given the diverse nature of potential
campaign organizers' perspectives and areas of expertise, it is likely that most
will lack the skills or resources to develop such systems. Our goal is to empower
campaign organizers, with limited or no software development experience, to
create their own crowdsensing applications.

To this end, we present Mobile Campaign Designer (MC Designer), an end-
user programming tool for creating and managing crowdsensing campaigns. MC
Designer provides a simple interface for campaign organizers to define characteristics of their crowdsensing campaign and generates a tailored mobile application.
This generated mobile application is capable of collecting and submitting data
using sensors commonly embedded in smartphones. To demonstrate that MC
Designer makes crowdsensing application development more accessible, we conduct a small user study. First, we evaluate the user's ability to use MC Designer
to create a crowdsensing application for a given scenario. Second, users compare
an existing crowdsensing application to one created using MC Designer. Our
results indicate that users can quickly and easily create applications with MC
Designer that are comparable in quality to existing crowdsensing applications.

2   Related Work

Crowdsensing stems from public participation in scientific research, or citizen science, in which volunteers collect data for a scientific purpose. Citizen science's
long history began with the National Audubon Society's annual Christmas Bird
Count (CBC) [27], an extremely successful data collection campaign that highlights the potential for citizen science. Over 63,000 volunteers submitted almost
65 million observations in the most recent CBC [19]. The results of the society's
112 years of citizen science has been used in 300 publications.

Crowdsensing extends citizen science by incorporating mobile phones, providing volunteers with sensors for sampling data. Crowdsensing has shown promise
for studying urban environments [25,6,7,34,24], social interaction [22,8], health
and wellness [33,12], education [9,11], and biology [4,20,28]. In order for crowdsensing to become widely available, however, mobile application development
needs to be simplified for non-technical campaign organizers. Many campaign
organizers will have domain expertise but lack the skills to create an industrial-
grade mobile application to support data collection, and may often lack the
resources to contract a professional software developer.

Some tools exist that aim to simplify application development, such as GUI-
based and end-user programming systems for mobile operating systems. For
example, MIT's App Inventor [23] provides simple GUI-based interactions for
creating mobile applications for the Google Android mobile operating system.

Microsoft's TouchDevelop [38] takes end-user programming one step further by putting the development environment on the mobile phone. However, both require a basic understanding of programming concepts and syntax to build any application. Also, both systems are general-purpose application-creation tools. Crowdsensing does not require most of these features (such as sprites for gaming), which distract from the goals of campaign organizers.

Close in spirit to our work are approaches specific to crowdsensing that attempt to eliminate the need for programming skills to create data collection campaigns. For example, Project Noah [29] is a tool for creating "missions" in which users can contribute images of wildlife. Campaign organizers register a mission on the website, and users simply upload their images from any camera via Project Noah's website. Similarly, Epicollect [1] allows the creation of campaigns specific to epidemiology and ecology. Participants collect data using the Epicollect mobile application, which provides an interface for collecting camera, GPS, and text-based data. While both Project Noah and Epicollect eliminate the need for developer skills, these systems are specific to their respective domains and do not provide general support for crowdsensing. Sensr [17] provides more generalized support by providing campaign organizers with a web interface for creating a campaign, which users then access via the Sensr mobile application. However, Sensr is limited to camera data and text-entry input. All three of these tools fail to provide access to many desirable sensors, including the accelerometer, camcorder, and microphone.

More sophisticated crowdsensing campaign creation tools have been explored as well, such as Campaignr [14], Medusa [30], PRISM [5], Code-in-the-Air (CITA) [31], and the Open Data Kit (ODK) [10]. Each of these provide high-configurability of campaigns by the end user, remove the user from the technical challenges of accessing phone sensors, and are robust to changes in the campaign. However, they still require some programming knowledge, including knowledge about the format and ordering of a document, correct use of the programming language's syntax, or infrastructure knowledge. In many cases, this may still present too large of a barrier for users. MC Designer was specifically designed to lower the barrier for the campaign organizer by providing an easy-to-use graphical user interface that allows users to create a mobile application simply by supplying relevant crowdsensing campaign parameters; MC Designer handles all configuration tasks based on the campaign organizer's description of the campaign. Furthermore, many of these systems require participants to use a single mobile application for all campaigns. MC Designer generates a stand-alone mobile application tailored specifically for each campaign. Lastly, MC Designer runs on mobile phones, allowing campaign organizers to quickly build campaigns from their smartphones in situ.

3   The MC Designer System Architecture

Our goal is to support the widespread adoption of crowdsensing by providing a tool that allows users to easily create a crowdsensing application. In this section, we describe the desired features that motivate our design choices. We then present the system architecture of MC Designer.

3.1   MC Designer Features and Design Motivation

MC Designer has two primary stakeholders: the campaign organizer and the campaign participant. The campaign organizer's goals are two-fold: gather data reported by participants using their mobile device and analyze the data to draw meaningful conclusions. The campaign participants' goals are to use their mobile device to contribute data to the campaign.

To meet these goals, MC Designer provides the campaign organizer with a mobile tool for defining all the parameters of a crowdsensing campaign, which are then used to generate a tailored mobile application serving the specific purposes of the campaign. Second, a campaign organizer needs participants to collect data; MC Designer addresses recruitment by providing the campaign organizer with a means to invite known parties or to recruit participants from a pool of identified participants through a *profile matching* system. The profile matching system allows interested volunteers to provide a profile that describes their interests and personal characteristics. These profiles are matched to new campaigns, and prospective participants are invited to join via email. Currently, the profile matching system allows users to be invited to campaigns based on an age range, gender, ethnicity, and geographic location. Future work will incorporate more sophisticated profile matching systems that evaluate potential partipants' trustworthiness based on their previous contributions, like those introduced in [32,13]. Once the crowdsensing application has been generated and potential participants have been recruited, the application is distributed to potential participants, who can use the app to collect and submit data samples.

Lastly, the campaign organizer must be able to access the collected data. The campaign organizer has two options: explore the data through a web interface dedicated to their campaign, or download the entire data set for offline analysis. Access to either option is available through the web interface on the MC Designer website.

Taking these goals and challenges into consideration, we designed MC Designer with five major subsystems:

1. **Mobile Campaign Manager:** interface for creating a crowdsensing campaign
2. **Application Server:** generates the tailored crowdsensing application
3. **Data Management Server:** receives data submissions from participants
4. **Web Interface:** interface for campaign organizers to access their data
5. **Campaign Application:** mobile application created by campaign organizer for collecting data

3.2   Mobile Campaign Manager

A campaign organizer uses the Mobile Campaign Manager (MCM) mobile client to define the parameters of their crowdsensing campaign. We chose to design

MCM as a mobile application for two reasons. First, mobile phones are quickly becoming the primary means of computing for many people thanks to their increased computing power, small form factor, and constant connectivity to the internet. Second, with this approach, the campaign organizer can create the mobile application in situ, instead of having to leave the field, facilitating on-the-fly campaign creation.

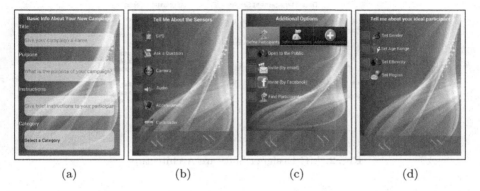

(a)　　　　　　　　(b)　　　　　　　　(c)　　　　　　　　(d)

Fig. 1. When defining a new campaign, the user configures relevant parameters in MCM: (a) basic information, (b), sensors, (c) participants, (d) profile matching for recruiting participants (optional), and additional options (optional, not shown). The user can review their campaign before submitting to the server.

Figure 1 shows the activities performed when creating a campaign. One of the most significant decisions the campaign organizer makes is the selection of sensors (Figure 1b). Because the energy consumption associated with a crowd-sensing app is a concern, MCM allows the campaign organizer to configure the sampling rate and other characteristics of data capture quality. Currently, MCM supports adjusting the polling frequency of the GPS receiver when selected by the campaign organizer. However, since the campaign applications are currently created for the Android OS, application-level adjustment of the sampling rate is limited for most of the other sensors. The Android OS optimizes the sampling rate of embedded sensors and allows programmers only to specify the polling rate of associated sensor listeners. In other words, Android only enables the sensor when a listener is registered to the sensor; the sensor operates at the frequency dictated by the OS, but only notifies a listener at the listener-specified polling frequency.

When the campaign organizer finishes defining their campaign, MCM generates an XML file that captures the campaign parameters and sends it to the application server, where it will be used to build a tailored application. MCM essentially acts as a centralized campaign management system; in addition to creating an app, the campaign organizer can install and launch existing campaign applications. Currently, MCM can be deployed on phones with Android OS 2.3.3 or newer.

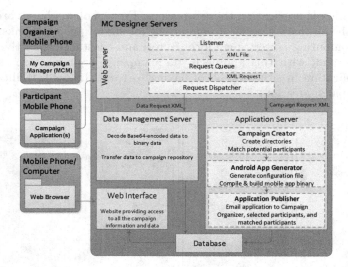

Fig. 2. MC Designer Software Architecture

3.3 The MC Designer Servers

The MC Designer server architecture is shown in Figure 2. First, all requests from MCM and the campaign applications are sent to a *web server* which responds to incoming HTTP requests. As processes become available, these XML requests are dispatched to either the application server or the data management server through the *request dispatcher*.

The Application Server. The application server is responsible for generating the source code and an executable for the crowdsensing application. The *campaign creator* parses the campaign request XML generated and sent from MCM, and creates a storage repository for the application source code and a directory for data submissions to the campaign. Next, a **constants** file is generated, which contains the configuration parameters that determine the user interface and resulting behaviors of the app, such as which sensors are available for use by the user. The constants file also stores important information about the campaign, such as identifiers for the campaign and the user, local storage directories, and HTTP parameters to connect to the server to submit data.

The source code and constants file are used by the *app generator* to build an application binary that can be installed on a mobile device. Each campaign application is given a unique package name, allowing multiple campaign applications to be installed on a single device. Should the campaign organizer want to make the application available via a mobile application market, the source code is made available to them. They are free to modify the code, sign the application, and place it in the market. After the application is created, the *application publisher* notifies the campaign organizer that her campaign is ready, and makes the campaign accessible through her instance of MCM. The application publisher also contacts all invited participants (directly through email or social networks, or via profile matching notifications) to give instructions for installing the application. Lastly, MC Designer organizes all information about campaigns and data submissions in a MySQL database.

The Data Management Server. Data submissions from campaign applications are also transferred to the server as an XML file packaged in an HTTP request. The data management server parses the request to determine the appropriate campaign and user information, decodes the data from the XML file, stores the data in the appropriate directory, and updates the database with the new submission. A campaign can use multiple sensors, and each piece of sensor data may have relationships with other sensor data (e.g., GPS data and an image, so the image can later be placed on a map). Each piece of sensor data is stored on the server as a separate file, but is tagged in the database with a session ID. The session ID is used to maintain the connection between data from a single data capture session so correlations between data points can be discovered during data analysis.

3.4 The Web Interface

MC Designer also consists of a website, which allows the campaign organizer to view and analyze data that has been submitted to the campaign. Each campaign has a web page that presents a campaign description, a link to download the campaign application, and summary information about the data collected (e.g., number of total submissions, coverage of a geographic area). The webpage also provides access to basic analysis tools, such as the ability to plot GPS points on a map and graph accelerometer data. Lastly, campaign organizers have the ability to download the entire data set.

3.5 The Campaign Application

Each time a campaign organizer defines and submits a campaign using MCM, a *campaign application* is created. The campaign application's primary purpose is to allow participants to collect data using the phone's sensors. The campaign organizer has six sensors (and their parameterized options) to chose from when defining their campaign: accelerometer, camcorder, camera, GPS, microphone, and text-entry. The application incorporates the correct combination of sensors and integrates their functionality to avoid conflicts (e.g., passing control of the microphone to a video capture session). Once the user has captured data, the campaign application allows the user to send these sensor readings to the server. To ensure a single interface between the campaign application and the server, all data is encoded into Base64, which converts any binary data into ASCII-based data. The encoded data is then added to an XML file. The use of XML is motivated by its widespread adoption and its ability to encode all data types in Base64, including potential future data types.

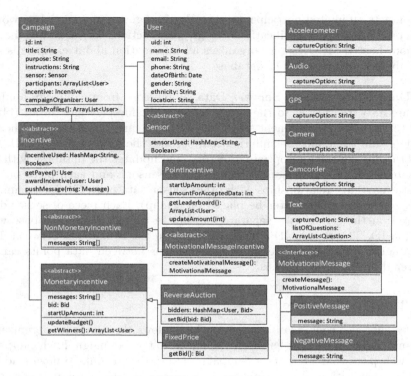

Fig. 3. MC Designer Class Diagram

3.6   Extending MC Designer

MC Designer incorporates many features for building crowdsensing apps and is extensible, with an API that provides hooks for incorporating emerging solutions in crowdsensing research. Figure 3 highlights some of the classes in MC Designer that contribute to this extensibility. For example, the `Sensor` abstract class and its concrete descendants provide access to the low-level physical sensors on the phone, and the `Sensor` class can be extended to provide MC Designer applications with access to higher-level sensors (e.g., utilizing sensor fusion). MC Designer also provides implementations of basic incentives (e.g., fixed price micropayments), and the `Incentive` class can be extended to incorporate more advanced mechanisms. MC Designer is open source and is available via an SVN repository (`https://subversion.assembla.com/svn/PSToolkit/`), allowing researchers to integrate their own implementations of crowdsourcing concepts into the tool.

4   Evaluating MC Designer

The motivation for creating MC Designer was to simplify development of crowdsensing applications. In our evaluation, then, we are concerned with 1) the ability of users with varying degrees of programming experience to develop crowdsensing applications with MC Designer, and 2) the expressiveness of MC Designer. We conduct a two-part user study, in which participants use MC Designer to create crowdsensing applications for a scenario and then evaluate the quality of the created applications as compared to existing implementations of custom-designed crowdsensing applications.

In part one of our study, users were provided with a mobile phone and asked to use MC Designer to create two mobile applications using scenario descriptions to guide their design. After creating the application with MC Designer, the study participant was asked to complete a survey to evaluate the application on two primary criteria: 1) is the application what you expected, and 2) based on your understanding of the scenario, does the application serve the purposes of the scenario?

Specifically, users in the study were presented with two scenarios describing a crowdsensing campaign:

> Scenario A: You are an astronomer interested in collecting data about meteor showers. Using your application, you would like to provide a method for users to provide textual input regarding the conditions during the meteor shower observation, such as sky conditions and visibility of stars (the camera and camcorder are not expected to be used to capture this data). You would also like to let the users record audio annotations as they are observing meteors. Lastly, users need to be able to input the number of times a meteor is spotted.

> Scenario B: You are a physical therapist, and you are constantly concerned about the conditions in which you use your bicycle every day. As such, you would like to build an app that allows users to capture data about their surroundings while riding. You would like to know the exact route taken, as well as the amount of noise encountered and the roughness of the road. Additionally, you'd like users to be able to take pictures or videos of dangerous encounters or other obstacles to bicycling.

These scenario descriptions were derived from real-world existing crowdsensing applications with publicly available implementations. Scenario A describes the Meteor Counter application [26], which was built for NASA to allow users to count meteors during a meteor shower. Users can enter information about the sky conditions, the star visibility, as well as use the microphone to provide audio annotations about each meteor. Scenario B describes Biketastic [34], which uses the GPS to track location, the microphone to record noise, the accelerometer to measure the roughness of the road, and the camera and camcorder to provide information about obstacles and points of interest along the bike route. These applications were selected because they incorporated numerous sensors and they have robust implementations that are publicly available.

In part two of the user study, the native implementations of the applications for both scenarios (Meteor Counter and Biketastic) were given to the user. For each, the user was asked to compare the custom-built implementation to an application generated by the research team using MC Designer. The purpose in providing the user with an app created by the research team was to 1) reduce any bias by the user, since they are the "creator" of the application and may have formed a sense of pride or ownership of the application, 2) ensure the MC Designer-created application mimics the real application as closely as possible, and 3) ensure a consistent evaluation of a single MC Designer-generated application across all users.

A pre-survey was issued to gauge the user's understanding of technology and familiarity with crowdsensing. The user was surveyed after each scenario in part one of the study, to gauge their perception of the campaign creation process. After each scenario in part two, the user was surveyed again to capture their observations while comparing the real application to the one created by MC Designer. Lastly, the user was surveyed at the end of the study to gauge their understanding of the process they'd just completed and their overall perception of the MC Designer system. Throughout the user study, participants were audio-recorded and asked to "think out loud" as they performed the activities. These recordings were reviewed to gain a better understanding of the user's thought process and perceptions of the system while using MC Designer.

5   User Study Results

The user study included 19 participants ranging in age from 18 to 55; 26% were female, 74% were male; all participants were either faculty, staff, administrators, or students at the university. Participants were evaluated on their technical competency prior to the study with a focus on their mobile and smart phone usage, since these are the primary tools used by MC Designer.

All users indicated they owned a mobile phone and used it frequently (more than once a day), and 79% of the users indicated they owned a smartphone. The majority of these users (70%) owned an Android-based smartphone, which is the mobile OS used in our study. When asked to rate their comfort level with software in general, learning to use new software, and their comfort level using a touch screen on a mobile phone, users ranked their comfort levels quite high (8.21, 8.00, and 8.21 out of 10, respectively). Given these observations, it is reasonable to assume that users were not greatly influenced by an unfamiliarity with mobile technology.

Users were also asked to rank their ability to create software using traditional programming languages (e.g., Java, C++, Python) and development tools. Overall, the average rating was 4.42 on a 10-point scale. Four users rated their ability to create software at 1 (no competency), and two users rated 10 (highly competent). The remaining 13 users rated themselves between 3 and 8, with the majority rating a 3, indicating that most users had some basic programming skills but did not feel they were "expert" programmers. We also compared the results excluding the two users who rated 10, and no significant differences in the results were identified. The remainder of this section reports on all 19 users.

5.1   Part I: Creating Applications with MC Designer

Part one of the study was designed to evaluate the user's ability to create a mobile application using MC Designer. Users were given the two scenarios and were asked for each to create a mobile app that served the purposes of the scenario. After creating the application, users explored the campaign application and described how well the application met their expectations. Surveys were issued after each scenario to capture 1) the user's level of confidence in MC Designer's ability to create a campaign application, 2) the actual and perceived accuracy of the application, and 3) the amount of time it took the user to create the application.

Confidence in MC Designer. In scenario A (Meteor Counter), users were confident in MC Designer's ability to generate a mobile application, despite having never used the system before, as shown in Table 1. Aside from question 4, users rated the mobile application they created above average in each category. Users were very confident (4.16 out of 5) that their campaign application used the correct sensors, and the system handled the use of multiple sensors well (4.05 out of 5). However, users felt feedback was an issue with data submissions (2.89 out of 5). Users commented that "I wasn't sure if my data was uploaded or not. I just assumed it worked." To address this issue, feedback mechanisms for crowdsensing and methods for effectively visualizing the sensor data on mobile phones are being explored.

In scenario B (Biketastic), users expressed significantly more confidence in MC Designer's usage of the sensors, feedback provided about the data being collected, and the handling of multiple sensors (questions 2, 4, and 5 of Table 1, respectively). Most significantly, user confidence that MC Designer was creating an application that served the purposed they expected (question 6 of Table 1) increased dramatically, implying that users became more comfortable with crowdsensing requirements and were able to create the application with ease after just one interaction with the tool.

Accuracy of the Created Applications. In our study, we define an "accurate" implementation as one in which the user incorporates all of the required sensors, and only those sensors, and inserting the appropriate text-based questions to address data that cannot be captured with sensors in scenario A (Meteor Count). In scenario A, only 2 of 19 users were able to create a mobile app that was exactly as the scenario described. The user's mistakes were most likely due to misinterpretations of the scenario and not an inability to configure the campaign. For example, multiple users entered the wrong number of text questions. They were capable of adding the questions in MCM, but they simply did not add everything the scenario described. A number of users also felt GPS was important to the scenario, despite no indication that GPS was required for the scenario. One user simply added the sensors he felt were "cool", almost entirely ignoring the scenario. Despite the low accuracy, users did feel as though they were creating the correct application, as evident by the 11 of the 19 users rating

Table 1. Perceptions of the campaign-creation process (1=strongly disagree, 5=strongly agree)

The mobile application generated by MC Designer:	Scenario A		Scenario B		p-value
	μ	σ	μ	σ	
1. used the sensors that I felt were needed for the scenario.	4.16	1.21	4.58	0.90	0.23
2. used the sensors appropriately for the scenario.	4.00	1.00	4.63	0.60	0.02
3. was able to collect data that was appropriate for the scenario.	3.95	1.13	4.42	0.96	0.17
4. provided me with feedback about my data.	2.89	1.20	3.58	1.17	0.08
5. handled the use of multiple sensors well.	4.05	0.91	4.53	0.84	0.10
6. served the purposes I expected.	3.58	1.30	4.53	0.70	0.01
Overall Average	3.77		4.38		0.04

"agree" or "strongly agree" to question 6 of Table 1, indicating MC Designer allowed them to create an application *they believed* was correct based on their understanding of the scenario.

In scenario B (Biketastic), 6 users were able to create the correct application, despite requiring twice as many sensors. Of the 19 users, 17 felt they created the correct application. Again, the large disparity between these findings are believed to be due to differing interpretations of the scenario and a lack of knowledge about the sensors, as opposed to an inability to add the sensor in MCM. For example, one user chose text-based entry as the appropriate method for capturing the roughness of the road. When asked why they chose that sensor, they responded, "I didn't know an accelerometer could capture the roughness of the road, so I didn't use it." These findings indicate MCM would benefit from hints that educate the campaign organizer about the features they are configuring, and points to the need for a wizard-like feature in MCM that will help the end-user programmer to validate their application in a user-friendly way.

Campaign Application Development Time. The time required to create the application with MC Designer was measured for each scenario (Figure 4). The average time to create an app was 6 minutes for Scenario A (Meteor Counter) and 4 minutes for scenario B (Biketastic). These results indicate that users are easily able to create a mobile application, even in their first experience with MC Designer. Figure 4 also compares user creation time to their pre-survey rating of their comfort level with creating software. Users who rated their comfort level at the lower end of the spectrum did not show a significant difference from users who rated higher, indicating that a lack of perceived technical competence did not impede the users' abilities to create an application using MC Designer. As one user noted, "I don't use apps so was coming at this as someone with no experience as a user and was still able to use the app maker."

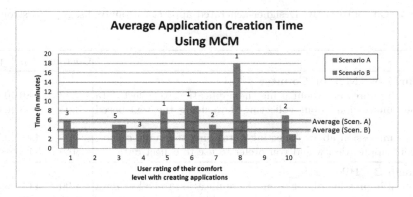

Fig. 4. Users' average creation time and comfort level with creating new software for scenario A (Meteor Counter) and scenario B (Biketastic). Bars are annotated with the number of users who rated themselves at a corresponding comfort level.

5.2 Part II: Comparing Custom Apps to MC Designer Apps

Part two of the user study is intended to evaluate expressiveness, captured by the user's comparison of the apps created using MC Designer and custom-built applications. Table 2 summarizes the results.

Comparison of Custom Apps and MC Designer Apps. In scenario A, both the Meteor Counter and MC Designer applications included an audio sensor and text-based input, but used them in slightly different ways. Meteor Count does not provide the user with a start or stop button to control recording audio. Recording begins when the user starts the data capture session, can be paused, and ends when the user uploads the contribution. The MC Designer app allows the user to explicitly start and stop the audio recording, but does not include the pause feature. Each press of the start button creates a new data collection session. For text-based input, Meteor Counter provides a slider option for entering predefined options for sky conditions and star visibility. To count meteors, the Meteor Counter app provides the user with a button to press each time a meteor is spotted. The MC Designer app captures these three entries by allowing the user to enter text.

Scenario B (Biketastic) included the accelerometer, audio, camcorder, camera, and GPS sensors. Again, differences exist between the way the Biketastic application and the MC Designer app incorporate each sensor. The Biketastic app collects accelerometer readings as a background task, and gives the user no feedback this data is being collected, whereas MC Designer displays the most current readings to the user. Similarly, audio is captured in the background in Biketastic, while MC Designer clearly displays "Recording audio" to the user. Camcorder and camera functions are very similar for the two apps; both use the built-in camera and camcorder APIs offered by the Android SDK. However, since riders should not be using these sensors while riding the bicycle, Biketastic automatically pauses the GPS, audio, and accelerometer sensors while camera

Table 2. Custom vs. MC Designer-generated apps (1=strongly disagree, 5=strongly agree)

	Custom	Clone	p
Scenario A - Meteor Counter			
1. Overall impression about using the application to collect data	4.42	3.89	0.05
2. Your impression about collecting data using the text-based input	3.95	4.05	0.49
3. Your impression about collecting data using the audio sensor	4.05	4.16	0.75
4. Which application would you prefer to use to collect data	50%	50%	
Scenario B - Biketastic			
5. Overall impression about using the application to collect data	4.00	4.05	0.84
6. Your impression about collecting data using the accelerometer	3.42	4.32	0.02
7. Your impression about collecting data using the audio sensor	4.05	4.21	0.60
8. Your impression about collecting data using the camera sensor	4.42	4.58	0.53
9. Your impression about collecting data using the camcorder sensor	4.32	4.42	0.72
10. Your impression about collecting data using the GPS sensor	3.84	4.37	0.16
11. Which application would you prefer to use to collect data	53%	47%	

functions are in use; MC Designer continues to collect this data. Also, Biketastic allows the user to upload multiple images or videos per a single data collection session; MC Designer allows only one per session. Lastly, GPS readings are converted to miles per hour and total distance when displayed to the user in Biketastic; MC Designer displays the most recent GPS location.

User Evaluations of Expressiveness. First, users were asked to compare the sensors used to collect data (i.e., "Rate your impression about the application's ability to collect data using the audio sensor") in each application. Overall, users rated the applications as equally able to capture data with two sensors (questions 2 and 3 in Table 2). These findings suggest that MC Designer can create apps that are *as good as* custom-built crowdsensing applications for capturing data.

Users were also asked to rate their overall impression of each application (question 1 in Table 2). For scenario A, the custom application rated significantly higher than the MC Designer app. Users were also asked to select the application they would prefer to use for data collection (question 4 of Table 2); the MC Designer app was selected by 50% of the users. When asked why one app was preferred, responses included "They are both good apps that capture data, you just have to play around with both to see how well they work," and "Basically the only difference is how it looks..." and "Both worked well but the NASA brand name made me biased." These results indicate that users were not only considering the application's ability to collect data when comparing the applications, but also the look-and-feel of the app. Clearly, crowdsensing applications that are built for a particular purpose will likely have a highly specialized user interface design that will tend to be more attractive. This is a trade-off that we expect, but we do plan to provide more options for customizing the UI with MC Designer in the future.

For scenario B, when asked to rate their overall impression (question 5 in Table 2), users had equally favorable impressions for each application. Question 11 aligns with these findings, with 47% of users stating that they preferred the MC Designer app for data collection. Responses from users included "The clone was more straightforward and I like the real time accelerometer data," and "The clone provided immediate feedback about the data the sensors were collecting, which is useful for an app like this," and "The clone seems to be just a simplified version of the actual app, which some people prefer."

The application's use of each sensor was also evaluated. Users rated use of the audio, camera, camcorder, and GPS sensors nearly equally across the MC Designer created application and the custom implementation in terms of their ability to collect data (questions 7-10 in Table 2). Users rated the accelerometer sensor (question 6 in Table 2) in the MC Designer app significantly higher than in the custom Biketastic app. User interviews indicate this is largely due to the fact that no real-time feedback about accelerometer data is provided by the Biketastic application. These findings indicate that for scenario B, MC Designer succeeded in being able to create an *equally functional* mobile application for data collection.

Lastly, users were surveyed on their overall experience while using MC Designer (Table 3). On average, users were pleased with MC Designer and felt they could create crowdsensing campaigns with ease. Users were very confident that MC Designer is able to create a mobile application for data collection (4.68 out of 5), and applications created using MC Designer use the phone sensors correctly (4.79 out of 5). Most importantly, users felt that MC Designer provided an easy-to-use interface for creating mobile applications (4.63 out of 5).

5.3   User Study Assumptions and Limitations

The user study was conducted under the following assumptions and limitations:

- This study focused on the user's ability to create a crowdsensing application that could be used to enable a sensor, capture a digital data sample, and upload the sample. Users were not asked to give input for recruitment and sensor sampling parameters.
- Users were provided with a description of each sensor in MC Designer (e.g., "the accelerometer measures motion in 3 dimensions, including shaking, turning, and rotating"). Users were then asked to apply sensors to the two scenarios. However, users often used a different sensor than expected (e.g., recording the roughness of the road with text-entry instead of the accelerometer). This likely contributed to the disparity between the accuracy and the user's perception of accuracy for the created application. We did not evaluate how well the users understood the scenario or sensor descriptions.
- Users did not submit data to the original apps. (We did not want users submitting synthetic/test data to the real Meteor Counter and Biketastic campaigns.) Future work will use a large-scale deployment of an MC Designer generated app to evaluate the utility of data collected.

Table 3. Perceptions of MC Designer (1=strongly disagree, 5=strongly agree)

Survey Question	Average Rating
1. I found the MCM application easy-to-use.	4.42
2. MCM is able to create a mobile application	4.68
3. MCM is able to incorporate phone sensors into a mobile application.	4.79
4. The mobile applications generated by MCM are the same as what I was expecting.	4.16
5. MCM allows me to define everything about the scenarios that I felt was important.	3.89
6. MCM provided me with an easy-to-use interface for creating a mobile application.	4.63
7. MCM included all the sensors I wanted to use for the scenarios.	4.53
8. MCM let me input all the information about the mobile application that I wanted to enter.	4.32

6   Conclusions and Future Work

We have presented MC Designer, a tool that enables end-users to create and manage crowdsensing campaigns from a mobile phone. MC Designer has a core set of constructs for building crowdsensing apps, and is designed with an extensible API with hooks for implementing emerging solutions in active areas of research, such as privacy [35,16], data analysis tools [33], and sensor and data fusion [3,36]. Since MC Designer is open source, researchers can integrate their own implementations of these concepts into the tool. Our evaluation of MC Designer indicates that users with varying levels of programming skill are able to use MC Designer to create an application that meets their expectations in an average of five minutes. Furthermore, the applications created by MC Designer were perceived as equivalent to or better than custom-built implementations of existing crowdsensing applications.

References

1. Aanensen, D., Huntley, D., Feil, E., Spratt, B., et al.: Epicollect: linking smartphones to web applications for epidemiology, ecology and community data collection. PLoS One 4(9), 6968 (2009)
2. Amazon.com, Inc. Amazon Mechanical Turk (June 2011),
   https://www.mturk.com/mturk/welcome
3. Beach, A., Gartrell, M., Xing, X., Han, R., Lv, Q., Mishra, S., Seada, K.: Fusing mobile, sensor, and social data to fully enable context-aware computing. In: Proc. of HotMobile (2010)
4. Center for Embedded Networked Sensing. What's Invasive! community data collection (2011), http://whatsinvasive.com/
5. Das, T., Mohan, P., Padmanabhan, V.N., Ramjee, R., Sharma, A.: PRISM: platform for remote sensing using smartphones. In: Proc. of MobiSys, pp. 63–76 (2010)

6. Eisenman, S.B., Miluzzo, E., Lane, N.D., Peterson, R.A., Ahn, G.-S., Campbell, A.T.: BikeNet: A mobile sensing system for cyclist experience mapping. ACM Transactions on Sensor Networks 6(1), 1–39 (2009)

7. Ganti, R.K., Pham, N., Ahmadi, H., Nangia, S., Abdelzaher, T.F.: GreenGPS: a participatory sensing fuel-e_cient maps application. In: Proc. of MobiSys, pp. 151–164 (2010)

8. Gaonkar, S., Li, J., Choudhury, R.R., Cox, L., Schmidt, A.: Micro-Blog: sharing and querying content through mobile phones and social participation. In: Proc. of MobiSys, pp. 174–186 (2008)

9. Griswold, W., Shanahan, P., Brown, S., Boyer, R., Ratto, M., Shapiro, R., Truong, T.: ActiveCampus: experiments in community-oriented ubiquitous computing. Computer 7(10), 73–81 (2004)

10. Hartung, C., Lerer, A., Anokwa, Y., Tseng, C., Brunette, W., Borriello, G.: Open data kit: Tools to build information services for developing regions. In: Proc. of ICTD, p. 18 (2010)

11. Heggen, S., Omokaro, O., Payton, J.: MAD Science: Increasing engagement in STEM education through participatory sensing. In: Proc. of UBICOMM (October 2012)

12. Hicks, J., Ramanathan, N., Kim, D., Monibi, M., Selsky, J., Hansen, M., Estrin, D.: AndWellness: an open mobile system for activity and experience sampling. In: Proc. of Wireless Health, pp. 34–43 (2010)

13. Huang, K.L., Kanhere, S.S., Hu, W.: Are you contributing trustworthy data?: The case for a reputation system in participatory sensing. In: Proc. of MSWiM (2010)

14. Joki, A., Burke, J., Estrin, D.: Campaignr: A framework for participatory data collection on mobile phones. Technical report, UCLA Center for Embedded Network Sensing (2007)

15. Kanjo, E., Bacon, J., Roberts, D., Landshoff, P.: MobSens: Making smart phones smarter. Pervasive Computing 8(4), 50–57 (2009)

16. Kapadia, A., Kotz, D., Triandopoulos, N.: Opportunistic sensing: Security challenges for the new paradigm. In: Proc. of COMSNETS, pp. 1–10 (January 2009)

17. Kim, S., Mankoff, J., Paulos, E.: Sensr: evaluating a exible framework for authoring mobile data-collection tools for citizen science. In: Proc. of CSCW, pp. 1453–1462 (2013)

18. Kim, S., Robson, C., Zimmerman, T., Pierce, J., Haber, E.M.: Creek watch: Pairing usefulness and usability for successful citizen science. In: Proc. of CHI, pp. 2125–2134 (2011)

19. LeBaron, G.: The 112th Christmas Bird Count. American Birds 66, 2–8 (2012)

20. Mediated Spaces, Inc. The WildLab: Use mobile technology to explore, discover, and share the natural world, http://thewildlab.org

21. Mendez, D., Perez, A., Labrador, M., Marron, J.: P-sense: A participatory sensing system for air pollution monitoring and control. In: Proc. of PerCom Workshops, pp. 344–347 (2011)

22. Miluzzo, E., Lane, N., Eisenman, S., Campbell, A.: CenceMe: Injecting sensing presence into social networking applications. In: Proc. of Euro SSC, pp. 1–28 (October 2007)

23. MIT Media Lab. App inventor for android, http://www.appinventor.mit.edu/

24. Mohan, P., Padmanabhan, V.N., Ramjee, R.: Nericell: using mobile smartphones for rich monitoring of road and traffic conditions. In: Proc. of SenSys, pp. 357–358 (2008)

25. Mun, M., Reddy, S., Shilton, K., Yau, N., Burke, J., Estrin, D., Hansen, M., Howard, E., West, R., Boda, P.: PEIR, the personal environmental impact report, as a platform for participatory sensing systems research. In: Proc. of MobiSys, pp. 55–68 (2009)
26. NASA. Meteor Counter (2011), http://meteorcounter.com/
27. National Audubon Society. The Christmas Bird Count (2012), http://birds.audubon.org/christmas-bird-count
28. NEON and the Chicago Botanic Garden. Project Budburst (2011), http://neoninc.org/budburst/
29. Networked Organisms. Project Noah, http://www.projectnoah.org
30. Ra, M., Liu, B., La Porta, T., Govindan, R.: Medusa: A programming framework for crowd-sensing applications. In: Proc. of MobiSys, pp. 337–350 (2012)
31. Ravindranath, L., Thiagarajan, A., Balakrishnan, H., Madden, S.: Code in the air: simplifying sensing and coordination tasks on smartphones. In: Proc. of Hot-Mobile (2012)
32. Reddy, S., Estrin, D., Srivastava, M.: Recruitment framework for participatory sensing data collections. In: Floréen, P., Krüger, A., Spasojevic, M. (eds.) Pervasive 2010. LNCS, vol. 6030, pp. 138–155. Springer, Heidelberg (2010)
33. Reddy, S., Parker, A., Hyman, J., Burke, J., Estrin, D., Hansen, M.: Image browsing, processing, and clustering for participatory sensing: lessons from a DietSense prototype. In: Proc. of EmNets, pp. 138–155 (2010)
34. Reddy, S., Shilton, K., Denisov, G., Cenizal, C., Estrin, D., Srivastava, M.: Bike-tastic: sensing and mapping for better biking. In: Proc. of CHI, pp. 1817–1820 (2010)
35. Shilton, K.: Four billion little brothers?: Privacy, mobile phones, and ubiquitous data collection. Communications of the ACM 52(11), 48–53 (2009)
36. Spanos, D.P., Murray, R.M.: Distributed sensor fusion using dynamic consensus. In: World Congress of the International Federation of Automatic Control (2005)
37. Thiagarajan, A., Ravindranath, L., LaCurts, K., Madden, S., Balakrishnan, H., Toledo, S., Eriksson, J.: VTrack: accurate, energy-aware road traffic delay estimation using mobile phones. In: Proc. of SenSys, pp. 85–98 (2009)
38. Tillmann, N., Moskal, M., de Halleux, J., Fahndrich, M.: TouchDevelop: programming cloud-connected mobile devices via touchscreen. In: Proc. of ONWARD, pp. 49–60 (2011)

Towards User Interface Components for Dashboard Applications on Smartphones

Marcus Homann, Vassilena Banova, Paul Oelbermann,
Holger Wittges, and Helmut Krcmar

Technische Universität München, Chair for Information Systems,
Boltzmannstr. 3, 85748 Garching, Germany
{marcus.homann,vassilena.banova,paul.oelbermann,
holger.wittges,krcmar}@in.tum.de

Abstract. Aim of this paper is to identify common functionalities of dashboard applications on smartphones. The findings are used to design reusable user interface components in order to improve the development activities for such applications. In order to identify common functionalities twelve existing dashboard applications for smartphones from different vendors were analyzed. The findings are illustrated using an UML use-case diagram. A grouping of different use-cases represents the foundation for the proposed reusable user interface components. The components are described using a structured format based on user interface patterns. The findings revealed that the analyzed dashboard applications offer similar functionalities that were categorized by ten use-cases. The groups of functionality were used to design seven user interface components that could be reused in future developments. An implementation of the proposed components for the iPhone revealed that the components are feasible.

Keywords: Mobile BI, Smartphone, Dashboard, User Interface Pattern, User Interface Component, Business Intelligence.

1   Introduction

Business intelligence applications become increasingly important as information volumes in enterprises explode. Today, driven by the increasing mobility of employees and the pervasive utilization of mobile devices in enterprise environments, the need for mobile business intelligence solutions is also growing. Mobile business intelligence (mobile BI) is the delivery of BI capabilities through mobile devices and offers a way of improving employee's productivity by using technology that employees already understand and are familiar with [1]. Recent market research shows that enterprises have already recognized the benefits of mobile BI such as operational efficiency, real-time analytics and customer responsiveness [2].

Current mobile BI solutions are mainly focused on information consumption, offering rich and interactive dashboards that generate a level of user engagement not usually seen in traditional desktop solutions [1]. During the implementation of mobile

G. Memmi and U. Blanke (Eds.): MobiCASE 2013, LNICST 130, pp. 19–32, 2014.

BI applications, different challenges related to the specific characteristics of mobile devices and distributed information consumption should be considered. The restricting effect of some of these challenges decreases over time because of technological enhancements – for example, the rapid development of wireless communication networks in the last years enabled the access of bigger amounts of data via mobile devices [3]. Nevertheless, there are other challenges, such as the limitations of data input, screen size and mobile device performance which still need to be considered as an important aspect in the scope of implementing mobile BI solutions.

The aim of this paper is to improve the development activities for mobile BI applications by offering reusable user interface components based on different use-cases of mobile BI. To identify common functionalities and develop the reusable interface components, twelve dashboard applications for smartphones from different vendors were analyzed. The findings of this paper will offer a systematic classification of different use cases of mobile BI. Moreover, the elaborated reusable user interface components will support and simplify the implementation process of mobile dashboard applications.

The paper is structured in five sections. Section two offers an overview of the different categories of dashboards and their utilization. Section three offers a better understanding on the topic of user interface patterns and components, their definition and relevance in the scope of this paper. This section is followed by the description of the selected use cases of dashboard applications on smartphones. Subsequently, the reusable user interface components are derived from the selected use cases, offering a significant simplification of the development process of mobile dashboard applications. Finally, the last section of the paper summarizes the lessons learned as well as the outlook towards potential future research projects in the area of mobile BI.

2   Dashboards

Before we begin to describe the analysis of different use cases and common user interface patterns for mobile dashboards, a common understanding on what a dashboard application is will be introduced.

Many different understandings on what a dashboard is exist. The common aspects in all these definitions are the following: a dashboard appears on computer screens and offers visibility into key performance indicators (KPI) through simple visual graphics [4]. The understanding on dashboards in the scope of this paper is based on the definition of Few [5], who considers all these aspects and captures them in one sentence: "A dashboard is a visual display of the most important information needed to achieve one or more objectives; consolidated and arranged on a single screen so the information can be monitored at a glance" [5]. An example of a dashboard is shown in figure 1.

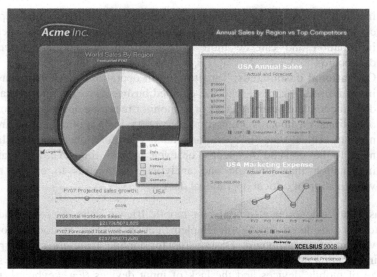

Fig. 1. Example of a dashboard [6]

Dashboards are commonly used by decision makers and have therefore the peculiarity of executive information systems. They are often seen as an addition to Online Analytical Processing (OLAP) Tools, offering more structured and easier to comprehend visualization of relevant information [6]. Dashboards can be categorized according to different aspects such as the type of information they visualize, the way they display information to serve a particular purpose and – related to this purpose – the target user group of the dashboard. In the scope of this paper we categorize different dashboard types according to their target group of use. Based on this categorization perspective three general dashboard types can be defined [6]:

1. **Strategic dashboards:** Target group of strategic dashboards are decision makers who need to get a quick overview of the current situation within the company. Strategic dashboards do not provide all the detailed information needed to make complex decisions, but focus on key figures which can help identify opportunities for further and more detailed analysis. Therefore they should offer a simple representation of the most important key performance indicators.

2. **Analytical dashboards:** Target group of analytical dashboards are mainly analysts or controllers. The data is here more detailed and more complex context can be displayed. Analytical dashboards provide information which enables the analysis of trends or even root cause analysis by drawing comparisons across multiple variables over time. To enable users to understand trends and why certain things are happening in an organization, analytical dashboards facilitate interactions with the data allowing the

increase of detail of the analyzed data, as well as time-dependent comparisons. Therefore, an analytical dashboard usually contains much more information and can be more complex than strategic and operational dashboards.

3. **Operational dashboards:** Target group of operational dashboards are users in operational business, who use detailed business process and transactional data to complete business tasks or to monitor real time operations. Moreover, operational dashboards are used to alert users, in case of deviations from the norm or critical states in operational data. Therefore, operational dashboards need to be updated frequently or even in real time. They contain less information than strategic and analytical dashboards to enable a clear visualization of critical operational data.

These dashboard categories also apply for mobile BI, yet there are some additional aspects to be considered during the implementation process in comparison to a desktop version of a dashboard. Dashboards for mobile BI users should provide relevant information that is easily processed on mobile devices. Moreover the smaller screen size of mobile devices and the lack of input devices (e.g. keyboard, mouse) should also be considered during the implementation of mobile dashboards. Since mobile BI user are viewing information on a small screen and do not have access to traditional interfaces, the dashboard's operational performance is one of the most relevant concerns to be addressed in the scope of developing mobile BI applications.

The consideration of these aspects during the development process of mobile BI applications is essential and therefore different guidelines addressing specific issues exist. The aim of this paper is to elaborate reusable user interface patterns and therefore the next section discusses the concept of user interface patterns and its use in the scope of a software implementation process.

3   User Interface Patterns and Components

Collected design knowledge about UIs is usually provided in form of guidelines, principles or patterns [7]. Principles such as the eight golden rules of Shneiderman [8] have a generic character, while guidelines are often platform specific [9]. Both tend to be difficult to use during the design process, because they suggest absolute validity [7]. On the contrary, UI patterns explicitly focus on context and are thus problem related [7]. They tell the designer when, how and why the provided solution is applicable [7].

The concept of design patterns was originated in urban architecture by Christopher Alexander [10], adapted to object-oriented software design by Beck and Cunningham [11] and became popular through the book of Gamma et al. [12]. In general, patterns are structured descriptions of an invariant solution to a recurrent problem in a certain context [13]. They follow a three-part rule which expresses the relation between a certain context, a problem and a solution [10]. The interest in patterns in Human-Computer Interaction dates back to 1994 [14]. According to a CHI workshop in 2000 an UI pattern "captures the essence of a successful solution to a recurring usability problem in interactive systems" [14]. Therefore patterns can be seen as descriptions of best practices which capture common solutions to design tensions and are thus by definition not novel [15].

A collection of UI patterns is often referred to as pattern catalogue or pattern language [9, 13]. Several UI pattern catalogues are focused on designing websites. However, there are also UI pattern collections available that deal with the design of smartphone applications, like [16, 17]. These patterns usually have a general orientation and are therefore suitable for a variety of application types. In contrast, domain-specific patterns focus on a specific application domain. The lack of general applicability of domain-specific patterns is affiliated with an easier handling and increased development productivity in the focused application domain [18, 19]. In software engineering, software components represent reusable program code fragments that could be used in various applications. Their usage generally increases the development productivity and improves the quality of the resulting applications. However, the identification of reusable components is challenging [20]. There is always a trade-off between usefulness on the one side and costs and quality on the other side [20]. Transferred to our context we understand user interface components as reusable building blocks to implement the user interface of dashboard applications on smartphones.

Similar to general software components the challenge is to identify a suitable degree of reusability with these components. In our approach we try to address this challenge by identifying recurring functionalities first. These are used to implement UI components afterwards.

4   Use-Cases of Existing Dashboard Applications on Smartphones

There are already several dashboard applications for smartphones available on the market. For our analysis we used a market overview of mobile dashboard applications from Gartner [21]. This report provides an overview of the most important vendors and their corresponding applications. Some vendors decided to implement native applications that are specialized on one particular mobile operating system like iOS or Android. Others use web technologies in order to implement cross-platform applications. This aspect is important for our analysis, because native applications can generally use a more extensive collection of UI elements. The report of Gartner revealed that the most dashboard applications are currently implemented as native iPhone applications. Therefore we decided to focus our analysis on the iPhone applications mentioned in the Gartner report. In summary, our analysis comprised twelve iPhone applications. Table 1 shows an overview of the analyzed applications, including vendor name, application name and version number.

Table 1. Analyzed dashboard applications for the iPhone

Vendor	Application Name	Application Version
Actuate	BIRT Mobile Viewer	3.2
Enterprise Signal	SurfBI	3.4
Extended Results	PushBI	3.5.1
Information Builders	Mobile Faves	2.2.0
Jaspersoft	JasperMobile	1.1.1
MeLLmo	Roambi Analytics Visualizer	4.4.3
Microstrategy	Microstrategy Mobile for iPhone	9.2.1.2.8
Oracle	Oracle Business Intelligence Mobile	11.1.1.5.0
QlikTech	QlikView	4.0.4
SAP	SAP BusinessObjects Explorer	4.0.8
SAP	SAP BusinessObjects Mobile	4.2.5
Yellowfin	YellowfinBI	6.12

In our analysis we examined the listed applications according their provided functionalities. Our results revealed that the analyzed applications offer a similar set of functionalities. The identified functionalities are illustrated using an UML use-case diagram in figure 2.

A large part of the identified functionalities is related to dashboard elements. According to [6] a dashboard element is a building block of a dashboard that visualizes a certain piece of information. In the analyzed dashboard applications the available dashboard elements are often presented in a single-column table (Use-Case: List Dashboard Elements).

Sometimes it is possible to sort the list according a certain criteria like in alphabetic order (Use-Case: Sort Dashboard Elements). In many cases a text based search for a certain dashboard element is provided (Use-Case: Search for Dashboard Element). In order to view a certain dashboard element the corresponding dashboard element must be selected within the table (Use-Case: View Dashboard Element). For the sake of organizing the dashboard elements some applications offer the possibility to manage a set of often used dashboard elements as so called favorites (Use-Case: Manage favorite Dashboard Elements). The visualized data is often received from a backend system such as a business intelligence server. Therefore, many of the analyzed applications offer the opportunity to update the displayed data by pressing a button or perform the update activities automatically (Use-Case: Show metadata of Dashboard Element). The most applications provide a set of parameters to maintain the access information to the associated backend system (Use-Case: Manage Backend Servers). Some applications provide the possibility to add comments to a dashboard element (Use-Case: Manage Comments). In several applications it is possible to share a dashboard element. Possible opportunities are via e-mail or as message using the multimedia messaging service (MMS) (Use-Case: Share Dashboard Element). Due to the limited space on smartphone displays some applications provide additional information about the dashboard element through separate screens or pop-up windows. Examples for this type of information are author or creation date of the dashboard element.

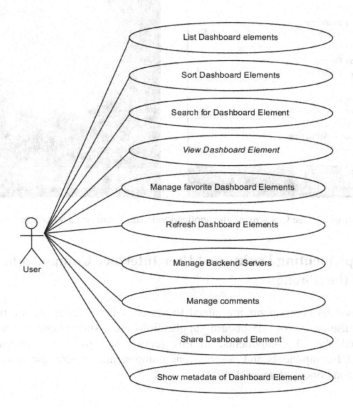

Fig. 2. Identified functionalities of dashboard applications on smartphones

Figure 3 illustrates an example of the use-cases List Dashboard Elements (left screen) and View Dashboard Element (right screen) using the application Roambi Analytics Visualizer as an example.

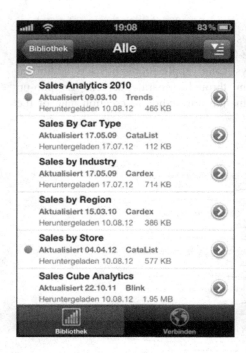

Fig. 3. Exemplary Use Cases using the application Roambi Analytics Visualizer as example

5   Implementing Dashboard User Interface Components for the iPhone

The proposed UI components are aimed to be reusable solutions for the previously identified use-cases of dashboard applications on smartphones. Overall we implemented six UI components. In this section we give an overview of the developed UI components and describe one component, the strategic & operational dashboard component, in more detail.

5.1   Implementing User Interface Components for the iPhone

Due to the different programming languages and libraries that are used to implement smartphone applications it is necessary to focus on a specific mobile platform. The iPhone was selected because it has been already used to identify our use-cases described in the previous section. The reason for choosing the iPhone was the fact that most of the dashboard applications were available for the iPhone when compared with other platforms. Applications for iOS are developed using the programming language Objective-C. The user interface is implemented with a set of programming libraries called Cocoa Touch. The used development environment is called Xcode.

All components can be integrated into new applications using a provided set of programming interfaces.

5.2   Overview of the Implemented Dashboard Components

In order to identify the functionality of the implemented UI components we used our previously proposed use-cases as foundation. Afterwards we analyzed, which use-cases have a semantic relationship with each other. This resulted in six UI components that are illustrated using an UML package diagram in figure 3.

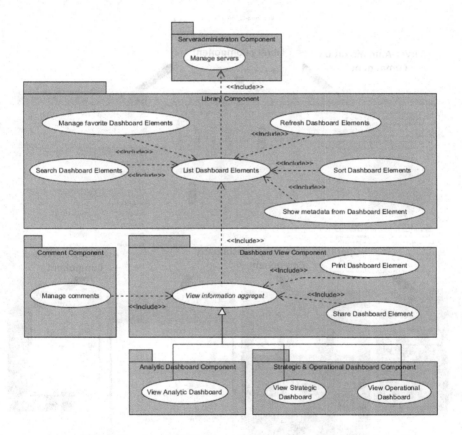

Fig. 4. Developed UI Components (Source: Own illustration)

The *Server-Administration Component* is responsible for the configuration of the backend connections. Configurable parameters are usually the network of a business intelligence server, used network port, used network protocol, username and password. The component offers the possibility to manage the connection data of several business intelligence servers.

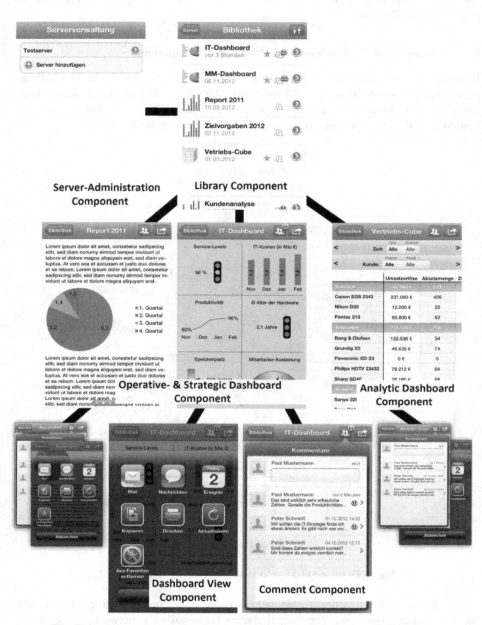

Fig. 5. Overview of the implemented UI components (Source: own illustration)

The *Library Component* manages the available dashboard elements. This is done within a single-column table. Each row of the table represents a selectable dashboard element. It is search for a specific dashboard element through keywords and to sort the list of available dashboard elements through attributes like used chart type or the name of the dashboard element.

The *Dashboard View* component is responsible for displaying the selected dashboard element. Depending on which type of dashboard element is selected, Analytical Dashboard Component or the Strategic & Operational Dashboard component is used to display the dashboard element. Thus, the Dashboard View Component is an abstract container for visualizing dashboard elements that provides common functionalities like share dashboard elements as pictures through e-mail or as short message or send the picture of a selected dashboard element to the printer.

The *Comment component* offers the possibility for the user to add some additional information to a dashboard element. An example could be additional explanations for the dashboard element and its visualized figures.

The *Analytical Dashboard* component aims to support data analysts, who need more sophisticated interaction possibilities like drill-down activities for selected datasets. This component is described in more detail in the next section of this paper.

The *Strategic & Operational Dashboard* component implements dashboard elements that support strategic decisions and operational activities. Although, both tasks are different, the used dashboard elements are pretty similar. The data is visualized with simple, easy to understand diagrams and in some cases enhanced with additional descriptions in text form. Sophisticated interaction possibilities like in the Analytical Dashboard component are not possible.

Figure 4 illustrates an overview of the user interface of the implemented components.

5.3   Example: Analytic Dashboard Component

In order to describe our implemented dashboard components we used the format of UI patterns to describe the components in a structured way. We also used the Apple's OS X documentation sets to generate an Xcode documentation that describes the usage of our components more detailed from a programmer's perspective. In the following we describe one of our components, the Analytical Dashboard Component, using the UI pattern format:

Name: Analytic Dashboard Component

What: The Analytical Dashboard component pattern can be used to perform sophisticated interactions with a data cube. It is possible to navigate within the predefined data space with the help of multiple interaction possibilities that are known from Business Intelligence applications like drill-down and roll-up, slicing and dicing or rotating the data cube [22].

Use When: The component can be used in analytical dashboard elements, in order to support the data analysis with the mentioned interaction possibilities on a selected data cube.

Why: Data cubes are well-known in business intelligence as well as the mentioned operations drill-down, roll-up, slicing and dicing, etc. The Analytical Dashboard component implements a data cube using a table UI element to display one dimension and additional superordinate row elements to navigate to the other dimensions of the cube.

Examples: Figure 5 illustrates examples of the offered interaction possibilities of the Analytical Dashboard component. The exemplary data cube has the dimensions time, customer and product. The table shows the revenues, sales and target volumes for individual products and product groups. Using a zoom gesture on the view shown in figure 5a the user can perform a drill-down. This results in a more detailed data. In the resulting view in figure 5b a pinch gesture can be used to perform a roll-up again.

Fig. 6. Exemplary operations implemented within the Analytical Dashboard component

Besides, there are some basic functionalities available. With swipe gestures the user can scroll horizontally or vertically trough the table (figure 5c). By tapping and holding on the left and right cell margins of the first row and subsequently swiping to the left or right, the user can change the column size. A double tap brings him back to the optimal column width. In addition, the user can also perform a slicing on multiple dimensions, which is called dicing [22]. To perform a slicing operation the user has to type on the field of the corresponding dimension first. This opens a pop-over dialog (figure 5d). Afterwards the user can choose how to slice the data cube. Figure 5e shows the result of the slicing process. By horizontal swiping on the dimensions shown at the top, the user can rotate the data cube. If the user pulls the customer dimension to the left, it is replaced by the remaining product dimension (figure 5f).

6   Outlook

In this paper, twelve selected mobile BI applications for the iPhone have been analyzed with the aim of identifying common functionalities. The analysis revealed ten use cases that were implemented across different applications. These use cases were grouped to UI components using their semantic relationship. Afterwards, the proposed components were implemented using the iPhone development environment Xcode, the programming language Objective-C as well as the necessary programming libraries like Cocoa Touch.

The implemented UI components can be used to implement new mobile BI applications. They can be parameterized through offered programming interfaces. The components are described using the format of UI patterns. These structured descriptions allow understanding their purpose. Additionally, the implemented components are also described using Apple OS X documentation sets, in order to describe their usage from a programmer's perspective.

Currently, the components are only implemented for the iPhone. Possible steps in the future could comprise the implementation of the elaborated reusable components also for other popular mobile platforms, like Android, BlackBerry OS or Windows Phone. Moreover, the implementation for tablet PC's like the iPad could be beneficial, although the larger form factor of tablet PC's should be considered in this case. In addition, HTML5-based programming libraries such as jQuery Mobile or Sencha Touch, which are becoming increasingly powerful, could be used to facilitate the implementation of cross-platform mobile BI components.

The usage of the proposed reusable components is currently done within the source code of the mobile BI application. For this purpose, programming skills are required. A useful future extension seems to be the development of a tool that avoids this prerequisite. Such a tool could enable non-programmers to develop or generate mobile BI applications for their purpose based on their own specification.

References

1. Tapadinhas, J.: Innovation Insight: Mobile BI Innovation Expands Business Analytics Boundaries. Gartner Research (2012)
2. Bensberg, F.: Mobile Business Intelligence. In: Bauer, H., Bryant, M., Dirks, T. (eds.) Erfolgsfaktoren des Mobile Marketing, pp. 71–87. Springer, Heidelberg (2009)
3. Zhu, X., Huang, Y.: A Framework for Mobile Business Intelligence Based on 3G Communication Environment. In: Jin, D., Lin, S. (eds.) Advances in FCCS, Vol. 2. AISC, vol. 160, pp. 75–81. Springer, Heidelberg (2012)
4. Rivard, K.C.: Doug: Are You Drowning in BI Reports? Using Analytical Dashboards to Cut Through the Clutter. DM Review 14, 26 (2004)
5. Few, S.: Information Dashboard Design. The Effective Visual Communication of Data. O'Reilly Media, Inc., Sebastopol (2006)
6. Hecht, S., Schmidl, J., Krcmar, H.: Xcelsius: Dashboarding mit SAP Business Objects. Galileo Press, Bonn (2010)
7. van Welie, M., van der Veer, G.C.: Pattern languages in interaction design: Structure and organization. In: Proceedings of Interact, Zuerich, Switserland (2003)
8. Shneiderman, B., Plaisant, C.: Designing the user interface: strategies for effective human-computer interaction. Addison-Wesley, Boston (2010)
9. Borchers, J.: A pattern approach to interaction design. Wiley, Chichester (2001)
10. Alexander, C., Ishikawa, S., Silverstein, M.: A pattern language: towns, buildings, construction. Oxford University Press, New York (1977)
11. Beck, K., Cunningham, W.: Using Pattern Languages for Object-Oriented Programs. In: Workshop on Specification and Design for Object-Oriented Programming, Orlando, FL, USA (1987)
12. Gamma, E., Helm, R., Johnson, R., Vlissides, J.: Design Patterns: Elements of Reusable Object-Oriented Software. Addison-Wesley, New Jersey (1995)
13. Dearden, A., Finlay, J.: Pattern Languages in HCI: A critical review. Human Computer Interaction 21, 49–102 (2006)
14. Rijken, D.: The Timeless Way.. the design of meaning. SIGCHI Bulleting 6 (1994)
15. Tidwell, J.: Designing interfaces. O'Reilly, Sebastopol (2011)
16. Neil, T.: Mobile Design Pattern Gallery. O'Reilly, Sebastopol (2012)
17. Hoober, S., Berkman, E.: Designing Mobile Interfaces. O'Reilly, Beijing (2011)
18. Homann, M., Wittges, H., Krcmar, H.: Towards user interface patterns for ERP applications on smartphones. In: Abramowicz, W. (ed.) BIS 2013. LNBIP, vol. 157, pp. 14–25. Springer, Heidelberg (2013)
19. Merrnik, M., Heering, J., Sloane, A.M.: When and how to develop domain-specific languages. ACM Computing Surveys 37, 29 (2005)
20. Caldiera, G., Basili, V.R.: Identifying and qualifying reusable software components. IEEE Computer 24, 61–70 (1991)
21. Gartner: Who's Who in Mobile BI. Gartner Research (2011)
22. Hecht, S., Jörg, S., Krcmar, H.: Xcelsius: Dashboarding mit SAP Business Objects. Galileo Press, Bonn (2010)

User-Centric Quality of Experience Measurement[*]

Bachir Chihani[1,4], Khalil ur Rehman Laghari[3], Emmanuel Bertin[1,4], Denis Collange[2], Noël Crespi[4], and Tiago H. Falk[3]

[1] Orange Labs, 42 rue des Coutures, 14066 Caen, France
[2] Orange Labs Sophia Antipolis, 905 rue Albert Einstein, 06560 Valbonne
firstname.lastname@orange.com
[3] Institut National de la Recherche Scientifique (EMT-INRS), Montreal, QC, Canada
[4] Institut Mines-Telecom, Telecom SudParis, CNRS 5157
9 rue Charles Fourier, 91011 Evry, France
firstname.lastname@mines-telecom.fr

Abstract. Quality-of-experience (QoE) produces the blue print of human perception, feelings, needs and intentions, while Quality-of-Service (QoS) is a technology centric metric used to assess the performance of a multimedia services and/or network. .It is quite important for service/content providers to understand user/customer experience requirements in order to improve the service quality or the content recommendation. With advent of 3G and 4G wireless networks, and efficient smart phones, the band-width hungry multimedia applications are becoming common in use on end-user devices. Thus,it is also important for telecom operators to understand the impact,if wireless network performances on the user experience in mobile environment. On the fly evaluation of user experience for multimedia services is a challenging problem especially in mobile environments. It implies the collection and the correlation of a mixture of variables on network conditions, on the service, as well as on the user itself. This paper proposes an innovative mobile application that can be used for measuring user quality-of-experience on the fly with a high accuracy and the consideration of multiple parameters about the user, the network and the system. This application takes advantages of current advances in mobile technologies to measure user experience directly on the user device. In addition, it aims to preserve the user privacy by transmitting only estimated quality-of-experience to the service provider.

Keywords: QoE, QoS, context, mobile computing, 3G UMTS, video streaming, machine learning.

1   Introduction

The wide spread deployment of Wi-Fi, 3G and 4G cellular networks has increased the use of smart phones, which has changed the landscape of information and

---

[*] A short abstract of this article has been accepted as a work-in-progress report in the IEEE Pervasive Computing magazine, Oct-Dec issue, 2012. [1]

G. Memmi and U. Blanke (Eds.): MobiCASE 2013, LNICST 130, pp. 33–46, 2014.
© Institute for Computer Sciences, Social Informatics and Telecommunications Engineering 2014

communications technology. Due to advanced operating capabilities of smart phones, multimedia applications are now being developed massively and made available through Google or Apple stores. These services have stringent Quality-of-Service (QoS) requirements. However, in a mobile environment, the user context (e.g. location) and network QoS change continuously, in turn continually influencing the user's behavior and experience. Thus, it is critical to identify requirements for mobile multimedia applications that are not only related to the wireless network QoS but also to the user context and feedback. These requirements can be derived from user Quality-of-Experience (QoE) demands that can be understood by mapping the user's subjective ratings to the objective QoS and contextual parameters.

We propose in this paper an innovative user-centric, context-aware solution that can be used for measuring QoE on smartphones. The objective is to design an intelligent and user-centric QoE measurement framework for Android-based smartphones. Such framework can be used to analyze and evaluate user experience requirements for multimedia services and applications in a mobile environment. In this paper, we propose a framework which is implemented with a standalone intelligent QoE application installed on smartphone. End-user usesa multimedia service, and s/he gives a QoE score using our framework. These subjective scores are correlated with QoS and context parameters. The resulting dataset is then analyzed locally by our proposed framework in order to generate a personalized QoE model to assess the user perception regarding the studied service. The generated QoE model is updated over time with respect to changes in the QoS or contextual parameters, i.e. network or application performance criteria. This application not only captures QoS, contextual parameters and the user ratings but also analyzes and generates the personalized QoE results for a given user session. Furthermore, QoE is never a fixed value; it keeps updated over the time with respect to changes in QoS or in contextual parameters.

The novelties of our solution are first, the collection of QoS, contextual and user ratings locally on user smartphones; and second, the client-side analysis of the collected data to generate a personalized QoE model locally on smartphones. The data are analyzed as soon as the user finishes interacting with the studied service or after a consequent change in the user perception.

2   Challenges and Motivations

From the telecom perspective [2], the network's performance can be monitored by collecting and investigating key performance indicators such as QoS parameters. These technical indicators are measured at the different levels in a wireless network. The examples of theseindicators collected at network layer are bandwidth, delay, jitter, packet loss rate, etc., and at end-user device level(e.g. noise/interference level, signal strength, connection establishment time, drop rate, etc.).

On the other hand, from the user perspective [2], the network's performance can be monitored by collecting user feedback, i.e. QoE data. In contrast to QoS, QoE provides an assessment of human perceptions, feelings, emotions and intentions with respect to a particular product, service or application [18]. QoE is affected by various technological, business and contextual factors [19] [3].

It is extremely difficult for telecom operators to measure QoE as it depends on various factors [4]: objective ones related to network condition and subjective ones related to user perception. For example, the QoE for a video streaming service depends on network conditions (e.g. bit rate, packet loss rate) and viewing conditions (e.g. type of used device, at home or work, etc.).

Moreover, it is quite challenging to establish an accurate QoS to QoE mapping method for different applications as it is hard to choose the relevant QoS parameters for a given application [5]. It is also challenging to evaluate feedback with respect to QoS and context data as acquiring these different parameters is difficult in a mobile environment. Another challenge [6] was due to the limited computing capabilities of user terminals which make QoE processing on these devices hardly possible. This challenge was valid for traditional featured phones as they were limited in terms of processing powers and not designed for calculation task. This is no longer valid as current smartphones have improved processing capabilities and they are equipped with flexible operating system allowing the development of advanced applications. For example, the Google Nexus runs the Android 4.1 operating system; it has 1 Gb RAM memory and 1.2 GHz CPU processor.

These improvements in mobile device capabilities as well as the fact that the mobile devices are the closest elements to end-user motivate our work for a full client-based QoE measurement framework. This proposed framework aims to collect and process both QoS and QoE data locally on the user device and create a personalized QoE model. Compared to QoS-based approaches, this approach is closer to user and provides better insights about user experience.

3   User-Centric QoE Measurement

Existing QoE frameworks tend to upload the data needed for generating QoE model from multiple users to a central server to process and aggregate them. Our objective is to avoid unnecessary Internet traffic generated by uploading data to a distant server by performing a local management of QoE parameters. This enables the generation of a personalized QoE model and better user privacy by storing and processing user information locally on his device. We propose a user-centric way for measuring QoE parameters, directly on the user device.

3.1   Framework Architecture

Our architecture is composed of an Android application running on the user Smartphone for measuring user QoE; multimedia server (e.g. YouTube) from which the videos will be streamed over a 3G/WiFi connection via Real Time Streaming Protocol (RSTP).

Figure 1 presents main components of the Android application responsible for QoE measurement, interaction with the end-user and with the remote multimedia service provider (MSP).

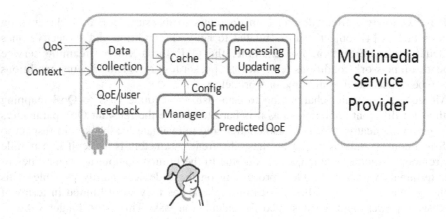

Fig. 1. Architecture of the Android application for QoE measurement

The manager component (MC) is the main component responsible for interacting with the outside world (user and service provider) and managing rest of the system components. The data collection component (DCC) is responsible for acquiring QoS (e.g. jitter, packet loss) and user context (e.g. GPS data) related information. The Cache Component (CC) is responsible of caching temporarily, a set of collected data (QoS, context and QoE) and the generated QoE model. The processing/updating component (PUC) works in two modes: learning and automation modes. In the learning mode, this component uses a supervised learning algorithm (for instance a linear regression) to generate a personalized QoE model and stores it into the cache component. The generated model is updated continuously with the cached data and each time the cached data is consumed, the cache is emptied.

In the automation mode, the component is responsible for predicting QoE parameters (e.g. did the user like the video content?), with the use of the cached QoE model. Thanks to this mode, a multimedia and telecom service provider can use our framework as an integrated component to its multimedia service to evaluate the the user experience regarding the usage of the service. In this case, the predicted QoE values can be for instance sent to the multimedia and telecom service provider in order to personalize the recommended videos.

3.2   Collected Parameters

Smartphones are a rich source of information about user and his/her environment. Table 1 summarizes the data we are collecting on the client-side for generating user QoE model. These collected data belong to the following categories.

User related information: input from user describing his satisfaction through various ratings after viewing a video;

Table 1. Collected parameters for QoE model generation

Parameter	Unit	Value	Sampling
User related information			
Satisfaction	state	[yes, no]	On thumbs up/down
Video Quality	integer	[1, 5]	When user stop watching
Video Content	integer	[1, 5]	When user stop watching
Application related information			
Watched	%	[0, 100]	When user stop watching
Error	%	[0, 100]	On error
Device related information			
CPU	%	[0, 100]	Each second
Memory	%	[0, 100]	Each second
Battery level	%	[0, 100]	Each second
Latitude	double	[0, 180]	On location changes
Longitude	double	[0, 90]	On location changes
Network related information			
Jitter	second	$[0, \infty[$	On RTSP packets arrival
Loss rate	%	[0, 100]	On RTSP packets reordering
Network Type	state	[WiFi,3G,LTE]	On changes
RSSI	dBm	$]-\infty, +\infty[$	On changes

Application related information: Video parameters like time spent watching the video (i.e. if or not the whole video was watched) or the moment when an error had happened (e.g. related to a bug in the application) while the user was watching the video;

Device related information: battery related information like level, its health (e.g. good), its status (e.g. charging); CPU usage (e.g. percentage consumed by our application); memory usage (e.g. amount of memory needed by our application); Location information like the name of the location provider, altitude, longitude, etc.

Network Performance related information like signal strength, QoS parameters like delay and jitter, received packets; network type (e.g. UMTS, LTE, GPRS);

In our implementation, there is no fix sampling rate as the Android platform allows applications to subscribe for specific events (e.g. network type/location changes) to be notified on their occurrence. This way, there is no need for a continuous polling of the event source (e.g. GPS sensor, network manager).

3.3   Implementation Details

The different components in Figure 2 are implemented as Android threads (i.e. AsyncTask) except the cache which is implemented as an Android ContentProvider able to store data locally into the Android SQLite database. The application has two Android activities: the first one displays a list of videos; the second one displays the chosen video. We used the YouTube API (Application Programming Interface) to stream videos from the multimedia service provider. Some Android APIs are used to get contextual information (e.g. location) and QoS parameters (e.g. jitter).

When the application is started, a list of videos is displayed from which the user can choose one video to watch. Two ways are provided to user to report his/her satisfaction (which is represented by the reported QoE score): While s/he is watching the video thanks to thumbs up (QoE score = 4) or thumbsdown (QoE score = 1) buttons, or at the end of the video by answering the questions (QoE score ranges from 0 to 5). The reported QoE will be stored in the cache to be processed later when there will be enough available data; i.e when the cache becomes full.

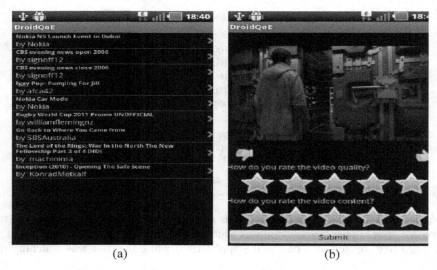

(a)   (b)

Fig. 2. Screenshots from the QoE measurement application

Figure 2 depicts a screenshot from an implementation of the QoE measurement frame work. The GUI (Graphical User Interface) showed in (a) displays a list of videos. The one in (b) is composed of a top area where the video is displayed. In the middle, the user can use the thumbs up/down buttons to express his current liking and disliking of the displayed video. At the bottom, there is a button for submitting this user survey.

3.4   Components Interaction

Figure 3, illustrates the framework sequence diagram. When the user reports its QoE, the Manager sends this value to the data collection component. In addition to the QoE value, it collects the current QoS and user context information, and stores them into the cache. When the stored examples in the cache reach a certain value (configurable parameter), the processing-updating component is notified to consume them and to generate an updated version of user QoE model.

When the multimedia service provider requests a QoE value for the currently streamed video, the manager component sends back the user reported QoE (if there is) or a predicted value generated by the processing-updating component.

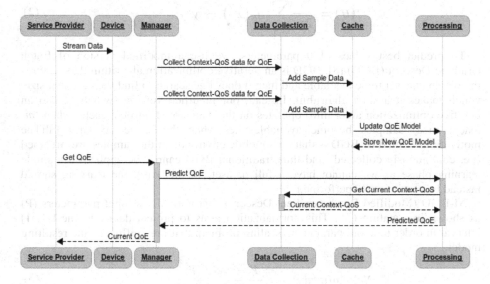

Fig. 3. Sequence diagram for QoE management

4   Learning and Processing

All the data is not available at a single time but it is gathered continuously and progressively over the time. Thus, the iterative nature of linear regression may help in building accurate model which fits our needs. Our learning algorithm, implemented by the processing/updating component, is based on the multivariate linear regression [7] where input parameters are QoS and contextual information and QoE is the output or target variable. For each learning phase, the size of the training set or number of samples is 'm' which is also the size of the cache. The hypothesis (h) represents the model to be learned for predicting future values of QoE ($y_{predicted}$) for a giving sample vector (X), i.e. $y_{predicted} = h(X)$. Mathematically, h is defined in equation (1), where x_i is an input parameter, n is the number of input parameters, and θ_j the weight of the corresponding input parameter. It is the set of weights that represent the parameters to be learned.

$$h(X) = \theta_0 x_0 + \theta_1 x_1 + \theta_2 x_2 + \ldots + \theta_n x_n \tag{1}$$

The learning algorithm tries to predict the best values of the hypothesis parameters (vector of θ values) minimizing the difference between the output QoE value and real value ($y_{predicted} - y_{real}$). Equation (2) defines mathematically the cost function 'J' which is based on a model (vector of θ values) to output the cost of this model by the summation of distances between predicted values $h_\theta(x)$ and real values y for all samples (rows) of the dataset.

$$J(\theta) = \frac{1}{2m} \sum_{i=1}^{m} (h_\theta(x^i) - y^i)^2 \qquad (2)$$

To predict best values of θ parameters, we use a modified version of Batch Gradient Descent (BGD) [8]. BGD is an iterative optimization algorithm that requires the whole data set to be available and then it does line search to find the best step size, which makes it a slow algorithm. Instead, our modified version (which is also an iterative optimization algorithm) operates on the data stored into the cache when 'm' (cache size) samples become available, i.e. when the cache becomes fullThe motivations behind M-BGD is that on a mobile environment the samples are streamed (i.e. continuously collected) and thus traditional BGD cannot be applied in a single learning phase as we cannot have a full dataset. In this case, the learning should instead be continuously performed.

M-BGD (Modified Batch Gradient Descent) first normalizes input parameters (P) as shown in equation (3).. This normalization aims to project data into the [-1, 1] interval in order to avoid parameters scaling problem that may influence the resulting model.

$$Normalized\ P = \frac{P - mean(P)}{\max(P) - \min(P)} \qquad (3)$$

Second, M-BGD updates θ values continuously until convergence or stagnation at a local minimum given the following algorithm:

```
Initialize θ parameters (e.g., to 0);

Repeat until convergence:
```
$$\theta_j := \theta_j - \alpha * \frac{d}{d\theta_j} J(\theta)\ j=1, n$$

By replacing J derivative with its value, the last loop becomes:
```
Repeat {
```
$$\theta_j := \theta_j - \alpha * \frac{1}{m} * \sum_{i=1}^{m} (h(X^i) - Y^i) * X_j^i$$
```
}
```

Where X^i is a vector representing the ith sample/input features, Y^i is the QoE value corresponding to the ith row of the training set, and θ_j represents the learned parameters corresponding to the jth feature/column. The latter are initialized the first time to zero. Then, after each training phase, θ_j are stored to be reused the next phase as initialization values. The 'α' regulate the convergence speed of θ_j values.

The cost function 'J' is a convex function; it has then a unique minimum which is the global minimum at which θ values are best values that gives the minimal distance between predicted and real output values. Convergence of θ_j to best values is guaranteed. But gradient descent is an iterative algorithm and it is known to be too slow as the all dataset is used many times during each iteration. The 'α' parameter needs to be well chosen to speed up the algorithm convergence.

5   Evaluation

Our first goal is to understand the impact of the modification brought to the original Batch Gradient Descent (BGD) algorithm with respect to the optimization of an objective function. In our case, this optimization aims to calculate the best weights that correspond to the QoS and context variables used in the objective function to measure the QoE score. We implemented the original Batch Gradient Descent (BGD) algorithm and our variant Modified BGD (M-BGD) algorithm to compare their performance in term of evolution of the output cost function (equation 2) after each algorithm step. Figure 4 depicts the graphs related to cost function calculated for each algorithm. To generate these graphs, we used some data collected from a QoE study of a multimedia service (video streaming) that involved 24 subjects (6 women and 18 men) aged between 20 to 35 years. The data is composed of output parameters (QoE values given by users) and input parameters including the video category ('0' for fast videos like football match, and '1' for slow videos like a ship moving in the large sea), and QoS parameters (packet loss, packet reorder, video bit rate).

In case of BGD, the cost function is calculated for the whole dataset each time and this is why its graph is smooth (it can be represented with a linear function) and the cost value is decreasing in a steady way. At the other hand, the cost function of M-BDG is calculated only for the available data in the Cache component which makes the cost value oscillate continuously as the model may fit current data while not perfectly fit the next set. The BGD need more data to output a low cost value, while M-BGD is able to output an acceptable cost (less than 1).

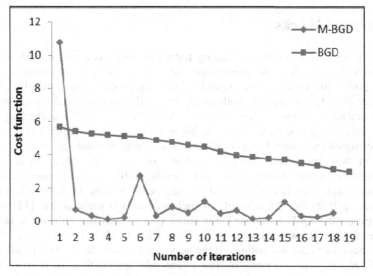

Fig. 4. Cost function graphs of two methods

A second goal is to understand the relation between QoS parameters and QoE scores. For this, we conducted a set of experiments with our framework to collect QoE scores under varied QoS conditions (network related). After aggregating the resulting data, the Figure 5 shows the relation between users QoE and network QoS. It is clear that the obtained QoE scores are inversely related to disturbance of QoS parameters as stated in [9].

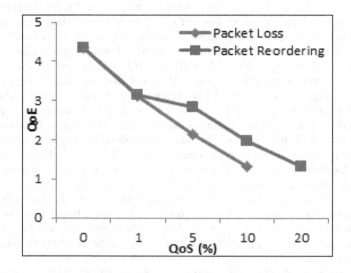

Fig. 5. Relationship between QoE score (y-axis) and QoS values (x-axis)

6   Related Works

Commonly, QoE is evaluated in Living Labs [9] which is a user-centric ecosystem that involves users in testing/assessing new services (e.g. multimedia, games). Another possibility for measuring QoE is to hire a representative panel of real users of the service (e.g. telephony). In both cases, the evaluation is based on questionnaires where users have to answer after a service usage session. After collecting multiple answers from the participant users, the Mean Opinion Score (MOS) [10] method is used to evaluate the overall QoE of the service. These methods are experimental and passive in way they need to: hire a group of users, put them in a controlled environment, experiment the service under study in different conditions, collect data from users and correlate them with experiments setups to finally generate an aggregated QoE model. An example of such approach is presented in [11] where the authors propose a QoE framework for smart phones and use subjective assessment technique for the measurement of QoE. Their framework is based on a client-server model. Once, user data are collected; the server side takes the control of all user data and analyzes it. The purpose of the client-side application is limited to video streaming and reporting user feedback data to the server side. It is not intelligent enough to make any analysis over data and/or produce personalized QoE results for smart phone users.

Objective QoE assessment methods represent another class of approaches which are more active [12] as they attempts to measure QoE by mapping it to some QoS parameters without end-user involvement. An example of such approaches is presented in [6] where the authors proposed a QoE measurements method for smart phones. The method is based on the collection and the processing of QoS data on the user terminal and reporting QoE based on objective (QoS) assessment. Hence they do not require any user feedback. However our work is based on a subjective assessment scheme and it provides more reliable and accurate user QoE. In fact, the generated QoE model is personal as it relies on user input as well as system and network information acquired directly from the user device. These methods rely heavily on QoS indicators to try to approximate the evaluation of the user perception ignoring user contextual information like location. Also, if a QoS to QoE mapping is accurate for a given class of applications, it may become obsolete for another class as different applications have different QoE/QoS requirements. For example, some application may be sensitive to jitter and delay like online video games while others are more sensitive to packet loss like file transferring.; some applications may need a quiet environment to be used (e.g. telephony), while others may need a suitable lighting arrangement (e.g., texting).

Table 2 summarizes the description of these two main QoE measurement approaches, and illustrates as well a comparison between them.

Table 2. QoE measurement approches comparaision

	Data Collection	Data Transmission	Comparison
Objective Methods	QoS	Huge data transmission	Generalized QoE (QoS- specific), Saves time. No User feedback, lacks accuracy
Subjective Methods	Surveyed QoS / QoE	No need for data transmission	Personalized QoE (User-Specific), Time consuming Reliable and Accurate QoE Based on user feedback

Most of the existing QoE measurement tools aims to analyze the user web browsing activities, especially video downloading as it represents a major part of the Internet traffic [13]. Some of these tools usually implement a polling interface to ask more or less interactively the users about their satisfaction. For instance, HostView [14] is an end-host tracing tool that implements a combination of objective and subjective QoE measurement methods. It collects network traffic, system performance information, and prompts also the user for feedback on network performance. Another tool combining both QoE assessment approaches is presented in [15]. This tool does not require any installation on the user side; it uses a heuristic approach to collect user feedbacks in an explicit way. It is able to infer the user impatience from collecting and analyzing the last flags of the TCP connections generated by the user activity as well as the end-to-end network performance. QOM frame work [20] combines both subjective and objective factors, but the most of the QoE processing and management is done at server side.

Typical examples of objective QoE measurement tools include: Netalyzr [16] and a modified version of FasterFox [17]. Netalyzr [16] is client-server application that allows the user to download an applet through which active tests are conducted and collected data are uploaded to some of the predefined Netalyzr servers. In [2] the authors attempted another deployment architecture based on plugins (e.g. browser plugin.); they modified FasterFox [17] which is a Firefox plugin originally developed to speed-up network performances. They used this plugin to collect data from the user browser and to report it to a remote server.

The existing tools relying on QoS data imply the transfer of an important quantity of low level data about network metrics. The aggregation made at the back-end side produce a generalized model about user experience which may lack accuracy. The tools combining objective with subjective measurement approaches provide an enhanced accuracy with a more personalized QoE assessment. Nevertheless, most of these tools do not consider information about user situation which may be important for a more precise user experience assessment. The following table summarizes the description of the presented QoE measurement tools and attempt to compare those tools regarding different implementation and operational characteristics.

Table 3. Summary of existing QoE measurment tools

	Architecture	Measurement technique	Personalization	Metrics
Z. Qia et al. [6]	Client side	Objective QoE Assessment	No	Network parameters
I. Ketykó et al. [11]	Client-Server	Subjective assessment	Partial	Network parameters User feedback
HostView [14]	Client-Server	Combined approache	Yes	Network parameters System performance User feedback
D. Collange et al. [15]	Network centric	Objective QoE	No	Network parameters
Netalyzr [16]	Client-Server	Objective QoE	Partial	Network parameters
J. Shaikh [2]	Client-Server	Objective QoE	No	Application parameters
Laghari et al.[20]	Client-Server	Combined approch	Partial	Network parameters Application params User information
Our proposal	Client side	Combined approache	Yes	Network parameters Device parameters Application params User information

Our proposed QoE framework is a simple, intelligent and self-functioning QoE framework which not only monitors contextual, QoS and user ratings but also makes QoE analysis and decisions on its own at the client side. It does not require any third party servers for data analysis and it produces run time QoE Evaluation. However, the used machine learning technique is rather simple which makes the accuracy of the generated QoE model relatively low. More advanced techniques (e.g. neural networks, Bayesian networks) should be used to enhance the accuracy. To our knowledge there are currently no robust and reliable libraries implementing these techniques on mobile Operating Systems. In further studies, we will investigate the possibility of using such advanced machine learning techniques on mobile platforms, like Android, by porting existing libraries in the Android environment.

7   Conclusion

In this paper, we propose a smartphone-based framework that enables the evaluation of the user experience regarding multimedia streaming services. We present the framework architecture and implementation details. The advantages related to our solution are twofold. First, from the service provider perspective, the framework provides a better user perception assessment as the processed technical and user parameters (QoS, context and user rating data) are collected close to user, directly from the his/her device. Second, from the user viewpoint, he/she has freedom to give his feedback about offered quality at any time through thumbs up/thumbs down icon and/or user rating, with respect to a particular service, and in any situation. Third, from the telecom operator perspective, our framework handles "monitor, analyze and decide" functions on user data on smartphone and it does not require any other server side for these functions, hence there is no need for bulk data transfer. Also, it may give a privacy control to user behavioral requirements. In a future work, we plan to investigate the possibility of using more advanced machine learning techniques (on an Android device) like neural networks to generate a QoE model with better accuracy.

References

1. Chihani, B., Bertin, E., Crespi, N.: Android-based QoE Management Framework. Work in Progress report, IEEE Pervasive Computing, Issue (October/December 2012)
2. Shaikh, J., Fiedler, M., Collange, D.: Quality of Experience from user and network perspectives. Annals of Telecommunications 65(1-2), 47–57 (2010)
3. Chihani, B., Bertin, E., Jeanne, F., Crespi, N.: Context-aware systems: a case study. In: International Conference on Digital Information and Communication Technology and its Applications, France (2011)
4. Hubbe, P., Kerboeuf, S., Leprovost, Y., Mahfoufi, Y.: An Innovative Tool for Measuring Video Streaming QoE. TECHzine Technology and Research E-ZINE (2011)
5. Serral-Gracià, R., Cerqueira, E., Curado, M., Yannuzzi, M., Monteiro, E., Masip-Bruin, X.: An overview of quality of experience measurement challenges for video applications in IP networks. In: International Conference on Wired/Wireless Internet Connections, Sweden (2010)

6. Qiao, Z.: Smarter Phone based Live QoE Measurement. In: 15th International Conference on Intelligence in Next Generation Networks (ICIN 2011), Berlin, Germany (2011)
7. Kaw, A., Kalu, E.: Numerical Methods with Applications: Abridged, 2nd edn. (2011) ISBN: 9780578057651
8. Nabney, I.: NetLab: Algorithms for Pattern Recognition. Springer (2002)
9. Rifai, H., Mohammed, S., Mellouk, A.: A brief synthesis of QoS-QoE methodologies. In: 10th International Symposium on Programming and Systems (ISPS), Algiers, Algeria (2011)
10. International Telecommunication Union, "Methods for Subjective Determination of Tranmission Quality," ITU Recommendation, p.800 (August 1996)
11. Ketykó, I., De Moor, K., De Pessemier, T., Verdejo, A.J., Vanhecke, K., Joseph, W., Martens, L., De Marez, L.: QoE measurement of mobile YouTube video streaming. In: Proceedings of the 3rd Workshop on Mobile Video Delivery (MoViD 2010), Firenze, Italy (2010)
12. Calyam, P., Ekicio, E., Lee, C., Haffner, M., Howes, N.: A gap-model based framework for online VVoIP QoE measurement. Journal of Communications and Networks 9(4), 446–456 (2007)
13. Schatz, R., Egger, S.: Vienna Surfing - Assessing Mobile Broadband Quality in the Field. In: Workshop on Measurements Up the STack (W-MUST), collocated with ACM SIGCOMM, Toronto, Canada (August 2011)
14. Joumblatt, D., Teixeira, R., Chandrashekar, J., Taft, N.: HostView: Annotating End-Host Performance Measurements with User Feedback. In: HotMetrics Workshop, collocated with SIGMETRICS, USA (2010)
15. Collange, D., Hajji, M., Shaikh, J., Fiedler, M., Arlos, P.: User impatience and network performance. In: 8th Euro-NF Conference on Next Generation Internet (NGI), Karlskrona, Sweden (June 2012)
16. Kreibich, C., Weaver, N., Nechaev, B., Paxson, V.: Netalyzr: Illuminating the edge network. In: ACM Internet Measurement Conference (IMC), Melbourne, Australia (2010)
17. FasterFox, http://fasterfox.mozdev.org/ (accessed on March 2013)
18. Laghari, K.U.R., Molina, B., Palau, C.E.: QoE Aware Service Delivery in Distributed Environment. In: IEEE Workshops of International Conference on Advanced Information Networking and Applications (WAINA 2011), March 22-25, pp. 837–842 (2011)
19. Laghari, K.U.R., Connelly, K., Crespi, N.: Toward total quality of experience: A QoE model in a communication ecosystem. IEEE Communications Magazine 50(4), 58–65 (2012)
20. Laghari, K.R., Pham, T.T., Nguyen, H., Crespi, N.: QoM: A new quality of experience framework for multimedia services. In: Proceeding of IEEE Symposium on Computers and Communications (ISCC), pp. 851–856 (2012)

Online Reviews as First Class Artifacts in Mobile App Development

Claudia Iacob[1], Rachel Harrison[1], and Shamal Faily[2]

[1] Oxford Brookes University
Oxford, United Kingdom
{iacob,rachel.harrison}@brookes.ac.uk
[2] Bournemouth University, Bournemouth, United Kingdom
sfaily@bournemouth.ac.uk

Abstract. This paper introduces a framework for developing mobile apps. The framework relies heavily on app stores and, particularly, on online reviews from app users. The underlying idea is that app stores are proxies for users because they contain direct feedback from them. Such feedback includes feature requests and bug reports, which facilitate design and testing respectively. The framework is supported by MARA, a prototype system designed to automatically extract relevant information from online reviews.

Keywords: Mobile apps engineering, app stores, online reviews.

1 Introduction

The mobile application market has grown considerably over the past five years: mobile application downloads are expected to reach 48 billion by 2015 [1]. Surprisingly, however, there is a dearth of work on what the implications of mobile app development might be. Arguably, the theory and practices underpinning classical software and usability engineering need to change. In many cases, individual developers act as both designers and developers as they bring their apps to market. Also, they may share characteristics with end-user developers [2], in that they may lack formal education in software engineering and HCI and build apps that initially satisfy their own requirements before bringing these apps to market. Once available on the market, apps are subject to reviews from their users. App stores provide a straightforward way for users to give feedback on the apps they use, reviews proving to be much more trusted by users than the descriptions that developers provide [3].

Several studies on the impact that online reviews have on users have been conducted [4, 7, 8, 9, 10], but there has been little interest on how online reviews could benefit developers. A tool for retrieving information relevant for developers from online reviews is described in [5], but no framework to incorporate the tool and make it directly available to developers has been presented. This work aims to fill this gap and introduce a framework for developing mobile apps, which relies heavily on app stores and, particularly, on online reviews from app users. The paper is structured

G. Memmi and U. Blanke (Eds.): MobiCASE 2013, LNICST 130, pp. 47–53, 2014.
© Institute for Computer Sciences, Social Informatics and Telecommunications Engineering 2014

as follows: Section 2 introduces the framework, while Section 3 describes supporting tools and their role in the framework; Section 4 briefly points out the scarcity of research in related areas. Lastly, the paper ends with conclusions and ideas for future work.

2   A Framework for Mobile App Development

App stores now have a place in the app development cycle. They collect direct feedback from users, including them indirectly in the whole development loop. In [5], the authors identified several recurring themes users report through online reviews. Such themes include feature requests and bug reports.

Feature requests inform design processes and support designers in eliciting users' requirements. In classical software engineering, such processes are usually supported by techniques such as focus groups, interviews, or questionnaires where users need to be present and are subject to questioning or analysis. App stores change this by providing direct feedback from users without them interacting with the actual designers. Even though such feedback is less structured, it is provided with little bias and in copious amounts. Writing a review does not require a user to be in laboratory settings and hence does not risk the possible bias, which may come from that context.

The deployment of apps is done on app stores. Users can use the app and evaluate it, and provide direct feedback on any possible malfunctions of the app. Such feedback is mostly expressed as bugs. Usually, evaluating an interactive system involves laboratory usability testing. In the case of apps, however, bugs get reported through reviews. At their own pace, users make use of apps and then report on the problems they encounter, feeding such data back to the designers and developers and also supporting the maintenance processes of apps. Thus app stores can be thought of as proxies for users.

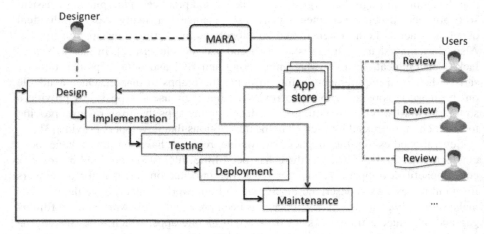

Fig. 1. A new model for app development

There are two challenges that this approach faces. On the one hand, the number of online reviews for an app may make it impossible for one developer to go through them all and manually identify relevant information for the development process or trends in such information. On the other hand, the language used in reviews rarely respects grammar norms and rules, making it difficult to apply Natural Language Processing techniques to automatically extract information from reviews.

We have developed a tool called MARA (Mobile App Repository Analyzer) to answer these challenges. In its first iteration (described in [5]) MARA was designed to: 1) retrieve all the reviews of an app as HTML pages directly from the app store, 2) parse the raw description of the reviews and extract their content and meta-data (e.g. the date the review was posted, user information, device information associated with the review, scores from users etc.), 3) store the content and meta-data, and 4) mine for feature requests in the review content. To better support the framework described in this paper, we extended the tool to extract other types of feedback as well.

3 MARA, Version Two

We extended MARA to extract other types of feedback as well as feature requests. We are particularly interested in mining for bugs. Therefore, we adapted and extended the tool's architecture to answer such needs. The mining algorithms (4 in Figure 2) takes as input: a) the content of a set of reviews (for example, all the reviews of a given app) and b) a set of linguistic rules defined to model the language used (e.g. the language for feature requests, bugs, customer support feedback, usability feedback, etc). It then outputs all the sentence fragments in the review content which match at least one linguistic rule in the set used as input (i.e. all feature requests, or bugs).

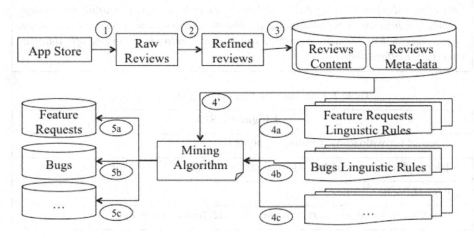

Fig. 2. MARA Architecture

3.1   Extracting Bugs

Based on the sample of 3279 randomly chosen reviews described in [5], we defined the set of linguistic rules associated with bugs. To do this, we manually extracted bug reports from the sample. We identified three categories of bugs: *major*, *medium*, and *minor* bugs and two main differences between these. First, they differ in the extent of the malfunctioning caused by the bug. *Major* bugs make it impossible to use the app. *Medium* bugs affect just one specific function of the app leaving the rest to function properly. *Minor* bugs are issues of only slight severity, which do not prevent the user from using any of the app's functions. Second, they differ in the level of frustration the users express. *Major* bugs are often expressed as *"forced shutdown many times"*, *"crashes at the end of the race"*, *"fails and loses entire workout"*, *"app is not working"*, or *"it won't open"*. *Medium* bugs are less intense and more specific, focusing on a particular aspect of an app - *"does not show any tracks of previous workouts"*, *"the Slovenian dictionary is missing even the basic words"*, *"miles do not add right"*, *"I did not create a password. Yet it asks me for my password"*. *Minor* bugs are merely observations related to a feature of an app - *"slight issue with GPS data"*, *"a little bug on the Persian keyboard"*, *"text overlaps for lower percentages"*. The majority of the bugs identified were major bugs (38.10%), while medium severity bugs accounted for 28.33% of the entire feedback reporting usage issues. 20.5% of the reported bugs were minor.

We aimed to identify linguistic rules defining each type of bug. Following the process described in details for feature requests [5], we associated each sentence labelled as a bug in the training sample with a keyword.

Table 1. Keywords for expressing major bugs

closes, can't/cannot/couldn't, don't/doesn't/does not/didn't, not, fail, crashes, lag, error, stopped, freeze, won't/will not, not able to, locks, unable to, erased, eliminated, impossible to, impossible to, glitches, reboot, annoying, problems with, bugs, causes, lost, restart, horrible, slows down, reloads, switches off, timeout, wouldn't, malfunction

Table 2. Linguistic rules for defining feature requests

Linguistic Rule
stopped {downloading, running, syncing}
{don't, doesn't, none, didn't} *work (since the update)*
impossible to <action>
will not (even) {open, start, execute, activate, install, show up}

We then identified all the keywords associated with more than 3 sentences in order to exclude accidental associations of keywords with sentences. The number of keywords we filtered in the case of medium and minor bugs was not conclusive enough to support further analysis. However, in the case of major bugs we identified 33 keywords (Table 1). The keywords filtered do not always point to bugs; therefore, we went through all the sentences associated with these keywords and identified the contexts in which these keywords are used. We further abstracted these contexts into 74 linguistic rules. A fragment of this set is shown in Table 2.

3.2   Evaluation

To evaluate this revised version of MARA, we replicated the evaluation approach described in [5], but for bugs rather than feature requests. We used precision (P)[1], recall (R)[2], and Matthews Correlation Coefficient (MCC)[3] to measure the performance of the algorithm when extracting bugs. We defined: a) true positives (TP) as the correctly returned bug reports, b) false positives (FP) as the returned results which are not the actual bug reports, c) true negatives (TN) as the non bugs not returned as results, d) false negatives (FN) as actual bug reports not returned as results. We evaluated the tool with the same testing sample described in [5]; this contained all the reviews of half of the non-free apps available on the Google app store. We selected paid apps mainly because they tend to receive more reviews. The sample consisted of 136,998 reviews in total. We ran the mining algorithm on the sample using the linguistic rules defined for the bug reports. For measuring precision, we randomly selected 3000 outputs of the algorithm and a human coder went through them to identify the true positives. Based on that, we computed a value $P = 0.91$ for bugs. For measuring recall and Matthews Correlation Coefficient, we randomly selected one app and we considered its reviews as our sample. The results we obtained are summarized in Table 3.

Table 3. Recall and MCC metrics

Inputs	R	MCC
778	0.89	0.91

4   Related Work

To the best of our knowledge, little research on online reviews has focused on mobile apps. However, there has been a keen interest among researchers in studying the impact of online reviews on both customer behavior [6] and product sales [4, 6, 7, 9, 10]. Based on an analysis of customer reviews of books from two different online bookstores, Chevalier et al. [6] found that a) in general, reviews are overwhelmingly positive, b) the popularity of different types of books is very similar across the two

---

[1] Precision is the ratio between the returned results which are actual feature requests (TPs) and the total number of returned results (TPs + FPs)

[2] Recall is the ratio between the returned results which are actual feature requests (TPs) and the total number of feature requests in the input (TPs + FNs)

[3] MCC value is between -1 and 1, with MCC = 1 for a perfect predictor, MCC = 0 for a random predictor, and MCC = -1 for a perfect inverted predictor.

sites studied, c) the impact of 1-star reviews is greater than the impact of 5-star reviews, and d) an improvement in a book's reviews leads to an increase in sales of that book on the site. Bounie et al. [4] analyzed the effect of online reviews of video games on purchasing decisions and compared them to personal and expert reviews. They found that offline information sources such as specialized magazines and trial versions as well as online information have a significant positive effect on video game purchases. When it comes to online reviews, half of the respondents claimed to always consult such reviews and 57% of them reported purchasing a video game after consulting the reviews.

The impact of a review's content and length on its helpfulness to a decision process are analyzed in [8]. The authors suggest that extremely negative reviews are perceived as less helpful than moderate ones and they classify products as search goods (i.e. a good for which it is easy to obtain information on product quality prior to interaction with the product) and experience goods (i.e. a good for which interaction with the product is necessary to obtain information on the product). Moreover, they found that the depth of a review has a positive effect on the helpfulness of the review, whereas the length of a review increases the helpfulness of a search good review more than that of an experience good review. We are not aware of studies looking into how manufacturers/developers make use of reviews to improve their products.

5   Conclusions and Future Work

In this paper, we argue that classic software engineering models and techniques may not be suitable for the development context of mobile apps. Online reviews of mobile apps hold a place in app development. The growth in the number of apps, the demographics of app developers, and the emergence of the app store distribution model mean that online reviews need to step forward and take a more productive role in the engineering of apps. In a move towards evidence based app engineering we introduce a framework which supports the full integration of user feedback reported through app stores in various phases of the app development process. During the design phase, feature requests from users are automatically extracted from reviews and the designer can then use them to guide future iterations of the app. During the testing and maintenance phases, bug reports coming from users are automatically extracted and used to help improve the apps.

As future work, we are designing studies for evaluating MARA involving app developers over longer periods of time. We are mainly interested in addressing the usability issues the tool might have and the impact its use has on the overall app development process.

References

1. http://cdn.idc.com/research/Predictions12/Main/downloads/IDCTOP10Predictions2012.pdf
2. Fischer, G., Giaccardi, E., Ye, Y., Sutcliffe, A.G., Mehandjiev, N.: Meta-design: a manifesto for end-user development. Commun. ACM 47(9), 33–37 (2004)

3. http://www.itu.int/ITU-D/ict/facts/
   2011/material/ICTFactsFigures2011.pdf
4. Bounie, D., Bourreau, M., Gensollen, M., Waelbroeck, P.: Do Online Customer Reviews
   Matter? Evidence from the Video Game Industry, Telecom ParisTech Working Paper No.
   ESS-08-02
5. Iacob, C., Harrison, R.: Retrieving and analyzing mobile apps feature requests from online
   reviews. In: Proceedings of the 10th Working Conference on Mining Software
   Repositories (MSR 2013), pp. 41–44 (2013)
6. Chevalier, J.A., Mayzlin, D.: The Effect of Word of Mouth on Sales: Online Book
   Reviews. Journal of Marketing Research 43(3), 345–354 (2006)
7. Dellarocas, C., Awad, N.F., Zhang, X.: Exploring the Value of Online Product Ratings in
   Revenue Forecasting: The Case of Motion Pictures. In: Proc. of ICIS 2004, pp. 379–386
   (2004)
8. Mudambi, S.M., Schuff, D.: What makes a helpful online review? a study of customer
   reviews on amazon.com. MIS Q. 34(1), 185–200 (2010)
9. Zhang, Z., Varadarajan, B.: Utility scoring of product reviews. In: Proc. of CIKM 2006,
   pp. 51–57. ACM Press (2006)
10. Zhang, X., Dellarocas, C.: The Lord of the Ratings: How a Movie's Fate is Influenced by
    Reviews? In: Proc. of ICIS 2006, pp. 1959–1978 (2006)

SaSYS: A Swipe Gesture-Based System for Exploring Urban Environments for the Visually Impaired

Jee-Eun Kim, Masahiro Bessho, Noboru Koshizuka, and Ken Sakamura

Interfaculty Initiative in Information Studies, The University of Tokyo,
7-3-1 Hongo, Bunkyo-ku, Tokyo, Japan
{kim,besshy,koshizuka,ken}@sakamura-lab.org

Abstract. Exploring and learning an environment is a particularly challenging issue faced by visually impaired people. Existing interaction techniques for allowing users to learn an environment may not be useful while traveling because they often use dedicated hardware or require users to focus on tactile or auditory feedback. In this paper, we introduce an intuitive interaction technique for selecting areas of interests in urban environments by performing simple swipe gestures on touchscreen. Based on the swipe-based interaction, we developed SaSYS, a location-aware system that enables users to discover points of interest (POI) around them using off-the-shelf smartphones. Our approach can be easily implemented on handheld devices without requiring any dedicated hardware and having users to constantly focus on tactile or auditory feedback. SaSYS also provides a fine-grained control over Text-to-Speech (TTS). Our user study shows that 9 of 11 users preferred swipe-based interaction to existing pointing-based interaction.

Keywords: Accessibility, mobile devices, visually impaired, touchscreens, location-based services.

1 Introduction

Traveling to unfamiliar places still remains one of the major challenges faced by people with visual impairments. Although many guidance systems providing turn-by-turn directions to predetermined destinations have been developed, such systems are inadequate in that they fail to address one of the most important navigational needs: exploring and learning one's surroundings [9, 23]. Visually impaired people often get knowledge about what is around them by walking with sighted people. However, it is important to enhance their ability to explore surrounding points of interest (POI) for making their travels more independent and enjoyable. This need is also recognized by large-scale field tests in our research project, carried over a decade, using ubiquitous computing technologies for enhancing mobility experience of the visually impaired [18, 19, 20].

Map exploration systems [21, 24] are one of the effective options for visually impaired people to learn an environment. They often adopt tactile or auditory feedback to interact with information on maps, and this may require dedicated hardware.

G. Memmi and U. Blanke (Eds.): MobiCASE 2013, LNICST 130, pp. 54–71, 2014.

Fig. 1. Participant searching for POIs using SaSYS by performing swipe gestures

These interaction techniques may be useful for learning an environment in detail, but are hard to apply to discover POIs while walking. Automatically notifying immediate surroundings could be another option [1, 3], but may not be useful when users want to retrieve POIs at their discretion. Thus, how to allow users to interact with the surrounding geo-located information space is the key to effectively support exploratory traveling [16]. To this end, we introduce a novel and simple touch-based interaction method, *swipe-to-search* that allows visually impaired users to select areas of interests. Users intuitively specify the direction (relative to the direction they are facing) and distance of areas of interest by swipe gestures on touchscreen. For example, users can find nearby POIs in front of them by performing short swipe-up gestures, and distant POIs on their right by performing long swipe-right gestures. In this paper, it is shown that swipe-to-search is usable and acceptable to visually impaired users. Pointing a smartphone towards areas of interest has been used for retrieving POIs [23], but this method could have usability issues. For example, the user might lose his sense of direction and spatial orientation because he must make a 180° turn while searching backward.

Based on swipe-to-search, we developed SaSYS (Swipe and Scan Your Surroundings) on a smartphone, which enables users to search for POIs such as restaurants and stores (Figure 1). SaSYS provides interaction methods that can be used to control audio information by allowing the user to draw shapes on touchscreen. For example, while listening to user reviews about some restaurants, the user can skip to the next review by drawing a triangle. SaSYS also offers auditory and olfactory features of POI such as "There is a café on the right, near which coffee aroma can be experienced".

This paper presents two major contributions. First, we present the design, implementation and evaluation of a swipe-based interaction technique that offers several benefits over the existing pointing-based approaches. Second, we designed and implemented speech feedback control feature on touch-based interface. Importance of speech feedback control has been recognized in the literature [6], but none of the existing systems presents any concrete implementation. We conducted a user study with 11 visually impaired users comparing SaSYS's swipe-based interaction against pointing-based interaction. We also investigated the usefulness of TTS (Text-to-Speech) controls provided by SaSYS.

The rest of this paper is organized as follows. In Section 2, we explore interaction techniques that help visually impaired users learn an environment. In Section 3, we describe the design of our interaction methods and implementation of SaSYS in detail. Section 4 and 5 present the design of a user study to verify the usability of our interaction techniques and its results. In Section 6, we discuss our findings and future work. Finally, section 7 concludes this paper.

2   Related Work

In this section, we investigate IT-assisted interaction techniques that support exploratory traveling for people with visual impairments. We also briefly investigate eye-free interaction techniques on touch-based mobile devices for exploring the potential of our approach to be used in map-based applications.

2.1   Exploration Support Systems

We investigated two major areas of work that give an opportunity for visually impaired users to explore and learn about their surroundings: (a) map exploration systems that enable users to learn spatial and geographic information, and (b) navigation and wayfinding systems that provide POI information in situ during navigation.

The BATS [13] project uses force-feedback and spatial sound to deliver spatial information with tactile input devices. Pielot et al. [14] developed an auditory city map that leverages computer vision technology to trace a tangible object regarded as the representation of the listener on a virtual map. Some map exploration systems allow the user to grasp layout of streets. Poppinga et al. [15] examined the use of vibration and speech feedback on handheld touch screens to make the road network accessible to the user. Timbremap [21] uses the sonification to guide the user's finger to trace routes on a mobile device. While map exploration systems listed above provide spatial information in detail, SpaceSence [24] offers high-level spatial relationships between two locations. It uses custom spatial tactile feedback hardware on a mobile device, which generates vibrations to the user's palm indicating location of POI. However, these techniques require the user to concentrate on sound and/or tactile feedback, which make them difficult to use while traveling. Furthermore, many of these systems need haptic input devices or dedicated hardware (costly and bothersome to carry). Thus, approaches in map exploration systems may not be useful for exploring urban environments.

Bellotti et al.'s tour guide system [1] and Chatty Environment [3] provide information when the user passes near the objects with a RFID tag. This type of push-based approach may be appropriate for providing POI information in situations such as museum or zoo tours. However, in urban environments, it would be more appropriate to allow the user to search for areas of interest at will. Yang et al. [23] addressed this issue by providing both push- and pull-based information retrieval. Their system automatically notifies the user of nearby POIs, and at the same time allows the user to search distant locations by pointing a handheld device. In this way, the system enhances the chance to discover POIs and encourages the user to learn the surroundings in the process of wayfinding. Pointing-based mobile interaction has been recognized as an effective means of location selection [4, 17], and adopted by several exploration and navigation systems for sighted people as well [16, 22]. However, as stated earlier, 'point-to-search' technique may have problems especially for visually impaired users. Furthermore, pointing allows the user to show only desired directions without any mechanism for specifying distance. Allowing the user to adjust the scope of search space could provide a better user experience when the user wants to search further or closer areas.

2.2   Touch-Based Mobile Device Accessibility

As handheld devices such as smartphones have gained widespread popularity, many research efforts have been investigating interaction techniques in order to make touch-based mobile devices accessible to visually impaired people. For example, SlideRule [8] uses multi-touch gestures to menu and item selection for applications such as e-mail clients, music players, and phone books. Also Apple's VoiceOver[1], screen-reading technology, allows visually impaired users to use iPhone. Text-based contents are getting accessible to the user, but visual-based contents (e.g., maps) still remain inaccessible [2]. While existing interaction techniques cover several useful applications such as a mobile messenger or a mobile player [10], little attention has been given to gesture-based interaction techniques for map-based applications (e.g., Google Maps, Yelp[2], etc.). Our swipe-to-search method has potential to be used for these map-based applications for visually impaired users.

3   SaSYS System

SaSYS is a location-aware system running on touch-based handheld devices that allows visually impaired users to discover POIs and get detailed information about them. To provide useful and easy-to-use interaction methods for searching and obtaining POI information, we designed SaSYS to achieve the following:

- SaSYS enables users to search for POIs in all directions, and allows them to adjust the scope of search areas at will.
- SaSYS enables users to obtain information effectively from auditory information, as needed, by allowing them to choose what to listen to.

Furthermore, we explored what kind of POI information could be useful for visually impaired people [5, 7]. SaSYS can provide olfactory and auditory features of POI (currently manually collected in a specific area).

The current system was developed through an iterative design process in consultation with a blind teacher of University of Tsukuba's Special Needs Education School for the Visually Impaired. Since he works with visually impaired students, his comments and suggestions were really helpful to incrementally improve our system. The system development process included three iterations of design, implementation,

---

[1] http://www.apple.com/accessibility/iphone/vision.html
[2] http://www.yelp.com/yelpmobile

testing and refinement. First, we conducted initial prototype test with the blind teacher to assess the feasibility of our swipe-to-search approach, and discover potential usability problems. He provided the following feedback for ensuring better user experience:

- *Only intentional touches should be recognized; the prototype should provide some kind of a 'touch trigger' to avoid accidental activation.* Therefore, we chose the volume keys on the side to act as a 'touch trigger', effectively ignoring touch inputs when one of the volume keys is not pressed.
- *Let users know what appears onscreen, and provide instructions in order not to get lost while navigating the application.* Thus, we give instructions for non-triggered touches as well. For example, if the POIs list shows up on screen, the following voice instruction is given: "POIs list. Swipe up and down to navigate POIs and double-tap to select one."
- *Minimize the number of drawings for TTS controls to remember them easily.* Therefore, we made the basic shapes to mean different interactions depending on whether or not they are drawn while the volume key is pressed. For example, while listening to audio information, drawing a greater-than sign with the volume-up key pressed would cause *speech rate up*, whereas doing the same with the volume-down key pressed would skip to the next sentence (Figure 4).

After refining the prototype as described above, we again consulted the blind teacher to ensure usability improvements before conducting a user study. Moreover, we demonstrated the refined prototype to 3 blind individuals at the 2013 TRON Enableware Symposium[3] to examine our swipe-based system's usability. One of them was iPhone user and the others had never experienced using smartphones. All of them could understand, and perform swipe-to-search with interest, indicating the potential of our interaction technique.

SaSYS interactions consist of two modes: scanning mode to retrieve POIs by swipe gestures, and content listening mode to listen details of selected POI information. The following sections present two modes illustrating how we achieve the design goals and describe implementation of SaSYS in detail, highlighting its novel interactive features.

3.1   Scanning Mode

Scanning mode allows the user to retrieve POIs and select one from the list of POIs. SaSYS's swipe-to-search interaction is derived from very simple and intuitive ideas. Suppose that you were asked to present a desired direction on the paper. Drawing an arrow might be one of the easiest ways to show the direction. Additionally what if you were asked to indicate the relative distances you want to know? You can intuitively express the sense of distance by drawing different lengths of arrows. We have implemented these ideas on a touch screen smartphone. The user first touches any point on touch screen, which is regarded as the current location, then draw a line towards a desired direction. This simple gesture gives the user a POIs list within the area of interest.

---

[3] http://www.tron-enableware.org/en/

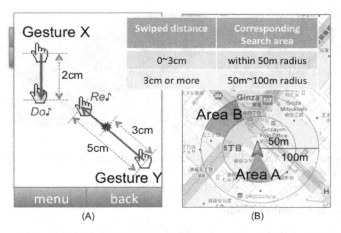

Fig. 2. Examples of swipe-to-search. (A) Gesture X retrieves POIs within Area A, and (B) Gesture Y retrieves POIs within Area B.

An example of swipe-to-search is illustrated in Figure 2. In the example, swiped distances between 0 to 3cm retrieve POIs within 50m radius, and 3cm or more retrieve POIs within from 50 to 100m radius in the 8 cardinal directions. The user can customize the swiped distances and their corresponding search radii. When the user performs a short swipe-down gesture ("Gesture X" in Figure 2A), SaSYS offers a POIs list within 50m behind the user (Area A in Figure 2B). Also, the user can retrieve POIs between 50m and 100m front-left by performing a long swipe gesture diagonally ("Gesture Y" in Figure 2A and Area B in Figure 2B). In this manner, the user can intuitively explore nearby places by short swipes and distant places by long swipes in all directions.

POI retrieval process includes three steps: (a) measure a direction and distance of a swipe gesture, (b) convert swiped distance to predetermined search ranges and calculate the latitude and longitude of the center of a target area, and (c) get POIs information within the area and read the search results via TTS.

In addition to explicit speech feedback about swipe gestures performed by the user, SaSYS provides vibrotactile and auditory feedback for assisting the user to perform swipe-to-search. For example, while performing Gesture Y as depicted in Figure 2A, the user will receive vibrotactile feedback as he advances from Area A to Area B, crossing the 50m radius of Area A (3cm gesture equivalent). The duration of the vibration will be in effect corresponding to $(3\pm\alpha)$cm, where α (currently 20mm) is a configurable parameter. It helps the user perform swipe gestures as he intended by allowing him to know how long he slid his finger. Auditory feedback, one of 7 notes in the major scale, is given according to the radius of search areas (e.g., Figure 2B has two areas, A and B) when the user's finger lifts off the screen after finishing the swipe gesture. Swipe gestures specifying further areas get higher notes; for example, if search space is divided into 3 areas, then swipe gestures searching for the third area play "Mi".

The user can perform swipe-up and swipe-down gesture to navigate the list of retrieved POIs. SaSYS reads brief description of the POI that includes the name and distance from user's current location. The user can select POI for detailed information by double-tap. We use hardware back button (standard for most Android phones) to go back to the swipe-to-search mode from navigating the POI list.

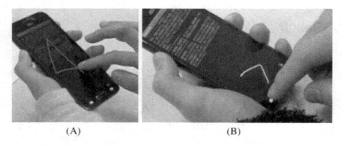

Fig. 3. Participants performing TTS controls: (A) skip by drawing a triangle and (B) forward by drawing a greater-than sign

3.2   Contents Listening Mode

After the user selects POI on the list, SaSYS provides more detailed information with several controls that make TTS repeat, forward, skip, etc. When sighted people search for POI using mobile applications (e.g., nearby restaurants for lunch), they might look over or into detailed information to filter information they want to get (e.g., the latest review). However, it is difficult for visually impaired users to get desired information efficiently through unilateral auditory information. The user may have to listen again from the beginning for missed information that sighted people may not need even a second to read again. Although the need for TTS controls has been reported [6], few systems provide this feature. Therefore, it is necessary to provide TTS controls feature for visually impaired users to obtain desired information effectively from TTS by allowing them to choose what to listen to.

We use gesture-based interactions that allow the users to control TTS by letting them draw shapes on touchscreen (Figure 3). TTS controls include play, pause,

Functionality	User Interface
Play and pause	Double tap with pressing the volume down key
Forward	Drawing ⟩ with pressing the volume down key
Backward	Drawing ⟨ with pressing the volume down key
Next content	Drawing  ▷ with pressing the volume down key
Previous content	Drawing  ◁ with pressing the volume down key
Change the information category	Drawing  ◁▷ with pressing the volume up key
Repeat	Drawing ℗ with pressing the volume down key
Speech rate up	Drawing ⟩ with pressing the volume up key
Speech rate down	Drawing ⟨ with pressing the volume up key

Fig. 4. The gesture set used for TTS controls

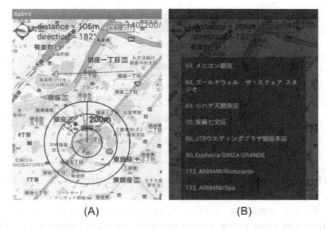

(A)   (B)

Fig. 5. A screenshot after performing 'swipe-to-search'. (A) The blue arrow shows the gesture performed by the user; the green and red dots present retrieved POIs but only red dots will be introduced to the user. (B) The list of retrieved POIs.

repeat, go forward and backward by the sentence, skip to the next and previous by the item (e.g., each customer review), and speech rate up and down. By providing various control features, SaSYS helps the user 'look over' or 'look into' detailed information. We initially assigned gestures to each TTS control in accordance with design guidelines for accessible touchscreens [10, 11]. For denoting gestures, Figure 4 shows a set of shapes provided by SaSYS. However, in the future, it would be desirable to enable the user to customize the gesture-shape mapping.

3.3   Implementation

SaSYS is implemented on Android platform, and currently running on Samsung Galaxy S2 and Galaxy Nexus. SaSYS makes use of smartphone's GPS-based positioning and a built-in compass to identify the user's current position and orientation. We used commercially available SOVOX Classic TTS engine with Japanese language pack to provide POI information and interact with the user. We also utilized Gesture Builder which is an application included in Android 1.6 and higher SDK platforms to create custom gestures used for TTS control interactions. Gesture Builder allows developers to create a library of pre-defined gestures that can be used in their applications.

When the user performs a swipe gesture, SaSYS retrieves POIs on the map (Figure 5A), and then immediately transit to the screen that shows the list of search results (Figure 5B). After the user selects POI, SaSYS moves to the screen that shows detailed information (Figure 3).

SaSYS offers rich information about points of interest. The current implementation of SaSYS supports a use case of practical importance of going around in Ginza, a famous shopping and entertainment district in Tokyo. We used Kokosil[4] API that provides local businesses information in Ginza. To help the user find desired information easily,

---

[4] `http://home.ginza.kokosil.net/en/`

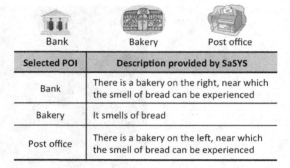

Fig. 6. Examples of contextual cues as auditory and olfactory features of POI

we categorized POI information into four types: general information, user reviews, advertisements (e.g., discount coupons, events, etc.) and contextual cues. The user can move between not only items but also categories so as to save time by listening to only information of interest. General information includes a short description about POI, business hours, address, regular holidays and additional features such as history of POI. User reviews and advertisements are retrieved from Kokosil and Twitter. Advertisements often contain URL for further information, but it can be tiresome for the user listen to the meaningless characters via TTS. Thus, SaSYS examines posts and removes URLs if any. Contextual cues are information about auditory and olfactory features of POI. For example, aroma of coffee near a café or sound of outdoor air conditioner units. This contextual information can be useful to visually impaired people when they get near to a desired POI. To the best of our knowledge, there is no content provider that offers auditory or olfactory features of POI. Therefore, we manually collected contextual information of POIs in Ginza. This information is created as a CSV file. When the user selects POI, SaSYS searches this file whether the POI has any contextual features. Figure 6 presents contextual cues provided by SaSYS.

4   User Study Design

To verify the usability of interaction techniques provided by SaSYS, we conducted experimental evaluation with 11 visually impaired participants in the laboratory. Our user study consists of three parts: A) verifying the ease-of-use and usefulness of swipe-to-search approach by comparing to point-to-search approach, B) verifying the effectiveness of TTS controls feature, and C) obtaining user feedback on the overall system. The whole process of the experiment was conducted in Japanese, and was video taped for later analysis.

4.1   Participants

Eleven visually impaired participants (4 male and 7 female; P1-P11) were recruited for the study. Their degree of visual impairments varied: 9 of them were blind and 2

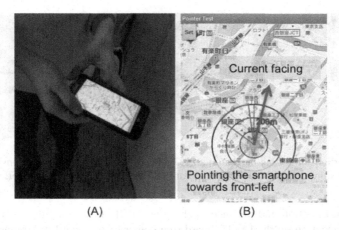

(A)   (B)

Fig. 7. An example of performing Pointer Test: (A) searching POIs on front-left by pointing the smartphone to that direction, and (B) a screenshot after performing (A)

had low vision. The average age of the participants was 23.09 (SD=8.1). 2 participants were iPhone users. The others are not smartphone users but 3 of them had experience with touchscreen mobile devices. All participants use white canes as mobility aids and 6 participants had experience with GPS navigation systems. The entire study took on average 2 hours.

4.2 Part A: Swipe-Based Interaction

For comparison with pointing-based interaction, we developed an Android application called 'Pointer Test' that provides the same functionalities as SaSYS, but using point-to-search. Pointer Test retrieves POIs by pointing the smartphone in a desired direction and double tapping on the screen (Figure 7).

To allow the users to develop a clear impression of both approaches, we asked them to perform the following task using both applications:

"Imagine that you stand at an exit of Ginza subway station. Before traveling, you want to know what is around you. Explore your surroundings with the given application. Please try to find four specific stores in Ginza and remember their locations. After 10 minutes, represent each location on a LEGO board with blocks, and tell us the names of each store"

Both SaSYS and Pointer Test used the same POIs set which consists of 66 POIs in Ginza within a 200m radius centered on the participant's simulated location. We divided SaSYS's search space into 3 areas by swiped distances: searches from 0 to 70m radius (corresponds to from 0 to 2cm swipes), from 70 to 140m radius (corresponds to from 2 to 4cm swipes), and from 140 to 200m radius (corresponds to over 4cm swipes). We limited the number of POIs for the experimental purpose because navigating too many search results was cumbersome to the participants. The participants were asked to

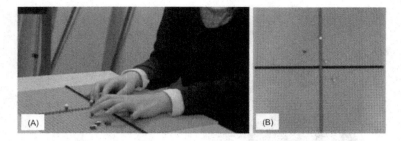

Fig. 8. (A) Participant putting blocks on a LEGO board to present spatial relationships among the location of stores. (B) Spatial relationship of POIs as perceived by a participant.

remember the direction and distance of the given POIs when they discover them and present their location on the LEGO board (the center of the board was regarded as the current position of the user) (Figure 8). We used LEGO to enable the participants to simply express the relative spatial relationships among stores. To avoid making the task into a test of how well the participants were able to remember the given locations, we allowed the users to ask the name of given stores while performing the task.

To minimize the influence of area familiarity from the former session, we set different current locations for each session (exit A3 at first and then exit B4 of Ginza subway station, regardless of which application would be used first). We randomly chose 6 participants to use swipe-to-search first and the others to use point-to-search first. At the beginning of each task, we conducted a training session for all participants until they became familiar with the application. After finishing the task for both applications, we asked the participants to answer the questionnaire about ease-of-use and usefulness of each approach.

4.3   Part B: TTS Controls

We asked the participants to answer three questions while listening to POI information about a restaurant. To avoid making the task too simple, we added more user reviews and advertisements manually, collected from social network services. The questions include *(Q1) What time does the restaurant close?, (Q2) how much the cheapest menu of the restaurant in the user reviews? and (Q3) what services does the coupon offer during lunch?*

We gave enough time to the participants to interact with TTS controls and give the answers. At the beginning of the task, we provided a training session for drawing shapes on the touchscreen until the participants could remember all controls and perform them. When the participants had difficulty in performing the task, the experimenter assisted them to draw the shapes.

After the participants finished the task, we asked them to answer the questionnaire about the effectiveness of TTS controls provided by SaSYS.

4.4   Part C: User Feedback on the Overall System Design

After the participants had completed the tasks we conducted an interview about the overall experience with SaSYS. We asked the participants to provide any comments on SaSYS including additional functionalities that they would like to have, potential use cases, gesture-based interactions on the touchscreen, etc.

We also investigated whether the auditory and olfactory features of POI provided by SaSYS could be useful for visually impaired people. Furthermore, we asked the participants to mention other helpful contextual information that they would like to acquire through SaSYS.

5   Results

5.1   Part A: Swipe-Based Interaction Results

The participants generally were able to complete the task using both applications. All participants could discover the given stores, but some participants had difficulties in remembering the location and name of the stores when they were asked to put the blocks on the LEGO board. 11 participants presented the location of 4 given stores using the 2 interaction methods, 88 items in total. They were able to properly put the blocks with the store names 71 times, only the locations without the names 4 times, and completely failed to put the blocks 13 times (8 times with SaSYS and 5 times with Pointer Test). After finishing both sessions, the participants rated each interaction method in terms of usefulness and ease-of-use using a 5-point Likert scale (1=Disagree strongly, 5=Agree strongly). The results are shown in Table1.

Table 1. The ratings on Ease-of-Use and Usefulness for each interaction method (Mean, SD)

Interaction method	Ease-of-Use	Usefulness
Swipe-to-search	3.91 (1.04)	4.36 (0.81)
Point-to-search	3.18 (1.33)	3.72 (1.19)

Although a Wilcoxon test did not find a significant difference regarding both ease-of-use ($z=1.26$, $p=.24$) and usefulness ($z=1.51$, $p=.14$), 9 of 11 participants preferred swiped-based interaction to pointing-based interaction (P9 chose swipe-to-search on the condition that search space is not divided by swiped distances) when they were asked to indicate their favorite of the two interaction methods.

We also asked the participants to comment on the reasons why they thought the method they chose was better than the other. The participants who liked *swipe-to-search* commented as follows:

- Easy to search backward while walking (P1, P6, P7, P8, P9 and P11).
- Pointing a device is not realistic in a crowded place, whereas swiping on the screen allows him to intuitively imagine his surroundings (P2).

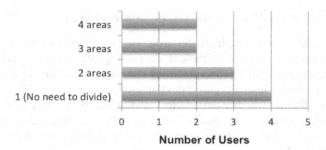

Fig. 9. Participants' preference of the number of areas they would like the search space to be divided into

- Pointing a device on the street would be embarrassing (P4).
- Adjusting search areas by swiped distances would be useful in different use cases (P10).

On the other hand, the participants who liked *point-to-search* commented as follows:

- Retrieving POIs by double tapping was easy to use and simple (P3 and P5)

Participants explicitly mentioned the concerns about losing their sense of direction and the awareness of their body position in relation to the surroundings when they turn around for searching backward with Pointer Test. P8 said, *"Compared to performing swipes, it is quite demanding to turn around with holding the device [for searching]. I found [Pointer Test] tiresome for having to change my body position."* P7 also pointed out, *"Turning the direction [of the device] or changing one's own body position would end up losing the sense of direction."*

Although most participants preferred SaSYS's swipe-based interaction method, some participants were either neutral or positive about Pointer Test's pointing-based interaction method. P2 noted, *"I think it would be useful to go to the [discovered] place by moving the device [with Pointer Test] after understanding the surroundings by moving the finger [with SaSYS]...So it is hard to say which one is better"* and added *"but surely, the one with moving the finger [swipe-based interaction method] is necessary as a means of imaging the surroundings."* Similarly, P6 commented, *"While I generally prefer swipe [based interaction] mode, it would be good to know [information about] a building right in front of me by pointing the device and double-tapping"* Integrating SaSYS with wayfinding systems such as TP3 [23] could respond to the needs.

Some participants found it difficult to control the distance by sliding their fingers on the touchscreen. P11 thought that dividing search space by swiped distances was not a desirable feature for him because he has a slight finger-motion impairment. However, P10 liked swipe-to-search because she could control search areas by swiped distances. We asked the participants about the desirable number of areas for this feature. The preference was varied (Figure 9). The result indicates that interaction designs for visually impaired users should take individual characteristics into account. Thus, the number of areas should be customized according to each user's preference.

5.2   Part B: TTS Controls Results

Overall, participants could easily remember the given drawings for each control and perform the task. 8 of 11 participants answered correctly to all the questions, but 3 participants gave a wrong answer only to one question each (both P1 and P6 answered incorrectly to Q(3), and P9 answered incorrectly to Q(2)). SaSYS takes 248 seconds to read the prepared POI information with normal speech rate. Participants used TTS controls on average for 504 seconds (SD=119) to find answers for the given questions. 10 of 11 participants found that they needed TTS controls when they were asked to indicate whether the TTS control feature is necessary.

We also asked the participants to rate the usefulness of each TTS control provided by SaSYS using a 5-point Likert scale (1=Disagree strongly, 5=Agree strongly). Overall, the participants found the given functionalities were useful. In particular, the 'speech rate' control was thought of as the most useful functionality whereas 'repeat' was thought of as the least useful among the given functionalities (Table 2).

Table 2. Results of questionnaire on usefulness of each TTS control functionality

Functionality	Average rating (SD)
Repeat	3.72 (1.19)
Forward	4.18 (0.75)
Backward	4.27 (0.79)
Speech rate	4.28 (0.4)
Skip to other items	4.27 (0.64)
Skip to other categories	4.36 (0.67)

Most participants liked the drawings we assigned and the recognition rates of the drawings were acceptable, but some participants had difficulty drawing swirls to repeat. P3 mentioned, *"It would be better to assign symbols less similar [to triangles to the repeat control] because swirls are recognized as triangles."* As noted earlier, it is important to allow the user to customize interactions as much as possible.

Overall, the participants liked gesture-based interaction to control auditory information. When we asked the participants about their preference between button-based interface and gesture-based interface, if the drawing recognition was not a problem, surprisingly 8 of 10 participants (who thought the TTS control feature was necessary) chose the gesture-based interface. This shows that symbol-based gestures have a potential to be used as an effective interface with touchscreen for the visually impaired.

5.3   Part C: User Feedback on the Overall System Design Results

Participants explicitly commented that SaSYS would encourage them to explore their surroundings and to participate in shopping and leisure activities. P6 said, *"I would like to use [systems like SaSYS] all the time. I would like to search stores right now."*

P11 who is currently using an iPhone compared SaSYS with existing navigation systems providing turn-by-turn instructions. P11 pointed out, *"Navigation systems require predetermined destinations...I think they are useless in situations like going around Asakusa (one of the famous districts in Tokyo)."* He also commented, *"I think I can use [SaSYS] like equipment for leisure time amusement. For example, when I want to go shopping or look for some restaurants in Ginza."*

We investigated additional features for improving the user experiences with SaSYS. Several participants thought that it would be better to share their findings (e.g., a bakery near the station) with other users. Some participants suggested that it is important to know the current direction they are facing.

We found that all participants thought contextual information (olfactory and auditory feature of POI) would be helpful when they get near to a desired POI (or destination). We also asked the participants to whether SaSYS requires any additional features. Several participants noted that information about the following would be helpful: shapes and types of entrances (e.g., whether it is a manual door or an automatic door), the position of the entrance (whether in the middle or the end of a building), whether there are steps or slopes near the entrances and the texture of the floor of the entrance hall (e.g., carpets, concrete, wood, etc.). Furthermore, some participants mentioned that the characteristics such as the colors of signboards or the shapes of buildings could be used as clues when they ask the way to sighted individuals. P6 and P11 suggested that the order of buildings in a city block with street names would be helpful. For example, "Your are on Harumi Avenue. You can find building A, B and C in order." Although the current prototype of SaSYS does not provide turn-by-turn navigation to POI, we believe that POI description should contain useful information for visually impaired people that sighted people may take for granted.

A number of participants enjoyed the experiences with SaSYS and our user study. P10 said, *"Overall, I enjoyed [the user study]. It would be very useful once I get used to smartphones."*

6   Discussion

Regarding part A of the user study, it was encouraging that participants intuitively understood the concept of swipe-to-search and were able to find POIs. Most participants preferred the swipe-to-search method, but two participants thought the point-to-search method was better for them because of its simplicity. We observed that they seemed to avoid touch input as much as possible, which made them feel the pointing-based interaction was simpler than swipe-based interaction. Several users also were positive to the point-to-search method. Further extension of SaSYS could add the pointing-based interaction method to allow users to select a proper mode according to their preferences or use cases.

Although several participants thought dividing search space by swiped distances could be useful, some participants found that it was difficult or tiresome to adjust swiping distances in order to select desired search areas. We found two possible explanations for why this feature was not well accepted: first, individual ability and attributes (e.g., spatial ability, tactile sensibility, age, etc.) could affect the performance [12]; and to perform the task, users had to interact much more with SaSYS. To scan all areas,

SaSYS required users to search 24 times (8 directions with 3 search areas), which made the system seem more tiresome compared to Pointer Test (which only takes 8 times to scan non-divided search space). Note that we extremely limited the number of POIs (66 stores) for the task. We believe that adjusting search areas is necessary when dealing with dozens of POIs within a specific area in real-world scenarios. This issue will be improved by allowing users to customize the number of search areas.

During part B of the user study, we observed that several participants spent much more time on finding the answer to $Q(3)$ (find a coupon available at lunch time) compared to $Q(1)$ and $Q(2)$. They seemed to have difficulty figuring out the starting point of each item (a coupon), whereas they easily distinguished items (user reviews) from each other because each review starts with the date of posting. We believe that numbering items or giving users feedback (e.g., vibration or auditory icons) at the end of each item could provide a better user experience in case of auditory information.

It was interesting that most participants used and rated the speech rate control the highest. Overall, users preferred speech rate up and down functionalities to quickly "look though" the contents rather than fast-forwarding or skipping functionalities. Participants seemed to be concerned about the possibility of missing out on important information. One participant used only speech rate controls to perform the task. This suggests that providing just the speech rate controls could allow users to obtain information effectively. On the other hand, the repeat control was thought relatively less useful because the recognition rates of swirl shapes were poor, and the backward control could substitute for the repeat functionality. We believe that assigning and registering custom drawings by the user could improve this issue.

Our study also confirmed that providing contextual information could benefit visually impaired users. Our current implementation of SaSYS provides only manually collected olfactory and auditory features of POIs in Ginza, but these features can be affected by certain situations (e.g., rains can affect olfactory senses). Furthermore, it would be desirable to provide richer contextual information anywhere and at any time suggested by participants. Future work should investigate into how to collect and manage contextual information for visually impaired users.

7   Conclusion

We presented a novel and intuitive interaction technique, *swipe-to-search*, to allow visually impaired people to search the surrounding geo-located information space. Based on swipe-to-search, we developed SaSYS, using off-the-shelf smartphone. SaSYS also provides text-to-speech control feature, which gives the users liberty to what to listen to. Our user study showed that swipe-based interaction method was accepted well by users as a means of location selecting. Users also preferred swipe-to-search method to existing point-to-search method. Moreover, we showed that TTS controls are highly useful to visually impaired users. Users thought the speech rate control was the most useful functionality. We also showed that olfactory and auditory features of POI would be helpful to visually impaired people. In short, participants found that SaSYS would be useful for exploring unfamiliar places and discovering surrounding POIs.

The user study revealed valuable insights into the design requirements of an effective location-based service like SaSYS. Based on these insights and the understanding of user interaction gained through our laboratory study, we are planning to conduct a field test in future in order to increase independence and enjoyment of traveling experience for the visually impaired.

Acknowledgment. The authors would like to thank Akiyoshi Takamura for his feedback on the early prototypes, and all of our participants for their time and effort. We would also like to thank Dr. Fahim Khan of the University of Tokyo for helping improve the clarity and focus of this paper.

References

1. Bellotti, F., Berta, R., De Gloria, A., Margarone, M.: Guiding visually impaired people in the exhibition. Mobile Guide (2006)
2. Buzzi, M.C., Buzzi, M., Leporini, B., Martusciello, L.: Making visual maps accessible to the blind. In: Stephanidis, C. (ed.) Universal Access in HCI, Part II, HCII 2011. LNCS, vol. 6766, pp. 271–280. Springer, Heidelberg (2011)
3. Coroama, V.: Experiences from the design of a ubiquitous computing system for the blind. In: Proceedings of CHI 2006 Extended Abstracts on Human Factors in Computing Systems, pp. 664–669. ACM, New York (2006)
4. Fröhlich, P., Simon, R., Baillie, L., Anegg, H.: Comparing conceptual designs for mobile access to geo-spatial information. In: Proceedings of the 8th Conference on Human-Computer Interaction with Mobile Devices and Services, pp. 109–112. ACM, New York (2006)
5. Golledge, R., Klatzky, R., Loomis, J., Marston, J.: Stated preferences for components of a personal guidance system for nonvisual navigation. Journal of Visual Impairment & Blindness 98(3), 135–147 (2004)
6. Guy, R., Truong, K.: CrossingGuard: exploring information content in navigation aids for visually impaired pedestrians. In: Proceedings of the SIGCHI Conference on Human Factors in Computing Systems, pp. 405–414. ACM, New York (2012)
7. Hersh, M., Johnson, M.A.: Assistive technology for visually impaired and blind people. Springer, Heidelberg (2008)
8. Kane, S.K., Bigham, J.P., Wobbrock, J.O.: Slide rule: making mobile touch screens accessible to blind people using multi-touch interaction techniques. In: Proceedings of the 10th International ACM SIGACCESS Conference on Computers and Accessibility, pp. 73–80. ACM, New York (2008)
9. Kane, S.K., Jayant, C., Wobbrock, J.O., Ladner, R.E.: Freedom to roam: a study of mobile device adoption and accessibility for people with visual and motor disabilities. In: Proceedings of the 11th International ACM SIGACCESS Conference on Computers and Accessibility, pp. 115–122. ACM, New York (2009)
10. Kane, S.K., Wobbrock, J.O., Ladner, R.E.: Usable gestures for blind people: understanding preference and performance. In: Proceedings of the SIGCHI Conference on Human Factors in Computing Systems, pp. 413–422. ACM, New York (2011)
11. McGookin, D., Brewster, S., Jiang, W.: Investigating touchscreen accessibility for people with visual impairments. In: Proceedings of the 5th Nordic Conference on Human-Computer Interaction: Building Bridges, pp. 298–307. ACM, New York (2008)

12. Oliveira, J., Guerreiro, T., Nicolau, H., Jorge, J., Gonçalves, D.: Blind people and mobile touch-based text-entry: acknowledging the need for different flavors. In: Proceedings of the 10th International ACM SIGACCESS Conference on Computers and Accessibility, pp. 179–186. ACM, New York (2011)
13. Parente, P., Bishop, G.: BATS: the blind audio tactile mapping system. In: Proceedings of the 41st ACM Southeast Regional Conference (2003)
14. Pielot, M., Henze, N., Heuten, W., Boll, S.: Tangible user interface for the exploration of auditory city maps. In: Oakley, I., Brewster, S. (eds.) HAID 2007. LNCS, vol. 4813, pp. 86–97. Springer, Heidelberg (2007)
15. Poppinga, B., Magnusson, C., Pielot, M., Rassmus-Gröhn, K.: TouchOver map: audio-tactile exploration of interactive maps. In: Proceedings of the 13th International Conference on Human Computer Interaction with Mobile Devices and Services, pp. 545–550. ACM, New York (2011)
16. Robinson, S., Eslambolchilar, P., Jones, M.: Sweep-Shake: finding digital resources in physical environments. In: Proceedings of the 11th International Conference on Human Computer Interaction with Mobile Devices and Services, pp. 85–94. ACM, New York (2009)
17. Rukzio, E., Leichtenstern, K., Callaghan, V., Holleis, P., Schmidt, A., Chin, J.: An experimental comparison of physical mobile interaction techniques: Touching, pointing and scanning. In: Dourish, P., Friday, A. (eds.) UbiComp 2006. LNCS, vol. 4206, pp. 87–104. Springer, Heidelberg (2006)
18. Sakamura, K., Ishikawa, C.: Internet of Things—From Ubiquitous Computing to Ubiquitous Intelligence Applications. In: Vermesan, O., Friess, P. (eds.) Internet of Things-Global Technological and Societal Trends From Smart Environments and Spaces to Green ICT, pp. 115–141. River Publishers (2011)
19. Sakamura, K., Santucci, G.: Japan-Europe Cooperation on ucode technologies. In: Smith, I.G. (ed.) The Internet of Things 2012: New Horizons. CASAGRAS2, Halifax, UK, pp. 340–351 (2012)
20. Sakamura, K.: Ubiquitous ID Technologies (2011),
http://www.t-engine.org/ja/wp-content/themes/
wp.vicuna/pdf/en_US/UID910-W001-110324.pdf
21. Su, J., Rosenzweig, A., Goel, A., de Lara, E., Truong, K.N.: Timbremap: enabling the visually-impaired to use maps on touch-enabled devices. In: Proceedings of the 12th International Conference on Human Computer Interaction with Mobile Devices and Services, pp. 17–26. ACM, New York (2010)
22. Wasinger, R., Stahl, C., Krüger, A.: M3I in a pedestrian navigation & exploration system. In: Chittaro, L. (ed.) Mobile HCI 2003. LNCS, vol. 2795, pp. 481–485. Springer, Heidelberg (2003)
23. Yang, R., Park, S., Mishra, S.R., Hong, Z., Newsom, C., Joo, H., Hofer, E., Newman, M.W.: Supporting spatial awareness and independent wayfinding for pedestrians with visual impairments. In: Proceedings of the 10th International ACM SIGACCESS Conference on Computers and Accessibility, pp. 27–34. ACM, New York (2011)
24. Yatani, K., Banovic, N., Truong, K.: SpaceSense: representing geographical information to visually impaired people using spatial tactile feedback. In: Proceedings of the SIGCHI Conference on Human Factors in Computing Systems, pp. 415–424. ACM, New York (2012)

Smartphone Interactions Change for Different Intimacy Contexts

Mattia Gustarini and Katarzyna Wac

Institute of Service Science, University of Geneva, 1227 Carouge, Switzerland
firstname.lastname@unige.ch

Abstract. Emerging mobile applications on a growing scale adapt their functionalities and the way these are provided, leveraging the user's contextual information, without the need of explicit settings setup from the users side. However, this contextual information, *e.g.*, location and other environmental information, may not fully represent the users' context. There are other contextual features related to the user's social context that may be considered. In this paper we introduce an example of such contextual information - the *intimacy* context information, and we investigate if smartphone users change the way they interact with their smartphones depending on their intimacy state. We performed a 4 weeks 20-users study, with participants using their own smartphones in daily life environments, and being sampled for their intimacy perception. Our results show how intimacy context changes and relate to the smartphone usage. Therefore our research contributes by introducing new context information - intimacy, which can be leveraged by developers to create mobile applications automatically adapting to provide different services, functionalities and content depending on the intimacy level of the situation the user is in.

Keywords: context-awareness, self-application adaptation, mobile application, interaction design, social context.

1   Introduction

Developers are designing mobile applications that can be customized by users to provide them with the best experience. The customization is usually made through a set of settings that offer the possibility to define some static cause-effect actions. A simple example can be a messaging application that provides the possibility for the users to customize how they are notified of new messages - via a full screen pop-up, with message preview and phone screen ON, simple notification icon, with or without message preview, any possible sound, vibration and LED light colors combination, or different combinations of all the above, depending on the contact or group of people, and so on. All these settings may overwhelm the users that may just do not explore all the functionalities of the application [1]. Users may not be able to fully exploit the potential of these applications, either because they are not aware on how to set up the application to enable different behaviors, or they just agree upon the default settings,

G. Memmi and U. Blanke (Eds.): MobiCASE 2013, LNICST 130, pp. 72–89, 2014.
© Institute for Computer Sciences, Social Informatics and Telecommunications Engineering 2014

because the set up seems to be cumbersome. In addition, usually these settings are static, so recalling the example, if the user decides that she/he wants a given new message notification type, the application will always notify the user in that way, in any situation. That can irritate the user, if this setting is not appropriate for some situations. The developers become aware of that and to address it, on a growing scale they develop new kinds of application-adaptations techniques to meet the users' needs and expectations [2–4]. Namely, developers are starting to use contextual information of the users to not only provide new functionality of their mobile applications, but also to adapt, based on the user's context, the applications functionalities and the way they are provided. There are mobile applications that after a very basic setup are automatically adapting to the user context, to the extreme example by *Google Now*, that is not even requiring a minimal set up, but acts autonomously from the beginning and "settings and preferences" of the application are mostly derived from the user's actions. However, the number of these mobile applications is still very little compared to the total available ones, and new techniques and a diverse types of user's contextual information is still to be explored [5]. To enable it, we need to research new contextual clues, in particular the ones that are considering the user as a human being with a set of motivational and attitude traits, and exploit these [6]. Towards this end, in our research we focus on one of such traits and hereby we investigate if the *intimacy context* of the users is relevant to mobile applications' adaptation. Supported by the literature [7, 8], we define the intimacy context of a user as *her/his level of comfort in her/his current contextual situation* [9]. For the purpose of this explorative research we let the users to interpret this definition themselves, and we have interviewed them for their understanding and operational definition of their intimacy context.

Supported by the literature [8], we assume that the intimacy context is composed by several contextual information such as the number and kind (*e.g.*, strangers, friends, family members) of people around the person, the familiarity of the current place, and so on. For example imagine being in a very busy public bus commuting from home to work, you will be with a lot of people, some that you see everyday (*i.e.*, commuting acquaintances) and a lot of them that are complete strangers for you. Now imagine being at home either alone, or with your significant others, having dinner around a table in a comfortable chair. In our research (at large) we aim to understand in which of the two situations, the users likely feel more intimate, thus more comfortable. We hypothesize that the intimacy context can be a very rich representation of the users' feelings about their current contextual situation, and can be then leveraged for an adaption of mobile applications provisioning.

In the research presented in this paper we particularly aim to answer the following questions: How the interaction of the user with a smartphone may change depending on her/his current intimacy context? What are the implications of understanding the user's intimacy on the mobile applications design?

Answering the questions above can bring new possibilities for developers that are striving to make their applications more usable and useful for their users, in different circumstances. If we consider our simple example about the messaging application, we may think how the notification of a new message may automatically be adapted to the user intimacy context. For example if the user is in an intimate situation (*i.e.*, at home, possibly with her/his family) the notification for a new message may be presented as a full screen pop up, with the content of the message displayed in it (given the assumption that there are less privacy issues when at home with people the user trust) accompanied by the smartphone screen ON, a longer notification sound and a LED blinking (to attract the user attention probably focused elsewhere). Instead, when the user is in a less intimate context (*i.e.*, in a bus full of strangers) the notification may need to be more discreet without showing the message content in a pop-up (so people around cannot read it), but just using the normal notification system of the smartphone, and without emitting a very long and loud sound or just vibrating. Of course these settings may be reversed or refined following the user needs and/or behavior patterns.

In this paper we focus on understanding the human perception of intimacy in daily life environments, and particularly we present an user study that we employed to understand if the interaction with the smartphone (*e.g.*, applications usage type and ways of interaction) changes depending on the users' intimacy context and if this intimacy context can be modeled from the users' behavior. In the rest of this paper we provide a description of the methods employed in our user study and the summary of data collected. We then present and discuss the results of the study, which show that intimacy is involved in how smartphones are used. Furthermore, we present related work on application adaptability using contextual information. Finally, we conclude this paper with a discussion on the future work opportunities.

2   User Study

In this section we present the methods employed to collect the intimacy ground truth and the parameters describing how the users were interacting with their smartphones.

2.1   Participants' Recruitment

We recruited 20 smartphone users, out of a total of 30 users that are participating in our Mobile Quality of Life Living Lab (mQoL)[1] at University of Geneva. 10 users were excluded, either because they are part of the faculty or because they did not accept to participate in the study. All the participants in this study were already using one of the Android OS smartphones provided by the Living Lab to them (Samsung Galaxy Nexus with Android OS 4.0+) for at least 6 months, so we assume they are expert smartphone users. The participants were involved in the study for 24 to 36 days (average of 29 days). There were 6 female and 14 male participants, aged 20 to 58.

---

[1] http://www.qol.unige.ch/mQoL.html

2.2   Study Methods

The study participants first were asked to visit our laboratory to install our study application on their smartphones. They were instructed on how to use it. The application is fully automated: starts when the phone boots, runs continuously in the background, stops when the battery level on the phone is low (less than 20%), and is able to auto-update. Participants were asked to run the application on their phones for at least 4 weeks.

To simplify the participants' task, the only requirement for them was to answer to an Experience Sampling Method (ESM) survey whenever notified by the application on their smartphone. The ESM approach assumes an automated annotation diary where the person does not need to remember to take note of her/his context (therefore minimizing the recall error), but is asked by the system to answer specific questions, *i.e.*, estimate her/his current context randomly during the day [10]. In addition to the users' answers to the ESMs, we automatically collected smartphone usage information that we explain in details in the following sections. All the answers to the ESMs and the usage information were recorded in the smartphone's internal memory and opportunistically sent over the network (when the user was connected to WiFi) to our dedicated server.

2.2.1   ESM: Collecting the Intimacy Ground Truth

Our ESM survey was issued every day with 8 random uniformly distributed survey notifications, between 8am-10pm, on the participant's smartphone. Additional ESMs appeared each time the participant plugged his/her phone for charging. We monitored how many surveys were issued and then actually answered and completed. The survey was composed by a single question asking about the participant's subjective feeling of intimacy, ranging from '*completely*' [intimate], '*yes*', '*more yes than no*', '*more no than yes*', '*no*', '*not at all*' [intimate]. These answers were designed based on the relevant literature in the domain [7, 8].

2.2.2   Smartphone Usage Information Collection

We automatically collected several information to derive how the smartphone was used such as when the screen was switched ON/OFF, when the user was interacting with the phone after the unlock phase (*i.e.*, after inserting the screen lock code), current applications running, and any touch that the user was performing on the screen [11].

2.2.2.1   Screen Events. We logged all the ON/OFF screen events provided by the Android OS. The ON event is triggered each time the screen is switched ON, i.e., when the user presses the smartphone button to wake it up from standby. The OFF event is triggered whenever the screen goes OFF, so the phone enters standby, and may be the consequence of the user pressing once again the ON/OFF button of the smartphone or when the phone reaches maximum time of screen ON before standby defined by the user in the settings of the OS. We were logging the event type, either ON/OFF together with its the timestamp.

2.2.2.2 Presence Events. We were collecting a user PRESENT event every time the user unlocked the phone (e.g., by inserting the unlock code, or simply by sliding the unlock button) and so started to interact with the smartphone. As before, we log this event together with its timestamp.

2.2.2.3 Applications Running. When a user was starting to interact with the phone (i.e., a PRESENT event was triggered) a log of all the applications used is created. There is not an explicit Android OS event signaling that an application is opened or closed. Therefore, we were launching a service that was monitoring which was the application on top of the stack of the running applications accessible with the Android OS API. We were performing this check every 10 seconds and whenever there was a switch in the stack top we were logging the current application as the current in use. In our log file we were registering, as reported by the Android OS: (1) the current timestamp (in ms), (2) the full package name of the application, (3) the unique ID (UID) assigned by the OS whenever an application is installed, (4) the current process ID (PID) on which the application is running, (5) a flag stating if the application has requested the permission to access the network, thus able to access the Internet.

2.2.2.4 Screen Touches. We were registering each time the user was touching the screen surface. The events were captured thanks an invisible overlay on the system UI.

2.3   Data Analysis

We conducted our analysis in a hierarchical way. We started by the analysis of *screen* and *presence* events, then we analyzed *applications* at their category level (we categorized application used using the same categories of Google Play store: Lifestyle, Social, Productivity, etc.), finally we picked the category, *Communication*, with the highest number of different and most used applications. *Screen Touches* were included transversally in all the steps.

The first step of the analysis was to define which were the valid transitions in which the smartphone can be following the paths given from the *screen* and *presence* events. This was necessary to remove some invalid records resulted from the data loss. Therefore, we defined the state machine depicted in Fig. 1 where we present the transitions that we are going to consider for our analysis (ON-OFF, ON-PRESENT, PRESENT-OFF, OFF-ON).

In a second step, for each single valid *transition* identified in the entire dataset (*i.e.,* all participants together) we derived (Fig. 2): (1) its day of the week and hour of the day (2) the transition duration (state-to-state time interval), (3) how many applications were switched in between PRESENT and OFF states (*app_switched*), (4) the number of touches, (5) the median of the intervals between touches (*m_touches*).

As a third step we analyzed each single *applications used* and for each of them we noted: (1) day of the week and hour of the day, (2) the application category (derived from Google Play store), (3) the usage time, (4) the number of touches, (5) the median of the intervals between touches (*m_touches*).

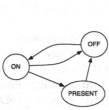

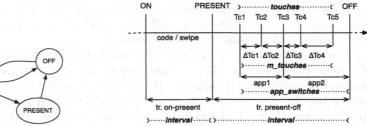

Fig. 1. State machine representing valid transitions between *screen* and *presence* events

Fig. 2. The transition model presenting variables considered in our research, especially in the present-OFF transition

The fourth step consisted of the assignment of the *intimacy state* (as declared by the participants answering the ESM survey) to each *transition* and *applications use*d. We considered an *intimacy state* valid for a window of 15 minutes (7.5 minutes before and 7.5 minutes after the ESM answer is specified, a reasonable time in which the intimacy state would remain constant). All the measurements of *transitions* and *applications used* falling inside these 15 minutes window were assigned to the current *intimacy state* of the user that generated the data. When there was no *intimacy state* specified, we marked the data with a "NA" *intimacy state*.

In the fifth step we performed a quantitative analysis of the *applications used*. We removed all the records without an *intimacy state* and we identified which were the most used categories of applications. We selected the category with the highest number of different *applications used*. As we are going to present in the results section, the *Communication* category was the most used.

Finally with all this information we created several models to observe the evolution of the *intimacy state* under different combinations of the data depicted in the previous steps. We are going to present the most significant model results together with basic statistics about the full data set in the Results section.

2.3.1   Modeling Methods
As first step we performed a cleaning of the data from extreme values for each subset: *screen* and *presence* events transitions, *applications used*, and *Communication category*. Then, we created our intimacy models using the variables we depicted above.

2.3.1.1 Data Cleaning. In order to avoid the influence of outliers in temporal variables (*i.e.*, resulting in long transition times), most probably generated by data loss when logging and transmitting the data to the server, we cleaned the dataset from extreme values for the subsets' variables, enabling us also to further define bounds of variables in which we want our data to be modeled. Data was removed either by considering the variable's distribution (*i.e.*, cutting the "long tails" by fixing a maximum value at the third quartile of the data) or by common sense (*i.e.*, removing the unreasonably long time intervals for some variables).

For the full set of data we considered only the records that were recorded from 5h in the morning to midnight (removed 5.2% of data) as most indicative, as Fig. 5 shows intimacy state ground truth are infrequent over night.

For *screen* and *presence* events transitions we removed all the data with any of the followings characteristics: (1) *interval*s longer than 180 seconds (8.8% of data meeting this condition), (2) more than 10 *app_switches* in the same session (0.1% of data meeting this condition), (3) the *m_touches* out of the third quartile, values less or equal 1.72 seconds (6.5% of data meeting this condition), and (4) the *m_touches* with NA value due to 0 or 1 touch in the interval considered (26.2% of data meeting this condition). As a result, in total we have removed 28.4% of the data (meeting one or several of the above conditions). In addition, given that apart the *interval* time of the session in the transitions *on-off*, *on-present*, and *off-on* there was no data (no interaction of the user with the smartphone) we also subset the data to deal manly with the transition *present-off*.

Then, for *applications used* we removed all the records with any of the following characteristics: (1) usage *interval*s longer than 180 seconds (16.8% of data meeting this condition), (2) we removed all the applications not belonging to the categories of: *Communication*, *Social*, and *System* as minor contributors in the data (25.4% of data meeting this condition, with the extra fact that we also removed our logger application records), (3) the *m_touches* out of the third quartile, values higher or equal 1.87 seconds (16.3% of data meeting this condition), and (4) the *m_touches* with NA value due to 0 or 1 touch for the app entry considered (65.2% of data meeting this condition), for a total of 75.4% removed data (meeting one or several of the above conditions). Finally, for the last data subset, given that the *Communication* category is a subset of the cleaned *applications used*, we did not need any further manipulation.

2.3.1.2 Modeling Procedure.

For each subset of data, *using all its data records*, we generated all the possible models defined by all the possible combinations without repetitions of the subset of variables. The model variables were combined using the additive method only (*e.g.*, with three variables: intimacy=var1+var2+var3). We processed these models' definition with the Ordinal Regression Model (ORM) approach [12], because of our ordinal intimacy scale, from 1="most intimate" to 6="least intimate". Then, for each subset we selected the most significant model (smallest χ^2 test p-value) using the *ANOVA's* χ^2 test [12] between each generated model and the baseline model. The baseline model is represented only by the intimacy threshold coefficients (*i.e.*, 1|2, 2|3, 3|4, 4|5, 5|6) without any model variables coefficient, *i.e.*, a model without description parameters, just based on the "raw" distribution of intimacy states. In addition we analyzed how all the models composed by a single variable were related to intimacy (*i.e.*, evaluating their χ^2 test p-value and confidence intervals).

The most significant models, presented in details, were recreated with 60% of randomly sampled data from the full data set and we tested against the remaining 40%. We generated the model and test data set 10 times (denoted in machine learning as 10x Cross Validation). When possible, we plotted the predictions probabilities for each intimacy state for the different model variables, and we obtained similar results between all the 10 different trials.

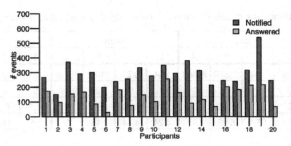

Fig. 3. Notified/answered ESM surveys per a participant

3   Results

We present the results divided in two main parts. In the first part, we present the basic statistics about the data set we collected (Section 3.1-2). In the second part, we present a more detailed view of the models used to analyze how smartphone's usage variables, as derived from the collected data, are related to intimacy (Section 3.3).

3.1   ESM Survey and Automatic Data Results

Overall a total of 5801 ESM notification surveys were randomly issued to the participants of the study. On average the answer rate was 48.62% (total answers: 2776) and in Fig. 3 we show how each participant contributed to these numbers. The participation is not uniform and some participants were slightly more active than others, however that did not influence our research at this stage, hence we do not discard any user as an "outlier".

In Fig. 4 we show how the participants answered their ESMs. Most of the time participants declared to be in an intimate state and less often in a non-intimate one. The overall probability distribution for each intimacy state is: 42.5% *completely* [intimate], 27.8% *yes*, 7.2% *more yes than no*, 7.4% *more no than yes*, 11.2% *no*, 3.9% *not at all* [intimate].

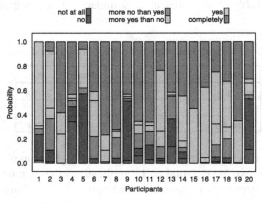

Fig. 4. Distribution of intimacy states per participant

Table 1. Basic statistics for transitions subset, 1=on-off, 2=on-present, 3=present-off, 4=off-on

Var. / Tran.	Max				Mean				Std			
	1	2	3	4	1	2	3	4	1	2	3	4
interval [s]	334	459	28870	39360	13.4	3.77	118.2	197.8	16.5	10.4	618.5	1084.8
app_switched	0	0	19	0	0	0	1.96	0	0	0	1.9	0
touches	9	7	1335	0	0.1	0.04	33.5	0	0.7	0.3	70.3	0
m_touches [s]	33.1	55.1	54.3	0	4.24	4.44	1.45	0	6.5	11.6	1.7	0

In general for *screen* and *presence* events transitions, before cleaning the data, we have a total of: 18048 ON-OFF, 19625 ON-present, 19357 present-OFF and, and 36923 OFF-ON for a total of 93953 transitions. We have removed the invalid transitions (*i.e.*, not following the transition model Fig. 1) resulting from some data loss, as follows: 271 OFF-OFF, 491 OFF-present, 153 ON-ON, 758 present-ON, and 1290 present-present, accounting for a total of 2963 (3.15%) discarded records. As expected ON-present and present-OFF transitions are almost symmetric and OFF-ON cover almost all other transitions starting with the *ON* event.

The number of transitions that were assigned with an intimacy state is 12181 (14.6% of the total) and the probability distribution is: 36.9% *completely* [intimate], 28.8% *yes*, 7.3% *more yes than no*, 6.6% *more no than yes*, 14.3% *no*, 6.1% *not at all* [intimate]. In Table 1 we present the statistics for the variables we extracted for each transition, before data cleaning, (as explained in the data analysis section above) taking in account all the participants and transitions being tagged with.

The general statistics for the *applications used* are as follows: in total we have identified 326 different applications being used by participants (over a total of 35 categories), but for the further analysis, we retained only the applications that were used at least 50 times (along the study) and only when intimacy state ground truth was available, leaving us with a total of 24 (7%) applications, with an intimacy states probability distribution for these, as follows: 41.2% *completely* [intimate], 27.9% *yes*, 7.2% *more yes than no*, 6.9% *more no than yes*, 12.4% *no*, 4.4% *not at all* [intimate]. The applications selection process leads to 7 (20%) different categories over a total of 35 categories. In Table 2 we present a summary of the variables selected for *application used*.

Table 2. Basic statistics for application used

Variable	Min	Max	Mean	Std
interval [s]	0	180400	455.5	3770.8
touches	0	1251	14.9	55.1
m_touches [s]	0.01	13580	4.756	162.4

Furthermore, the *Communication* category has the highest number of *applications used*. In this category we have a total of 11 applications that can be further separated in 4 sub-categories: *Browser* (3 apps), *Email* (3 apps), *Phone* (1 app), and *Messaging* (4 apps).

3.2   Intimacy in Time

Two variables in common for *screen* and *presence* events transitions and *applications used* that relate to the time of interaction with the smartphone are: the day of the week and the hour of the day. In Fig. 5 we plot the probabilities for each intimacy state (from 'completely' to 'not at all', in different colors) for each *day of a week* (separate graphs, Sun-Sat) and *hour* (X axis). From the graph we can note how the period from midnight to 5h is not well covered by the intimacy state ground truth, *i.e.*, there were not many ESM responses from the participants. This is partially due to the fact that our random ESM events where issued only in waking hours, *i.e.*, from 8h to 22h, and usually people sleep at this time of the night. The intervals from 5h to 8h and from 22h to midnight are covered by the fact that the survey is issued whenever the phone was un/plugged from the charger and potentially by the fact that some of these are also late answers to earlier-triggered notifications in the interval 8-22h. From Fig. 5 we conclude that the general trend for study participants is to be more intimate in the early morning and in the evening and, additionally Sunday seems to be the most intimate day in a week. The least intimate hour seems to be the ones around noon in a weekdays and Saturday.

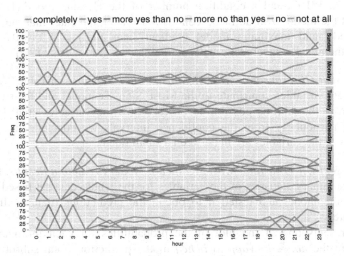

Fig. 5. Frequency for each intimacy state for each hour and day

3.3   Intimacy Models Results

We present the intimacy models divided in three main categories: (1) Present-Off transaction models, (2) Applications used models, and (3) Communication category models.

3.3.1   Present-Off Transition Models

For the data concerning the *transitions event present-OFF* we generated models with the combination of the variables: *hour*, *day*, *interval*, *app_switched*, *touches*, and *m_touches*. We obtained a total of 63 models (combinations without repetition of the

Table 3. Most_Sign_Tr model variables significance (0 '***', 0.001 '**', 0.01 '*', 0.05 '.', 0.1 ' '), confidence intervals (CI)

Variable	P-value (*chisq*)	CI 2.5%	CI 97.5%
hour	$8.9*10^{-6}$ ***	-0.058	-0.023
day	0.001 **	0.025	0.107
app_switched	0.001 **	-0.180	-0.044

6 variables from this subset, taking 1, 2, 3, 4, 5, 6 variables at time). Out of 63 models, 4 were not significant (p-value > 0.05), 59 were significant (among them 41 had p-values < 0.001). The models composed by a single variable contributed in the following way (p-value ordered from most to least contributing): $p=2.4*10^{-5}$ variable *hour* (rank 28), $p=2.3*10^{-3}$ for *day* (rank 44), $p=2.4*10^{-3}$ for *app_switched* (rank 45), $p=2.3*10^{-2}$ for *interval* (rank 57), $p=1*10^{-1}$ for *touches* (rank 61, not significant), and $p=3.7*10^{-1}$ *m_touches* (rank 63, not significant).

For space reasons we present details of only the most significant model: denoted as *Most_Sign_Tr* build based on the variables *hour+day+app_switched*. The model has a p-value < $2.3*10^{-8}$, and a condition number of the Hessian (cond.H) = $1.7*10^{4}$ (measures if the model is ill defined; cond.H > 10^{6} [12], indicates that the model can be simplified), and maximum model gradient (max.grad) = $6.38*10^{-13}$ (a value indicates if the model converges: usually for value max.grad < 10^{-6} [12])).

3.3.1.1 Present-Off Transition Most Significant Model Details. In Table 3 we present how the single variables contribute to the Most_Sign_Tr model and their confidence intervals. From the table is possible to observe how the variables contribute to the models and particularly from the confidence intervals we conclude that the most likely values of the variables are in between a small range.

3.3.1.2 Present-Off Transition Most Significant Model Prediction Results. In Table 4 we present summary statistics of the variables for the whole data set based on which we defined the model and tested it to obtain the predictions (data is divided per intimacy state).

Fig. 6 presents one of the plot of the probabilities for each intimacy state as resulted from the *hour+day+app_switched* model prediction (total subset size 1957 records, data to define the model 1174 and testing size 783). Across the Fig. 6, we can note how the probability to be *completely* intimate increases with the hour of the day, changes depending on the day of the week (in particular *Sunday* is more intimate than the rest of the week, as already observed from Fig. 5), and has different behaviors depending on how many applications are switched in the *present-off* transition. The more applications are switched, the higher the probability to be in a *completely* intimacy state.

3.3.2   Applications Used Models

For the *applications used* we generated models with the combination of the variables: *hour, day, interval, application, category, touches,* and *m_touches,* we obtained a total of 127 models. Out of them one was not significant (p-value > 0.05), 126 were

Table 4. Basic statistics of Most_Sign_Tr model data after cleaning

Var	Stat	\multicolumn{6}{c}{Intimacy State}					
		1	2	3	4	5	6
hour [5h-23h]	min	5	5	6	6	5	5
	max	23	23	23	21	22	23
	mean	13.7	13.9	14.2	12.4	12.2	12.9
	std	4.8	4.2	4.2	3.5	4.3	4.2
day	min	0	0	0	0	0	0
	max	6	6	6	6	6	6
	mean	2.8	3	3.7	3	3.1	2.8
	std	2	1.9	1.9	1.7	1.8	1.9
app_switched	min	0	0	0	0	0	0
	max	9	9	6	6	7	7
	mean	1.7	1.8	1.5	1.8	1.6	1.5
	std	1.2	1.2	1	1.2	1.3	1.5

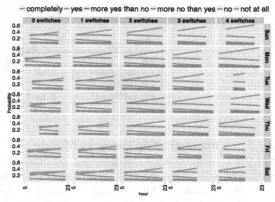

Fig. 6. Probability (left Y axis) for each intimacy state depending on *hour* (bottom X axis), *day* (right Y axis), and *app_switches* (top Y axis)

significant (among them 118 p-values < 0.001). The models composed by a single variable contributed in the following way (p-value ordered from the most to least contributing): $p=1.4*10^{-14}$ for *application* (rank 63), $p=8.5*10^{-5}$ *touches* (rank 107), $p=1.5*10^{-4}$ *hour* (rank 110), $p=2.1*10^{-4}$ *m_touches* (rank 111), $p=1.4*10^{-3}$ *day* (rank 122), $p=7.6*10^{-3}$ *interval* (rank 125), $p=2.2*10^{-1}$ *category* (rank 127, not significant). As before, we present details of the most significant model denoted as *Most_Sign_App* composed by the variables: *hour+day+app+touches*, with its p-value $< 2.9*10^{-19}$, cond.H $= 5.4*10^{6}$, max.grad $= 1.95*10^{-7}$.

3.3.2.1 Applications Used Most Significant Model Details. In Table 5 we present how the single variables contribute to the Most_Sign_App model and their confidence intervals. Also in this case we have variables that are significant for the models, in particular application and hour. Application CI are omitted, due to lack of space, i.e., we would need to list results for 20 applications. Differently from the other models we are not going to plot results of predictions for this case. Due to model size (4 variables) is difficult to plot these results, needing 4 + 1 (probability) dimensions.

Table 5. Most_Sign_App model variables significance (0 '***', 0.001 '**', 0.01 '*', 0.05 '.', 0.1 ' ') and confidence intervals (CI)

Variable	P-value (*chisq*)	CI 2.5%	CI 97.5%
hour	0.005 **	-0.041	-0.007
day	0.011 *	0.012	0.090
application	$1*10^{-9}$ ***	omitted	omitted
touches	0.034 *	-0.004	-0.000

Table 6. Most_Sign_Com model variables significance (0 '***', 0.001 '**', 0.01 '*', 0.05 '.', 0.1 ' ') and confidence intervals (CI)

Variable	P-value (*chisq*)	CI 2.5%	CI 97.5%
day	0.06 .	-0.003	0.103
sub_cat [Email]	0.002 **	-0.959	-0.050
sub_cat [Messaging]	0.002 **	-0.851	-0.226
sub_cat [Phone]	0.002 **	-1.667	-0.342
touches	0.003 **	0.430	1.174

3.3.3   Communication Category Models

For the *Communication category* we generated models with the combination of the variables: *hour, day, interval, sub-category, touches,* and *m_touches*. We obtained a total of 63 models. Out of them 2 were not significant (p-value > 0.05), 61 were significant (among them 51 p-values < 0.001). The models composed by a single variable contributed in this way (p-value ordered from the most to least contributing): p=$3.3*10^{-4}$ for *sub-category* variable (rank 42), p=$3.3*10^{-4}$ *m_touches* (rank 43), p=$4.5*10^{-4}$ *touches* (rank 45), p=$2.4*10^{-2}$ *interval* (rank 59), p=$2.4*10^{-2}$ *day* (rank 60), p=$3.2*10^{-1}$ *hour* (rank 63, not significant). As before, we present details of the most significant model, this time denoted as *Most_Sign_Com* based on the variables *day +sub_category+touches*, with its p-value < $8.1*10^{-6}$, cond.H = $4.8*10^{5}$, and max.grad = $1.91*10^{-12}$.

3.3.3.1 Communication Category Most Significant Model Details. In Table 6 we present how the single variables contribute to the Most_Sign_Com model and their confidence intervals. In this case for the Most_Sign_Com model we have the day variable, presenting not significant contribution to the model. Instead, sub_category and touches are significantly contributing to the model. CI shows how, in general, variables are supported by their values enclosed in a small interval.

3.3.3.2 Communication Category Most Significant Model Prediction Results. The predictions for the Most_Sign_Com model are presented in Fig. 7 (total subset size is 1213 records, model definition size 728 and testing size 485). In Table 7 we provide a summary of statistics about the two variables of the model for the data from which we sampled the model definition and testing data.

The *Messaging sub_category* is the one related to the most of the touches per its usage session, and particularly on *Sunday. Email* and *Phone* have very little interaction, *i.e.*, very few touches per session. *Browser* has a regular short number of *touches* across the week. The intimacy states change with the number of *touches* (particularly in *Messaging*, but also in *Browser*). In *Messaging*, the *completely* intimacy state probability increases by increasing the number of touches. Instead in *Browser* with very few *touches* we have a higher probability for the *no* intimate state that decreases slightly when the *touches* increase (*Saturday* may indicate a general trend for the week).

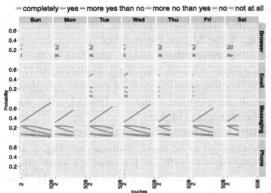

Fig. 7. Probability (left Y axis) for each intimacy state (colored lines) depending on *touches* (bottom X axis), *sub_category* (right Y axis), and a *day* (top Y axis)

Table 7. Basic statistics of *Most_Sign_Com* model data after cleaning (f=frequency)

Var	Statistics	Intimacy State					
		1	2	3	4	5	6
day	min	0	0	0	0	0	0
	max	6	6	6	6	6	6
	mean	2.9	3.2	3.9	2.8	3.2	2.9
	std	2	1.8	1.9	1.7	1.9	2.6
sub cat.	f(Browser)	54	45	7	9	36	18
	f(Email)	43	25	10	5	17	4
	f(Mess.)	372	285	57	57	107	29
	f(Phone)	19	9	5	5	4	0
touches	min	2	2	2	2	2	2
	max	865	584	223	313	336	112
	mean	53.7	48.9	39.9	52.2	36	33.5
	std	76.1	68.3	46.9	60.2	44.4	25.6

4   Discussion

Based on the results, we conclude that there are some differences on how users interact with their smartphones depending on which intimacy context they are in. Effects of these interaction changes are mostly visible at the extreme intimacy states *completely* and *no*. Users are switching more applications when in a high intimacy context, writing shorter messages when in lower intimacy, and so on.

The *hour* and *day* variables are contributing to all the most significant models, from which we conclude that this time variable, together with the other variables we presented in this paper, is relevant to identify different user's intimacy patterns. *Hour* and *day* are very significant in the *present-OFF transition* as single variable in models of intimacy (high rank for single models variable), However, if we look at the *application used* set, time variables loose the significance, and they become even less relevant for the *Communication category* where *hour* alone is not even significant. We may conclude that probably time variables are also related to smartphone usage variables, as the usage of the smartphone is also influenced by the *hour* of the day and the *day* of the week. They become usage variables themselves. An extra note on these variables is that they are related and most probably they could be treated as an input to the models as interactive variables, instead of just addictive model terms, as we have done. These could be verified with further ANOVA tests on such model definition compared to the one we have already performed.

For the **present-OFF transition** model the only variables that alone are not significant to derive a single variable model for this set of data, are *touches* and *m_touches* that are related to each other. Namely, there are no particular changes on the number of touches or the interval between them for different intimacy states along the *present-OFF* interaction section with the smartphone. Also, as the *interval* variable alone is not so powerful, we conclude that the interaction time is also not a very good indicator for the user's intimacy state.

Furthermore, the *app_switched* variable changes depending on the intimacy context. In particular, as reported in Fig. 6 the higher the number of switches, the higher is the probability to be in the *completely* intimate state and less in the *no* intimate state. An interaction with the phone without switching applications (*i.e.*, when the user lands straight at screen application after the *present* event is generated) can indicate that the user may not be in an intimate situation. Instead, after four applications switches the probability to be intimate is higher.

Additionally, the *day* variable is mostly contributing for the differences between weekday and weekends, as on Sunday users tend to be more intimate (see Fig. 6 and Fig. 5). Finally, *hour* is the single variable most significant for intimacy state given our set of data. When one uses the phone in the morning he/she tends to be less intimate than when using it in the evening (Fig. 5).

For **applications used** model the application's *category* and *interval* variables are not significant for the intimacy state. Also *day* and *hour* variables, although they are present in the most significant models do not seem to contribute so much, as well as *m_touches*.

To indicate the most significant variables, *touches* and *application* we have plotted two sub-models of the most significant model: *hour+touches+app* and *hour+day+app* (not presented here for space reasons). From both plots we can observe how depending on which *application* is used we have a different probability on being on the *completely* intimate state. We can divide the 20 applications in two groups: one, composed by 14 of them (Email (2 apps), Messaging (4 apps), App Launcher (3 apps), Browser (1 app, small amount of data available), Contacts (1 app), Phone (1 app), Settings (1 app), and Social Contact (1 app)), where the *completely* intimate state is distinct from the other states. For an additional group of six apps (Browser (2 apps), Email (1 app), System (1 app), App Market (1 app), Social Network (1 app)), the probability of *completely* state is very close to the other most probable states, *i.e.*, such applications can be used in any state. For the moment we did not investigate further these differences.

Finally, for the other variables present in these models (as well as being the most significant ones), *hour*, *touches* and *day* are contributing as follows: *hour* as increasing high intimacy when reaching the end of the day, increasing number of *touches* increasing *completely* intimate probability, and *day* as the least contributing and significant only for Sunday.

For the last subset of data defining the **communication category** model, the temporal variables *hour*, *day* and *interval* are the least significant ones, probably because the temporal effect is reduced by the more equally distributed use of *Communication* applications across time. These variables are followed by *touches* and *m_touches* that relate to how the user interacts with the phone. In particular, in this data subset the number of *touches* depends on the *sub-category* variable. This *sub-category* variable combined with the *touches* and the *day* creates the most significant model of this subset. From Fig. 7 we can notice that for the *Messaging* (4 apps) sub-category, the longer are the messages or the conversation time (more *touches* to write longer messages or longer threads), the higher is the probability that the user is intimate. We can rationalize this finding as follows. We interact or text longer messages when we feel more confortable and secure in the environment we are at that moment (*i.e.* at home). From *Browser* (3 apps) we see that we tend to navigate with the mobile browsers when we are not intimate. If we do that with more *touches* (*e.g.*, we interact more by clicking on several links or we do not use bookmarks, but we type the website fully) it probably means, that we are more intimate. This assumption cannot be fully confirmed from our data, because the *Browser* interaction, in term of *touches*, is quite short.

4.1 Study Limitations

There are some limitations that are conditioning our approach. Particularly, self-selected applications and interactions, the participants were performing, may influence significantly the generalization of results. Additionally, by asking the current user intimacy randomly during the day is possible that the participant were mostly answering when they were mostly intimate, maybe more willing to interact with the smartphone (as the results of this study show). We assume that if a user is not intimate, *i.e.*, interacting with someone that she/he does not know or does not consider as a significant other, it is not really socially acceptable to interact with the smartphone. The solution to get less biased ground truth, could be to collect the ground truth much more often, but this will probably decrease the participant adherence to the study in the long term. Another important point about the ground truth is the subjectivity of the participants in stating their intimacy. We group all the data from all users in one single set of data from which we derived the three smaller data sets, as we have presented (namely, *transitions present-OFF*, *applications used*, and *Communication*). It would be interesting to see how our models perform using mixed models instead of just fixed effects models. In our future work, we will consider each user as a random variable and add it to our models and observe how our models behave.

With respect to the interaction variables collected, we can imagine that there are other ways to observe how a smartphone is used. For example we could include the battery [11, 13], device memory, and processing unit logs. It was for purpose to keep the set of variables small to perform this initial research exploration.

Furthermore, adding extra questions to the ESM survey, such as number of people around, who are these people, where is the participant, and so on. These questions would probably significantly contribute to understanding on how the phone is used with respect to these factors assumed to be determinant for intimacy.

Finally, the results suggest that we may need to redefine the scale of the intimacy states to a simpler one, like: *high*, *medium*, *low* intimacy levels. To better understand if this is the right direction a similar analysis performed for the results presented in this paper must be done by grouping *completely* and *yes* state in the *high* level, *more yes than no* and *more no than yes* in *medium* level, and *no* and *not at all* in *low* level.

5   Related Work Areas

There exist some related work in the area of the context, in which smartphone applications are used and, similarly to our approach, how it can help to adapt mobile apps. To best of our knowledge, no related work exists on the modeling of the intimacy context for mobile applications users. Only in our previous work [9], where we studied the possibility to use smartphones to determine the intimacy state of the user, we have a first attempt to define intimacy as contextual information. Differently from this work, in [9] we did not have any ground truth to confirm our assumptions. Shin *et al.* [14] widely analyses context factors in relation of the use of mobile apps. They performed a user study where they collected GPS and cellular network location (for location), app open/close events (for time), and battery charging patterns, and so on. They used the data to predict the next app used, thus be able to adapt the apps menu. Böhmer *et al.* [15] did an analysis on mobile apps' usage. The data was collected from over 4100 users. 22'626 different apps were used and 4.92 million events of app usages (*e.g.*, install, opened, closed) were collected. They analysed apps' usages with respect to the location, time, and chain of app usages context information. They presented how the analysis of this information can be used to improve the design of mobile apps, which it is also one of the goals of our future work. Ickin *et al.* [16] also investigated mobile apps' usages regarding the location (semantic place), time of the day, and connectivity (Quality of Service analysis). When participants were interviewed, they admitted that they learn how to maximize their own experience based on their previous apps usage experience, connectivity options and app needs at hand. There is definitely a need to provide to users automated mechanism to adapt the use of their smartphones and mobile apps. Floch *et al.* [17] presented the European research project MUSIC describing typical context (*e.g.*, noise, light, network, location, users interactions) and adaptation features (*e.g.*, alternative user interaction and provided functionalities) that are relevant for developing self-adaptive mobile apps. They propose a framework to help developers to make use of contextual information to reduce the development complexity of self-adaptive mobile apps. Intimacy could definitely be leveraged as the contextual information for application self-adaptation.

6   Conclusions

In conclusion, this paper presents a study on the intimacy context of smartphone users and applications usage patters in different intimacy states. Intimacy is new contextual information, directly related to the human being behavior and social context. We show that even considering a small set of variables we can model the interaction of the user with the smartphone and its change along her/his current intimacy. In particular, we present how the probabilities of being intimate or not are changing when considering variables as *day* of the week and *hour* of the day for *when* the smartphone is used, or *number of applications switched*, *application* used, or the number of *touches* performed for *how* the smartphone is used.

The future work areas relate to (1) investigating additional smartphone usage variables like social activities, battery information, memory usage logs, and so on and their relation to intimacy, (2) dividing the users in groups to identify different relations between their perception of intimacy in different contexts, (3) find methods and approaches to automatically estimate the intimacy perception from the data available from the smartphone, and (4) explore how knowledge of the intimacy context can imply the mobile applications' design decisions.

Acknowledgements. AAL projects (MyGuardian, WayFiS) and UniGe-CUI grant supported this work.

References

1. Tossell, C., Kortum, P., Shepardb, C., Rahmati, A., Zhong, L.: An empirical analysis of smartphone personalisation: measurement and user variability. Behav. Inf. Technol. 31, 995–1010 (2012)
2. Geihs, K., Wagner, M.: Context-awareness for self-adaptive applications in ubiquitous computing environments. In: Vinh, P.C., Hung, N.M., Tung, N.T., Suzuki, J. (eds.) ICCASA 2012. LNCIST, vol. 109, pp. 108–120. Springer, Heidelberg (2013)
3. Efstratiou, C., Cheverst, K., Friday, A.: An Architecture for the Effective Support of Adaptive Context-Aware Applications. In: Tan, K.-L., Franklin, M.J., Lui, J.C.-S. (eds.) MDM 2001. LNCS, vol. 1987, pp. 15–26. Springer, Heidelberg (2000)
4. Geihs, K.: Self-Adaptivity from Different Application Perspectives. In: de Lemos, R., Giese, H., Müller, H.A., Shaw, M. (eds.) Software Engineering for Self-Adaptive Systems. LNCS, vol. 7475, pp. 376–392. Springer, Heidelberg (2013)
5. Evers, C., Kniewel, R., Geihs, K., Schmidt, L.: Achieving user participation for adaptive applications. In: Bravo, J., López-de-Ipiña, D., Moya, F. (eds.) UCAmI 2012. LNCS, vol. 7656, pp. 200–207. Springer, Heidelberg (2012)
6. Pei, L., Guinness, R., Chen, R., Liu, J., Kuusniemi, H., Chen, Y., Chen, L., Kaistinen, J.: Human behavior cognition using smartphone sensors. Sensors 13, 1402–1424 (2013)
7. Gerstein, R.S.: Intimacy and privacy. Ethics 89, 76–81 (1978)
8. Reiman, J.H.: Privacy, intimacy, and personhood. Philos. Public Aff. 6, 26–44 (1976)
9. Gustarini, M., Wac, K.: Estimating People Perception of Intimacy in Daily Life from Context Data Collected with Their Mobile Phone. Nokia workshop at Pervasive (2012)
10. Raento, M., Oulasvirta, A., Eagle, N.: Smartphones: An Emerging Tool for Social Scientists. Sociol. Methods Res. 37, 426–454 (2009)
11. Rahmati, A., Zhong, L.: Studying Smartphone Usage: Lessons from a Four-Month Field Study. IEEE Trans. Mob. Comput. 12, 1417–1427 (2013)
12. Haubo, R., Christensen, B.: Analysis of ordinal data with cumulative link models — estimation with the R-package ordinal
13. Ferreira, D., Dey, A.: Understanding human-smartphone concerns: a study of battery life. Pervasive Comput., 19–33 (2011)
14. Shin, C., Hong, J.-H., Dey, A.K.: Understanding and prediction of mobile application usage for smart phones. In: UbiComp, p. 173. ACM Press, New York (2012)
15. Böhmer, M., Hecht, B., Schöning, J., Kruger, A., Bauer, G.: Falling asleep with angry birds, facebook and kindle: a large scale study on mobile application usage. In: MobileHCI (2011)
16. Ickin, S., Wac, K., Fiedler, M., Janowski, L., Hong, J.-H., Dey, A.K.: Factors influencing quality of experience of commonly used mobile applications. IEEE Commun. Mag. (2012)
17. Floch, J., Frà, C., Fricke, R.: Playing MUSIC—building context-aware and self-adaptive mobile applications. Softw. Pract. Exp., 359–388 (2012)

Geometric Layout Analysis in a Wearable Reading Device for the Blind and Visually Impaired

Roman Guilbourd and Raul Rojas

Free University Berlin
{guilbour,rojas}@mi.fu-berlin.de

Abstract. Blind and visually impaired people can use a mobile device for accessing printed information, which is ubiquitous in everyday life. Thus, there is a need for a mobile easy-to-use reading device, capable of dealing with the complexity of the outdoor environment. In this paper a wearable camera based solution is presented, aiming at improving the performance of existing systems through the use of an integrated approach for the document processing. This particular publication covers the segmentation phase of the processing chain as well as geometric analysis of the layout. Using a highly efficient approach we were able to overcome the limitations of a mobile computing environment without compromising on the robustness of the result. In order to demonstrate the advantages of the presented algorithm for the specific field of application we compare its output to the results obtained by a state-of-the art commercial solution.

Keywords: Wearable device, healthcare assistance, OCR, document processing.

1 Introduction

In our project we are developing an eyewear system for blind and visually impaired people, which would automatically detect, localize and process text documents in both in- and outdoor environments. Most of the currently available standard solutions in this area require a significant amount of user involvement, in particular during the acquisition phase, when the capturing device has to be oriented towards the document. This might be one of the major reasons for the continuing prevalence of stationary reading devices that was indicated by our survey.

Apart from the stationary solutions there exist numerous smartphone-based aids, which, however, can be difficult to handle for people with limited spatial vision due to its handheld nature. The mobility requirement poses a considerable challenge in terms of robustness and efficiency of the algorithms utilized in the document processing chain. Table 1 illustrates the additional effort necessary to achieve a result that would be comparable with that of a scanner-based reading device. Compounding the problem are the limited computational resources of a mobile platform, which are a result of the miniaturization effort. Therefore, an efficient and highly integrated approach was developed through optimization of the entire processing chain as a whole. Several steps of the procedure have already been presented in [1]. This current paper is focused on the segmentation phase showing how different parts of the chain interact in order to

G. Memmi and U. Blanke (Eds.): MobiCASE 2013, LNICST 130, pp. 90–97, 2014.
© Institute for Computer Sciences, Social Informatics and Telecommunications Engineering 2014

reduce overall processing time. In the following we will briefly introduce the proposed document processing routine and then discuss image segmentation and text detection in more detail, demonstrating the links between the different stages of the pipeline. In conclusion, some evaluation results are presented and the benefits of the proposed algorithm for the particular application are explained.

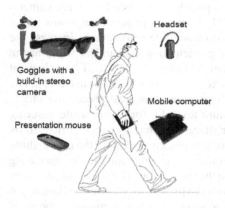

Goggles with a
build-in stereo
camera

Presentation mouse

Headset

Mobile computer

Fig. 1. System components

Table 1. Stationary vs. Mobile Systems

Stationary	Mobile
Position of the document is determined	Text localization required
Lighting conditions are controllable(scanner)	Calibration required
Distance to the document is fixed	Auto-focusing required
Distortion is negligible	De-warping required
No motion artifacts	Prevention required

2 Related Work

Several multiresolution approaches for segmentation of document images have been suggested by different authors. In [2] the performance of wavelet packet spaces is analyzed in terms of sensitivity and selectivity for the classification of textures in general. In particular, a comparison of energy and entropy based signatures is performed and, as a result of an experimental analysis, energy representations computed from the standard set of wavelet nodes is shown to be sufficient for texture classification. In the work of Etemad at al. [3] wavelet based features are utilized for the specific case of textures presented in a printed document with four kinds of layout elements considered as different classes: text, image, graphics and blank areas. In the suggested method every sub-block of a document image is pre-classified using a multilevel feed-fordward neural network. After that the results of the classification are combined by means of a soft decision integration approach. The author also mentions, without going into more detail, that wavelet based features can indicate font size of characters contained in a text block. Distribution of the wavelet coefficients in high frequency bands are analyzed in [4] in order to identify text and non-text regions of a document. The presented classification approach follows the assumption that a histogram of the coefficients from a text area should be of a highly discrete nature. Several authors [5] [6] have proposed an approach, where the quadtree-representation of an image in the position domain is combined with the FWT-decomposition of the signal in the frequency domain. The problem of font size estimation basing on the distribution of the FTW-coefficients is addressed in [7]. The author introduces a method for detection of text areas using third andfourth central moments of the corresponding scalogram pdf. However, no information is provided on the efficiency of the implementation.

3 System Description

The system presented in this paper comprises a goggle with a build-in stereo camera, a mini ITX computer featuring a 1.6 GHz CPU, a wireless presentation mouse and a headset (as seen in figure 1). By using a stereo camera we were able to increase the field of view of the device, thus alleviating the orientation difficulties, while at the same time tackling some of the most prominent problems in the field of document processing like text tracking, de-warping of text regions and exact focusing [1]. The whole chain can be divided into two stages: capturing phase and processing phase. The capturing phase serves to detect and capture textual information while ensuring a suitable quality of the image as required for successful character recognition. In its initial state the system scans the environment for text objects providing the user audible feedback upon detection. After the notification the user can either initiate the processing of the detected textual information or go back to the initial loop. This basic functionality can be accomplished by using just two buttons on the presentation mouse, whereas two more buttons are needed to access some advanced services such as permanent storage of the recognized text and text navigation. Pending a decision, the systems keeps tracking the detected regions and produces a warning, if a text block has reached a boundary of the visible image area. After the user has initiated the processing, optimal camera settings and orientation are determined utilizing the measurements from the tracking phase.

The second phase includes a preprocessing of the stereo image, an actual OCR (optical character recognition), a TTS (text-to-speech) transformation and the output of the result. It starts with a segmentation of the two high resolution images as well as a classification of the separated regions. Unlike in the case of the real-time text detection algorithm from the capturing phase, the completeness and accuracy of the result are of crucial importance for the layout analysis. In order to meet the requirements a novel document image segmentation algorithm based on the Fast Wavelet Transformation (FWT)[8] and quadtrees [9] was developed and integrated into the processing chain. After the segmentation is completed, a binarization of the regions [10] and extraction of the text lines is performed in a combined approach involving connected component analysis. The set of the extracted components is then analyzed in order to reliably identify text regions, which are to be further processed. First, the structure of the documents in the images is recognized and every text block is labeled as a component of the logical layout. Basing on the result of the layout analysis, a proper reading order for the text regions is obtained and an OCR is accomplished according to that order. Using the text specific features extracted in the previous steps, de-warping and stitching of the regions can be performed [1] prior to the character recognition, when necessary. Finally, an OCR and a TTS-conversion are carried out using commercial solutions [11]. The output is initiated immediately after the first text block is ready, while the processing is continued in the background.

4   Image Segmentation and Text Detection

4.1   Specific Requirements

Segmentation of the images is the first step of the presented document processing chain, so no information about the content of the images is available at the time. While a reliable recognition of text regions depends upon a correct segmentation, some data on text specific properties are required to support the segmentation. In order to be able to deal with this mutual dependency a few general assumptions about the text regions are made prior to the segmentation step:

- (initially)bimodal distribution of the pixel values in document areas
- (nearly) uniform distribution of character heights in a single text region
- (nearly) uniform distribution of inter-character and interline spacing in a single text region
- the distance between two lines in a text block is relative to the average inter-character spacing in the lines and is at least twice as large as its maximum
- the distance between two text regions is relative to the average inter-line spacing and is at least twice as large as its maximum

A coarse estimation of the possible font size presented in the segments is required, since some of the subsequent steps of the processing such as text line extraction and binarization [10] rely on it.

The main motivation of developing a mobile reading device is that it could be used in an outdoor environment, where the user is confronted with a wide variety of different presentations of textual information. Compared to the special case of printed documents, distinguishing between text and non-text elements, that are embedded in a dynamic natural environment, can be a much more difficult. Unlike most of the related works presented above, our segmentation algorithm does not include a comprehensive classification of the segments. After connected components of a region are extracted as part of the binarization procedure, identification of text areas can be accomplished in a more straightforward way.

4.2   Image Segmentation

For reasons of robustness, reliability and efficiency a multiresolution FWT-based approach is utilized for image segmentation. In the position domain a quadtree decomposition is performed [12], so each stage of the FWT has a corresponding level in the tree. The pattern of distribution of the energies over the scales

$$Energy_i = \sum_j \left| \alpha_i^j \right|^2,$$

with α^i denoting the FWT coefficients from ith decomposition level, is analyzed to determine the similarity between subregions. Energy representations computed from the standard set of wavelet nodes have been shown to be sufficient for texture classification [2]. In addition, locations of the peaks in the energy distribution indicate such important text specific properties of regions as possible font size (as seen in figure 2) and text flow direction, that are both required for the subsequent steps of the processing. The feasibility of the conclusions follows directly from the scaling property as well as energy conservation property of the FWT [8], since differences in the font size can be considered as shifts in the frequency spectrum of the image signal.

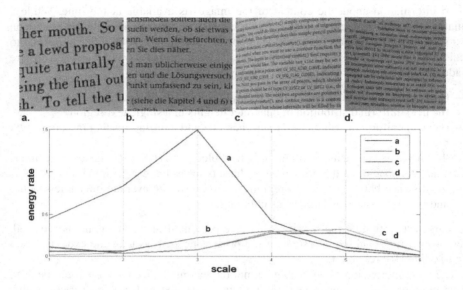

Fig. 2. Correspondence between font size and peaks in the FWT energy distribution

The segmentation of the image is carried out as follows:

1. Energy distribution signature of the subregions is computed up to the corresponding decomposition level.
2. Homogeneous background areas are identified using a variance threshold.
3. Neighboring subregions are incrementally merged taking into account the background areas.

The recognition of the homogeneous subregions occurs by means of the universal threshold $\lambda_u = \sqrt{2 \ln N} \hat{\sigma}$, that was first introduced and frequently utilized for noise reduction [15]. Here is N - number of the FTW-coefficients in the region and $\hat{\sigma}$ - median absolute deviation (MAD) of all coefficient values on the respective decomposition level. Since computation of MAD is quite a time consuming operation, variance σ of the coefficients is used to approximate $\hat{\sigma}$ instead:

$$\sigma^2\left(\alpha_i\right) = E\left(\alpha_i^2\right) - \left(E\left(\alpha_i\right)\right)^2 = \tfrac{1}{N_i} Energy_i - \left(E\left(\alpha_i\right)\right)^2,$$

E denotes here the expected value whereas $Energy$ denotes the overall energy of the coefficients α on the level j. This way, no additional time is needed to determine the threshold λ_u, however, the accuracy of the classification can be compromised by potential outliers. At this point of computation it is especially important to avoid false positive results (as seen in figure 3), so that the threshold is scaled by a factor $\gamma < 1$.

Nodes in the tree that correspond to the homogeneous subregions are then marked as background. According to the assumptions about text regions presented above, two text blocks should be separated by an interval at least twice the width of the inter-line spaces of the blocks. As a consequence, homogeneous areas from within the regions should be located on a lower tree level than blank areas from the intermediate spaces. Moreover, the assumptions also imply, that the width of a spacing interval should correspond to the font size in the surrounding text blocks and therefore to the "peak" scale of the energy distributions in the neighboring tree nodes. With that in mind we can merge detected background areas and filter out most of the false positives by applying following strategy:

1. Starting with the leaves follow the tree up until the "peak" scale level is reached.
2. If a "peak node" has any background neighbors mark them as border regions.
3. Propagate the signature $\{h\left(R_{max}\right), o\left(R_{max}\right)\}$ of the "peak nodes" down to the leaves, where h denotes distribution of the energy over the scales, o denotes distribution of the energy over the FWT subbands corresponding to the ridge orientation and all feature vectors are assumed to be normalized.
4. Traverse the tree one more time and mark all the descendants of the border region according to the scale of the "peak-node".
5. Apply marker-controlled watershed segmentation algorithm [13].

   - Use the mismatch between the propagated "peak node" scale and the current level of the marked border regions as the segmentation function.
   - Use the signature-based similarity function to obtain foreground markers:
     $sim\left(R_1, R_2\right) = h\left(R_1\right) \cdot h\left(R_2\right) + o\left(R_1\right) \cdot o\left(R_2\right).$
   - Use the "peak-node"-scale to obtain background markers.
   - for each foreground marker perform a region growing operation on the corresponding tree level.

4.3 Text Detection

Utilizing the approach presented above we not only managed to perform a text specific segmentation of the image, but also to estimate the font size in the segments, thus being able to parameterize the scale sensitive binarization algorithm [10]. The subsequent analysis of the extracted regions is carried out on the binarized image of the positive translation energies. The blocks are then scanned in the direction perpendicular to the estimated orientation of the text lines (as determined by means of the FWT energy distribution) and foreground objects are extracted using [16]. Provided that the measurements of the characters are distributed uniformly, it can be easily shown, that the characters of a single line are detected in the sequential order as long as the orientation error does not exceed certain limits, e.g. $45°$ in case that the maximum height difference and the maximum gap size between two neighboring characters are both limited to the height of the smaller character. During this operation the contours of the components are marked to avoid rediscovering already known elements and the size of the elements is estimated by bounding volumes. After the scanning process is completed, the coefficient of variation of heights of the bounding boxes is computed to verify the "uniformity" condition: $\sigma(h_s)/E(h_s) < 2$, where $\sigma(h_s)$ - the standard deviation and $E(h_s)$ - the expected value. In case the requirement is not fulfilled, the segment is classified as non-text and discarded. Otherwise, the characters are arranged into lines and the distances between the characters are analyzed in a similar way to how character size distribution was analyzed before. Since the characters of a line are discovered in an order close to the sequential, only few characters from the current end of each line need to be considered as potential predecessors of a text line element to be sorted.

5   Result and Evaluation

In this paper a document processing chain for a wearable reading system is presented of which the segmentation stage is discussed in more detail. The overall result of the initial layout analysis includes positions, measurements and specific characteristics of the text blocks, text lines and single characters contained in the image. Thanks to the integrated approach, we were able to incorporate the binarization algorithm into the segmentation operation for their mutual benefit. The ability of the segmentation algorithm to systematically differentiate between inter-line and inter-region spacing basing on the font size is particularly important in outdoor environments, where text regions are tightly embedded into the scene and could be partly obscured by non-text objects. A special effort was made in order to optimize the procedure in terms of the efficiency. The execution time average for the combined approach including segmentation, binarization, text line extraction and classification of the segments given two 8 Mpx images on a 1.6 GHz processor is at 1 ms per extracted component. After these steps the amount of text to be recognized and output at a single round of reading can be dynamically determined with a precision up to a single word, depending on the estimated processing time for the subsequent region. The *response* time of the system for a document containing 10000 symbols is around 20 s, whereas the overall processing time can exceed two minutes.

OmniPage Capture SDK 16, which is used to perform character recognition in our system, also features geometric layout analysis making it possible to evaluate the

Fig. 3. Segmentation result

Table 2. Evaluation result of the algorithm

	Our approach	OmniPage
MediaTeam DB 1793 regions	91% 1625	95% 1702
Additional images 128 regions	77% 99	31% 40

accuracy of the proposed approach. Two different data sets were used for evaluation purposes: a publicly accessible document database [14] presenting a wide variety of layout/font types and 14 images of severely distorted documents made outdoors under realistic lighting and environmental conditions. The rating was explicitly designed to detect oversegmentation and region merging by evaluation of coordinates of the extracted bounding boxes. While in the public data set ca. 90% (as seen in Table 2) of the text regions were localized and classified correctly, the success rate for the second set containing document images of a poorer quality was about 80%. In contrast, the performance of the OmniPage layout recognition module on images of distorted documents dropped dramatically, even though the recognition rate on the images from the MediaTeam document database was slightly higher than that of our implementation.

References

1. Guilbourd, R., Yogev, N., Rojas, R.: Stereo camera based wearable reading device. In: Proceedings of the 3rd Augmented Human International Conference, vol. 1. ACM (2012)
2. Laine, A., Fan, J.: Texture Classification by Wavelet Packet Signatures. IEEE Trans. Pattern Anal. Mach. Intell. 15, 1186–1191 (1993)
3. Etemad, K., Doermann, D.S., Chellappa, R.: Multiscale Segmentation of Unstructured Document Pages Using Soft Decision Integration. IEEE Trans. Pattern Anal. Mach. Intell. 19(1), 92–96 (1997)
4. Li, J., Gray, R.M.: Context-based multiscale classification of document images using wavelet coefficient distributions. IEEE Trans. Image Process. 9, 1604–1616 (2000)
5. Lee, S.-W., Ryu, D.-S.: Parameter-Free Geometric Document Layout Analysis. IEEE Trans. Pattern Anal. Mach. Intell. 23(11), 1240–1256 (2001)
6. Cheng, H., Bouman, C.A.: Multiscale bayesian segmentation using a trainable context model. IEEE Trans. Pattern Anal. Mach. Intell. 10(4), 511–525 (2001)
7. Gupta, P., Vohra, N., Chaudhury, S., Joshi, S.D.: Wavelet Based Page Segmentation. In: Indian Conf. on Computer Vision, Graphics and Image Processing, pp. 20–22 (2002)
8. Rioul, O., Vetterli, M.: Wavelets and Signal Processing. Signal Processing Magazine 8(4), 14–38 (1991)
9. Finkel, R., Bentley, J.L.: Quad Trees: A Data Structure for Retrieval on Composite Keys. Acta Informatica 4(1), 1 (1974)
10. Block, M., Rojas, R.: Local Contrast Segmentation to Binarize Images. In: International Conference on the Digital Society, vol. 1(1) (2009)
11. OmniPage Capture SDK 16, Nuance Communications, Inc.
12. Choi, H., Baraniuk, R.G.: Multiscale image segmentation using wavelet-domain hidden Markov models. IEEE Trans. Image Process. 1309–1321 (2001)
13. Najman, L., Schmitt, M.: Geodesic saliency of watershed contours and hierarchical segmentation. IEEE Trans. Pattern Anal. Mach. Intell. 18(12), 1163–1173 (1996)
14. Sauvola, J., Kauniskangas, H.: MediaTeam Document Database II. CD-ROM collection of document images, University of Oulu, Finland,
   http://www.mediateam.oulu.fi/MTDB/index.htm
15. Donoho, D.L., Johnstone, I.M.: Ideal Spatial adaptation via wavelet shrinkage. Biometrika 81, 425–455 (1994)
16. Suzuki, S., Abe, K.: Topological structural analysis of digitized binary images by border following. Computer Vision, Graphics, and Image Processing 30(1), 32–46 (1985)

Ring GINA: A Wearable Computer Interaction Device

Joseph Greenspun and Kristofer S.J. Pister

Department of Electrical Engineering and Computer Science
University of California, Berkeley
Berkeley, CA, USA
greenspun@berkeley.edu

Abstract. The Ring GINA platform is capable of sensing and interpreting a user's hand and finger movements to emulate and enhance the functions of classic input methods to smartphones, tablets, and heads-up displays. A wearable platform frees the user from the need to know hand position relative to a keyboard or touchscreen, and grants the ability to perform gestures in open space or on any surface. Here, a method is presented that utilizes these rings as a text input system. In moving forward, efforts are being focused on creating a library of gestures to perform additional tasks, as well as further miniaturizing the mote and ring.

Keywords: wearable computing, sensor networks, input device, ring GINA.

1 Introduction

Mobile text entry is a challenege that constantly plagues cell phone users. Typically text entry is done on a standard QWERTY keyboard displayed on a touchscreen. The QWERTY keyboard layout works well for a standard desktop or laptop computer because the typist's fingers are constantly acquiring feedback as to their position. The typist does not need to constantly look at the keyboard because he/she obtains tactile feedback during the entire text entry process, is aware when two keys are hit instead of one, et cetera. This feedback is absent when typing on a smartphone touchscreen. The screen might vibrate when a key is pressed, but this vibration gives no valuable feedback; It does not help reorient the user or inform which key was pressed. Additionally, due to device size, users are typically forced to type with just their thumbs, and often with just a single thumb if one hand is occupied.

In an attempt to address these issues, we present Ring GINA which allows users to enter text using just a single hand. A wireless sensor enabled ring is worn on each finger and allows the user to input text requiring neither a special surface nor direct contact with the target device. The first smart ring was published in 1997[1]. This device uses a one-axis accelerometer on each finger. These accelerometers are physically wired to a computer where the signals are

G. Memmi and U. Blanke (Eds.): MobiCASE 2013, LNICST 130, pp. 98–103, 2014.

interpreted. Since then there have been numerous advances in the capability and functionality of smart rings[3,4,5]. Perng et al.[8] created an accelerometer sensing glove. This glove contains a two-axis accelerometer on each fingertip and can be used to determine static hand poses. These acceleromters are also wired to a receiving computer.

2   Ring GINA Platform

The Ring GINA system is comprised of four identical rings that are worn on the fingers of the dominant hand. Figure 1 shows the components that make up a single ring. Each one is 3D printed with a custom plastic (VisiJet) using a ProJet 1500. A custom PCB, Figure 1b, fitted with a 20 mAh battery and connector is fixed into the top of the ring. Lastly, a GINA[7] mote, 1c, is plugged into the connector and the ring is fully assembled and functional, 1d. GINA is comprised of all off-the-shelf components. It contains two three-axis accelerometers, a three-axis gyroscope, a three-axis magnetometer, a microprocessor, and an 802.15.4 radio.

Each ring is part of a simple OpenWSN[6] based wireless network. This wireless protocol allows each ring to reliably transmit the salient information gleaned from processing the inertial data obtained from the various sensors on the mote. The wireless communication is low bandwidth, transmitting only a few bits per second. As discussed in section 3, all of the gesture recognition signal processing occurs on the motes themselves. This removes the need to transmit the raw sensor data which decreases power comsumption on the ring and reduces the computational load on the receiving device. For all experiments performed in this paper, the receiving device is a laptop with an accompanying 802.15.4 USB dongle as is shown in Figure 2.

Fig. 1. Teardown of a ring. (a) A 3D printed ring. (b) PCB and battery. (c) GINA mote. (d) Fully assembled device.

Fig. 2. Ring GINA System

3 Signal Processing

Text entry is performed by abstracting a chorded keyboard from finger taps. The user taps on any surface with one or more fingers to input characters. With four rings worn on a single hand, there are 15 different possible chords that a user can type. When the inertial data is processed, and it is determined that a user has tapped a finger, that ring sends a signal to the target device. Figure 3a shows a chord being typed wherein the pointer finger and ring finger are tapped and the remaining two fingers are not. For each gesture, a four-bit binary signal is created with ones corresponding to tapped finers and zeros corresponding to non-tapped fingers.The fingers are aligned in order, with the pointer finger being the most significant bit and the pinky finger being the least significant. The signal from each ring is sent to the host device where it is referenced against a lookup table, Figure 3b, to determine what letters or actions to type or perform.

This technology hinges on the ability to reliably detect these tapping gestures. Though there is a wealth of inertial sensors on the mote, the signal processing is done entirely on a single axis of the accelerometer. The z-axis of the accelerometer is orthogonal to the plane of the mote, and thus aligned with the axis in which the finger tap occurs. Therefore a tap produces a strong signal on this axis of the accelerometer. Figure 3c shows traces of the z-axis of the accelerometers from each of the four rings during a 300 ms time period in which the gesture shown in 3a was performed. It is clear that the signals from the pointer finger and ring finger (the fingers that were tapped) are much stronger than the signals of the two fingers that were not tapped. However, a simple threshold would not be sufficient to selectively determine when taps occur. If a user were to wave his/her hand around while wearing the ring, or possibly even just tilt the ring and change how the acceleration of gravity aligns with the accelerometer, a tap event might be detected.

To ensure that the tap detection algorithm is robust to various motions, the algorithm ensures certain characteristics are present before declaring a tap and sending the appropriate signal. The algorithm determines a dynamic baseline signal by applying a low pass filter to the input stream and averaging. The user's hand may reorient with respect to gravity, and this will throw off the sensing if not taken into consideration. From this baseline, the algorithm searches for deviations in the accelerometer data that exceed a certain threshold. This threshold is calibrated for each finger and mote. Lastly, once the potential tap is complete, the accelerometer signal must return to a value within 5% of the baseline. This is important in ensuring that the user is not simply gesticulating or performing some unrelated hand motion. If all of these criteria are met, a tap has occurred, and the mote sends a signal to the host device.

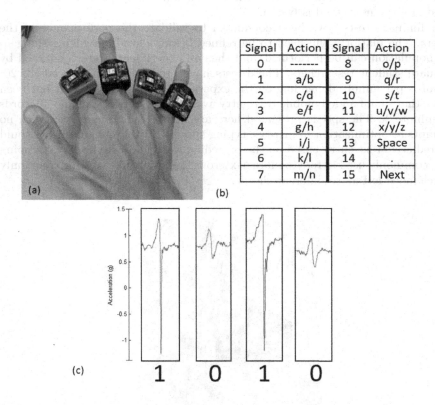

Signal	Action	Signal	Action
0	-------	8	o/p
1	a/b	9	q/r
2	c/d	10	s/t
3	e/f	11	u/v/w
4	g/h	12	x/y/z
5	i/j	13	Space
6	k/l	14	.
7	m/n	15	Next

Fig. 3. Chorded input. (a) A user typing a chord. (b) Table correlating each chorded input signal with output letters or action. (c) Traces from the accelerometer of each ring, over a 300 ms period, with corresponding binary signals.

4   User Application and Performance

The host device runs an application that receives the signals sent from each ring and displays the desired text to the user. Each four-bit signal from the rings corresponds to either one action or a series of characters. Actions can be "Next," entering a space, or entering a period. If the user wants to type the word "cot" for example, the user would type the chords 2-8-10 (see Figure 3b), and the search algorithm would determine that the word made from the letter combinations c/d, o/p, and s/t is cot. If the user actually meant to type the word "dot", which would be the same chord combination, the user would type the chord 15, which corresponds to the "Next" action. This "Next" command would display the next word that corresponds to that same chord combination, if one exists. Once the user selects the desired word, a space or period can be typed and the next word is begun.

Preliminary tests have been conducted to validate the performance of the system. The platform will need to be refined before a study involving the general population can be performed, and thus all experiments were conducted by graduate student researchers. These tests have produced typing speeds of 20-30 words per minute depending on the experience level of the user. It has been shown that dual handed mobile text entry averages are between 20 and 40 words per minute[2]. The speeds presented here are within that range, even with no attempts at optimization to increase typing speed. Possible enhancements could be predictive text entry based on the preceding word and user history, mapping more commonly used letters to more dexterous fingers, and separating commonly interchanged letters to different chords.

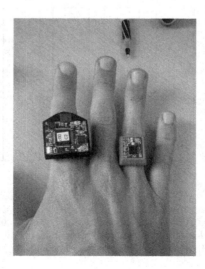

Fig. 4. Side by side comparison of two GINA boards

5   Conclusion and Future Work

Text entry for smart devices has lagged considerably behind the incredible advancements in mobile computing as a whole. The trend in mobile electronics is that smaller and less obtrusive is better, but that leaves the big challenge of how to actually interact with the devices. One goal for this technology is to pair Ring GINA with a smart watch. The combination of this always available display and this novel input system could revolutionize how we respond to emails and text messages in non-standard situations. The motes used throughout this paper all contain an 802.15.4 radio, however a new board has recently been spun that is less than half the size of the original board (see Figure 4) and uses a Bluetooth 4.0 radio. These new motes have already been shown to pair natively with various Bluetooth 4.0 enabled smart phones and tablets. The previously mentioned algorithms will be ported to the Bluetooth enabled rings and truly mobile applications can start to be developed. There is an abundance of unused inertial data that will eventually be utilized to create a richer library of gestures which will lead to the development of even more advanced and interesting mobile applications.

References

1. Fukumoto, M., Tonomura, Y.: Body Coupled FingeRing: Wireless Wearable Keyboard. In: CHI, pp. 147–154 (1997)
2. MacKenzie, S., Kober, H., Smith, D., Jones, T., Skepner, E.: LetterWise: Prefix-based Disambiguation for Mobile Text Input. In: UIST, pp. 111–120 (2001)
3. http://www.kickstarter.com/projects/mycestro/mycestrotm-the-next-generation-3d-mouse
4. Ogata, M., Sugiura, Y., Osawa, H., Imai, M.: iRing: Intelligent Ring Using Infrared Reflection. In: UIST, pp. 131–136 (2012)
5. Ashbrook, D., Baudisch, P., White, S.: Nenya: Subtle and Eyes-Free Mobile Input with a Magnetically-Tracked Finger Ring. In: CHI, pp. 2043–2046 (2011)
6. Watteyne, T., Vilajosana, X., Kerkez, B., Chraim, F., et al.: OpenWSN: a standards-based low-power wireless development environment. Transactions on Emerging Telecommunications Technologies 23(5), 480–493 (2012)
7. Mehta, A., Pister, K.: WARPWING: A complete open source control platform for miniature robots. In: The 2010 IEEE/RSJ International Conference on Intelligent Robots and Systems, pp. 5169–5174 (2010)
8. Perng, J., Fisher, B., Hollar, S., Pister, K.: Acceleration Sensing Glove (ASG). In: Intl. Symposium on Wearable Computers, pp. 178–180 (1999)

Intelligent Energy-Efficient Triggering of Geolocation Fix Acquisitions Based on Transitions between Activity Recognition States

Thomas Phan

Samsung Research America - Silicon Valley
San Jose, CA USA
thomas.phan@samsung.com

Abstract. Location-based applications (LBAs) running on smartphones offer features that leverage the user's geolocation to provide enhanced services. While there exist LBAs that require continuous geolocation tracking, we instead focus on LBAs such as location-based reminders or location-based advertisements that need a geolocation fix only at rare points during the day. Automatically and intelligently triggering geolocation acquisition just as it is needed for these types of applications produces the tangible benefit of increased battery life. To that end, we implemented a scheme to intelligently trigger geolocation fixes only on transitions between specific modes of transportation (such as driving, walking, and running), where these modes are detected on the smartphone using a low-power, high-resolution activity recognition system. Our experiments show that this approach consumes little power (approximately 225 mW for the activity recognition system) and correctly triggers geolocation acquisition at transitional moments with a median delay of 9 seconds from ground-truth observations. Most significantly, our system performs 41x fewer acquisitions than a competitive accelerometer-assisted binary classification scheme and 243x fewer than continuous tracking over our collected data set.

1 Introduction

Location-based applications (LBAs) running on modern commodity smartphones offer features that leverage the user's current or past physical location to provide some enhanced service. For example, commercial smartphone LBAs currently exist that automatically acquire geolocation fixes (represented as latitude, longitude coordinates) in order to keep the user's health statistics [10], derive vehicular traffic conditions [38], and warn drivers of nearby hazards [36].

While such capabilities are compelling, they are limited in practice due to the high rate of energy consumption from the geolocation fix acquisition process. A fix can be attained through GPS, which has high precision outdoors but cannot function indoors, or trilateration using WiFi or cellular towers, which can work indoors but with typically lower precision depending on the density of surrounding signal sources [5,35,13].

G. Memmi and U. Blanke (Eds.): MobiCASE 2013, LNICST 130, pp. 104–121, 2014.
© Institute for Computer Sciences, Social Informatics and Telecommunications Engineering 2014

Although our work is relevant to either means of geolocation positioning, we note that GPS achieves the most accuracy but at the highest battery cost. Studies have shown that continuous use of GPS can deplete a smartphone's battery within one day [20,29,21]. As a result, researchers in the area of energy-efficient geopositioning have looked at better ways of performing fix acquisitions, for example through duty-cycled scheduling with accelerometer-assisted motion detection [1,39,22]. However, such approaches are based on the fundamental assumption that LBAs need *continuous geolocation tracking*.

In this paper we focus on LBAs that require automated geolocation fixes only at specific points of the day to facilitate user engagement, thereby allowing an underlying system to trigger fix acquisition *very rarely*. Examples are:

- Location-based reminders: Smartphone applications like Apple's voice-driven Siri [2] allow the user to set reminders whose UI alert is activated only at a target location, such as an alert for "Remind me to finish writing the report when I get home."
- Location-based advertising: Advertisement offers, such as coupons, can be proactively pushed to users who are in the vicinity of a business [32].
- Location-based tourist recommendations: Tourists who drive and walk through a city can be shown recommended places to visit [6].

Because these types of LBAs require only rare geolocation fixes, namely at the location where the user becomes engaged with the LBA, continuous tracking is wasteful. Instead, battery power could be conserved if the geolocation software could trigger a fix acquisition in a just-in-time manner. Using a location-based reminder as an example, an ideal oracle system would acquire a fix right as the user reaches the target location, and the resulting proximity would then activate the reminder.

In this paper we approximate such an oracle by defining transitional periods between transportation modes to be opportune points to acquire a geolocation fix. For example, if the user has been driving and then transitions to walking, then most likely the user has parked his car and gotten out to walk, and that moment would be an opportunity to acquire a fix. Other identifiable transitions would also be good opportunities.

We implemented the above scheme to intelligently trigger geolocation fixes only on transitions between specific modes of transportation, where the modes are detected on the smartphone using a low-power, high-resolution activity recognition system that acquires real-time 3-D accelerometer data, performs signal processing to extract features, and applies a trained machine learning model to determine the most likely means of transportation (such as driving, walking, running, bicycling, or idling). Our experiments show that this approach consumes little power (approximately 225 mW for the activity recognition system) and correctly triggers geolocation acquisition at the correct transitional moments with a median delay of 9 seconds from ground-truth observations. Most significantly, it performs 41x fewer acquisitions than a competitive accelerometer-assisted binary classification scheme and 243x fewer than continuous tracking over our collected data set.

The rest of this paper is organized in the following manner. In Section 2 we discuss related work in the area of energy-efficient geolocation positioning. In Section 3 we provide an overview of our system, and in Sections 4 and 5 we describe our high-resolution activity recognition component and our transition-triggered geolocation fix acquisition systems, respectively. We show experimental results in Section 6 and then conclude in Section 7.

2 Related Work

Our work differs from previous research in the area of energy-efficient geolocation acquisition (e.g. [8,17,39]) in that we do not make the assumption that LBAs require continuous tracking. Instead, we focus on LBAs that need a geolocation fix only at specific and rare points in the day.

Previous researchers in this area have observed that (continuous) geolocation acquisitions can be disabled during phases of the day when the user is idle, such as when the user is asleep. One approach to implementing this scheme is to use the accelerometer at a coarse-grained resolution to detect only two states: idle versus non-idle [1,39,34,16,27]. These works do not exploit the fact that non-idle states can be broken down further to identify transitions between them. Other approaches detect non-idle states by using GPS itself as a sensor [17,37,11].

The work in [22] uses high-resolution activity recognition with the accelerometer to identify different modes of activity, which can then be used to inform GPS duty-cycle scheduling. Again, this work differs from ours is that they assume a need for continuous tracking; specifically, they look to expend a battery energy budget. The work in [26] uses the accelerometer to distinguish between standing and sitting to assist localization down to stores in which people tend to stand or sit (such as grocery stores and coffee shops).

In our work we define a finite state machine (FSM) that uses specific transitions between known user state vertices to trigger geolocation acquisition. The work in [37] also uses a FSM but for the opposite problem: they use sensors (including GPS) to determine the unknown user state.

Previous efforts have also looked at exploiting historical data. For example, the work in [28] adapts GPS duty-cycling based on whether location uncertainty has exceeded a threshold for a given location and time historical combination. The work in [25] discovers association rules that allow low-power sensors to replace high-power sensors. Our work differs in that our system does not require accumulated history.

Our system uses an activity recognition component to determine the user's mode of transportation so that transitions between them can be detected. Activity recognition is the process of inferring the user's physical behavior from sensor data and stems from work in the body-sensor community. Early research (e.g. [4,31,19,7,15]) relied on custom sensor hardware mounted on the human body. Modern smartphones with built-in sensors are now the platform of choice for mobile activity recognition research. Recent work (e.g. [23,22,18,33]) has demonstrated that on-device recognition is feasible and benefits from the fact that users carry smartphones with them throughout most of the day.

3   Design Overview

While there exist many location-based application (LBA) domains that require continuous geolocation tracking, such as health monitoring and vehicular traffic aggregation, we instead focus on LBAs for which continuous tracking is superfluous and unnecessarily depletes the battery; indeed, such LBAs may need a geolocation fix only at rare points during the day. Automatically and intelligently triggering geolocation acquisition just as it is needed for these types of applications produces the tangible benefit of increased battery life for users.

As a concrete example, consider a user who wants to set a location-based reminder. While the user is at work, he creates an alert that should activate when he arrives at his targeted home. We make the assumption that his home's address is in his smartphone's addressbook and has already been resolved to a geocoordinate. Such a reminder can be implemented in a number of ways:

- **Continuous tracking.** The system can continuously track the user as he drives from work to home. To save power, it can use coarse-grained but lower-power cellular tower geopositioning to determine the user's location with an error of about 300m to 400m [8]. When the user is within that error range to his home, the system may switch to GPS to get accuracy to within 10m. Once the user is within a proximity tolerance of the target, the reminder system activates the alert.
- **Just-in-time fix.** The system can, somehow, trigger *one* geolocation fix just as the user arrives at his home, and because he is within a proximity tolerance, the reminder system activates the alert.
- **Sensor fingerprinting to derive semantic location.** The system can use sensor fingerprints (i.e. features extracted from on-device sensors) to infer that the user has arrived at his home, which is a semantic location rather than a geocoordinate. Previous work has looked at WiFi, Bluetooth, audio, light, and other sensors as inputs to a classifier [3,9]. Since this approach requires training fingerprints to be taken, its generalizability is still an open question.

Our scheme follows the just-in-time approach. While triggering a geolocation fix acquisition before knowing that the user has arrived at a location may seem oracular, we posit that such triggering can be implemented in a general manner by observing transitions between user activity states, where each state represents a mode of transportation. Our key assumption is that particular transitions are indicative of moments in time when the user is amenable to engagement with an LBA, and so a fix should be triggered on these transitions.

We implemented our scheme on Android smartphones, and Figure 1 shows a block diagram of the system. At the bottom-most layer, a low-power accelerometer-only activity recognition component generates a continuous stream of inferred human modes of transportation. This component uses a supervised machine learning

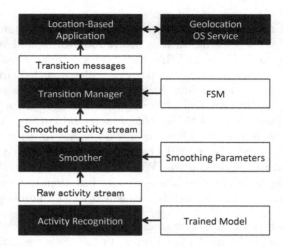

Fig. 1. High-level architecture of our system. The black boxes are software components while white boxes are data or models.

classifier that loads a trained C4.5 decision tree model into memory, reads real-time accelerometer signals, and produces a classification label. While the activity recognition is accurate on single-activity behavior in lab environments, it produces endemic misclassification errors when faced with real-world, mixed-activity behavior. To address this problem, we apply a smoothing window. The activity recognition is discussed in Section 4.

The transition manager listens to the stream of smoothed activity labels and manages a finite state machine (FSM) to detect relevant transitions. The vertices and edges in the FSM have labels that correspond to the possible activity recognition labels. The transition manager is discussed in Section 5.

The output of the transition manager are transition messages sent to any listening application, and in our Android-specific implementation, these messages are realized as Android Intents. Upon receiving such a message, the listening LBA should then acquire a geolocation fix and check to see if the the resulting geolocation coordinate satisfies its LBA-specific logic. For example, the coordinate could trigger a location-based reminder or a location-based advertisement.

An alternative implementation could have the transition manager acquire the geolocation and then include the resulting coordinates in its Intent message to all listeners. However, this approach would bypass Android's security and privacy model where each application must declare its use of geolocation services (in its manifest file), which is then surfaced to the user in the application's description before it can be downloaded from the Google Play store.

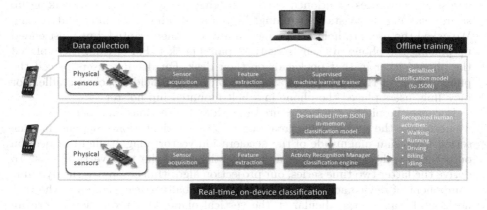

Fig. 2. Activity recognition end-to-end data collection, training, and classification

4 High-Resolution Activity Recognition

Smartphone-based physical activity recognition [4,22,18] infers human activities by analyzing on-board smartphone sensor signals, and in our framework we use supervised machine learning to make these inferences. The end-to-end system comprises two distinct phases, as shown in Figure 2. First, in an offline training phase, test participants perform various physical activities while wearing smartphones that run data-collection software. After extracting relevant sensor features, the model is then trained that maps such features back to the physical activities. Second, in an online classification phase that runs on a smartphone, the model is deployed onto smartphones and loaded by our activity recognition manager component to perform on-board, real-time classification of sensor data that can drive higher-level applications.

The activity recognition manager's sole input is the accelerometer, and the periodic output is a callback containing an activity represented as a string, such as *Running*; downstream clients then implement callback listener functions to receive them. We defined the following activities: *Walking*, *Running*, *Driving*, *Bicycling*, and *Idling* (which comprises standing and sitting).

4.1 Offline Model Training

To train the machine learning model, we had users perform single-activity, scripted behavior while an Android application (running on a Samsung Nexus S smartphone) recorded tri-axis accelerometer readings at 32 Hz and labelled them with the user's activity.

In each resulting file, we trimmed off the first 10 and the last 10 seconds' worth of samples. There were 17 total users, all from our research lab and in the age range of late-20s to 50s. The data totalled 397 minutes, or over 6 hours, across the activities mentioned earlier: walking (on a flat surface), walking up stairs, walking down stairs, running, bicycling, driving, standing, and sitting. We asked the users to hold the phones in any way they wanted, but most ended up placing the phone in their front right pants pocket. For sitting, users placed the phone either in that pocket or on their desk. For driving, users placed the phone either in that pocket, in a bag, or on a windshield-attached cradle. For bicycling, users placed the phone in a belt-mounted hip holster.

Because the phone can be oriented in different directions on a person's body, we normalize the accelerometer readings into three orientation-independent time series: Cartesian magnitude of the acceleration vector; magnitude of projection onto the true horizontal plane; and projection onto the true vertical axis. To derive the latter two time series, our projection algorithm computes the dynamic component of device acceleration in the true global vertical plane and the true horizontal plane perpendicular to the vertical plane. Our projection algorithm is based on past work [24,22].

The resulting three time series (Cartesian magnitude of the acceleration vectors, magnitude of projection onto the true horizontal plane, and projection onto the true vertical axis) are then captured with a 128-sample sliding window with 50% overlap.

For each of the three time series, we computed features using both the time and frequency domains. To obtain frequency domain information, we ran an FFT and follow standard steps to compute a correctly-scaled magnitude frequency response. We are constantly evaluating new features, but at the time of this writing, the features we use are:

- time-domain mean
- time-domain standard deviation
- time-domain real-valued discrete power
- time-domain entropy
- frequency-domain energy
- the frequency f_{max} with the highest magnitude
- the magnitude of f_{max}
- the frequency $f_{weighted-mean}$ calculated as the weighted mean of the top-5 highest-magnitude frequencies weighted by magnitude
- the weighted variance of the top-5 highest-magnitude frequencies weighted by magnitude.

These 9 features are extracted from each of the 3 time series, resulting in 27 total features that are concatenated together into one feature vector.

We used the Weka [14] off-the-shelf machine learning program to build our model offline on a desktop computer. The software provides a variety of different machine algorithms, including Naive Bayes, SVM, and kNN, and after testing them, we found that the C4.5 multi-class decision tree [30] produced the best results. Additional benefits of using a decision tree are that its memory footprint is low (less than 10 kB resident in memory) and its time to classify a feature vector is small (on the order of milliseconds), characteristics that are important when executing on a phone. Classifying a real-valued feature vector is a matter of walking down a tree structure and making a single floating-point comparison at each level, and in our work the decision tree never grew taller than 10 levels. The resulting trained model is serialized to a JSON file that contains data structures, statistics, and other metadata that are deserialized later on the phone by the activity recognition manager. The serialization format is JSON rather than binary, resulting in a file that is portable and can be can be deployed and updated separately from the other activity recognition components.

4.2 On-Device Classification System Architecture

The on-device classification system comprises several software stages and a trained model. Referring back to Figure 2, the sensor acquisition layer is the interface between the classification system and the sensor API provided by the smartphone's operating system. This layer is responsible for (i) reading the physical hardware sensors, such as the accelerometer (and other sensors like the microphone and compass in future work), and (ii) preparing the data into a structure for later processing.

The activity recognition manager runs as a system-wide singleton service that (i) loads the JSON-encoded classication model built during the training phase, (ii) reads accelerometer input from the sensor acquisition layer to extract features, and (iii) executes the real-time activity classification. Clients register themselves as listeners to the manager, which then invokes client callback functions whenever a relevant activity has been recognized by the classifier.

4.3 The Need for Smoothing

We augmented our classifier with an smoothing algorithm that improves classification for real-world usage. As we show later in Section 6, the system achieves a 10-fold cross-validated accuracy of 98.4%. While this result is appealing and is in alignment with the methodology and results reported in other activity recognition work (e.g. [22,18]), it is misleading because it applies only to the single-activity, scripted activity behavior recorded during the training phase. Even with the use of cross-validation, two problems arise: (1) the built model may be overfit for the data; and (2) mixed-activity, naturalistic human behavior contains many motions and transitions that were not captured during training. As a result, the classifier can return incorrect labels in real-world use.

To avoid any such choppiness, we implemented a simple smoothing algorithm with a majority vote within a trailing window (of parameter size N). As we show later, this choice of N affects the trade-off between the number of geolocation fix requests and the delay (in terms of time and distance) between the fix request and ground-truth observed transitions.

Fig. 3. Geolocation fixes are triggered only on major activity transitions controlled by a finite state machine. A fix is acquired on transitions indicated by the solid edges.

5   Activity Recognition Transition-Triggered Geolocation Fix

Given the availability of the low-power activity recognition system described in the previous section, we can use its output states (comprising recognized modes of transportation) as input into our just-in-time geolocation fix component.

As mentioned in Section 3, we posit that certain transitions between modes of transportation are indicative of points in time which are more conducive to user engagement with LBAs. For example, when the user makes the transition $Driving \rightarrow Walking$, it may indicate that he has gotten out of his car after having arrived at a desired destination. This spot would then be a good opportunity for an LBA to acquire a geolocation fix to see if it satisfies its LBA-specific logic.

Note that in the case of a location-based reminder with the user's home as the target destination, this approach will still trigger a geolocation acquisition if the user stops somewhere else first, such as at a gas station. Nonetheless, as we show show in Section 6, these additional acquisitions are still less frequent than continuous tracking.

Referring back to Figure 1, a transition manager component observes the smoothed activity recognition stream and keeps track of the current and immediately previous user state. By observing these two states, the manager can identify transitions between certain activities, where these transitions are represented in our system as edges within a finite state machine (FSM).

Our reference FSM is shown in Figure 3. Note that most of the vertices in the system correspond to the available known activity labels that can be produced by the activity recognition component. The only special vertex is the one for long idling, which we define to be idling (that is, sitting or standing) for more than 20 minutes.

When a transition between states is detected by the transition manager, the FSM is checked to determine if the transition qualifies for a geolocation fix acquisition. The solid edges in the FSM are those transitions that we selected to trigger an acquisition. They were heuristically selected to be those where an LBA would most likely take advantage of a new geolocation.

Different FSMs defining different transitions can be used in place of this one. In the future we will also look at ways to discover appropriate transitions automatically rather than heuristically; building a Hidden Markov Model is one such approach.

Note here the advantage of using a high-resolution accelerometer-only activation recognition system such as the one we implemented. Unlike previous work [1,39,34,27] where accelerometers are used to differentiate between only binary states (idling vs. non-idling), our work leverages the distinction between multiple classes of non-idling, such as between driving and running. Note further that being able to be detect these distinctions using only the accelerometer provides a battery consumption advantage over other approaches that use GPS as a sensor[17,37,33,11].

However, the use of transitions to trigger geolocation acquisition suggests a clear limitation. If the user does not change his mode of transportation, then our system will not be able to detect any transitions at all. For example, it may be the case that the user continuously walks from his home to work, never stopping at any point. To address this problem, we additionally implemented an optional background service that performs fixed duty-cycling with a parameterized period to serve as a backup.

6   Evaluation

We implemented and ran our system on two commodity Android smartphones, a Samsung Galaxy S II (released in the U.S. in May 2011) and a Samsung Nexus S (released in the U.S. in December 2010). The key result from our experiments is that while our activity recognition transition-triggered design incurs more delay to identify ground-truth events versus competing schemes, it requires *significantly* fewer geolocation fix acquisitions, up to 41x fewer acquisitions than an accelerometer-assisted binary classification scheme and 243x fewer than continuous tracking over our collected data.

6.1   Activity Recognition Results

Our activity recognition system, described in Section 4, generates the raw user activity stream indicating the user's mode of transportation. Using our training data set collected from 17 users, our system demonstrates a 98.4% per-window classification accuracy over our activities with 10-fold cross-validation. The confusion matrix is shown in Table 1. We found that walking up and down stairs were confused often with walking on a flat surface, so we aggregate them together into our final classifier. Similarly, standing and sitting are aggregated into idling. The end result is an output of five activities: *Walking*, *Running*, *Driving*, *Biking*, and *Idling*.

Table 1. Confusion matrix for activity classification. Overall accuracy is 98.4%.

		Predicted							
		Walking	Sitting	Running	Standing	Driving	StairsDown	StairsUp	Biking
Actual	Walking	**99.05%**	0.00%	0.09%	0.06%	0.12%	0.15%	0.34%	0.18%
	Sitting	0.00%	**99.24%**	0.00%	0.51%	0.13%	0.00%	0.00%	0.13%
	Running	0.42%	0.00%	**99.48%**	0.00%	0.00%	0.00%	0.00%	0.10%
	Standing	0.00%	1.33%	0.00%	**97.52%**	1.14%	0.00%	0.00%	0.00%
	Driving	0.16%	0.06%	0.00%	0.13%	**99.00%**	0.00%	0.00%	0.65%
	StairsDown	16.83%	0.00%	0.00%	0.00%	0.00%	**80.20%**	2.97%	0.00%
	StairsUp	29.63%	0.00%	0.00%	0.00%	0.00%	7.41%	**62.96%**	0.00%
	Biking	0.56%	0.00%	0.00%	0.00%	2.33%	0.00%	0.00%	**97.11%**

We further evaluated the power consumption of the activity recognition system using a Monsoon Solutions Power Monitor, a hardware power meter that directly provides electricity through connected leads and measures the resulting power draw. The results from both test devices are shown in Table 2. We found that the continuous recognition consumes up to approximately 225 mW. Note that the activity recognition's signal processing, feature extraction, and classification consume very little power, whereas the baseline idle CPU (kept alive with a wake lock to ensure that the system continues to run even if the screen is off) consumes the most. As point of reference, the power consumption of the Galaxy S II to acquire a GPS fix is 771 mW, including the baseline CPU.

Table 2. Power consumption of the activity recognition system on commodity smartphones, where the phones were run in "airplane mode" with no WiFi and the screen off. Total power on the Galaxy S II is 224.92 mW.

Smartphone	Baseline idle CPU with wake lock	Accelerometer sampling to 32 Hz	Feature extraction and classification
Samsung Nexus S	167.15 mW	18.03 mW	4.49 mW
Samsung Galaxy S II	184.34 mW	35.53 mW	5.05 mW

6.2   Activity Recognition Transition-Triggered Geolocation Fix

The following subsections provide an evaluation to quantify the performance of activity recognition transition-triggering against competing schemes. Note that the system runs successfully on our test smartphones and correctly triggers geolocation acquisition fixes on transitions between specific modes of transportation; however, to fully evaluate the system with varying parameters, we recorded data traces and ran offline experiments to expedite our work. Both the online and offline execution used the same software code base.

In these experiments we asked users to carry two clock-aligned Android phones to collect two streams of data over the course of entire days, including overnight. First, to collect **ground truth transitions**, users carried a phone running a program that could record the immediate time and geocoordinate when a button is pressed. We asked users to press this button at transition moments between modes of transportation which could be appropriate for a LBA to acquire a fix. Second, to collect **traces of sensor data**, users carried another phone which they kept with them in any position they wanted. The program on this phone continuously recorded accelerometer data and geolocation data. Note that both the ground truth transitions and sensor data collection could have been performed on the same phone, but we did not want the physical interaction for ground-truth marking to produce anomalous sensor data.

In this data set we collected sensor readings totaling 547,583 minutes (or 6.34 days). During this time, users also collected 124 ground-truth transition events of their choice that they believed represented opportunistic locations where a LBA could provide value. These locations turned out to include the users' home, workplace, shopping malls, gas stations, restaurants, and other places. Geolocation fixes were acquired through either GPS or WiFi/cell tower trilateration.

Given the two data streams, we evaluated our system against competing geolocation-triggering schemes along the following dimensions:

1. What is the recall of each scheme – that is, what fraction of ground-truth transitions were correctly recognized?
2. What is the delay between the ground-truth observation and the triggered geolocation fix acquisition in terms of time and distance?
3. How many fix acquisitions are triggered by each scheme?

6.3   Geolocation Fix Acquisition Triggering Schemes

We evaluated four algorithms for triggering a geolocation fix acquisition:

- **Continuous Tracking.** This approach triggers a geolocation fix as often as possible, where the collected data came directly from the sensor-collection phone as described earlier. To enable this approach, we used Android's LocationManager class and asked for callbacks from either GPS or network services, where the callbacks are set with a minimum time of 1 millisecond and minimum distance of 0.1 meters. However, as we show later, the callback minimum time is not necessarily honored by the underlying location service.
- **Continuous Tracking with Fixed Duty Cycling.** This approach triggers acquisitions with a 15-second inter-acquisition period.
- **Accelerometer-Assisted, Binary States.** This approach is representative of current state-of-the-art research work [1,39,34,27] where the accelerometer is used to detect idling versus non-idling. Here, we evaluate a 4-second segment of accelerometer data, and if the user is idling, then geolocalization is deactivated, whereas if the user is not idling (that is, moving), then the geolocation fixes are acquired as often as possible (using the same settings as Continuous Tracking).
- **Activity Recognition-Triggered, Window N.** This approach represents our work, where we apply our activity recognition software on the collected sensor data and apply a smoothing window of size N (which varies between 5 and 40). The system then triggers a geolocation fix acquisition only on the transitions shown in the FSM of Figure 3.

6.4   Recall

We first evaluate the recall of each triggering scheme by quantifying the fraction of the 124 ground-truth transition events that were correctly identified for geolocation triggering. We say that a true-positive identification of a ground-truth event occurs when the scheme performs triggering within 60 seconds of the ground-truth, where a particular triggering can be associated with only one other ground-truth event. In Table 3 we show the recall of each triggering scheme.

Table 3. Recall of ground-truth observations for each triggering scheme

Triggering Scheme	Recall
Continuous Tracking	0.8952
Continuous Tracking w/Fixed Duty Cycling	0.8952
Accelerometer-Assisted, Binary States	1.0000
Activity Recognition-Triggered, Window 5	1.0000
Activity Recognition-Triggered, Window 10	0.9677
Activity Recognition-Triggered, Window 20	0.9274
Activity Recognition-Triggered, Window 30	0.8306
Activity Recognition-Triggered, Window 40	0.7097

Most surprisingly, Continuous Tracking, with and without Fixed Duty Cycling, performed relatively poorly despite the fact that they supposedly trigger geolocation fixes often. The problem is that while the Android API allows the developer to set the minimum time between the automatic geolocation callbacks, it is only a *hint* to the underlying system software or device driver [12], which may instead provide the callbacks as it sees fit (for example, it may aggressively try to reduce power by conserving geolocation fix invocations). Indeed, we occasionally observed long lapses (on the order of 15 minutes) between consecutive geolocation fixes with Continuous Tracking regardless of whether the user was moving or not. In the future we look to explore this issue more fully.

The Accelerometer-Assisted, Binary States scheme performs well with 100% recall, which is representative of the fact that transitions between transportation modes are captured by the binary accelerometer classifier.

Our Activity Recognition-Triggered, Window N scheme exhibits 100% recall with a window size of 5 but suffers decreasing recall with increasing N. The recall diminishes because a longer smoothing window causes activity recognition convergence to take longer, resulting in missed ground-truth transitions.

6.5   Delay

We next evaluated each scheme with respect to the delay between the ground-truth transition events and the triggered geolocation acquisition. Figure 4 shows the median time delay in units of seconds. We observe that the Continuous Tracking scheme has a low time delay, and as expected the Continuous Tracking with Fixed Duty Cycling set to a 15-second period has a longer delay. The Acceleration-Assisted, Binary States has the lowest time delay, again illustrating its ability to turn on triggered geolocation fixes as soon as it detects any movement. Our Activity Recognition-Triggered, Window N scheme incurs longer delay than, but is competitive against, both Continuous Tracking and the Accelerometer-Assisted Binary States scheme with N=5. Note, though, that it again demonstrates decreasing performance with increasing window size. Activity recognition simply responds slower when the smoothing window is large.

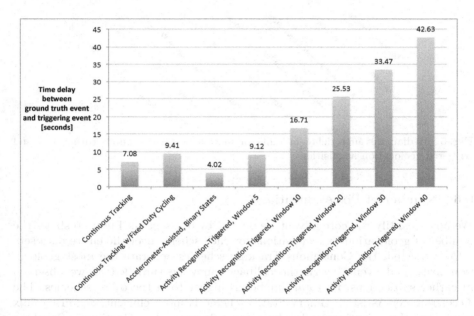

Fig. 4. Median time delay in units of seconds between ground-truth event and triggered geolocation acquisition

Figure 5 shows the median distance delay in units of meters, where we calculated the Haversine distance from the latitude and longitude coordinates. Note that any distance between the time of the ground-truth event and the time of the triggering is dependent on the mode of transportation; for example, walking will most likely produce a shorter distance than driving. Nonetheless, we observe similar relative behavior between the schemes as with the time delay. It is important to further note that the small distances involved here, on the order of 30-40 meters, is close to the 10m accuracy of GPS and at or below the known accuracy of cellular network trilateration.

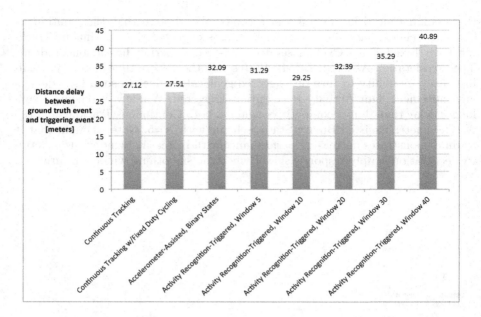

Fig. 5. Median distance delay in units of meters between ground-truth event and triggered geolocation acquisition

6.6 Number of Fix Acquisitions

We now quantify the core advantage offered by our system. Figure 6 shows the number of geolocation fix acquisitions for each scheme over the entire data set.

As expected, the Continuous Tracking schemes generate the most geolocation fixes, and even though the callbacks may be throttled as we observed in earlier subsections, its total number is higher than the other schemes. The Accelerometer-Assisted, Binary States scheme is more efficient, acquiring 5.9x fewer fixes than Continuous Tracking and 1.6x fewer than Continuous Tracking with Fixed Duty Cycling; its main advantage is that it disables geolocation fixes when the user is idle, such as when the user is sleeping.

It can be seen that our Activity Recognition-Triggered scheme is even more efficient and significantly reduces the number of geolocation fix aquisitions. With N=5, our scheme produces 243x fewer fixes than Continuous Tracking and 41x fewer than Accelerometer-Assisted, Binary States.

The advantage of our scheme here stems from its intelligent transition-based triggering. Continuous Tracking acquires geolocation fixes without regard for user events because it is missing the high-level information offered by sensor fusion, for example when coupled with the accelerometer. The Accelerometer-Assisted, Binary States scheme improves upon Continuous Tracking, but while it can eliminate geolocation fixes when the user is idle, it can neither distinguish with sufficient detail nor exploit the transition movements that humans emit.

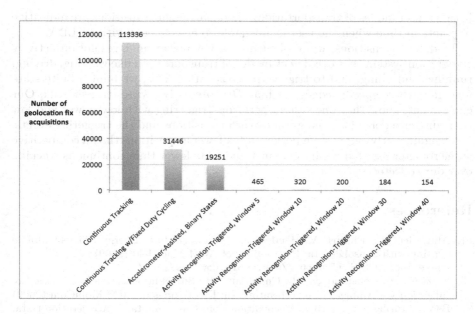

Fig. 6. Total number of triggered geolocation fix acquisitions over the data set

Additionally, we observe that the longer windows for the Activity Recognition-Triggered schemes reduce the number of geolocation fixes. A longer window will provide more smoothing over the raw activity stream produced by the classifier, reducing choppiness and spurious transitions due to mixed user activities. Note, though, that this smoothing and its apparent reduction in fix acquisitions cause longer delays and reduce recall (due to more missed events), as seen in previous experiments. Nonetheless, we note that the N=40 configuration triggered 3x fewer fixes than the N=5 configuration. In the future we will continue looking into ways of achieving high recall and low delay while invoking fix acquisition as seldom as possible.

All the schemes require that the CPU be active, and in the absence of a precise power-consumption model we rely on the number of geolocation fix acquisition as a close proxy for power usage. In the future we look to develop a power model [29] to study the schemes' battery usage trends.

7   Conclusion

In this paper we consider a subset of location-based applications (LBAs) that require geolocation fix acquisition only at specific and rare points in the day. For LBAs like location-based reminders, performing continuous tracking wastes battery power; instead, the most efficient solution is to able to trigger a single geolocation fix at the target location, which would then activate the LBA-specific logic. We make the assumption that such triggering can occur on transitions between user modes of transportation, where particular transitions are indicative of points in time when the user is amenable to engagement with an LBA.

To detect transitions, we implemented a low-power, high-resolution activity recognition system that can detect modes of transportation like walking, driving, running, and idling, and to trigger the geolocation fixes, we built a finite state machine, where specific edges (such as $Driving \rightarrow Walking$) trigger a fix. Our experiments show that our system performs triggering with low power and low time/distance delay between ground-truth transitions and the triggering events. Most significantly, our system performs 41x fewer acquisitions than a competitive accelerometer-assisted binary classifier and 243x fewer than continuous tracking over our collected data set.

References

1. Abdesslem, F., Philips, A., Henderson, T.: Less is More: Energy-Efficient Mobile Sensing with SenseLess. In: Proceedings of ACM MobiHeld (2009)
2. Apple, Inc. "iOS Siri," http://www.apple.com/ios/siri/
3. Azizyan, M., Constandache, I., Choudhury, R.: SurroundSense: Mobile Phone Localization via Ambience Fingerprinting. In: Proceedings of ACM MobiCom (2009)
4. Bao, L., Intille, S.S.: Activity Recognition from User-Annotated Acceleration Data. In: Ferscha, A., Mattern, F. (eds.) PERVASIVE 2004. LNCS, vol. 3001, pp. 1–17. Springer, Heidelberg (2004)
5. Chen, Y., Chawathe, Y., LaMarca, A., Krumm, J.: Accuracy Characterization for Metropolitan-Scale Wi-Fi Localization. In: Proceedings of ACM MobiSys (2005)
6. Cheverst, K., Davies, N., Mitchell, K., Friday, A.: Experiences of Developing and Deploying a Context-Aware Tourist Guide: The GUIDE Project. In: Proceedings of ACM MobiCom (2000)
7. Consolvo, S., McDonald, D., Toscos, T., Chen, M., Froehlich, J., Harrison, B., Klasnja, P., LaMarca, A., LeGrand, L., Libby, R., Smith, I., Landay, J.: Activity sensing in the wild: a field trial of ubifit garden. In: Proc. of ACM CHI (2005)
8. Constandache, I., Gaonkar, S., Sayler, M., Choudhury, R., Cox, L.: EnLoc: Energy-Efficient Localization for Mobile Phones. In: Proceedings of IEEE Infocom Mini-Conference (2009)
9. Dousse, O., Eberle, J., Mertens, M.: Place Learning via Direct WiFi Fingerprint Clustering. In: Proceedings of IEEE MDM (2012)
10. Endomondo application, http://www.endomondo.com
11. Fang, S., Zimmerman, R.: EnAcq: Energy-efficient GPS Trajectory Data Acquisition Based on Improved Map Matching. In: Proc. of ACM SIGSPATIAL (2011)
12. Google Android LocationManager documentation,
    http://developer.android.com/reference/
    android/location/LocationManager.html
13. Google Indoor Maps, http://maps.google.com/help/maps/indoormaps/
14. Hall, M., Frank, E., Holmes, G., Pfahringer, B., Reutemann, P., Witten, I.: The WEKA Data Mining Software: An Update. SIGKDD Explorations 11(1) (2009)
15. Huỳnh, T., Blanke, U., Schiele, B.: Scalable recognition of daily activities with wearable sensors. In: Hightower, J., Schiele, B., Strang, T. (eds.) LoCA 2007. LNCS, vol. 4718, pp. 50–67. Springer, Heidelberg (2007)
16. Kim, D., Kim, Y., Estrin, D., Srisastava, M.: SensLoc: Sensing Everyday Places and Paths using Less Energy. In: Proceedings of ACM SenSys (2010)

17. Kjaergaard, M., Langdal, J., Godsk, T., Toftkjaer, T.: EnTracked: Energy-Efficient Robust Position Tracking for Mobile Devices. In: Proceedings of ACM MobiSys (2009)
18. Kwapisz, J., Weiss, G., Moore, S.: Activity Recognition Using Cell Phone Accelerometers. In: Proceedings of SensorKDD (2010)
19. Lester, J., Choudhury, T., Borriello, G.: A practical approach to recognizing physical activities. In: Fishkin, K.P., Schiele, B., Nixon, P., Quigley, A. (eds.) PERVASIVE 2006. LNCS, vol. 3968, pp. 1–16. Springer, Heidelberg (2006)
20. Lin, K., Kansal, A., Lymberopoulos, D., Zhao, F.: Energy-accuracy trade-off for continuous mobile device location. In: Proceedings of ACM MobiSys (2010)
21. Liu, J., Priyantha, B., Hart, T., Ramos, H., Loureiro, A., Wang, Q.: Energy Efficient GPS Sensing with Cloud Offloading. In: Proc. of ACM SenSys (2012)
22. Lu, H., Yang, J., Liu, Z., Lane, N., Choudhury, T., Campbell, A.: The Jigsaw Continuous Sensing Engine for Mobile Phone Applications. In: Proceedings of ACM SenSys (2010)
23. Miluzzo, E., Lane, N., Fodor, K., Peterson, R., Lu, H., Musolesi, M., Eisenman, S., Zheng, X., Campbell, A.: Sensing Meets Mobile Social Networks: The Design, Implementation and Evaluation of the CenceMe Application. In: Proceedings of ACM SenSys (2008)
24. Mizell, D.: Using gravity to estimate accelerometer orientation. In: Proceedings of ISWC (2003)
25. Nath, S.: ACE: Exploiting Correlation for Energy-Efficient and Continuous Context Sensing. In: Proceedings of ACM MobiSys (2012)
26. Ofstad, A., Nicholas, E., Szcodronski, R., Choudhury, R.: AAMPL: Accelerometer Augmented Mobile Phone Localization. In: Proceedings of ACM MELT (2008)
27. Oshin, T., Poslad, S., Ma, A.: Improving the Energy-Efficiency of GPS-based Location Sensing Smartphone Applications. In: Proc. of IEEE TrustCom (2012)
28. Paek, J., Kim, J., Govindan, R.: Energy-Efficient Rate-Adaptive GPS-based Positioning for Smartphones. In: Proceedings of ACM MobiSys (2010)
29. Pathak, A., Hu, C., Zhang, M.: Where is the Energy Spent Inside My App? Fine Grained Energy Accounting on Smartphones using Eprof. In: Proceedings of EuroSys (2012)
30. Quinlan, J.: C4.5: Programs for Machine Learning. Morgan Kaufmann (1993)
31. Ravi, N., Dandekar, N., Mysore, P., Littman, M.: Activity recognition from accelerometer data. In: Proceedings of IAAI (2005)
32. Reardon, M.: Location information to make mobile ads more valuable. CNET.com news (April 15, 2013), http://news.cnet.com/8301-1035_3-57579746-94/location-information-to-make-mobile-ads-more-valuable/
33. Reddy, S., Mun, M., Burke, J., Estrin, D., Hansen, M., Srivastava, M.: Using mobile phones to determine transportation modes. ACM Transactions on Sensor Networks (2010)
34. Shafer, I., Chang, M.: Movement Detection for Power-Efficient Smartphone WLAN Localization. In: Proceedings of ACM MSWiM (2010)
35. Skyhook Wireless, http://www.skyhookwireless.com
36. Trapster application, http://www.trapster.com
37. Wang, Y., Lin, J., Annavaram, M., Jacobson, Q., Hong, J., Krishamachari, B., Sadeh, N.: A Framework of Energy Efficient Mobile Sensing for Automatic User State Recognition. In: Proceedings of ACM MobiSys (2009)
38. Waze application, http://www.waze.com
39. Zhuang, Z., Kim, K.-H., Singh, J.: Improving Energy Efficiency of Location Sensing on Smartphones. In: Proceedings of ACM MobiSys (2010)

Fine-Grained Activity Recognition of Pedestrians Travelling by Subway

Marco Maier and Florian Dorfmeister

Mobile and Distributed Systems Group
Ludwig-Maximilians-University Munich
Oettingenstraße 67, 80538 Munich, Germany
{marco.maier,florian.dorfmeister}@ifi.lmu.de

Abstract. With the now widespread usage of increasingly powerful smartphones, pro-active, context-aware, and thereby unobstrusive applications have become possible. A user's current activity is a primary piece of contextual information, and especially in urban areas, a user's current mode of transport is an important part of her activity. A lot of research has been conducted on automatically recognizing different means of transport, but up to know, no attempt has been made to perform a fine-grained classification of different activities related to travelling by local public transport.

In this work, we present an approach to recognize 17 different activities related to travelling by subway. We use only the sensor technology available in modern mobile phones and achieve a high classification accuracy of over 90%, without requiring a specific carrying position of the device. We discuss the usefulness of different sensors and computed features, and identify individual characteristics of the considered activities.

Keywords: Mode of Transport Recognition, Mobile Phone, Context Awareness, Activity Recognition.

1 Introduction

Context-aware applications and services have the ability to adapt to a user's environment. Although the term has already been coined in 1994 by Schilit and Theimer [6], only since the advent of smart mobile devices like today's smartphones, we can see a more wide-spread move towards context-aware computing. Besides *location, identity* and *time, activity* is regarded as a primary piece of information for characterizing a user's context [1].

There are many possibilities to get to know a user's current activity, ranging from manual input by the user to automatic recognition. The latter has been a major research topic for several years, but it many ways still is limited to very basic activities.

The first wave of attempts to perform automatic activity recognition often required the attachment of dedicated sensors like accelerometers or heart rate monitors [10] to the human body. However, with the proliferation of smartphones with their integrated sensors such as gyroscopes, compasses or barometers, it has

G. Memmi and U. Blanke (Eds.): MobiCASE 2013, LNICST 130, pp. 122–139, 2014.
© Institute for Computer Sciences, Social Informatics and Telecommunications Engineering 2014

become feasible to recognize a user's activity without any additional devices, promising a more convenient and ubiquitous user experience.

1.1   Mode of Transport Recognition

Especially in urban areas, a key information of a user's activity is her current *mode of transportation*, e.g., whether she is walking, cycling, driving a car, or travelling by any means of public transport like bus or subway. One can imagine a multitude of use cases including personal activity and health monitoring (e.g., *quantified self-tracking* [9]), creating ecological profiles of one's travelling habits, and first and foremost applications and services which automatically adapt their functionality to the user's current mode of transportation (e.g., interactive maps which focus on subway lines when travelling by subway).

There have been several attempts to automatically distinguish between different modes of transportation, which perform reasonably well. However, to the best of our knowledge, to date there exists no work aimed at recognizing activities and transportation phases on a finer-grained level, e.g., to tell apart entering, being on and exiting a subway train.

1.2   Fine-Grained Activity Recognition When Using the Subway

In this work we focus on recognizing several fine-grained activities and transportation phases when travelling by subway, i.e., walking in the subway station, walking upstairs/downstairs, using an escalator (up and down without walking, up and down while walking), using an elevator (up and down), waiting, waiting while the subway arrives, entering the subway train, standing in the subway while parking/accelerating/driving/decelerating, and exiting the subway train. In total, we try to recognize 17 different activities.

The subway as a means of transportation is interesting not only because it is an essential part of public transport in larger cities, but also because it is subject to restrictions such as the unavailability of GPS-based positioning. Beneath the previously mentioned use cases, finer-grained activity recognition while travelling by subway could enable pro-active services like reminding of getting off the subway train, or offering paperless ticketing on public transport (using recognized activities either directly for tracking/billing or indirectly as a means of fraud detection).

Being able to recognize activities and transportation phases while travelling by subway not only enables activity-aware services but also might solve the inherent positioning problem without GPS below ground: Patterns of entering a subway, accelerating, driving, decelerating and exiting could be matched to maps and subway timetables, leading to estimates about the user's current position.

1.3   Preconditions, Requirements and Contributions

We state the following preconditions and requirements for this attempt to fine-grained activity and transport phase recognition:

1. The solution should be realizable with the sensor technology of current smartphones, without any additional peripheral devices.
2. The user should not be required to carry the smartphone in a specific position.
3. Recognition of the current activity should be completed in a short timeframe, i.e., analyzing a large interval of sensor data afterwards in an offline manner is *not* sufficient[1].

In the following, we present a solution for this problem statement. By employing a supervised machine learning approach, we recognize 17 different activities with a high accuracy of over 90%. In our concept and evaluation, we try to infer qualitative statements which are generalizable to other scenarios and use cases. We include experimental results, and we describe and explain our experiences and observations regarding

- how sensor data should be collected and pre-processed
- which types of sensor data correlate with which activities in what way
- which computated features are suitable to represent these correlations

The rest of this paper is structured as follows: In section 2, our experimental setup and the data collection process is described. After that, we outline the general concept of our approach (section 3). In section 4, we describe insights regarding individual activities and their correlation with specific sensor data and features, and we assess the performance of our recognition approach. In section 5, we have a look at related work in the field of activity and transportation mode recognition, before we finish with a conclusion and an outlook at future work (section 6).

2   Experimental Setup and Data Set

In order to examine the characteristics of different activities and transportation phases of the subway, we collected a data set in the subway system of Munich, Germany. In this section, we explain the data collection procedure as well as the properties of the resulting data sets.

2.1   Hardware and Logging Application

We used Android-based Google Nexus 4 smartphones as test devices to collect the sensor data. Up to four devices were used in parallel to capture sensor data at different positions at the human body.[2] Each device was running a custom made logging application, recording the following information and sensor data:

---

[1] This requirement does not rule out offline training phases of machine learning algorithms. However, our goal is that once trained, the solution should not require more sensor data than what is available in a reasonable timeframe for near-realtime usage.

[2] Notice that we collected this data at four different positions only for the purpose of performance comparison, not for sensor fusion algorithms or the like.

- timestamp
- accelerometer (three axis)
- gyroscope (three axis)
- magnetometer (three axis)
- barometer
- GPS
- audio (microphone)

The sampling frequency was set to the maximum value (i.e., the corresponding listener of the Android application was set to SENSOR_DELAY_FASTEST).

To synchronize the recordings of all devices, they were linked via WLAN. We used an additional smartphone as the *master* device which set up the WLAN and was used to broadcast the current activity label[3]. The latter was done by sending a message via UDP to the *client* devices when a new label was selected at the master device. Client devices were required to confirm the new label, in order to ensure a data collection and labeling process as accurate as possible.

2.2 Data Collection

As stated in section 1.3, we aim for a solution which is independent of the carrying position of the smartphone. Therefore, we equipped a male test person with four devices, carried at the following positions:

- left front shirt pocket
- right front trouser pocket
- lying in the backpack
- held in the right hand

Additionally, the test person was holding the master device in his left hand, which he used to assign a label to the current situation. The test person could quite easily perform the labeling without bigger distractions, both mentally and concerning the other smartphones' sensor data readings.

2.3 Activities

We used a set of 17 different activities which we regard as important in the given scenario. The corresponding labels are summed up in table 1. The activities include those which can happen anytime outside the subway train (i.e., walking, waiting), typically occur when entering or leaving the subway station (i.e., walking downstairs or upstairs, maybe using escalators or elevators), and those which are linked to the transportation phases of the subway (i.e., entering, accelerating, driving, decelerating, exiting).

---

[3] The activity labels were used for our supervised learning approach later on.

Table 1. Overview of labels/activities which were recorded

label	meaning
walk	walking outside the subway, on even ground
walkup	walking upstairs
walkdown	walking downstairs
rollupwalk	walking on escalator, upwards
rolldownwalk	walking on escalator, downwards
rollup	standing on escalator driving upwards
rolldown	standing on escalator driving downwards
walkwait	standing still, on static ground
driveup	using elevator driving upwards
drivedown	using elevator driving downwards
subarrive	standing still (waiting) while subway train arrives
subenter	walking into the subway train
subwait	standing in the subway while not driving
subaccel	standing in the subway while accelerating
subdrive	standing in the subway while driving
subbrake	standing in the subway decelerating
subexit	walking out of the subway

2.4   Final Datasets

We performed three test drives in Munich. Experiments were started above ground, then entering the subway station, getting on an subway train, driving an arbitrary number of stations, exiting the train, returning above ground, re-entering the subway station, and so on.

In total, we collected 279 minutes of travelling by subway in Munich (in which the label changed 717 times). The pre-dominant label (*walk*) comprises 32.9 % of the collected dataset, i.e., simply always guessing that label would result in such a classification accuracy (which therefore serves as a baseline to be beaten by a more sophisticated approach).

3   Concept

We use a supervised machine learning approach to recognize the activities. After a suitable data set has been collected, such an approach typically requires the following steps:

1. Pre-Processing
2. Windowing
3. Cleansing
4. Feature Computation
5. Feature Selection
6. Choosing a Classifier

In the following, we describe our methods and choices in each of these steps.

3.1   Pre-processing

The hardware sensors on current Android devices typically have a sampling rate of about 20 to 80 Hz. Combined with the uncertainty of when different sensors return a new measurement, the actual sampling rate is fluctuating. In order to get a more stable sampling rate, we transformed the recorded values into an equidistant series of measurements. By filling in the missing values, we arrived at a synthetic sampling rate of 1000 Hz. It is important to note that we only performed this "up-sampling" to make feature computation easier. We did *not* employ any features using higher sampling frequencies than the sensors physically could provide.

Since the devices were carried at various orientations, the absolute values of the three axis of the accelerometer, the gyroscope and the magnetometer were not really meaningful. In each case, we combined the three values into a orientation-independent value by computing the norm of the three-element vector (i.e., $a = \sqrt{a_x^2 + a_y^2 + a_z^2}$).

3.2   Windowing

Raw measurements of sensor data usually cannot be used directly with machine learning algorithms but have to be combined by computing features on larger data intervals of certain length. In related work for transportation mode recognition, such windows often are eight seconds or longer [11]. Approaches for pure activity recognition typically use shorter windows like one or two seconds [13]. Regarding requirement 3 of section 1.3, windows should not be too wide, so that the lag for recognizing an activity does not get too long. However, they have to be big enough to capture periodicity in movements, etc. Therefore, we experimented with windows of length 1024 ms, 2048 ms and 4096 ms.[4] In each case, windows were overlapping 50%, which is a common approach in related work.

3.3   Cleansing

The windowing procedure sometimes resulted in windows with multiple labels assigned. These were removed from the dataset. Some recordings furthermore had unlabeled windows at their beginning (due to a lag between starting the recording and assigning the first label), which were also deleted.

3.4   Feature Computation

We computed a large set of features for each window to be able to examine the correlations of certain activities with certain features. There are features in both the time domain and the frequency domain (after performing an FFT on the respective data). We considered the following components:

---

[4] Using a multiple of 2 increases computation performance of the FFT used later on.

- norm of acceleration values
- norm of gyroscope values
- norm of magnetometer values
- pressure

and computed the following statistical features for each of them

- maximum, minimum, mean, standard deviation, 75th percentile
- root mean square
- number of zero crossings

For each combination, we also computed the difference to the respective value of each of the previous ten windows and of the following window. We then performed an FFT on each of the four components as well as on the audio data, and computed the following measures on the obtained coefficients:

- maximum, minimum, mean, standard deviation, 75th percentile
- dominant frequency
- root mean square
- energy, defined as

$$\frac{1}{n} \sum_{i=1}^{n} x_i{}^2$$

- entropy, defined as

$$-\sum_{i=1}^{n} P(x_i) log_b P(x_i)$$

- ratio of the mean to the mean of the complete spectrum
- ratio of the energy to the energy of the complete spectrum
- ratio of the entropy to the entropy of the complete spectrum

The above values were not only computed on the respective complete frequency spectrum but on the frequency intervals

1-3, 3-5, 5-8, 8-11, 11-16, 16-22, 22-29, 29-37 and 37-50 Hz

for the sensor data, and on the frequency intervals

1-20, 20-50, 50-100, 100-200, 200-500, 500-900, 900-1400, 1400-2000, 2000-2700, 2700-4000, 1-500, 500-1500 and 1500-4000 Hz

for the audio data.

The frequency intervals for the audio features partly were chosen according to certain characteristics we observed while visually investigating the recorded audio data. Figure 1 shows a short section of one of the audio recordings, visualized as a spectrogram.

There a several interesting moments in that recording. At time (1), we marked the beginning of a repeated signal tone (*beep*) which is played before the subway train's doors close. These short tones result in the signal peaks at about

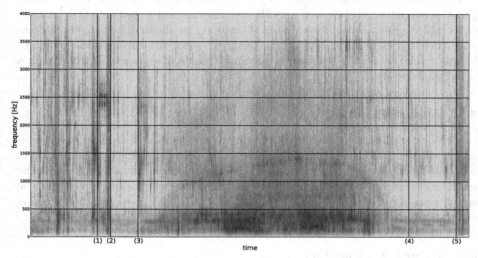

Fig. 1. Spectrogram of the audio signal recorded while driving by subway. At (1), the signal tone of the subway train is played (indicating doors closing). At (2), doors are closed. From (3) on, the subway train is accelerating, then driving and then decelerating until it stops at about (4). At (5), doors are opened.

2.5 kHz. After the signal, the doors close, indicated by a short "noisy" moment at time (2). This noise is caused by the pneumatic closing of the doors. Then there is a more silent period when the doors are closed but the subway train is still not moving. At time (3), the subway starts to accelerate, which results in an overall increased amount of energy in the signal spectrum. Interestingly, one can even visually conceive the sound of accelerating, driving and decelerating, which constitutes the near-semicircle in the frequency range from 1.0 kHz to 1.5 kHz. At about time (4), the subway has reached its parking position, again followed by some seconds of "silence" until the doors open. At time (5) the noise burst signifies the pneumatic opening of the doors.

Of course, these characteristics like the presence or the frequency of the signal tone can vary among traffic systems in different cities. However, the general idea to leverage these audio signatures can be adopted. Therefore, we not only included the aforementioned audio features but added some more features specifically targeted at the signal tone. To be more precise, we computed the maximum, mean, energy and root mean square of the frequency spectrum in the range of 2.4 kHz to 2.6kHz of the previous n windows ($n \in \{5, 10, 20, 30\}$) and added that values as features to the current window. The meaning of these features simply is that the "signal tone occured in the near past of the current window".

Preliminary tests showed that orientation-independet values of the gyroscope and the magnetometer do not provide any information beyond what is already observable in the accelerometer data. Therefore, we did not include those components in our evaluation. Making use of the gyroscope and magnetometer might be interesting when the position of the smartphone is known or is inferred in a pre-processing step [2].

3.5   Feature Selection

In total, we started with a set of 632 features, based on accelerometer, barometer and audio data. This large number of features on only a few raw data sources naturally tends to providing redundant information. Therefore, we reduced the number of features by performing a correlation-based feature subset selection [3] which resulted in a set of about 80 features which were used for the following evaluation.

3.6   Choosing a Classifier

We experimented with several types of classification algorithms, namely decision trees (J48), support-vector machines (SMO), bayesian networks, instance-based learning (kNN) and random forests. Preliminary tests showed best results with the random forest classifier, which therefore was used for most of the evaluation (where not stated otherwise).

4   Evaluation

In this section, we explain the influence of the window size as well as of the carrying position of the smartphone. After that, the merit of including the audio features is examined. We outline the usefulness of a hierarchical classification approach, show general results of different classifiers, and finally have a look at some interesting features which led to a good classification performance.

The evaluation was performed using the WEKA data mining software [4], and all the results have been obtained doing 10-fold cross validations on our dataset.

4.1   Window Size

We evaluated the performance of the three window sizes 1024 ms, 2048 ms and 4096 ms. The results are shown in figure 2a. One can see a slight increase of correct classifications with growing window sizes. Regarding requirement 3 from section 1.3, we opted for a window size of 2048 ms as a compromise, since larger windows might not be useful in practice.

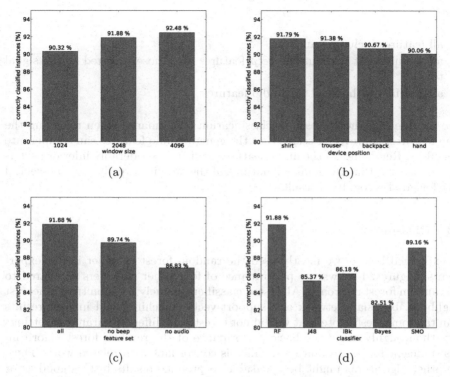

Fig. 2. Correctly classified instances by (a) window size, (b) device position, (c) feature set (with or without specific audio features) and (d) classifier (random forest (RF), decision tree (J48), k-nearest neighbour (IBk), bayes net (Bayes) and support-vector machine (SMO))

4.2 Carrying Positions

Regarding the different carrying positions, there is not much difference between the four choices (see figure 2b). The shirt pocket seems to be the most suitable position, probably due to a good combination of little mobility and less damping of the audio signal, e.g., compared to the trouser pocket. In general, a more stable position is better than a free one because this allows to better reflect the movement of the whole body.

Summing up, the chosen features with a special focus on orientation-independency allow for usage of the system in any of the tested positions.

4.3 Influence of Audio Features

As explained in section 3.5, some of the audio features were chosen based on observations in the frequency spectrum of the audio data. We therefore evaluated the influence of the audio features. Figure 2c shows the classification results when using

1. all features including audio
2. all features but without the *beep* features (i.e. those targeted at the signal tone)
3. all features without all the audio features

One can see a slight decrease in classification performance when removing the beep features. However, it seems that the general audio features can compensate this effect. Removing all the audio features leads to considerably inferior performance, proving that the audio signatures of the activities really are an essential part for good recognition results.

4.4   Classifiers

As explained before, we mostly used the random forest classifier in our experiments. Figure 2d shows the performance of four other classifiers compared to the random forest approach. All tested classifiers, namely decision tree, k-nearest neighbour, bayesian network and support-vector machine yield inferior results than random forest. Note that we did not investigate different parameter settings very thouroughly, since the basic performance of the random forest algorithm was sufficient for our evaluations, which is concordant with related work. Thus, the other algorithms might be tweakable to produce results just as good as or even better than the random forest.

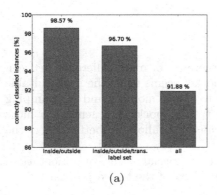
(a)

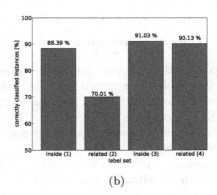
(b)

Fig. 3. Correctly classified instances when (a) grouping instances together and (b) performing a hierarchical classification (3+4) compared to a flat classification (1+2)

4.5   Hierarchical Classification

Although the general recognition results look good with the number of correctly classified instances above 90%, the results are a bit skewed due to an uneven distribution of the observed activities. Naturally, the activity "walking" occurs far more often than e.g. entering or exiting a subway train.

In order to more thoroughly assess the recognition rates of certain activities, we define four subgroups of activities:

- *outside*, which are activities happening outside the subway train (i.e., *walk, walkup, walkdown, rollupwalk, rolldownwalk, walkwait, rollup, rolldown, driveup, drivedown*).
- *inside*, which are activities happening inside the subway train (i.e., *subwait, subaccel, subdrive, subbrake*).
- *transition*, which are activities happening between *outside* and *inside* activities (i.e., *subarrive, subenter, subexit*).
- *related*, which are activities related to the subway train (i.e., the union set of *inside* and *transition*).

In a first step, we replaced the individual labels of the activities with the respective choice of either *outside, inside* or *transition*. Figure 3a shows the classification results when only trying to distinguish between *outside* and *inside* activities, and when categorizing into *outside, inside* and *transition* activities.

In both cases, over 95% of all instances where classified correctly. Considering the unavoidable inaccuracy in the data collection and labeling process, we regard this value as a reasonable maximum. Thus, classification into the three main categories is as good as can be.

We then examined the classification performance of the labels contained in the *inside* and *related* subsets when performing the classification on the whole dataset. The results can be seen in figure 3b in bars (1) and (2). The *inside* category yields quite good results, whereas the recognition rate of the *related* category drops down to about 70%. The reason is that activities such as entering or exiting the subway can easily be confused with ordinary walking. Furthermore, the number of available training instances is quite low in that category, so the differences compared to the *walk* activity are hard to grasp.

In order to solve this problem we opted for a hierarchical approach. By first applying a coarse-grained categorization into *outside, inside* and *transition* activities, we can quite accurately identify and rule out *outside* activities and apply a second classification to groups of *inside* or *related* activities. Using this procedure, we obtain recognition rates of over 90% for both the *inside* or the more general *related* activities (which include the problematic labels such as *subenter* and *subexit*). The results are shown in figure 3b in bars (3) and (4).

4.6   Interesting Features

In the following, three interesting features will be discussed exemplarily because they either had a huge influence on classification performance or were more or less suprising.

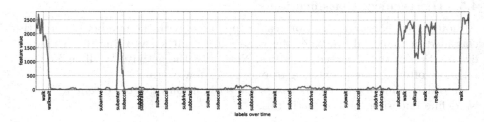

Fig. 4. Mean of frequency coefficients of accelerometer signal in range 1-3 Hz over time

In figure 4, one can see the mean value of the frequency coefficients of the accelerometer signal in the range from 1 to 3 Hz over time. This feature actually describes how present the frequencies from 1 to 3 Hz are within the window. Trying to group activities for which this feature exhibits larger values and those which only show values near zero, one can identify the disjoint groups of activities which involve "walking" and activities which do not. The reason is that frequencies of that range correspond to the typical step frequency of pedestrians.

This is an important feature to tell apart the activities *subenter* and *subexit* (which exhibit "walking" characteristics) from the other activities contained in the *related* subset (which do not).

One of the most difficult differentiations is between the activites *subaccel* and *subbrake* because they both simply are a kind of acceleration. Since we cannot rely on a specific orientation of the mobile device, we cannot tell apart positive (*subaccel*) from negative acceleration (*subbrake*).

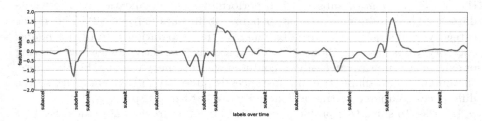

Fig. 5. Difference of mean pressure in window compared to the 3rd previous window over time

One feature to distinguish between these two activities is visualized in figure 5, which shows the difference of the mean pressure in the current window and the mean pressure in the 3rd previous window over time.[5]

---

[5] We observed the same pattern with each *i*th previous window, the 3rd previous one only showing the clearest peaks in this case.

In general, the features related to air pressure where included to better indentify activities which involve going up- or downstairs. However, we can also spot an interesting pattern concerning the activities *subaccel*, *subdrive* and *subbrake*. When accelerating, the pressure is going down (i.e., the difference to the previous window is negative). When driving, the ratio is normalizing to zero. Finally, when decelerating, the pressure is increasing (i.e., the difference to the previous window is positive).

This pattern is observable throughout our dataset. Nevertheless, we aim to investigate this behaviour more thouroughly in future work, since the pattern might be dependent on the exact location at which the user is standing within the subway (i.e., in the front or in the back).

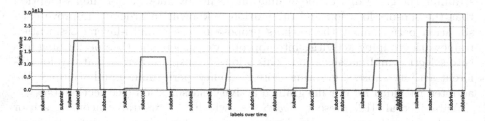

Fig. 6. Maximum energy of "beep" within last 30 windows over time

Another characteristic to tell apart the *subaccel*, *subdrive* and *subbrake* activities is the signal tone, as explained in section 3.4. Figure 6 shows the maximum energy of the signal tone's frequency range within a window's previous 30 windows over time. One can clearly see that the signal tone results in a peak in the following windows. Considering 30 windows of length 2048 ms with 50% overlap results in a timeframe of 30 seconds, which seems to correspond quite well to the typical acceleration length of the subway trains in Munich. Of course, this rather perfect mapping is biased, but the general idea is feasible.

In general, we found that several distinct features of both accelerometer and barometer values were chosen by the classifiers, with features concerning acceleration mostly being a variant of "energy in a certain frequency interval", and features concerning barometric pressure mostly being a variant of "difference to a certain previous window".

Summing up, we can state that our presented approach provides excellent results to recognize 17 important activities related to travelling by subway. Using position-independet features, we do not require a specific carrying position. A window size of 2048 ms enables responsive applications. We have shown that considering the audio signal leads to better results, and that a hierarchical classification approach renders high classification accuracy possible even for easily confusable activities such as "entering the subway train".

5   Related Work

In this section we have a look at existing approaches for activity recognition, especially the ones aiming at determining a user's current mode of transportation based on her mobile device's sensors.

Zhang et al. [13] aim at identifying the most important features for human activity classification, facing the problem that not all of the features available are equally useful for activity classification. Therefore, the authors evaluated the performance of three different algorithms for feature selection. The nine different activities the authors were trying to detect were walking forward, left, right, going upstairs and downstairs, as well as jumping, running, standing and sitting still. The recording device was attached to the users' hip, thereby somehow constraining the generality of the evaluation results by allowing for the assumption that the sensors location and orientation is known. In order to improve classification performance, the authors propose to use a multi-layer classification framework grouping activities into appropriate subsets and then performing feature selection and classification. This allows for using different features for different activity subsets, granting more flexibility, performance and accuracy. We adopted this idea for our finegrained activity classification (see section 4.5).

Yatani et al. [12] present *BodyScope*, which is a wearable acoustic sensor recording sounds from a user's throat area and classifying them into activities, such as eating, drinking, speaking, laughing, and coughing. Using a SVM-based classfication technique, the authors are reaching a combined F-score of about 79% for all of their twelve different activities. For classification, the authors use the zero-crossing-rate as a time-dependent feature, as well as several frequency-dependent features such as total spectrum power, brightness, spectral rolloff and spectral flux. With the F-measure resulting in 49.6% with the Leave-one-participant-out technique and 79.5% with Leave-one-sample-per-participant-out, the authors conclude that their classifier has to be trained individually on a per-user-basis.

Sun et al. [8] are making usage of the accelerometer readings in a current smartphone in order to monitor the daily activities of the smartphone's user. Just as we do, the authors put great effort in determining a user's current activity independent from the smartphone's orientation and different pocket locations. The features used are the three accelerometer axes as well as their magnitude's mean, variance, energy and entropy as well as the four components' correlation, summing up to 22 features per frame. The authors try to recognize seven everyday human activities such as being stationary, walking, running, bicycling, ascending and descending stairs as well as driving a car. Following a SVM based approach, the authors reach an overall F-score of over 93%. As their evaluation shows, however, classification results are even more accurate assuming that the pocket location is known in advance.

Quite similiar to our approach, Reddy et al. [5] aim at determining a user's current mode of transportation based on her mobile phone's sensor data readings alone. The authors are making usage of the phone's GPS module and accelerometer recordings in order to determine whether the user is sationary, walking, running, biking or in motorized transport. As a means for classification, the authors deploy a decision tree, postprocessing its output with a first-order hidden markov model, resulting in classification accuracy over 90%. Just as with our approach, this work is not making any assumptions about the phone's pocket location and orientation, making it generically applicable. Features in use are the user's speed derived from her GPS module, as well as her accelerometer readings' energy, variance and the sum of FFT coefficients lower than 5 Hz. According to their evaluation, accelerometer and GPS data readings should be used complementary, leading to accuracy gains of up to 10%. With their two stage approach consisting of a decision tree and a HMM, the authors reach classification results over 98% accuracy. However, the authors are not able to differentiate between different kinds of motorized transport or making any fine-grained assumptions for any subactivities such as entering a vehicle or accelerating. Moreover, relying on GPS data such as the speed received from the GPS module, this approach is not applicable to underground activity classification.

Going one step further, Zhang et al. [14] try to make more fine-grained assumptions about a user's mode of transportation. They base their classification on both mobile phones and wearable foot force sensors. Hence, the authors are not only using a smartphone (GPS), but also some specialized kind of sensing hardware mounted to a user's feet. The different modalities they try to recognize are walking, cycling, as well as being a bus passenger, car driver and car passenger. Their activity classification is hence more detailled than Reddy's, but is also relying on the GPS module and a specialized sensor placed on the user's foot. They reach a 95% accuracy with 10 different individuals. In order to save on the smartphone's computation and battery capacities, the authors primarily focus on using time-domain features. These include mean, maximum and standard deviation of the GPS speed of a window, as well as mean, maximum and standard deviation of both feet's foot force sensors. The authors compared Naive Bayes, Decision tree and decision table techniques against each other. For all five modes of transportation, the decision tree allows for an overall classification accuracy of 97.3%. Evaluating the different motorized modes only, DT still reaches 87.5% accuracy.

Stenneth et al. [7] examine the possibility of transport mode detection using mobile phones and GIS data. The classification algorithm takes a smartphone's GPS readings and map information of the underlying transportation network as input. Based on these data, the authors try to determine different modes of transportation, namely by car, bus, train, walking, cycling and being stationary. In contrast to all other works, the authors additionaly provide real time information of time and location of public transport vehicles in order to achieve higher classification accuracy. As new and innovative classification features, the authors are making usage of average bus location closeness, candiate bus location closeness, average rail line trajectory closeness and bus stop closeness rate. Additionally, standard features such as average speed, average heading change, average acceleration and average accuracy of GPS coordinates are used. Using all available information in a Random Forest classifier, the authos are able to reach an average classification accuracy of 93.7%. However, it is not possible to make fine-grained assumptions for a single mode of transportation or subway based transportation.

6 Conclusion and Future Work

In this work, we presented an approach to automatically recognize 17 important activities related to travelling by subway, using only the sensor technology of a modern smartphone. To the best of our knowledge, this is the first attempt to perform a really fine-grained recognition of different activities and phases of a user's mode of transport.

We achieve a high classification accuracy of over 90% even for problematic activities such as "entering the subway train", which can easily be confused with ordinary "walking", all without requiring a specific carrying position of the mobile device and while preserving the potential for near-realtime applications.

Despite the promising results, this work certainly is only a first step towards a deployable system. One major shortcoming is the lack of a larger data set comprising a lot more test users. Although we tried to focus on features which should be rather user-independent in theory, only a more thorough evaluation will prove that sentiment.

Another aspect which will be tackled in future work are the temporal dependencies amongst the individual activities. So far, we do not make use of facts like "entering the subway happens before exiting the subway". We are convinced that introducing a higher level, reasoning layer could be able to compensate for a drop of classification accuracy which might be observed when having a larger user base without that sophisticated training data as we had in our evaluation.

Finally, related aspects such as energy consumption, privacy and security of the system have to be considered in future work.

All in all, the presented work and our evaluation of the activities' characteristics with regard to certain features can be used as a basis for investigating fine-grained activity recognition in other fields, especially regarding other means of transportation.

Acknowledgement. We would like to thank our student Uwe Müller for collecting large parts of our data set during his bachelor thesis.

References

1. Abowd, G.D., Dey, A.K., Brown, P.J., Davies, N., Smith, M., Steggles, P.: Towards a better understanding of context and context-awareness. In: Gellersen, H.-W. (ed.) HUC 1999. LNCS, vol. 1707, pp. 304–307. Springer, Heidelberg (1999)
2. Fujinami, K., Kouchi, S.: Recognizing a mobile phone's storing position as a context of a device and a user. In: Zheng, K., Li, M., Jiang, H. (eds.) MobiQuitous 2012. LNICST, vol. 120, pp. 76–88. Springer, Heidelberg (2013)

3. Hall, M.A.: Correlation-based Feature Subset Selection for Machine Learning. PhD thesis, University of Waikato, Hamilton, New Zealand (1998)
4. Hall, M., Frank, E., Holmes, G., Pfahringer, B., Reutemann, P., Witten, I.H.: The weka data mining software: an update. ACM SIGKDD Explorations Newsletter 11(1), 10–18 (2009)
5. Reddy, S., Burke, J., Estrin, D., Hansen, M., Srivastava, M.: Determining transportation mode on mobile phones. In: Proceedings of the 2008 12th IEEE International Symposium on Wearable Computers, ISWC 2008, pp. 25–28. IEEE Computer Society, Washington, DC (2008)
6. Schilit, B.N., Theimer, M.M.: Disseminating active map information to mobile hosts. IEEE Network 8(5), 22–32 (1994)
7. Stenneth, L., Wolfson, O., Yu, P.S., Xu, B.: Transportation mode detection using mobile phones and gis information. In: Proceedings of the 19th ACM SIGSPATIAL International Conference on Advances in Geographic Information Systems, GIS 2011, pp. 54–63. ACM, New York (2011)
8. Sun, L., Zhang, D., Li, B., Guo, B., Li, S.: Activity recognition on an accelerometer embedded mobile phone with varying positions and orientations. In: Yu, Z., Liscano, R., Chen, G., Zhang, D., Zhou, X. (eds.) UIC 2010. LNCS, vol. 6406, pp. 548–562. Springer, Heidelberg (2010)
9. Swan, M.: Emerging patient-driven health care models: an examination of health social networks, consumer personalized medicine and quantified self-tracking. International Journal of Environmental Research and Public Health 6(2), 492–525 (2009)
10. Tapia, E.M., Intille, S.S., Haskell, W., Larson, K., Wright, J., King, A., Friedman, R.: Real-time recognition of physical activities and their intensities using wireless accelerometers and a heart rate monitor. In: 2007 11th IEEE International Symposium on Wearable Computers, pp. 37–40. IEEE (2007)
11. Wang, S., Chen, C., Ma, J.: Accelerometer based transportation mode recognition on mobile phones. In: 2010 Asia-Pacific Conference on Wearable Computing Systems (APWCS), pp. 44–46. IEEE (2010)
12. Yatani, K., Truong, K.N.: Bodyscope: a wearable acoustic sensor for activity recognition. In: Proceedings of the 2012 ACM Conference on Ubiquitous Computing, UbiComp 2012, pp. 341–350. ACM, New York (2012)
13. Zhang, M., Sawchuk, A.A.: A feature selection-based framework for human activity recognition using wearable multimodal sensors. In: Proceedings of the 6th International Conference on Body Area Networks, pp. 92–98. ICST (Institute for Computer Sciences, Social-Informatics and Telecommunications Engineering) (2011)
14. Zhang, Z., Poslad, S.: Fine-grained transportation mode recognition using mobile phones and foot force sensors. In: Zheng, K., Li, M., Jiang, H. (eds.) MobiQuitous 2012. LNICST, vol. 120, pp. 103–114. Springer, Heidelberg (2013)

Reconciling Cloud and Mobile Computing Using Activity-Based Predictive Caching

Dawud Gordon, Sven Frauen, and Michael Beigl

Karlsruhe Institute of Technology (KIT), Karlsruhe, Germany
Firstname.Lastname@kit.edu

Abstract. Cloud computing has greatly increased the utility of mobile devices by allowing processing and data to be offloaded, leaving an interface with higher utility and lower resource consumption on the device. However, mobility leads to loss of connectivity, making these remote resources inaccessible, breaking that utility completely during offline periods. We present a concept for reconciling the fragile connectivity of mobile devices with the distributed nature of cloud computing. We predict periods without connectivity on the mobile devices before they occur and cache process states for applications running on distributed cloud back-ends. The goal is to maintain partial or full utility during offline periods, and thereby to enable an improved user experience. We demonstrate prediction must include real-time behavioral information in addition to location and temporal models. The approach is implemented for mobile phones which learn to quantify human behavior using activity recognition, and then learn patterns in that behavior which lead to disconnectivity. We evaluate it for a streaming music scenario, where data is cached before the user goes offline, allowing seamless playback. The results show that theoretically we can successfully predict 100% of disconnection events on average 8 minutes in advance (std. dev. 46 secs.) with minimal false-positive caching in this scenario, although in the wild these events could prove more difficult to predict.

Keywords: predictive caching, activity recognition, mobile cloud computing, connectivity prediction, mobile apps.

1 Introduction

Smart phones have become pervasive and ubiquitous technology in first and second-world countries. These phones have a tremendous utility in our daily lives, changing the way we conduct many activities [3]. A great deal of this innovation is due to the combination of cloud and server-side computing with local user interfaces on the mobile devices. Cloud computing allows resource consumption to be distributed across many machines. The location of a certain piece of data or execution is not of interest, nor is it known to the user, as long as they maintain connectivity with those instances [9]. This allows the scale of operations to be increased and distributed across many machines, reducing the time for computation for certain types of operations [9]. Pervasive mobile devices

G. Memmi and U. Blanke (Eds.): MobiCASE 2013, LNICST 130, pp. 140–157, 2014.

on the other hand are drastically different in terms of their usage modality. Devices are carried or worn by users, meaning their physical location is of the utmost importance [3]. The devices present an interface to the user, where the interface itself cannot be distributed or remote. Furthermore, since the devices are carried with the user, they are therefore mobile, where mobility inherently implies that loss of connectivity is inevitable [3].

The disparity between these two concepts leads to a conundrum: cloud computing greatly enhances the utility of smart phones when they are connected, but their mobility means at times this connection will be lost. Furthermore, often this increased utility is most needed during times of high mobility, for example using map services while traveling. We present a novel approach for maintaining utility during periods of mobile disconnectivity in order to reconcile these two concepts with each other. In order to solve this problem, resources normally accessible in the cloud must be relocated locally to remain usable when the device is offline. Once the device has lost connectivity, it is already too late to fetch the required resources, therefore the connectivity change must be predicted. Allowing users to explicitly do this themselves is a possibility, but as the number of devices and applications which we use daily grows, this becomes infeasible. The reconciliatory concept we propose is as follows: we look to predict disconnection events before they occur, allowing required resources to be pre-fetched and thereby maintaining at least some utility during offline periods.

The goal is to predict changes in connectivity and detect events which result in insufficient connectivity for applications. Algorithms on the devices monitor the behavior of the human using the device's sensors, generating a time line of quantified human behavior. Within this time line, algorithms then search for and recognize patterns in that behavior which lead to connectivity events. When one of these patterns is identified in real time, the device is alerted before the event occurs, allowing applications running on the device to precache data. Predicting connectivity has been conducted successfully using location [13,15] and time of day [14] as indicators of connectivity patterns. However, for this scenario that information alone does not contain the necessary cues for caching.

Take for example leaving your house every day, where you lose wifi connectivity when you leave. Your location barely changes before you leave the area of connectivity, meaning location-based systems will only be able to react to loss of connectivity, instead of proactively predicting it. While time of day would quite often be a good predictor for leaving, e.g. going to work every day, one often leaves the house at irregular times of day as well. These unscheduled events would not be predictable and would have the same repercussions as not having a prediction-based caching solution for cloud apps. Furthermore, leaving a friend's house would cause the same problems because you don't do that every day, and the location is different than previously recorded [15]. However, identifying someone leaving the house based on observations of their behavior is almost trivial and could be done by any child: putting on your shoes, maybe a jacket as well, leaving the apartment, going down the stairs, etc.. Therefore, we argue that any system which honestly attempts to bridge the gap between cloud and mobile computing must take all three parameters into account: time, location and human behavior information. We implement a proof-of-concept which runs on a mobile device and attempts to do exactly this using applied machine learning techniques. Since connectivity prediction using location and time of day are large fields and have both been explored independently and in conjunction [13,14], we look at cases in which activity can be used to recognize connectivity state changes which are otherwise unpredictable. We evaluate the approach by observing the performance of the algorithm as it adapts to the behavior of an individual in an experiment described in Sec. 4. The experiment replicates a situation where temporal and location-based connectivity approaches fail, thereby showing the added benefit of using physical behavior as a further indicator.

This evaluation is carried out in two phases and the results are presented in Sec. 5. First we evaluate how well the system performs using the user's own annotations of his behavior as a basis for prediction. We then evaluate the performance of the same system using a timeline of behavioral information inferred from activity sensing data by the device itself.

Using annotated information, the results indicate an overall f-score of only 0.56 for predicting changing connectivity. However, with respect to periods of no connectivity the system performed much better, with a 100% prediction success rate with an average of 8.2 minutes grace period, an f-score of 0.78 and precision of 0.97. Using inferred behavior information caused little change with f-score staying at around 0.58, where the success rate remained at 100% with an average grace period of 8.28 minutes before the event. Based on a behavioral recognition f-score of 0.85 with respect to the annotated labels, precision dropped to 0.79, indicating more false positive predictions, causing damage in terms of unnecessary caching. The final message is that even with imperfect behavior data we can still predict offline periods successfully, but have a higher cost due to unnecessary caching. As behavioral recognition approaches perfection, this overhead approaches 0, allowing systems to seamlessly integrate periods of disconnectivity.

2   Related Work

Sensors integrated into wearable computing systems such as mobile devices can be used to sense human behavior through activity recognition [1,4]. Using activity recognition to quantify human behavior allows devices, systems and applications to detect these activities or contexts in real time and adapt themselves to that behavior, for example by predicting and highlighting the correct app on a mobile device [16]. Using those sensor signals, statements can be made about what that behavior will look like in the future through a process called activity prediction [8]. At the same time, a timeline of recognized and quantified behavior can also be used for predicting future properties, where using symbolic behavioral data in place of numeric sensor data is advantageous in terms of memory and computation for mobile devices [17].

Human beings are creatures of habit [4], making a history of human behavior a good basis for predicting future activities. Using histories of mobile device connectivity to predict future connectivities however does not yield optimal results due to the fact that "fluctuations of radio quality are too large to make long-term predictions" [5]. There are however other methods for predicting connectivity which serve this purpose better, most focusing on location or time information [15]. Location-based systems work on the basis of connectivity at different locations [13], however, standard behavior at unknown locations causes poor predictions [15]. Research has shown that modeling mobility patterns independent of temporal information (e.g. weekend / weekday) will inevitably lead to sub-optimal connectivity predictions [10]. Using temporal information alone however can also be effective [2], but will inevitably fail if the subject changes their routines or does something out of the ordinary.

Best results can be obtained when combining location with temporal information for predicting connectivity [15]. However even this approach may fail if the subject performs activities at unknown locations, as temporal information only helps to refine location models, or outside of normal temporal routines when connectivity may vary from the normal experience for certain locations [5]. Also, as demonstrated in the introduction, there are still situations in which both time and location are not enough to determine the future state of connectivity.

Resources and execution can be offloaded into the cloud conserving local resources and increasing device utility [6]. However when connectivity is lost, any processes still offloaded are lost and utility suffers. One method for counteracting the loss of utility is to cache resources before going offline. Approaches which use explicit input from the user to cache required resources (data) go back as far as 15 years [11]. More recently automated approaches have been introduced where browsing habits can be used to evaluate and cache links which will probably be clicked [19]. More recently, this concept has been adapted to allow automatic pre-fetching of items with a high probability of being viewed based on a users history and the current network state [7]. The concept we put forth here is to incorporate physical human behavior into temporal and location-based prediction models. We propose a scenario in which both temporal and spatial models would fail, and demonstrate the added benefit of behavioral-based systems.

3   Methods

In order to demonstrate the novel concept for reconciling cloud and mobile computing, we have constructed an archetype for predictive caching. Our system quantifies human behavior using an activity recognition framework designed for embedded recognition. This framework is based on previous work [4] and will not be detailed here. The important aspect for this work is that it quantifies human behavior from motion sensor signals, in this case using supervised machine learning approaches.

In order to preemptively cache resources from the cloud onto a mobile device before we lose connectivity, the device must monitor the following states. The observable state of the sensors embedded in the device S, also known as the evidence, and the connectivity state of the device C. Based on these observations, models can be built by the device from its own experience.

3.1 Behavioral Quantification

The first model required describes human behavior as a function of the sensor signals, allowing the device to recognize and quantify that behavior. This model M consists of models $m \in M$ for each distinct type of behavior $\alpha \in A$ of the form $p(S|a)$, where $s \in S$ are observations from the sensors of the device. Using this model, a prior distribution, and given a set of observations s, the device can calculate a probability distribution over these models, or $p(a|s)$ using Bayesian inference and the law of total probability [12]. For each discrete type of human behavior α, we model the belief function over the evidence, or extracted sensor features, as a probability density function (PDF):

$$m_\alpha = P(S|\alpha) = \sum_{k=1}^{K} \pi_k \mathcal{N}(S|\mu_k, \Sigma_k)$$

We then use these PDFs to generate a posterior probability distribution across behavioral states using the law of total probability and a prior distribution:

$$p(\alpha|S) = \frac{\frac{P(S|\alpha)p(S)}{p(\alpha)}}{\sum_{\alpha_i}^{A} p(\alpha_i|S)}$$

Using this posterior, we can then recognize human behavior by selecting the most probable model at any given time as the behavior for that time slice:

$$\arg\max_\alpha p(\alpha|S)$$

This inference, or activity classification, is conducted periodically, generating a time line of human behavior $\boldsymbol{A}$.

3.2 Connectivity Prediction

Based on the observations of the network connectivity states $c \in C$, transitions $\phi \in \Phi$ between network states can also be observed. By observing $\boldsymbol{A}$ and $\boldsymbol{\Phi}$ in parallel, $\boldsymbol{A}$ can be mined for behavioral patterns which occur directly before specific transitions in $\boldsymbol{\Phi}$. Due to the temporal relationship between the two, a pattern in $\boldsymbol{A}$ which is an antecedent to specific ϕ can be observed as having a causal relationship with that transition. For a given pattern length t_p, we model the causal behavioral patterns for transitions with the same resulting state as a Markov chain. Specifically, we model segments of behavior of length t_p leading up to those transitions.

In other words, the periods of behavior leading up to a change in network connectivity state into a specific state are modeled together in order to be able to later predict a transition into that state. This set of models is then used for predicting future changes in network state. Because we also model the null transition, we can use the law of total probability again to generate a distribution of probability across the models. The model with the highest probability is then output as the predicted connectivity transition.

Each ϕ_{ij} represents a switch from network state c_i to state c_j. The model is then built by observing a history of transitions $\boldsymbol{\Phi}$ between these states, and calculating the transitional probabilities as a Markov process. The result is a Markov model of transitional probabilities between all connectivity states of the mobile device. For each transition ϕ_{xi} *into* a new connectivity state c_i regardless of the previous state c_x, the activity time line of length t_p leading up to the transitions $\boldsymbol{A}_{t-t_p,t}$ are modeled together in Markov model $\omega_{c_i} \in \Omega$.

These activities are modeled as a Markov chain, where the model for transition into connectivity state c_i takes the following form: $\omega_{c_i} = (A, \lambda)$. where A are the states, namely one each quantization of the human behavior (recognized activity) extracted previously. λ are the transitional probabilities between activities, modeled on the data $\boldsymbol{A}_{t-t_p,t}$ leading up to the connectivity transitions, or:

$$\lambda : A \times A \to A, \text{ where } \lambda_{ij} = p(\alpha_t = \alpha_i | \alpha_{t-1} = \alpha_j)$$

For each connectivity state c_i we now have a Markov chain modeling the human behavior which "causes" transitions into that connectivity state, ω_{c_i}. For a given timeline of behavior $\boldsymbol{A}$ of length t_p, we now need to be able to calculate the probability that this history will lead to a transition, and if so which one. To do this, all Markov chains are traversed in parallel by taking the product of the transition required given $\boldsymbol{A}$ as evidence. Using the law of total probability, the probabilities are normalized across all models, and the most probable model is output as the prediction of the future connectivity state for the device:

$$\text{Prediction} = \arg\max_c \frac{p(\omega_c | \boldsymbol{A})}{\sum_{c_i}^C p(\omega_{c_i} | \boldsymbol{A})}$$

3.3 Predictive Caching

The combined approaches for recognition and prediction are shown in Fig. 1. Once the framework has predicted the future network connectivity state, this information is provided to every software entity on the device which is interested. At this point each application must then form its own decision about the appropriate action to take. The first input into this decision making process is the level of connectivity required in order to deliver the user experience which is wished. For example, for certain applications such as background data synchronization tasks, low speed and bandwidth may be acceptable, while for others such as streaming video applications, even slight reductions in connectivity may be unacceptable. Once the threshold in connectivity for the app has been predicted, the app can then decide to prepare itself for an offline period by prefetching resources from the cloud.

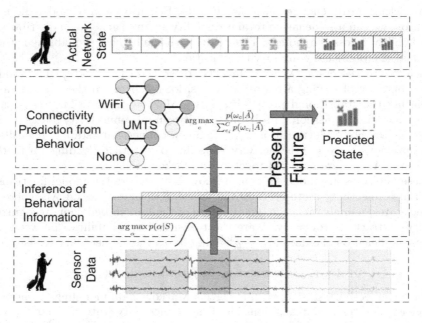

Fig. 1. The architecture of the proposed concept

The next decision is what to prefetch and cache. This decision is also based on what is required for optimal performance, and what is predicted. For example, using mobile map services with a slow connection may be enough to perform online searches comfortably if the map data has been cached. For the scenario evaluated here, as soon as the connectivity drops below the minimum for streaming music, the user experience plummets and the data must therefore be cached. Not only the type of data must be selected, but also which instance, e.g. which song or songs, or which map area. Each app using the framework is best equipped to understand what the usage profile of the user for that app is, and therefore which resource is required to restore the local process' state and preserve the experience as best as possible. How much of the experience and the utility can be preserved is dependent on the type of app, the user and the scenario, and is therefore not evaluated. We examine how well the framework provides apps with information about future connectivity, and the correctness of that information.

3.4   Evaluation Metrics

In order to evaluate the system we need to first define what we want from it, and then create metrics for assessing that [18]. What we want from the system is to inform us of the connectivity changes in the future based on a pattern of human behavior. What we know is the length of time over which these patterns occur, namely t_p. Based on this information we can define metrics to evaluate the system.

We define a **true-positive (TP)** prediction for a connectivity change to state c_i as the existence of transition $\exists_x | \tau_{xi} \in t_p$ within the time frame t_p of prediction. If the predicted transition to state c_i does not appear within t_p, or $\nexists_x | \tau_{xi} \in t_p$, this is then classified as a **false-negative (FN)** prediction. A prediction of the null transfer τ_{nc} when no transfer occurs $\forall_{x,y} | \tau_{xy} \notin t_p$, or the prediction of a transfer to the current state of the system, are both counted as a **true-negative (TN)**. If the predictor predicts any transition $\tau \neq \tau_{nc}$ and no transition occurs, or $\nexists_{x,y} | \tau_{xy} \neq \tau_{nc}, \tau_{xy} \in t_p$, this is **false-positive (FP)** (i.e. FP of 'no connection' results in unnecessary caching). Using these values we can calculate accuracy, precision, recall and f-score [12].

When evaluating the performance of prediction for transitions to a single class alone, the evaluation is slightly adapted. The metric is applied only to instances of that class alone, where all other classes are grouped together in a single class, as a two class problem. The reason for this is that transition to and between other states should not affect the results for a single class evaluation, which is not the case without this exception. Transitions into other classes within t_p are no longer counted as false-positives, as when observing only that class and the null class, these are then true-negatives.

These metrics allow us to evaluate the overall system performance. However they do not capture one critical aspect of system behavior. Take the example of retrieving something from the basement of an apartment building. In the apartment we have WiFi and in the stairwell we have a mobile data connection. In the basement for a short period we have no connection, followed by mobile connectivity on the stairs and WiFi again in the apartment.

In this scenario, if the behavioral pattern window t_p is larger than the length of the offline window, then completely missing the prediction of the connectivity loss would still result in an f-score of 1 as long as the other transitions inside the window are correctly predicted. In order to account for this, a different metric is required, which takes this into account. We define the prediction **success rate** as the number of transitions to that state which are predicted inside of t_p before they occur, divided by the total number of network transitions. Note that as with the other metrics, success rate can also be applied to a single transition type.

In addition to whether or not a specific transfer is successfully predicted, it is also important to note how far in advance the prediction came. Here we introduce the **time-to-event** metric to evaluate how long the system has to react to prediction information. The metric is defined as for all successful predictions, the time between the window and the occurrence of the connectivity transition event. It is important to note that as a result of the definition of success rate, this value will always be less than t_p. This information is especially critical for predictive process state caching, as it indicates whether the system is actually able to cache the required information in time before the connectivity event.

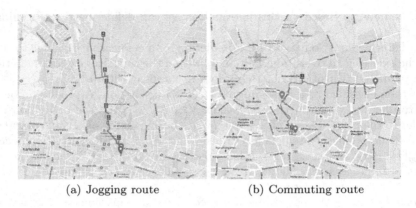

(a) Jogging route   (b) Commuting route

Fig. 2. The jogging route and the commute path taken in the data set

4   Experiment

In this work we propose to reconcile the concept of cloud computing with the fragile connectivity of mobile devices. To evaluate behavior-based precaching as a way to address these differences, we conducted an experiment in a specific usage scenario with a cloud-based streaming music service.

4.1   Scenario

During a normal jogging route, the subject jogs through an open park where there is little or no connectivity. He prefers to use a streaming music service which tailors a playlist for him based on his preferences and those of his friends. However, when he is in the park the slow connection is not sufficient to stream music. He is a student, and therefore does this at different times of day, meaning it is difficult to predict the event of jogging using temporal models. The beginning of his jogging route is along the same path as his trip to campus, making it difficult to differentiate the two using location models alone (see Fig. 2). Even the speed at which he travels does not differentiate between going to campus and going for a run, as he sometimes walks or rides his bike depending on his mood and the weather. However, when looking at the physical behavior, there are subtle differences between going to work and going jogging.

The challenge is that by the time the user enters the park, it is already too late to begin precaching, meaning this information must be present beforehand. At the time when the signal for precaching is required, both location and temporal features for going to work and going jogging are indiscernible from each other. In this case however, an intelligent version of the music service would not have a problem deciding what needs to be cached (the process state) in order to continue execution offline: the play-list.

Fig. 3. Left: mobile phone running the novel framework and the SmartWatch showing prediction state (color) and behavioral history. Right: the view for labeling activities and controlling the framework state.

4.2 Framework

For this experiment an HTC Desire Bravo was used as a mobile sensing device. The device contains a light and temperature sensor for sensing the environment, as well as an acceleration and orientation sensor for sensing physical behavior. The device was carried in the users pocket with the same orientation throughout the entire experiment. Paired with the device was a SONY SmartWatch[1] which was used to visualize the state of the mobile device without disturbing it for the purpose of activity recognition. The SmartWatch was also used as an input device for the predictive framework. The application for the SmartWatch and connected Android device can be seen in Fig. 3, where both the system output and input mode can be seen. This device allows the subject to interact with the monitoring device without having to physically touch it, thereby disturbing the behavior monitoring as little as possible.

The prediction of future connectivity was realized with a software framework running entirely on the device. The framework is implemented as a service for Android which runs in the background. All sensors are sampled at a dynamic sampling rate which is controlled by the operating system, with real sample rates averaged around 30 Hz for the behavior sensors.

Signal features are extracted over 2 second windows of sensor data, with a 50% overlap between windows, outputting a feature vector every second. The features calculated by the system are signal mean, median, standard deviation, min-max difference, signal entropy, FFT frequency peak and FFT entropy. These are calculated for each axis of the acceleration and orientation sensors individually as well. In practice only a subset of these features is required to achieve the same accuracy or negligible reductions, reducing computational load on the device. The necessary features were identified using standard feature selection algorithms [12].

Each second these features are classified into 6 different motion classes, standing, sitting, walking, climbing stairs, running and 'other'. This is done using a

---

[1] http://www.sonymobile.com/us/products/accessories/smartwatch/

probabilistic classifier which models the data for each activity as a mixture of Gaussians, where the number of components is estimated by the system using expectation maximization [12]. For this purpose, naive Bayes classifier was adapted to be trained and to classify on the Android device. The framework is based on previous systems which run on a mobile device and carry out both recognition and prediction actions simultaneously [4].

4.3   Data Set

The data set collected here is from one individual and was collected of the course of several weeks. The subject is male, 26 years old, 187 cm tall, weighs 87 kg, and is an Information Management student. The concept here is not to deploy a single system which works for all subjects (generalized), but to research an approach which allows devices to learn and adapt to their users over time (personalized). We argue that to demonstrate this concept, a longer term data set from a single subject is more suitable than having several shorter-term instances from multiple subjects. The data set contains sensor data from the acceleration, magnetic field, and GPS (not used for recognition) sensors on the device. Activities performed were labeled by the subject himself, using a touch-screen interface on the SmartWatch designed for this purpose. Network connectivity was also recorded and is annotated in the data set. Each trip is stored in a separate file where the type of trip, either jogging or commuting to or from campus, is indicated in the file name.

From this data we selected 1450 minutes of sensor data to use for this experiment. This contains 10 jogging runs of approximately 65 minutes each, including a period of time before departing from, and after arriving at the apartment. The daily trip to campus and back was also recorded, in total 10 round-trip commutes, approximately 20 minutes each way. During jogging, loss of connection was simulated using a geo-fencing approach. Crossing the boundary of the wooded area caused the mobile phone to lose network connectivity, motivating the scenario. In practice the system encountered and quantified the connectivity states of WiFi, UMTS, EDGE and NONE, but as EDGE did not occur at all in the traces, and because it is also not sufficient for streaming music purposes, this state was excluded from the evaluation and used as NONE whenever encountered. The daily commute begins with a similar pattern as going for a run, but does not lose connectivity. This data set has been made public as part of the contribution of this work[2].

5   Evaluation

In this section the performance of the predictive caching algorithms during the course of the study will be evaluated. The data presented here is generated using a leave-one-out evaluation approach. For each different type of trip (either

---

[2] www.teco.kit.edu/~gordon/precaching/data_set.zip

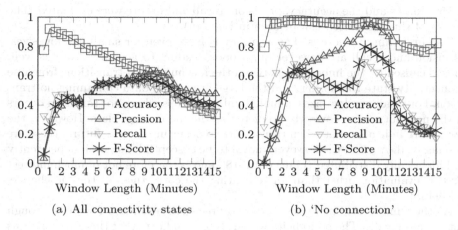

(a) All connectivity states　　　　　　(b) 'No connection'

Fig. 4. Results over t_p using behavior labels

jogging, going to campus, or going home), one trip is set aside and the others are used for learning with respect to activity recognition and the behavioral pattern for causal transition modeling. The performance is then evaluated using the data that was set aside. This process is repeated until each trip instance has been used for evaluation once and the results are averaged across all iterations.

The evaluation is two fold. First we evaluate the ability of the reference implementation to predict future connectivity. This is done using behavioral annotations provided manually for the prediction process, representing the minimum of error possible for behavioral information: the ability of a human to discern these behaviors. Although these annotations contain only human error, a system which attempts to recognize behavior automatically will introduce further error into the behavior annotations. At best, the system will learn to decipher these behaviors, but will never be able to perform better than the human, as it uses the human labels for training, and is evaluated by how well it is able to fit them. For this reason, the second part of the evaluation is concerned with investigating the performance of the same system using the error-bound output of a behavioral recognition system for prediction.

5.1   Proof-of-Concept

In this section we evaluate if behavior is indeed an indicator of future connectivity. The basis for prediction in this section is a time line of activity labels as annotated by the user through the SmartWatch interface. In the next section the performance when using error-bound activity data will be evaluated. In order to assess which behavioral patterns best allow us to predict connectivity changes, we dynamically changed the length of time before the change in connectivity state which was modeled t_p. This parameter was varied from 30 seconds to 15 minutes and the accuracy, precision, recall and f-score were evaluated. The results of this evaluation can be seen in Fig. 4(a).

The first thing to note is that accuracy is high, even for small window sizes. Precision and recall are however quite poor, leading to a poor f-score as well. This is caused by the imbalance between the few number of transitions from one connectivity state to another, and the large amount of data containing no transition. For small window sizes, a high number of steps where no transition occurs in the near future are correctly predicted as the 'no change' class. However, the low f-score indicates that when transitions do occur in the near future, these are misclassified. Accuracy is however known to be susceptible to non independently and identically distributed (i.i.d.) data [18], and is therefore not of much interest for this evaluation other than for indicating the correctness of the 'no-change' prediction.

As the window size increases so too do precision, recall and f-score, although not monotonically. The periodicity would seem to indicate that there are patterns of different lengths which are tell-tales of connectivity transitions, or possibly different harmonics of the same pattern. As the number of 'no-change' windows is reduced (longer patterns mean predictions extend longer into the future), the accuracy falls. F-score reaches an optimum of around 0.56 at 9 minutes, indicating the length for the most decisive patterns for predicting transitions in this scenario. Nonetheless, the initial values here appear to be a negative result, as an f-score of 0.56 would seem to indicate the inability of the system to allow prefetching of distributed resources.

This would appear to be confirmed by Fig. 4(b) which shows the results only for the specific transition to 'no connection'. Again accuracy is not an indicator of actual performance as the number of negative instances far outweighs the number of positive instances. The f-score however far exceeds overall values in Fig. 4(a), with an optimum at around 0.78 at a window length of 9 minutes. Interestingly, the precision for the unconnected state prediction is exceptionally high at that point as well at 0.93. This indicates that only in exceedingly few instances would an app cache resources unnecessarily. The next step is to evaluate how many instances of no connectivity were actually predicted ahead of time (success rate), and how far ahead of time (time-to-event). We then evaluate the success rate over the same window sizes to see what the user would experience from system performance. Despite the poor results indicated by the the recall metric which shows only 0.67 in Fig. 4(b) for a window length of 9 minutes, the success rate is 100% with all offline periods being successfully predicted. So how is a perfect prediction success rate possible with such low recall?

The low recall rates come about when many instances which should be predicted as 'no connection' are predicted as something else. The cause of these low recall rates is that after having correctly predicted the loss of connectivity in the future, the pattern for maintaining the loss of connectivity (the 'no change' model) becomes more dominant than the pattern for losing connectivity. However, while the transfer from a connectivity state to no connectivity is in the near future, this is judged as a missed prediction. High precision however indicates

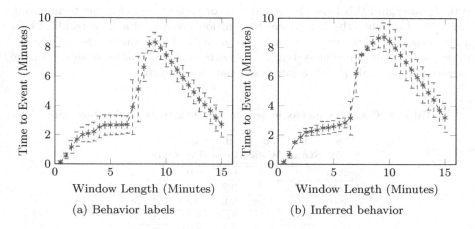

(a) Behavior labels   (b) Inferred behavior

Fig. 5. Time-to-event over t_p using behavior labels (a) and inferred behavior (b).

that the system is not generating false positive predictions, meaning that our streaming application is not caching when it doesn't have to. While this would not directly affect the user's experience of the system with respect to listening to music, it would have repercussions with respect to resource consumption. Most importantly, caching when not necessary causes battery consumption due to processing, storage and wireless communication, which will at some point negatively affect user experience.

Now the next question is, did the predicted warning arrive in time to allow the device to cache the playlist? In Fig. 5(a) the time-to-event for predicted loss of connectivity is shown across window length. Here we can see clearly that for the optimal behavioral pattern window of 9 minutes, a mean time-to-event of 8.20 minutes with a standard deviation of 46 seconds are obtained. Before the offline periods the device uses mobile internet. The measured connection at the location during caching is 1000 KBit/s, or 125 KByte/s, meaning 60 MB. Assuming 3.5 MB and 3 minutes play time per song, that equates to around 17 songs, or 51 minutes of music. The offline periods themselves last for 9.4 minutes on average, meaning the user would even have the luxury of being able to skip 13 songs they don't like.

5.2   Error-Bound Behavior Data

In the section we evaluated the performance of the system when using error-bound behavior data as recognized by the system using the sensors. The recognition system is based on a previously published embedded classification system for android phones [4] which has been simplified to the level described. During the leave-one-out evaluation, the training data is used to model classifiers for recognizing the behavior in real time from device sensors. The results of the 10-fold cross-validation are shown in Tab. 1. Here the classification errors can be seen, representing error in the activity time line. The accuracy of the system is 0.97, but again this is not representative of system behavior due to non-i.i.d. data [18]. In reality the behavioral recognition system achieves a recall of 0.91 and precision of 0.80, yielding an f-score of 0.85. These values are realistic for many activity recognition systems, and better rates are often achieved in the literature [1,4], making this a fair evaluation of the system.

Table 1. Confusion matrix in percent for the activity recognition chain

a Sit	b Stand	c Walk	d Stairs	e Jog	f Other	
99.2	0.0	0.0	0.0	0.0	0.7	a
0.0	92.5	1.7	3.9	0.0	1.9	b
0.0	2.1	87.9	9.6	0.2	0.4	c
0.0	0.9	7.1	91.1	0.2	0.8	d
0.0	0.1	0.3	0.1	99.4	0.1	e
0.0	14.2	0.8	11.1	0.0	73.9	f

When observing overall system performance, using recognized behavior for prediction does not appear to have drastic consequences for the systems. This can be seen when comparing Fig. 6(a), containing the results using recognized behavior, with Fig. 4(a) which was achieved using labeled behavior. The maximum f-score of the one is 0.56 compare to 0.58, both at window lengths for pattern modeling of 9 minutes. This would seem to indicate that although the data is to some extent flawed, the predictor trained on a timeline containing these flaws is able to nonetheless predict connectivity correctly.

However, when observing the prediction of the 'no connection' state, we can see that this is not entirely the case. Fig. 6(b) contains the results for prediction

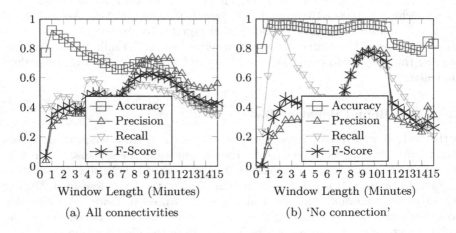

(a) All connectivities   (b) 'No connection'

Fig. 6. Results over t_p using inferred behavior data

of these state transitions alone. When comparing the same results using labeled data in Fig. 4(b), we see a drop in maximum f-score from 0.78 to 0.71, and a far more drastic a drop in precision from 0.93 to 0.79. This indicates that using error-prone behavior data for prediction causes a higher false-positive rate, causing the system to cache unnecessarily. Again though, across the board and also at a window length of 9 minutes, the system achieved a success rate of 100% even using error-bound behavioral data.

Finally, we looked at time-to-event occurrence for inferred behavioral data, the results of which are shown in Fig. 5(b). Here for window lengths of 9 minutes, 8.28 minutes with a standard deviation of 49 seconds was achieved between predictions and the occurrence of the offline event. This is a few seconds more than the same value using labeled data, and is also sufficient for the scenario.

6   Discussion

Prediction of the 'no connection' state performed better than overall system prediction. This indicates that for other connectivity classes the system did not perform as well. For no connectivity there is only a single behavioral 'cause' in this scenario, namely jogging through the woods, where for others there were multiple causal patterns, e.g. leaving the house and emerging from the woods cause switching to UMTS. Here, we selected simple models for their ability to perform on the mobile device [4], and all behavioral patterns leading to the same connectivity change were modeled together. In reality, this generalization worsens prediction, and different types of behavioral patterns should be modeled separately.

In this work we have shown that observing behavior can allow a system to predict connectivity when temporal and location models fail. In general however, spacio-temporal models perform quite well, and can be effective in situations where behavior-based prediction would fail, e.g. predicting connectivity for jogging in the woods versus jogging through the city. Activity and behavior modeling is not a substitute for spatio-temporal modeling, and would probably perform worse in a generalized study. The work done here solely demonstrates that in situations where location and temporal models fail, behavior modeling can improve prediction. Integrating these different types of modeling and prediction is however not part of this work and is the subject of further research.

The system presented here uses explicit activity definitions and labels along with supervised machine learning to quantify human behavior (prediction training is unsupervised). In this work, supervised learning with explicit labels was used in order to quantify the performance of the reference implementation (f-score of 1 for labeled ground truth, v.s. 0.85 for recognized activities). The semantic and ontological meaning behind the activity labels is not required for, or used in, this process. This seems to indicate that the system could perform as well or better using unsupervised learning techniques, making it far more attractive for real world use as users must not provide any explicit input train the system. The system observes behavior and connectivity using unsupervised clustering techniques, and learns interdependencies.

7   Conclusion

Cloud computing has greatly enhanced the functionality and utility of pervasive mobile devices in recent years. Although initially the focus was on offloading data and processing to the cloud to support processes on the device, this process is now irreversible such that losing connectivity means many processes and applications cease to function. We have presented a concept which allows these processes to continue to perform offline, maintaining at least reduced functionality and utility. Our approach is to use prediction technology to inform processes and apps on the mobile device in advance of the disconnection events. We reason that behavior information is necessary in certain situations where location and temporal information do not suffice for predicting disconnection events. Our use case is based on a jogging scenario through a wooded area where the user has no connectivity for a period of time.

We first looked at how well our system performs if correct behavior information annotated explicitly by the subject is presented to the system. The results presented show that the hypothesis was correct, as offline periods were predicted 100% of the time with an average of about 8.5 minutes ahead of time, giving the system more than enough time to cache process state information from the cloud and continue operation locally. Furthermore, with a recall of 0.97, the amount of unnecessary caching was also reduced to a minimum.

We then evaluated how the system performs using behavioral information which it extracts from sensor signals using activity recognition techniques. Here we used an activity recognition toolchain which was able to correctly recognize behavior with an f-score of 0.85, containing non-negligible error. The results indicated that the system was still able to predict periods without connectivity 100% of the time, 8 minutes ahead of time on average, but with a drop in precision to 0.79, indicating an increase in unnecessary caching. We demonstrated that predicting disconnectivity in advance and caching necessary resources from the cloud can allow processes to be continued locally in an offline state. This preserves partial utility across the offline event horizon, reconciling the mobility of pervasive devices with the distributed nature of cloud computing.

Acknowledgment. This work was partially funded by the EIT ICT Labs.

References

1. Bao, L., Intille, S.S.: Activity recognition from user-annotated acceleration data. In: Ferscha, A., Mattern, F. (eds.) PERVASIVE 2004. LNCS, vol. 3001, pp. 1–17. Springer, Heidelberg (2004)
2. de Araño, G.M., Pinto, A., Kaiser, J., Becker, L.B.: An evolutionary approach to improve connectivity prediction in mobile wireless sensor networks. Procedia Computer Science 10, 1100–1105 (2012), ANT 2012 and MobiWIS 2012
3. Forman, G., Zahorjan, J.: The challenges of mobile computing. Computer 27(4), 38–47 (April)

4. Gordon, D., Czerny, J., Miyaki, T., Beigl, M.: Energy-efficient activity recognition using prediction. In: 2012 16th International Symposium on Wearable Computers (ISWC), pp. 29–36 (June 2012)
5. Kobayashi, K., Matsunaga, Y.: Radio quality prediction based on user mobility and radio propagation analysis. In: International Symposium on Personal, Indoor and Mobile Radio Communications, pp. 2137–2141. IEEE Computer Society Press, Los Alamitos (2009)
6. Kumar, K., Lu, Y.-H.: Cloud computing for mobile users: Can offloading computation save energy? Computer 43(4), 51–56 (2010)
7. Lungaro, P., Segall, Z., Zander, J.: Contextshift: A model for efficient delivery of content in mobile networks. In: 2010 IEEE Wireless Communications and Networking Conference (WCNC), pp. 1–6 (April 2010)
8. Mayrhofer, R., Radi, H., Ferscha, A.: Recognizing and predicting context by learning from user behavior. Radiomatics: Journal of Communication Engineering, Special Issue on Advances in Mobile Multimedia 1(1), 30–42 (2004)
9. Mell, P., Grance, T.: The NIST Definition of Cloud Computing. Technical report (July 2009)
10. Motahari, S., Zang, H., Reuther, P.: The impact of temporal factors on mobility patterns. In: 2012 45th Hawaii International Conference on System Science (HICSS), pp. 5659–5668 (January 2012)
11. Mummert, L.B., Ebling, M.R., Satyanarayanan, M.: Exploiting weak connectivity for mobile file access. SIGOPS Oper. Syst. Rev. 29(5), 143–155 (1995)
12. Murphy, K.P.: Machine Learning: A Probabilistic Perspective (Adaptive Computation and Machine Learning series). The MIT Press (August 2012)
13. Nicholson, A.J., Noble, B.D.: Breadcrumbs: forecasting mobile connectivity. In: Proceedings of the 14th ACM International Conference on Mobile Computing and Networking, MobiCom 2008, pp. 46–57. ACM, New York (2008)
14. Rahmati, A., Zhong, L.: Context-based network estimation for energy-efficient ubiquitous wireless connectivity. Mobile Computing 10, 54–66 (2011)
15. Seneviratne, A., Pedrasa, J., Rathnayake, U.: Network availability prediction: Can it be done? In: Global Information Infrastructure Symposium (2011)
16. Shin, C., Hong, J.-H., Dey, A.K.: Understanding and prediction of mobile application usage for smart phones. In: Proceedings of the Conference on Ubiquitous Computing, pp. 173–182. ACM, New York (2012)
17. Sigg, S., Gordon, D., von Zengen, G., Beigl, M., Haseloff, S., David, K.: Investigation of context prediction accuracy for different context abstraction levels. IEEE Transactions on Mobile Computing 11(6), 1047–1059 (June)
18. Ward, J.A., Lukowicz, P., Gellersen, H.W.: Performance metrics for activity recognition. ACM Trans. Intell. Syst. Technol. 2(1), 6:1–6:23 (2011)
19. Yang, Q., Zhang, H.H.: Web-log mining for predictive web caching. IEEE Trans. on Knowl. and Data Eng. 15(4), 1050–1053 (2003)

Towards Smartphone-Based Assessment of Burnout

Christiana Tsiourti and Katarzyna Wac

Institute of Service Science, University of Geneva,
1227 Carouge, Switzerland
{Christiana.Tsiourti,Katarzyna.Wac}@unige.ch

Abstract. In this paper, we present work in progress on VITAL-IN, a pervasive mobile application that aims to operationalize and assess multi-dimensional risk factors increasing a person's chance of developing the burnout syndrome. To date, there are no conclusive scientific results of what causes burnout, yet some factors are evident. We propose VITAL-IN application, enabling the analysis of distributed, variable order, sensor input and ecological momentary self-assessment towards "just-in-time" inference of an individual's behaviour and state, and future burnout risk prediction. Understanding the risk factors and the developmental trajectories leading to burnout could facilitate its early recognition and help to determine the most effective strategies and the most appropriate time for prevention and intervention efforts.

Keywords: Mobile computing, behaviour modelling, burnout prevention, personalized health, self-monitoring, wellbeing, context awareness.

1 Introduction

In many contemporary work environments, in western, as well as developing countries, sedentary workers are suffering from chronic stress due to intensive workload, poor social support and insufficient personal resources to deal with daily life challenges [1]. These conditions are known to elicit a state of distressful psychophysiological arousal that may lead to negative health consequences [2] and facilitate the onset of burnout, a syndrome with devastating influences on the individual's psychological and physical health, cognition, and behaviour [3], as well as negative impact on an organization's effectiveness. In contrast to many occupational diseases that have their origin in exposure to particular hazardous agents, burnout is a highly multifactorial and dynamic psychophysiological process. Early stage symptoms look like normal fatigue, while in the late stages they overlap with major psychiatric disorders, such as depression and neurasthenia [4]. To date, a precise description of etiologically involved factors for burnout is lacking [5] and there is an on-going debate concerning the symptoms which belong to the syndrome, the use of appropriate measurements and how to make a proper diagnosis [6].

Self-administered paper inventories (*i.e.*, [7–9]) are currently the most typical burnout assessment form. These rely mainly on subjective past symptoms, which are summarized by patients over some period of time and are assessed when they visit

G. Memmi and U. Blanke (Eds.): MobiCASE 2013, LNICST 130, pp. 158–165, 2014.
© Institute for Computer Sciences, Social Informatics and Telecommunications Engineering 2014

their doctors. Despite being widely accepted, self-report by recall has an intrinsic problem; due to biases, such as mood states, people are not be able to accurately recall past experience, particularly experiences that are frequent, mundane, and irregular [17]. Moreover, to assess progressive biological, psychological or behavioural processes, multiple assessments over relevant time periods are necessary, as opposed to cross-sectional or global reports [18]. To address these gaps, we turn towards ICT and particularly towards recent advances in mobile computing and sensor devices.

In this work-in-progress paper we present our approach to operationalize the major risk factors for the onset or prevalence of burnout in healthy sedentary workers to provide reliable assessment and prediction of risk exposure (*i.e.*, "now" vs. "future"), which permits early recognition and preventive intervention. We thoroughly examine known burnout risk factors in order to identify which of these can be operationalized via ICT-based tools and particularly quantified by leveraging unobtrusive sensors and Ecological Momentary Assessment (EMA) methods [10]. To increase awareness of how different aspects of lifestyle impact the risk of burnout exposure, we design VITAL-IN, an evidence-based personal smartphone application, to monitor and assess multi-dimensional events, subjective symptoms as well as physiological and behavioural variables in the natural daily work settings of the individual.

The rest of the paper is organized as follows. Section 2 gives a brief overview of the etiology of burnout (which is presented in further detail by Aydemir and Icelli in [11]) and describes our approach to operationalize and quantify risk exposure. In Section 3 we describe the design of the VITAL-IN application and propose a user-based evaluation in the field. Finally, concluding remarks are presented in Section 4.

2 Risk Factors' Quantification for Burnout Assessment

There is an increasing availability of commercial and research-based unobtrusive personal sensing devices (*i.e.*, psychophysiological, bio-kinetic, ambient), either standalone or embedded in smartphones that can be used to track large quantities of sensory inputs in the user's natural settings [12]. These devices allow observing physiological signals, as well as unreported aspects of an individual's behaviour, interactions (*e.g.*, nonverbal actions) and context (*e.g.*, in a crowd) offering a complex picture of his/her status at a certain point in time. As an example, the Android Remote Sensing app (AIRS) [13], which gathers contextual factors such as location and noise levels and combines it with information on the user's social events and communication spikes to provide an overview of the user's day, aims to help stress and activity management before chronic disease develops. In addition to sensing devices, EMA, which permits to report symptoms, affect and behaviour close in time to experience, has been recently proposed by the personality/social psychology research as a reliable sampling method to assess stress-related diseases [14].

Input Sources and Data Quantification. Our work is based on a comprehensive review of the literature on risk factors that are consistently related to and may accelerate the development of burnout. Table 1 summarizes the factors considered by VITAL-IN and presents how we propose to operationalize these by leveraging o ff-the-shelf unobtrusive sensors, smartphone applications and computerized EMA.

Table 1. Factors, input sources for its quantification and data sampling rates.

Factor	Source(s) to Quantify the Factor	Sampling Rate
Job Settings [11]		
Work overload	Virtual sensors	Continuous, Static
	Work hours / week, Contract type	
Lack of control		
Insufficient reward	Quality of working life -	
Conflicting values	Self-assessment scales	Time-contingent
Job insecurity		
Absence of fairness		
Working Conditions [11]		
Human-Computer Interaction	Virtual sensors	Continuous
Involvement with People	Outgoing/incoming phone calls/SMS	Signal-contingent
	EMA self-assessment, Sociometer	Signal-contingent
Daylight/Artificial illumination	Ambient light sensor	Time-contingent
Shift work	Digitalized shift calendar	Time-contingent
Ambient noise	Microphone-based noise quantification	Continuous
	EMA self-assessment	
Overcrowding	Bluetooth devices in vicinity	Continuous
	EMA self-assessment	Signal-contingent
Physical and Spatial Context		
Location information	Smartphone (GPS, WLAN, Cell info)	Continuous
Distance travelled	Smartphone (GPS)	Signal-contingent
Posture	Bio-kinetic sensor	Continuous
Activity / Intensity level	Bio-kinetic sensor	Signal-contingent
Neurobiological Features [11]		
Genetic factors	Genetic tests	Static
Biomarkers	Micro-biometrics	
Socio-demographic Features [11]		
Age		
Gender		
Marital / Education status	Structured questionnaires	Static
Occupation type		
Personality traits		
Psychophysiological Context		
Heart rate (HR) / Var (HRV)	Ambulatory electrocardiogram	Continuous /
Arousal	Skin conductance level	Event-contingent
Current mood	EMA self-assessment	

VITAL-IN readings are repeated multiple times over a day/week. Following the principles of Ambulatory Assessment [15] the data sampling can be continuous (*e.g.*, in the case of physiological assessment), event-contingent (*e.g.*, initiated by the individual or automatically by change of physiological signals detected by monitoring device), signal-contingent (*e.g.*, initiated by a signal given to the person at random times), time-contingent (*e.g.*, initiated on specified time intervals: hourly, daily, weekly, monthly), as well as combinations of these. Wherever possible, passively monitored context information is additionally acquired to support and verify the self-assessment scores. For example, for a social interaction assessed as anxious and stressful, additional objective measures could be skin conductance level as an indicator of arousal or affective information transmitted through speech. Pitch appears to be an index of arousal, while prosody [16] and non-linguistic vocalizations (e.g., laughs, cries) can be used to decode affective signals such as stress, boredom, and excitement. Zeng et al. [17] present a survey on audio-based affect recognition systems.

Environmental Risk Factors for Burnout. The environmental risk factors are influences external to the individual. Although these factors (enumerated in Table 1) are not necessarily negative, they become job stressors when they require a physical and/or psychological effort, either cognitive or emotional, that produces negative effects [18].

Job Settings comprise mostly of subjective measures (*i.e.*, insufficient reward, job insecurity) which can be assessed by standardized scales related to the quality of working life [19]. Objective variables such as the number of hours worked per week or the contract type give information about the work overload. Additional indirect information can be collected using virtual sensors instrumented on the user's smartphone (*i.e.*, total interaction time, number of sessions) [20] or workstation (*i.e.*, keyword-based filtering of keystrokes, applications used).

Working Conditions, including the physical settings of the organizations have the potential to directly or indirectly affect the health of the individuals [11]. Artificial and inadequate illumination, one of the major problems in work settings, can be quantified using a smartphone ambient light sensor. Noise, a source of stress for workers in overcrowded environments can be measured by a number of commercial and research applications which turn smartphones into mobile noise level sensors (*e.g.*, NoiseTube [21]). Professionals of interpersonally demanding jobs tend to have less satisfaction with their work and experience burnout. Information about the user's social interaction can be inferred from sound/voice analysis (direct interaction), as well as PC instrumentation (*i.e.*, emails, chat programs) and smartphone call and messaging history (*i.e.*, total number and duration of calls, number of SMS, number of different contacts) for an indirect interaction. Research by Pentland using a device he termed the "Sociometer" [22] has shown the potential of using wearable sensors to track, analyse and even predict behaviour in social situations (via advanced sound/voice analysis).

Physical and spatial context, including factors such as bad posture and lack of exercise have serious health implications and impact on work performance. Bio-kinetic sensors deliver real-time feedback about body posture (*e.g.*, lumoBACK [23]) and the intensity of physical activities (*e.g.*, FitBit [24], accelerometer bracelet). The approximate distance travelled by an individual (*i.e.*, by foot or bike) can also be estimated from smartphone location data.

Individual Risk Factors for Burnout. Current literature indicates the possibility that stressful aspects of the work environment are more important burnout predictors than personality [3]. Nevertheless, knowledge of the individual characteristics implicated in the etiology of burnout is of considerable importance [11].

Neurobiological features. There are some predispositions and risk for burnout, with which we are born. Recent advances in micro-biometric (*i.e.*, UBIOME [25]) and genetic tests (*i.e.*, 23andme [26]) which report genetic health conditions and traits can contribute to the study for genetic predisposition to burnout.

Socio-demographic features may influence the risk of burnout. The syndrome is more prevalent in younger age groups and is experienced differently by men and women [11]. Questionnaires encompassing demographic and work-related information and measures of personality (*i.e.*, Big Five) are used to collect data.

Psychophysiological parameters such as skin conductance, blood pressure, heart rate (HR) and heart rate variability (HRV) have been statistically correlated as biomarkers for work stress. Smartphone applications with diagnostic capabilities are currently available and can be leveraged for long-term unobtrusive monitoring of psychophysiological parameters. Commercial examples include Tinké [27] a cardiorespiratory health and stress monitor for iOS devices or the Vital Signs Camera from Philips [28] that performs contactless HR and breathing rate measurements using a smartphone.

3   Application Design and Evaluation Plan

Given the above approach to operationalize burnout risk factors, we introduce the overall design of VITAL-IN, a field-configurable smartphone application for real-time monitoring and data acquisition, analysis and state assessment deployed over long-range wireless networks. Key aspects we consider for the design include the accuracy and reliability of data collection, maximizing battery energy efficiency and minimizing the monetary cost (*i.e.*, data uploading should only occur if cheap networking is available). VITAL-IN relies on a limited number of wearable sensors; both because of the amount of additional processing they require, as well as to prevent a cumbersome solution which might cause discomfort and stress, and alteration of the user's natural behaviour.

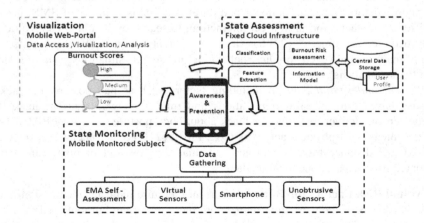

Fig. 1. VITAL-IN platform design and information flow

Figure 1 illustrates the preliminary conceptual design of the complete VITAL-IN solution. The monitored person is equipped with a commercial smartphone (usually carried in the pocket throughout the day) [29], which is used for collecting, interpreting, visualizing as well as remotely exchanging information, and small, cheap, minimally intrusive sensors located on-body or in-clothes or personal accessories, i.e., in the vicinity of the body and moving around with the person, thus enabling continuous ambulatory monitoring of his/her state and that of the environment (*i.e.*, workplace) [30].

State monitoring occurs continuously without requiring the attention of the individual. Input is collected in different formats and it is filtered and uploaded on a trusted server in a cloud infrastructure, which supports data storage and analysis. Theoretically, analysis can be deployed on the smartphone, however to facilitate separation of functionalities and system scalability it is common practice to deploy a separate processing node [30]. A rule-based system and various knowledge bases (related to the mentioned context dimensions) are used for data processing and extraction of semantic labels (*e.g.*, loud ambient noise, crowded). Information that something unusual happened at a certain time (*e.g.*, elevated heart rate) coupled with context information (*e.g.*, people present, activity information) should enable the user to deduct own conclusions and become more aware of the impact of their actions on their risk exposure. Semantic information is further processed to assess the burnout scores of the user on a given long timescale. Appropriate cut-off points will be established to allow classifying between various levels of risk exposure. Individual's behaviour is expected to unfold, as well as change over time, thus static predefined models that map inputs to trend predictions are of limited use in this case; models and useful features in the data should be learned over time. Users have access to a web portal to access the acquired data, visualize it (*i.e.*, current and historical burnout scores) and possibly perform further analysis. For sake of simplicity, in this paper we focus on operationalizing and monitoring constructs for assessment and we do not consider nor discuss the feedback/intervention functionality of the system.

Evaluation in the Field. In this section we discuss our plans for establishing a relevant and valid evaluation in order to demonstrate the feasibility of VITAL-IN for monitoring multi-dimensional burnout risk exposure in a reliable, privacy-conscious and unobtrusive manner. For that, we initially plan experiments designed to deal with issues introduced by data collection and inaccuracies when monitoring user context, activities and psychophysiological parameters. We will validate the monitoring accuracy of our application by comparing the results with gold-standard methods and with similar smartphone sensing experiments conducted with large numbers of subjects. For monitoring parameters such as social interaction, we may randomly select days during the week and require the subjects to keep a detailed log of their social interactions at work. From such an experiment we can conclude if VITAL-INN underestimates or overestimates a person's involvement with people.

The precision of the burnout assessment scores is critically important to the overall performance and user acceptance of the application, thus we will perform a series of experiments to assess the consistency of the scoring and classification models against the gold standard methods used nowadays for burnout assessment. The most predominant measure is the Maslach Burnout Inventory [7], a self-administered questionnaire designed to assess burnout as a continuous variable, ranging from low to moderate to high degree. In the long term, to evaluate the potential of VITAL-IN to deliver significant benefits to users, we propose a longitudinal study where healthy adult office-workers leading a sedentary lifestyle in the Geneva area in Switzerland will use the system, by means of smartphones and wearable sensors, in their natural daily work environments for a period up to one year. Trials will be carried out in collaboration with medical practitioners from the mental health and epidemiology centres of the University Hospital of Geneva aiming at the detection of patterns in behaviour, which could precede the appearance of even sub-clinical physical or mental discomforts associated with burnout.

4   Conclusive Remarks

In this work-in-progress paper we proposed a smartphone-based instrument and application called VITAL-IN to assess the individual's environmental situation and individual characteristics possibly leading to increased burnout risk. Our primary aim is to exploit existing empirical knowledge on risk factors and developmental trajectories that lead to burnout and investigate how to operationalize these in a minimally obtrusive way, using off-the-shelf smartphones, applications and sensors. VITAL-IN detects stressors momentarily as they occur, by sensing an individual's environmental and psychophysiological status, in correlation with subjective self-assessments captured by computerized EMA. In collaboration with medical practitioners, we plan to conduct a large-scale user study to better understand how people with different lifestyles can benefit from this application helping them determine the most appropriate and effective strategies for prevention and behaviour-change based intervention. VITAL-IN will support users in self-awareness and self-understanding of their current actions and behaviours, by paying immediate attention to any of the warning signals associated to burnout.

Acknowledgments. Support of MyGuardian (AAL-2011-4), WayFiS (AAL-2010-3-014) and CaMeLi (AAL-2012-5) projects is acknowledged by the authors.

References

1. Von Känel, R.: The Burnout Syndrome: A Medical Perspective. Praxis 97, 477–487 (2008)
2. Karasek, R., Theorell, T.: Healthy Work: Stress, Productivity, and the Reconstruction of Working Life. Basic Books (1990)
3. Maslach, C., Jackson, S.E.: The Measurement of Experienced Burnout. Journal of Organizational Behavior 2, 99–113 (1981)
4. Nuallaong, W.: Burnout Symptoms and Cycles of Burnout: The Comparison with Psychiatric Disorders and Aspects of Approaches. In: Bährer-Kohler, S. (ed.) Burnout for Experts, pp. 47–72. Springer US (2013)
5. Kaschka, W.P., Korczak, D., Broich, K.: Burnout: A Fashionable Diagnosis. Deutsches Ärzteblatt International 108, 781–787 (2011)
6. Weber, A., Jaekel-Reinhard, A.: Burnout Syndrome: A Disease of Modern Societies? Occupational Medicine 50, 512–517 (2000)

7. Maslach, C., Jackson, S.E., Leiter, M.P.: Maslach Burnout Inventory (1986)
8. Kristensen, T., Borritz, M., Villadsen, E., Christensen, K.: The Copenhagen Burnout Inventory: A New Tool for the Assessment of Burnout. Work Stress 19, 192–207 (2005)
9. Gil-Monte, P.R., Olivares Faúndez, V.E.: Psychometric Properties of the "Spanish Burnout Inventory" in Chilean Professionals Working to Physical Disabled People. The Spanish Journal of Psychology 14, 441–451 (2011)
10. Moskowitz, D.S., Young, S.N.: Ecological Momentary Assessment: What it is and Why it is a Method of the Future in Clinical Pychopharmacology. Journal of Psychiatry Neuroscience 31, 13–20 (2006)
11. Aydemir, O., Icelli, I.: Burnout: Risk Factors. In: Bährer-Kohler, S. (ed.) Burnout for Experts, pp. 119–143. Springer US, Boston (2013)
12. Wac, K.: Smartphone as a Personal, Pervasive Health Informatics Services Platform: Literature Review. Yearbook of Medical Informatics 7, 83–93 (2012)
13. Trossen, D.: Can your Phone Double-up as your Life-Coach? (2012), http://www.cam.ac.uk/research/news/can-your-phone-double-up-as-your-life-coach
14. Stone, A.A., Shiffman, S.: Ecological Momentary Assessment (EMA) in Behavorial Medicine. Annals of Behavioral Medicine 16, 199–202 (1994)
15. Trull, T.J., Ebner-Priemer, U.: Ambulatory Assessment. Annual Review of Clinical Psychology (2012)
16. Juslin, P.N., Scherer, K.R.: Vocal Expression of Affect. In: The New Handbook of Methods in Nonverbal Behavior Research, pp. 65–135. Oxford University Press (2005)
17. Zeng, Z., Pantic, M., Roisman, G.I., Huang, T.S.: A Survey of Affect Recognition Methods: Audio, Visual, and Spontaneous Expressions. IEEE Transactions on Pattern Analysis and Machine Intelligence 31, 39–58 (2007)
18. Lorente Prieto, L., Salanova Soria, M., Martínez Martínez, I., Schaufeli, W.: Extension of the Job Demands-Resources Model in the Prediction of Burnout and Engagement Among Teachers Over Time. Psicothema 20, 354–360 (2008)
19. Warr, P., Cook, J., Wall, T.: Scales for the Measurement of Some Work Attitudes and Aspects of Psychological Well-Being. Journal of Occupational Psychology 52, 129–148 (1979)
20. Falaki, H., Mahajan, R., Kandula, S., Lymberopoulos, D., Govindan, R., Estrin, D.: Diversity in smartphone usage. In: Proceedings of the 8th International Conference on Mobile Systems, Applications, and Services, p. 179. ACM Press, New York (2010)
21. Maisonneuve, N., Stevens, M., Niessen, M., Steels, L.: NoiseTube: Measuring and Mapping Noise Pollution with Mobile Phones. In: Information Technologies in Environmental Engineering, pp. 215–228 (2009)
22. Pentland, A.(S.): Honest Signals: How They Shape Our World (2008)
23. LUMO BodyTech Inc., http://lumoback.com/
24. Fitbit: The Wireless Activity and Sleep Tracker, http://www.fitbit.com/
25. uBiome, http://ubiome.com/
26. Genetic Testing for Health, Disease & Ancestry, https://www.23andme.com/
27. Zensorium, http://www.zensorium.com/
28. Philips Vital Signs Camera, http://www.vitalsignscamera.com/
29. Dey, A.K., Wac, K., Ferreira, D., Tassini, K., Hong, J., Ramos, J.: Getting Closer: An Empirical Investigation of the Proximity of User to their Smart Phones. In: 13th International Conference on Ubiquitous Computing, pp. 163–172. ACM, Beijing (2011)
30. Wac, K., Dey, A.K., Vasilakos, A.V.: Body Area Networks for Ambulatory Psychophysiological Monitoring. In: Proceedings of the Fifth International Conference on Body Area Networks, p. 181. ACM Press, New York (2010)

An Improvement of NFC-SEC with Signed Exchanges for an e-Prescription-Based Application

Mohamad Hamze[1], Fabrice Peyrard[2], and Emmanuel Conchon[3]

[1] University of Burgundy, Le2i
9 avenue Alain Savary, BP 47870, 21078 Dijon France
Mohamad.Hamze@u-bourgogne.fr
[2] University of Toulouse, IRIT/ENSEEIHT
2 rue Charles Camichel, BP 7122, 31071 Toulouse Cedex 7 France
Fabrice.Peyrard@irit.fr
[3] University of Toulouse, IRIT/ISIS
Rue Firmin Oules, 81100 Castres, France
Emmanuel.Conchon@irit.fr

Abstract. In the context of an aging population, drug intake can be a potential source of errors leading to death in some cases. Almost all of these errors are unintentional and come from incorrect prescriptions, unsuitable dosages for the patient or incompatibility with other treatments. To limit these risks which are especially important in the elderly or pre-dependency, we propose a secure system for drug treatment through the NFC (Near Field Communication) contact-less communication technology. The proposed system provides security mechanisms such as integrity, authentication, encryption and non-repudiation. To ensure this security, an extension of the international standard ISO/IED 13157 (NFC-SEC) is proposed to handle electronic signature based on a public key infrastructure.

Keywords: NFC, e-prescription, Security, e-signature, ISO/IEC 13157, healthcare application.

1 Introduction

Everyday our health system is improving so that elders can now have a longer life expectancy. Nonetheless, for many of them, seniors require an assistance to improve their quality of life leading to a strong effort in this direction by the research community. In this context, to support the autonomy of elderly people, we choose to focus on the risk of medication errors. More specifically, we choose to highlight three common sources of medication error. First is when the physician is writing his prescription: the patient may inadvertently omit to tell the doctor about another medication he is taking for the treatment of another disease. Second, during the pharmacist dispensation, a prescription may be poorly written so that the pharmacist may misread the prescription leading to the dispensation of the wrong drug or of the wrong dosage for instance.

G. Memmi and U. Blanke (Eds.): MobiCASE 2013, LNICST 130, pp. 166–183, 2014.
© Institute for Computer Sciences, Social Informatics and Telecommunications Engineering 2014

Third, when taking his medication, the patient can make an error with the dosage, the schedule or even with the drug he takes. The risk associated with each of these three sources is very different from one to another with a probability of occurrence which increases from source 1 to source 3. Indeed, a good physician (doctor) and a good pharmacist should ask the relevant questions to avoid most of these risks. However, the third case depends only of the patient and has therefore a great probability to occur especially in the case of the elderly.

We present in this paper a process of development and use of electronic prescribing (e-prescribing) in an ubiquitous environment to reduce the risk of medication errors. Indeed, potential errors induced by the prescriber or pharmacist can be limited with the use of an electronic prescription (e-Rx) system. The drug intake phase is assisted by an ambient intelligence system in order to reduce the associated risks.

The ubiquitous system is based on electronic prescription and on a NFC (Near Field Communication) contact-less communications technology between patient, prescriber, pharmacist and drug boxes. The originality of our contribution relies on the following points: (1) the use of a single wireless technology NFC throughout the overall process, (2) a natural behavior of the patient through the process by being vigilant at every stage at the acceptability of the system, (3) a secure design ensuring the confidentiality of patients personal data (ethics), the traceability and the non-repudiation of the data exchanges.

In this paper, it has been chosen to highlight the security issues of the NFC technology and to propose a solution that tackles these issues for a healthcare system. A big part to ensure the patient safety is the necessity to track every people, devices and medication involved in the medical treatment. Indeed, misidentified patient or medications can cause serious, or even fatal, errors in medication care [25]. In addition, for a secure system several other requirements have to be filled: confidentiality, integrity, availability and non-repudiation of the exchanged data.

An NFC communication is usually done through an insecure channel which is not satisfactory from a security standpoint as shown as in [18][27]. To tackle this issue, several security standards have been published. For example, the International Standard ISO/IEC 13157 (NFC-SEC) [2][3] published in 2010 enables two NFC devices to establish a secure channel in Peer-to-Peer mode. Nonetheless, they still do not provide a solution for every security requirements. For instance, the NFC-SEC standard does not provide entity authentication. In addition, it cannot ensure non-repudiation because it does not contain any functionalities to sign the exchanged data. To deal with this problem, we propose to extend the NFC-SEC standard with the use of an electronic signature delivered by a Public Key Infrastructure (PKI).

The remaining of this paper is organized as follows: in section 2, the proposed ubiquitous system to improve drug intake based on e-Rx is presented; in section 3, the NFC technology is introduced with a focus on the security issues for healthcare applications; in section 4, the proposed security architecture and the extension of the NFC-SEC standard are presented; finally, a conclusion and some future works are provided.

2   Proposed Communication Process

2.1   System Overview

The proposed system is based on a recommendation made in 2012 by the CLIO (Comité de Liaison Inter-Ordres) Santé, which is the liaison committee of French medical regulatory authorities. In this note, the CLIO has presented a solution for the introduction of e-prescription (e-Rx) in the French e-health organization.

Currently, this system mainly relies on two electronic health records (EHR): The shared personal medical record (DMP) and the pharmaceutical record (DP).

- The DMP is the French shared patient record where the health professionals (medical doctor, surgeon etc.) can exchange medical information about the patient. This EHR stores labs exams, medical background, letters between physicians, medical images but no e-Rx. It has to be noticed that the patient can hide some information in this record and, for instance, only allow the access to a small subset of information for a specific doctor.
- The DP is handled by pharmacists and stores information about every medication that have been delivered to the patient in the last 36 months.

The information is split between the DMP and DP and a e-Rx system should be suitable to establish a link between them to carry the information between doctors and pharmacists. Therefore, the CLIO recommendation is to have a third repository dedicated to e-Rx.

The new CLIO healthcare pathway is presented in Figure 1 from step (1) to step (6). Once the doctor is authenticated on the system, he can access to the DMP of his patient to collect information (step (1)). Both the identity of the patient and of the doctor are ensured with a smart card (see section 2.3). After the medical exam, the doctor can edit a new e-prescription (e-Rx) and sends it to the e-Rx national repository (step (2)). He also gives a paper-based prescription to the patient. With his prescription, the patient goes to the pharmacy of his choice to receive his medication. In the pharmacy, the patient gives his smart card to the pharmacist who can then access to the DP and can receive the e-Rx to deliver (step (3) and (4)). He can substitute some drugs for generic ones. If so, he updates both the DP and the e-Rx registries (step (5) and (6)).

This system seems to be an effective and cost-saving way to reduce several errors (transcription for instance) and to ease the exchange of information between the doctor and the pharmacist. But, this system has no direct impact on the way the patient deals with his own medication.

As depicted on Figure 1, we propose to extend this proposition with a dedicated solution to provide new services to the patient among which is the possibility to make the intake of medicines easier. This solution is not to be opposed to the centralized e-Rx repository but can rather be viewed has a complementary tool to enforce the patient safety and security.

To provide these new functionalities, the patient has to received the e-Rx. To do that, we choose to use a NFC contact-less technology (see section 3.1). Indeed, the NFC technology is of growing interest and is present in most of modern phones.

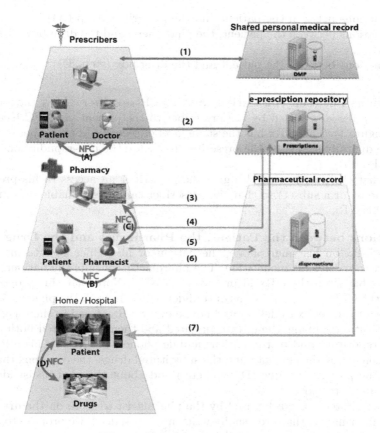

Fig. 1. Global system architecture

This technology is an extension of the RFID technology and provides a peer-to-peer communication mode which can be used for the exchange of e-Rx. Moreover, the range of communication is very short (below 10cm) so that the communication link has to be willingly established keeping the social interactions that currently exist and helping in the memorization of the transmission by the patient.

This e-Rx is then stored on the patient smartphone and can then be used to have reminders of his drug intakes for instance. Nonetheless, this NFC system has to be as secure as the system based on the centralized repository for e-Rx.

2.2   System Communication Architecture

Three kinds of actors have been defined: the patient, the prescriber (i.e. the health professional which can be a doctor or a nurse for instance) and the pharmacist. In addition to this three actors, the drug box also has a preeminent role as it contains a big part of the information (i.e. the intelligence) of the ambient system. The system is split in three parts where different interactions can occur:

- interactions between the patient and the prescriber (step (A)),
- interactions between the patient, the pharmacist and the drug box (step (B) and (C)),
- interactions between the patient and the drug box (step (D)).

Interactions between the Patient and the Prescriber. After the medical exam, the e-Rx is provided by the prescriber to the patient via NFC (see step (A) on Figure 1). This e-Rx has the same level of security as the paper one and has to be digitally signed by the prescriber to ensure the non-repudiation of the contained data.

Note that the patient can also give the prescriber an access to his previous prescriptions (or a subset) so that the prescriber can have valuable information to write his e-Rx.

Interactions between the Patient, the Pharmacist and the Drug Box. With his e-Rx on his smartphone, the patient or his helper goes to his usual pharmacy to receive his medication. The pharmacist consults the national e-Rx repository based on the e-Rx id provided via NFC. Note that this proposition enforces the CLIO system in terms of confidentiality. Indeed, the pharmacist has only access to the e-Rx to deliver and not to every e-Rx stored in the repository. If a substitution is made, the e-Rx is updated and then transmitted both to the national repository and to the patient mobile phone with NFC. This e-Rx has information about the current date, the substituted drugs, the drug box that are given to the patient (Unique ID, type etc.) and about the pharmacist identity for traceability purpose.

Moreover, the e-Rx can be used by the pharmacist to store on the drug box memory, information that are usually written on it. Indeed, we propose to add a NFC-tag to the drug box to store information about the patient, the prescriber, the dosage and the date of the prescription as well as the date of the dispensation.

At the end of this step, the patient has an updated e-Rx on his mobile phone and has received several smart drug boxes. All of these elements will allow the proposition of new services for the patient.

Interactions between the Patient and the Drug Box. With the e-Rx on his smartphone, the patient will then be allowed to receive scheduled reminders to take his drugs. When an alert is received, the patient has to pass the phone over the drug box (i.e. to tag) to acknowledge the drug intake. The drug box tag is read by the smart-phone to ensure first that the box contains the drug the patient is supposed to take and second that the box belongs to him. Alzheimer patients for instance can forget what their medication box looks like even after years of usage of this same drug. If the patient uses the correct drug box, the time and date are stored in the box tag. If a box is tagged without any reminder issued by the smart-phone, this date is used to compute the time between the last intake and the current one. If this time interval is too short leading to a risk for the patient health, an alert is generated in order to cancel the drug intake.

Every validated drug intake is then logged on the smart-phone to provide a historical overview of the patient behavior. This overview can be used by the doctor to adjust the medical treatment with more information than with an interview only. For Alzheimer patients, this overview can also be used by helpers to keep a track of the drugs taken. Moreover, a functionality is provided to allow the patient to add specific information during every drug intakes explaining why he did or did not take the prescribed drug (side effects for instance).

Information stored on the drug box can also be used to enforce the overall traceability from the dispensation standpoint (to recover some box within a contaminated lot for instance) and from the drug intake standpoint. Indeed, this information can be used by the patient to start over a new overview even if he looses his smart-phone or his e-Rx. Without an e-Rx, the patient will still be able to know if a drug box belongs to him, if the drug intake is possible at the current time and even find the prescribed dosage on the drug box.

To sum up, two kinds of communication can occur. Peer-to-peer communications between the doctor (e.g the pharmacist) and the patient and communications between the patient and the drug box.

2.3   Security Considerations

In the proposed system several security issues can be pointed out. First, as the e-Rx is considered in France as a medical information, it has to be encrypted and transmitted in a secure way to prevent eavesdropping. Similarly, the data stored on the box has to be encrypted. Moreover, every actors of the system has to be identified. For every communication the exchanged data has to be signed in order to ensure the non-repudiation. Furthermore, the use of the digital signature will help to detect potential modification of the information stored in the e-Rx or on the drug box.

In the French health system, health professionals and patients are equipped with a smart card that can be used to ensure the basic operation for our system: the 'CPS Card' and the 'Carte Vitale 2'.

CPS Card. *ASIP santé* is a national registration and certification authority that ensures trust in the exchange of health data. It delivers to each health professional a smart card called CPS (Carte des Professionnels de Santé) used as an electronic certificate. A CPS card is a professional electronic identity card. It helps holders to prove their identities and their professional qualifications. It is protected by an individual PIN code. A CPS card is the key for e-health services now and in the future in France. It enables healthcare professionals to: (1) Identify themselves and avoid identity theft; (2) Add electronic signatures to documents; (3) Send electronic treatment forms to the mandatory state health and supplementary insurance organizations; (4) Create, add to and refer to the electronic health records of their patients; (5) telemedicine; (6) Use a secure messaging service for healthcare professionals; (7) Thanks to contact-less technology, it can also be used for other applications such as accessing premises.

Carte Vitale 2. The *Carte Vitale 2* is the health insurance card in France used for the reimbursement of treatment costs by the national social security agency. With the *Carte Vitale 2*, health professionals can electronically transmit sheets to care health insurance. The *Carte Vitale 2* is supposed to guarantee the identification of the insured person and allows him to sign the electronic care sheet. It must be presented for each visit to the doctor and for every purchase of medication. At the time of writing, the identification is made by the health professional based on the name of the card holder and his photography printed on the card. But, it can be noticed that the card already offer cryptographic functionalities which could be used to ensure security of the exchange and the holder authentication if activated.

So, the CPS card empowered every health professional with digital certificates that can be used for encryption or signature. But, the communication technology has to support also encryption and signature to ensure the overall security of the system.

3   Backgrounds

3.1   Near Field Communication (NFC) Technology

NFC is an extension of RFID based on contactless communication standards. NFC provides short-range communication on a high frequency (13.56 MHz) and is used by devices with low capacity of memory and of computing. It allows data to be exchanged between devices that are within a few centimeters (10 cm) and supports data transfer rates of 106, 216, 424, and 848 Kbit/s. NFC allows the use of small tags that made it possible to be used with small products. Moreover the communication does not require a direct line of sight.

NFC in mobiles can operate in three different modes determined by the application used; it can communicate with another active NFC mobile in Peer-to-Peer mode, or communicate with a passive RFID/NFC tag in reader/writer mode, or communicate with an NFC reader in card emulation mode [30]. Our work in this paper concerns NFC mobiles in Peer-to-Peer communication mode.

Standardization. NFC is standardized in ISO/IEC 18092 [6] and ISO/IEC 21481 [7] that define communication interfaces and protocols between two NFC devices. For easier integration, NFC has been derived from the same platform as ISO/IEC 14443 [4][5], or from *proximity cards* that define the communication with contact-less integrated circuits (IC). NDEF (NFC Data Exchange Format) defines the logical formats for data exchanges.

3.2   NFC Survey

In Healthcare. Alemdar [8] presents in 2010 a state of the art of sensor networks for healthcare where the BAN (Body Area Network), PAN (Personal Area Network), gateway to wide networks, wide networks, and end-user healthcare monitoring application are described. This study is a large overview of the different wireless technologies. The presented work on contact-less technology in particular RFID and NFC, highlights the support for activities of daily living detection , the support of location tracking and the support of medication intake.

On this last point, Ho [19] is one of the first to propose a prototype integrating a sensor network and RFID technology for the in-home medication monitoring. Pang [28] recently proposed iPackage: a pervasive healthcare solution for medication noncompliance problem . This prototype allows to tag individual tablets of a medicine box. The proposed solution is cumbersome and the performances obtained do not fully meet the authors expectations.

Ilie-Zudor [20] published in 2011 a journal article which is also a state of the art of applications with unique identifications. It categorizes fifteen application areas including healthcare. The advantages of RFID-based applications are presented including pharmaceutics where RFID can be used as a substitute of bar-codes or can be used for hospital equipment and personnel tracking, for patient medical history or for implant prosthetic and elderly care. It is stated that RFID technology can reduce human errors in the process.

In their work Jara and al. [22,21,23] present architectures for AAL (Ambient Assisted Living) based on IoT (Internet of Things). In [22], Jara and al. present the need for secure communications in a medical environment based on symmetric ciphers and on DESFire tag for specific smartphones applications. In [21], the focus is on IoT with the use of NFC to ensure compatibility between drugs. Finally, in 2011, they published [23] a very interesting journal article where a system for diabetes therapy management has been proposed. This system defines a solution for a secure therapeutic monitoring based on a personal health NFC card of the patient.

Garcia and Bravo [16] proposed in 2011 a solution to assist the intake of medication for elderly people with cognitive disabilities. The objective of the system is to remind, guide and motivate the person to take his medication. NFC technology is used as a carrier to help identify boxes of drug.

In [10,11] Bravo and al. use NFC technology to assist people with Alzheimer's disease in their daily lives. It is based on tags that are embedded in the environment of the person enabling him to be guided and assisted thanks to a NFC smartphone.

Finally, the work of Lahtela [25] deals with a secure mechanism for the use of medications in a hospital environment. With NFC technology identification, the proposed system can reduce human errors in medication.

The closest work with our solution has been proposed by Vergara and al.[31]. In this work, the authors provide a mobile prescribing solution using a smartphone with interaction between the medical doctor and drug boxes. However, it does not consider the process as a whole (patient, doctor, pharmacist, drug manufacturer). Moreover, the security of exchanged data is not taken into consideration neither is the traceability of exchanged documents with NFC.

It can also be noted that Garcia and Bravo [16] project which supports strategies to improve the treatment compliance of elderly with ambient intelligent systems could be coupled with our own support and control system of e-prescribing and drug intake solution to have a complete system dedicated to the elderly with cognitive disabilities resulting from Alzheimer or Parkinson disease as well as people with head trauma.

Security Issues. Although the NFC communication range is limited to a few centimeters, it is not enough to ensure security. Indeed, three safety axis for NFC are to ensure: (1) Security of mobiles (NFC devices and applications); (2) Safety of the communication channel; (3) System Security (reader and tag).

Mifare Classic cards are one of the most popular solution with more than 200 million copies worldwide. These inexpensive cards implement the symmetric security algorithm Crypto-1 whose vulnerability was demonstrated in 2009 by Garcia [15]. He showed four possible attacks on this kind of card. The most significant result is the attack of the secret key in less than a second. Courtois [12] has also shown how to clone this type of card in 1 second. With such a low time rate, the spoofing of an ID tag can be easily done for instance.

In 2006, Hancke [17] proposed relay attack on an RFID system (tag/reader). In 2010, Francis et al. [13] showed the feasibility of this same relay attack between NFC smartphones. They proposed the use of an information system based on the mobile devices location coupled with a digital signature to counter this attack.

Madlmayr et al. [26] studied the security and the confidentiality of NFC devices. They call for the integration in applications of encryption and authentication mechanisms not only of terminals but also of people. More recently Roland [29] in 2010 proposes in his paper a digital signature records for NDEF NFC layer to ensure messages integrity and authenticity. In other works, Francis et al. [14] offer a Security applications Framework for e-identification, e-payment and e-ticketing with NFC reader/tag mode. This framework offers a CPTI (Communication Protocol Translator Interface) protocol for secure P2P transactions with token between terminal and cards. It is based on an asymmetric encryption mechanism and digital signature.

In addition, commonly known threats to the NFC security [24] are: (1) Eavesdropping, where a third party can receive a signal using an antenna. (2) Unwanted activation, which is somewhat similar to eavesdropping. Third party attacker tries to activate the card without the owner's knowledge; (3) Data Corruption, or modification of transmitted data using an NFC device working with the valid frequency; (4) Data Modification, where the attacker is sending valid, but altered data to the receiving NFC device; (5) Data Insertion, where attacker tries to insert a new message into a NFC communication; (6) Man-in-The-Middle-Attack, where two parties who want to establish communication are tricked into communicating with or via the third party which is therefore enabled to record the entire conversation; (7) Denial of service, where the attacker tries to interfere with the RF field, in order to prevent the transaction. Also, Haselsteiner and BreitfuB [18] show multiple attacks against NFC-based systems that rely on the lack of link level security of the NFC technology.

3.3   NFC Security Standard ISO/IEC 13157

NFC (Near Field Communication) data exchanges pose a security problem that the International Standard ISO/IEC 13157 published in June 2010 addresses. It consists of two parts: 'NFC-SEC: NFCIP-1 security services and protocol' [2] and 'NFC-SEC cryptography standard using ECDH and AES' [3]. This NFC-SEC cryptography Standard specifies cryptographic mechanisms based on the Elliptic Curves Diffie-Hellman (ECDH) protocol for key agreement and the AES algorithm for data encryption and integrity.

This standard enables the encryption of exchanged data based on a symmetric algorithm where the shared secret is generated from digital certificates of the communicating entities. This process can be split in four steps as depicted as in Figure 2.

- *Step 1:* Key agreement: enables the establishment of the shared secret (z) from the derivation of a part of the private key of the transmitter and derivation a part of the receiver's public key. It begins with the generation of an Elliptic Curve (EC) Key Pair and the validation of the EC public key. Each NFC-SEC entity generates a random nonce (N) which will be used to provide more entropy for the keys derivation. N is then concatenated ($\|$) with the EC public key (Q) and the result is sent to the other entity (Fig. 3). z is then computed by the ECDH derivation Primitive [1] from the user's private key and the public key of the other entity.

  With the properties defined in Table 1, two Key Derivation Functions (KDF) are specified; one for the Shared Secret Service (SSE) and one for the Secure Channel Service (SCH).

  1. SSE establishes a shared secret MK_{SSE} between two NFC-SEC entities. This secret must be cryptographically uncorrelated from any shared secrets established beforehand or afterwards (Fig. 3);

$$MK_{SSE} = KDF_{SSE}(N_S, N_R, z, ID_S, ID_R) \tag{1}$$

  2. SCH provides a secure channel between two NFC-SEC entities with link keys MK_{SCH}, KE_{SCH}, KI_{SCH}, and subsequently protect all communications in both direction across the channel.

$$\{MK_{SCH}, KE_{SCH}, KI_{SSH}\} = KDF_{SCH}(N_S, N_R, z, ID_S, ID_R) \tag{2}$$

- *Step 2:* Key confirmation: Both NFC-SEC entities check that they indeed share the same key. Each entity generates a key confirmation tag (MacTag) based on a Message Authentication Code (MAC) and sends it to the other entity. Both then verify the key confirmation tag upon reception.
- *Step 3:* PDU security: The NFC-SEC entities (Fig. 4) protect data exchange using encryption. This mechanism involves (a) Sequence Integrity, (b) Confidentiality and Origin authentication and (c) Data integrity. **No signature mechanism of packets is supported in the standard.**

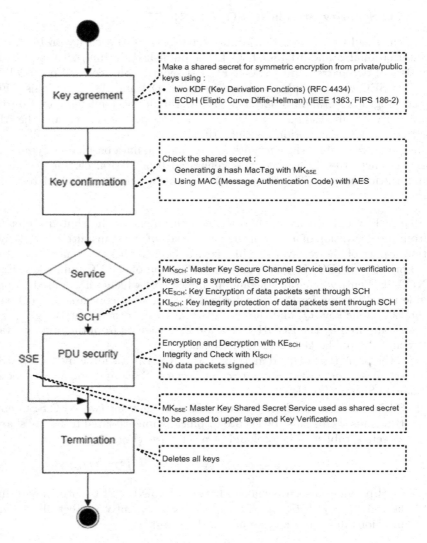

Fig. 2. General flow of the NFC-SEC services

(a) NFC-SEC provides a sequence integrity mechanism in accordance with the following: each NFC-SEC Entity maintains its SNV (Sequence Number Variable), then upon SCH establishment, the receiving entity initializes its SNV to the same initial value as the Sender's SNV. This SNV is then enclosed in every exchanged data to ensure the sequence integrity.

(b) As previously mentioned, the data encryption algorithm used is AES with counter CTR mode. At first, to avoid the exchange of the initial value (IV) of the CTR counter, the IV must be computed by both entities from the exchanged nonces with equation:

Table 1. Cryptographic properties of standard NFC 13157

Actions	Algorithms
Key agreement	ECDH P-192, IEEE 1363 and FIPS 186-3
Key Derivation Fonction	AES-XCBC-PRF-128, RFC 4434 (IPSEC v2)
Key confirmation	AES-XCBC-MAC-96, RFC 3566 (IPSEC v2)
Encryption	AES-128-CTR, IV init: AES-XCBC-PRF-128
Integrity	AES-XCBC-MAC-96

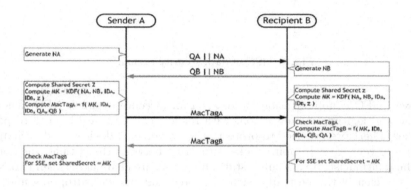

Fig. 3. MSC of establishing of a shared secret MK_{SSE}

$$MAC\text{-}IV(MK_{SCH}, KI_{SCH}, N_S, N_R) \tag{3}$$

The data must be encrypted or decrypted using the symmetric encryption key KE_{SCH} :

$$EncData = ENC_{KE_{SCH}}(Data) \tag{4}$$

$$Data' = DEC_{KE_{SCH}}(EncData) \tag{5}$$

(c) Integrity of all encrypted data transferred on the SCH is preserved through a MAC (Message Authentication Code) (i.e a fingerprint) generated with the symmetric key KI_{SCH} and the AES algorithm.

- *Step 4:* Finally, The NFC-SEC entities terminate SSE and SCH and destroy the associated shared secret and the link keys. Indeed, the MK_{SSE}, MK_{SCH}, KE_{SCH} and KI_{SCH} keys must be different for every NFC-SEC transaction.

More details on the standard can be found in [3].

4   Proposed Secure and Trust Architecture

4.1   A Need for Secure Communications

According to the architecture presented in Fig. 1, we propose to use NFC technology to transmit e-Rx between doctors (or pharmacists) and patients.

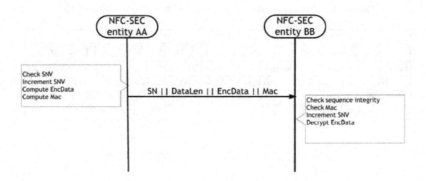

Fig. 4. MSC of data security exchange

However, NFC communication is done via an insecure channel. NFC tags can be read and legitimate transactions with readers can be heard by a third party attacker. Therefore, we need to protect privacy, personal devices, and exchanged data to prevent eavesdropping and ensure trust between the patient, the doctor and the pharmacist. As a result, establishing a secure channel between two NFC devices is clearly the best approach to protect against eavesdropping and any kind of data modification attack.

We propose the use of NFC-SEC to ensure security communication. The confidentiality and integrity are ensured by the symmetric keys MK_{SCH}, KE_{SCH} and KI_{SCH} that are derived from equation (2) and used in equations (4) and (5) and by the MAC computed from equation (3). This is ensured because if the attacker can find N_A, N_B, ID_A and ID_B, he still can't find the shared secret z. Indeed, the shared secret z is calculated from a user's private key and the public key of the other. Without the private key, the attacker can't reverse the process.

NFC-SEC enables two NFC devices in Peer-to-Peer mode to establish a secure channel but does not provide all requested security features.

Firstly, NFC-SEC standard does not provide authentication [9] mechanisms which is a strong weakness to fight against Man-In-The-Middle attacks as demonstrated by Haselsteiner and al. [18].

Secondly, doctor or pharmacist or patient must not be able to deny that they exchanged information at some point (to respect non-repudiation). In addition, 'e-Rx' must not be modified by an attacker when exchanged or stored in the patient smartphone (to respect integrity). Thus, when the patient goes to the pharmacy, the pharmacist must ensure that the received 'e-Rx' is not altered and is delivered by a doctor. Therefore, any data exchanged between users has to be signed.

As previously, stated NFC-SEC does not provide functionality to sign the exchanged nor stored data failing to ensure authentication and non-repudiation.

4.2   Proposed Trust Architecture

To deal with this problem, we proposed to use a digital signature (e-signature) to sign every exchanged of e-Rx at communication time. This method ensures a trust between the different parts of the communication due to the reliability of the signature checks, authentication and authorization required for both receiver and sender. It insures integrity of data, easily traces transactions between parties, and insures that any actor can not deny that he sends a signed information.

The e-signature relies on the utilization of a public-private key pair with a hash function. First, the sender uses the hash function to calculate a footprint of data to be signed. He uses the private key to encrypt (i.e. sign) this footprint. Then, he sends the message containing the clear data and the signature to the receiver. Upon receiving this message, the receiver decrypts the signed footprint using the public key of the sender. He calculates the footprint of the clear data with the hash function and compares the result with the decrypted footprint. If they are equals then the receiver is sure that the data were not altered (integrity) during the communication and that the sender is who he claims to be (non-repudiation).

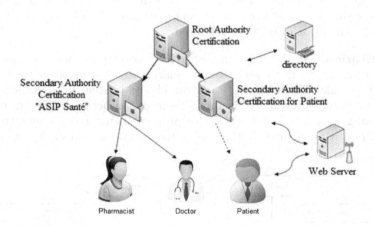

Fig. 5. Architecture of Public Key Infrastructure

Public Key Infrastructure (PKI). We propose a PKI (Fig. 5) to deliver e-signatures. This PKI is composed of the following equipments:

1. A root Certification Authority (AC_root) that self-generates its own certificate (key pair).
2. Two secondary certification authorities (AC_sec) which could be integrated into the social security system:
   - The *ASIP santé* (section 2.3) which delivers certificates for CPS user and which already exists.
   - An authority that distributes electronic certificates to patients.

3. A directory to manage valid and usable public keys and those which are on the CRL (Certificate Revocation List).
4. A Web server is used for:
   (a) The reception of a request for a certificate from the user, and its sending to the secondary authority.
   (b) Sending a certificate received from the secondary authority to the user with the addition of the public key in the directory.
   (c) Receiving information (public key, identifier...) sent by a user to check :
       - If a public key is on the CRL or is under use
       - If it is signed by the secondary authority, and if the authority's public key is signed by the root authority.
   (d) Sending a user public key based on the request of another user.
   (e) The return of the verification results.

These authorities distribute signing certificates (C_{sig_pat}, C_{sig_doc}, C_{sig_pha}) for (patient, physician, pharmacist) that contains actor key pair ($K_{pub\_sig_{pat}}$ / $K_{pri\_sig_{pat}}$, $K_{pub\_sig_{doc}}$ / $K_{pri\_sig_{doc}}$, $K_{pub\_sig_{pha}}$ / $K_{pri\_sig_{pha}}$).

These certificates are stored as follow: For the doctor and pharmacist, they are stored on the CPS card. While for the patient, they are stored in the smartphone. Note that we could store the patient certificates in 'Carte Vitale 2' if the cryptography functionalities were activated.

Authentication. At the beginning of a NFC communication, N and Q are exchanged among peers to generate the shared secret z in order to establish the secure channel. Therefore, to avoid the classical threat in unauthenticated key agreement protocols and to insure authentication between different entities before establishing a secure channel, we propose to use e-signatures (Fig. 6). First, each entity generates N then signs the concatenation of N and Q and

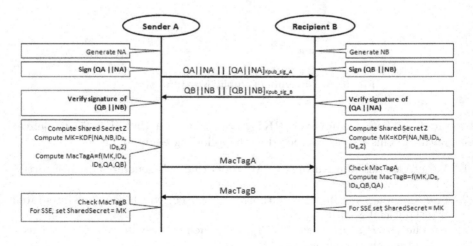

Fig. 6. MSC of authentication entities before communication

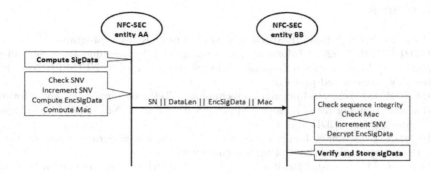

Fig. 7. MSC of trust exchange and data storage

append the resulting e-signature to the data to transmit. Next, each entity sends the result to the other for verification. Finally, if there were no alteration during the communication (verification of the fingerprint and of the e-signature), they compute the shared secret z and establish a secure and trust channel.

Trust Exchange and Data Storage. Next, the patient is going to exchange and store the signed data such as '*e-Rx*'. Therefore, we propose to sign these data first and then send them in a secured manner with NFC-SEC (Fig. 7). After signing the '*data*', we obtain '*SigData*'. Then, we encrypt '*SigData*' using the NFC-SEC encryption protocol and we obtain '*EncSigData*'. Finally, we apply the MAC on information and send them to the receiver using NFC-SEC. Finally at the reception, by applying the protocol NFC-SEC, we obtain the initial signed data '*SigData*' that can be verified or stored for a later check.

5 Conclusion

In this paper, we have presented a new system based on e-Rx to assist people with their daily medication intakes. This system relies on the NFC technology which has been enhanced to provide all requirements for a secure healthcare application (among which is confidentiality, authentication and non-repudiation). We have proposed an extension of the NFC-SEC standard to support electronic signature in order to authenticate and to ensure the non-repudiation every exchanged data. This extension relies on a PKI which can be seamlessly integrated in the existing French e-health system to deliver electronic certificate to every actors.

At the time of writing, an Android prototype has been developed and it is planned in future works to evaluate the impact of the e-signature extension on the communication process in terms of energy consumption, bandwidth and delays and to compare it with the NDEF e-signature mechanism. Finally, we are planning to extend our proposition to enable a e-signature support in reader tag communication in order to strengthen security in the communication between user and drug box.

References

1. IEEE 1363:2000, Standard Specifications for Public-Key Cryptography
2. ISO/IEC 13157-1:2010 Information technology – Telecommunications and information exchange between systems – NFC Security – Part 1: NFC-SEC NFCIP-1 security services and protocol
3. ISO/IEC 13157-2:2010 Information technology – Telecommunications and information exchange between systems – NFC Security – Part 2: NFC-SEC cryptography standard using ECDH and AES
4. ISO/IEC 1443-1:2008, Identification cards – Contactless integrated circuit(s) cards – Proximity cards – Part 1: Physical characteristics
5. ISO/IEC 1443-2:2001, Identification cards – Contactless integrated circuit(s) cards – Proximity cards – Part 2: Radio Frequency power and signal interface
6. ISO/IEC 18092:2004, Information technology – Telecommunications and information exchange between systems – Near Field Communication – Interface and Protocol (NFCIP-1)
7. ISO/IEC 21481:2004, Information technology – Telecommunications and information exchange between systems – Near Field Communication – Interface and Protocol (NFCIP-2)
8. Alemdar, H., Ersoy, C.: Wireless sensor networks for healthcare: A survey. Computer Networks 54(15), 2688–2710 (2010)
9. Alshehri, A., Briffa, J., Schneider, S., Wesemeyer, S.: Formal security analysis of NFC m-coupon protocols using casper/fdr. In: 5th International Workshop on Near Field Communication, Zurich, Switzerland (2013)
10. Bravo, J., Hervas, R., Fuentes, C., Chavira, G., Nava, S.: Tagging for nursing care. In: Second International Conference on Pervasive Computing Technologies for Healthcare, PervasiveHealth 2008, January 30-February 1, pp. 305–307 (2008)
11. Bravo, J., Hervás, R., Gallego, R., Casero, G., Vergara, M., Carmona, T., Fuentes, C., Nava, S.W., Chavira, G., Villarreal, V.: Enabling NFC technology to support activities in an alzheimer's day center. In: Proceedings of the 1st International Conference on PErvasive Technologies Related to Assistive Environments, PETRA 2008, pp. 81:1–81:5. ACM, New York (2008)
12. Courtois, N.: The dark side of security by obscurity - and cloning mifare classic rail and building passes, anywhere, anytime. In: Fernandez-Medina, E., Malek, M., Hernando, J. (eds.) Proceedings of the International Conference on Security and Cryptography (SECRYPT 2009), pp. 331–338. INSTICC Press, Milan (2009)
13. Francis, L., Hancke, G., Mayes, K., Markantonakis, K.: Practical NFC peer-to-peer relay attack using mobile phones. In: Ors Yalcin, S.B. (ed.) RFIDSec 2010. LNCS, vol. 6370, pp. 35–49. Springer, Heidelberg (2010)
14. Francis, L., Hancke, G., Mayes, K., Markantonakis, K.: A security framework model with communication protocol translator interface for enhancing NFC transactions. In: Proceedings of the 2010 Sixth Advanced International Conference on Telecommunications, AICT 2010, pp. 452–461. IEEE Computer Society, Washington, DC (2010)
15. Garcia, F.D., van Rossum, P., Verdult, R., Schreur, R.W.: Wirelessly pickpocketing a mifare classic card. In: Proceedings of the 30th IEEE Symposium on Security and Privacy, SP 2009, pp. 3–15. IEEE Computer Society, Washington, DC (2009)
16. García-Vázquez, J.P., Rodríguez, M.D., Andrade, A.G., Bravo, J.: Supporting the strategies to improve elders' medication compliance by providing ambient aids. Personal Ubiquitous Computing 15(4), 389–397 (2011)

17. Hancke, G.: Practical attacks on proximity identification systems. In: IEEE Symposium on Security and Privacy, pp. 328–333 (May 2006)
18. Haselsteiner, E., Breitfuß, K.: Security in near field communication (NFC). In: Workshop on RFID and Lightweight Crypto, RFIDSec 2006 (2006)
19. Ho, L., Moh, M., Walker, Z., Hamada, T., Su, C.F.: A prototype on rfid and sensor networks for elder healthcare: progress report. In: Proceedings of the 2005 ACM SIGCOMM Workshop on Experimental Approaches to Wireless Network Design and Analysis, E-WIND 2005, pp. 70–75. ACM, New York (2005)
20. Ilie-Zudor, E., Kemény, Z., van Blommestein, F., Monostori, L., van der Meulen, A.: A survey of applications and requirements of unique identification systems and rfid techniques. Computers in Industry 62(3), 227–252 (2011)
21. Jara, A., Alcolea, A., Zamora, M., Skarmeta, A., Alsaedy, M.: Drugs interaction checker based on iot. In: Internet of Things (IOT 2010), pp. 1–8 (December 2010)
22. Jara, A., Zamora, M., Skarmeta, A.: An architecture based on internet of things to support mobility and security in medical environments. In: 7th IEEE Consumer Communications and Networking Conference (CCNC 2010), pp. 1–5 (January 2010)
23. Jara, A.J., Zamora, M.A., Skarmeta, A.F.: An internet of things—based personal device for diabetes therapy management in ambient assisted living (aal). Personal Ubiquitous Computing 15(4), 431–440 (2011)
24. Jovanovic, M., Organero, M.: Analysis of the latest trends in mobile commerce using the NFC technology. Cyber Journals: Multidisciplinary Journals in Science and Technology, Journal of Selected Areas in Telecommunications (JSAT) May Edition, 1–12 (2011)
25. Lahtela, A., Hassinen, M., Jylha, V.: RFID and NFC in healthcare: Safety of hospitals medication care. In: Second International Conference on Pervasive Computing Technologies for Healthcare (PervasiveHealth 2008), pp. 241–244 (February 2008)
26. Madlmayr, G., Langer, J., Kantner, C., Scharinger, J.: NFC devices: Security and privacy. In: Third International Conference on Availability, Reliability and Security (ARES 2008), pp. 642 –647 (March 2008)
27. Mulliner, C.: Vulnerability analysis and attacks on NFC-enabled mobile phones. In: 1st International Workshop on Sensor Security, pp. 695–700 (2009)
28. Pang, Z., Chen, Q., Zheng, L.: A pervasive and preventive healthcare solution for medication noncompliance and daily monitoring. In: 2nd International Symposium on Applied Sciences in Biomedical and Communication Technologies (ISABEL 2009), pp. 1–6 (November 2009)
29. Roland, M., Langer, J.: Digital signature records for the NFC data exchange format. In: Second International Workshop on Near Field Communication, pp. 71–76 (April 2010)
30. Coskun, V., Ok, K., Ozdenizci, B.: Near Field Communication: from theory to practice. Wiley (2012)
31. Vergara, M., Diaz-Hellin, P., Fontecha, J., Hervas, R., Sanchez-Barba, C., Fuentes, C., Bravo, J.: Mobile prescription: An NFC-based proposal for AAL. In: 2010 Second International Workshop on Near Field Communication (NFC), pp. 27–32 (2010)

KeySens: Passive User Authentication through Micro-behavior Modeling of Soft Keyboard Interaction

Benjamin Draffin*, Jiang Zhu, and Joy Zhang

Department of Electrical and Computer Engineering
Carnegie Mellon University
Moffett Field, CA, USA
benjamin.p.draffin@vanderbilt.edu, {jiang.zhu,joy.zhang}@sv.cmu.edu

Abstract. Mobile devices have become almost ever-present in our daily lives and increasingly so in the professional workplace. Applications put company data, personal information and sensitive documents in the hands of busy nurses at hospitals, company employees on business trips and government workers at large conferences. Smartphones and tablets also not only store data on-device, but users are frequently authorized to access sensitive information in the cloud. Protecting the sensitivity of mobile devices yet not burdening users with complicated and cumbersome *active authentication* methods is of great importance to the security and convenience of mobile computing. In this paper, we propose a novel passive authentication method; we model the micro-behavior of mobile users' interaction with their devices' soft keyboard. We show that the way a user types—the specific location touched on each key, the drift from finger down to finger up, the force of touch, the area of press—reflects their unique physical and behavioral characteristics. We demonstrate that using these micro-behavior features without any contextual information, we can passively identify that a mobile device is being used by a non-authorized user within 5 keypresses 67.7% of the time. This comes with a False Acceptance Rate (FAR) of 32.3% and a False Rejection Rate (FRR) of only 4.6%. Our detection rate after 15 keypresses is 86% with a FAR of 14% and a FRR of only 2.2%.

Keywords: Keystroke Dynamics, User Authentication, Passive Authentication, Multi-factor Authentication, Continuous Authentication, Biometrics, Micro-behavior, Soft Keyboards, Mobile Security, Android.

1 Introduction

Imagine a nurse has been using a mobile tablet to access and record sensitive patient information (such as in Figure 1). She is suddenly called away for an urgent question and without realizing it she leaves the tablet on the table—unlocked

---

* This work was done while the first author interned at Carnegie Mellon University, Silicon Valley under the supervision of Jiang Zhu and Joy Zhang.

G. Memmi and U. Blanke (Eds.): MobiCASE 2013, LNICST 130, pp. 184–201, 2014.

and still in the medical application. A curious or even malicious bystander picks up the tablet and searches though medical histories; they get unfettered access to private, personal information with not so much as a warning. Consider also the case where the nurse *did* lock the tablet; this attentive bystander may have easily learned a short PIN just by watching, passing right through traditional security barriers [9]. Active authentication can help protect devices at rest, but mobile, dynamic environments need mechanisms to detect and stop these security breaches in real-time. *Passive, behavioral authentication* measures are needed to counter these threats. We envision an application, *KeySens*, that develops a model of a user's micro-behavior and can detect when the phone is in a different person's hands. This application could then limit access or prompt for additional authentication upon detection. Towards that end, we have developed a proof-of-concept application and analysis models that demonstrate that users *do* have distinctive typing micro-behavior.

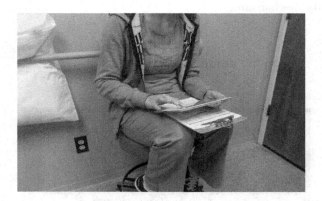

Fig. 1. Mobile devices such as iPads have become very popular among professionals. In this example, a nurse working at a dermatology clinic uses an iPad to take photos of a patient's skin, add notes, fill in forms and upload directly to the cloud.

1.1   Authentication Techniques

Authentication is the process of confirming that something or someone is what they say they are. The processes for authentication are many and diverse, and they have existed in the computing world since the beginning. Over time, the security field has categorized these into three primary groups [1]:

Something you know e.g. a password, security question, or ID number
Something you have e.g. a security token, ID card, or trusted device
Something you are e.g. a physical or behavioral trait such as a fingerprint or
    a keystroke dynamics model [14]

Most of these categories rely on *active authentication*, requiring direct user attention and input. While an effective protection schema to restrict unauthorized access, traditional active authentication procedures are of limited use on mobile platforms. Users switch between tasks rapidly and are authenticating with dozens of services every day. Pausing and asking for passwords each time gets tedious and frustrating; users may choose to switch to less secure services with lower barriers to entry.

Passive authentication procedures are needed—ones that allow for transparent, low-friction authentication for known users but can detect and block unknown ones. Micro-behavior metrics are seen as a promising avenue for tackling this challenge. They are inherent or *latent characteristics* of the user and as such, they are very hard to impersonate. It is extremely challenging to fake a fingerprint, a retina, a vein pattern, a facial structure, or a hand geometry [9]. It also turns out that it is challenging to fake a micro-behavior metric such as signature, voice timbre, or a user's keystroke dynamics [4]. Mobile phones, equipped with a variety of powerful sensors and empowered with fairly substantial computing resources, are a perfect domain for deploying behavioral analysis to bolster their current security mechanisms.

Fig. 2. Screenshot from an early version of the soft keyboard application comparing user typing patterns. In this example, a new user "Ed" presses different locations on keys (shown as yellow dots) than the normal user (grey dots) of this mobile device.

1.2   Contributions of This Research

This paper addresses how micro-behavioral metrics can be used to differentiate between users on mobile devices. This will be used for the development of a soft-keyboard application that can *passively authenticate* users in real-world environments. Keyboards and *keystroke dynamics* have been the subject of a wide body of prior research, looking to identify users based on *how* they type, not just *what* they type. We extend this research to the mobile platform and leverage data available only on touchscreens to develop user models that work in real-world environments. A trial application has been developed that collects raw keypress information to be analyzed offline. Figure 2 is a screenshot from an early version of this application, visualizing how a new user ('Ed') may have different typing patterns than the typical user ('Mr. Grey Dots').

In contrast to traditional keyboard dynamics research, we analyze not only how rapidly a user types, but also a variety of soft-keyboard specific micro-behavior features. These include *where* on the key the user pressed, how much the user *drifts* over the course of a keypress, and the *orientation* of the phone.

Using this data, plus a variety of statistical tools, we can generate a *certainty score* of whether the user's phone is in a stranger's hands. This score, when combined with a larger application and decision engine, will be used in future work to block access to applications or ask for additional authentication information when an non-authorized user is detected. For this demonstration we leverage other users' keypress data to help train the micro-behavioral model, but we envision a system where all data is collected and stored on the phone and a model is trained offline separate from other user data.

1.3   Applications

With the potential to provide passive, transparent authentication on any mobile device with very little inconvenience, micro-behavior metrics have a wide range of target applications. Environments where sensitive data is accessed by busy, mobile people—one of the hardest areas to secure—can be further protected with these models. A few examples:

- Companies can help protect their data hosted on employees' phones (whether the hardware is company-owned or personally owned);
- Delivery persons or IT administrators who may need to place their tablets down to carry things can reduce risk of unauthorized access;
- Parents who lend their devices to children or friends can feel comfortable knowing they are protected against impersonating emails or other messages;
- Business travelers have reduced risk upon loss or theft of their device;
- Nurses who carry mobile devices to maintain patient records can be protected from prying eyes if they were to place the device down;

Additionally, with a content-agnostic and always aware view of typing patterns, these environments can be protected even in the event a non-authorized user learns the primary user's password through shoulder surfing, discovery of a note, or social engineering.

2   Related Work

While to our best knowledge there has not been prior published research on this particular topic, there has been a wide variety of high-quality, instructive research on similar topics. These areas include desktop keystroke dynamics using traditional methods [1], mobile phone keypress dynamics using traditional methods [18] and key inference using side-channel sensors [13]. This research can focus on either *structured text* such as passwords/shared secrets or *dynamic text* that tracks keystroke patterns over the duration of a typing session. The testing environment in these studies could be either *controlled* or *uncontrolled*, describing whether the users are in a lab or on their personal machines. Additionally, studies can either focus on *authentication* of a single user or *identification* from among a pool of users [1]. They can also study a wide variety of features, depending on researcher interest and the capabilities of the target equipment.

2.1   Desktop Keystroke Dynamics

Desktop computer keystroke dynamics research has a long and rich history. A wide variety of extracted features, learning algorithms, success metrics and testing environments have been studied [1,14]. While more research has been focused on static text that can observe the patterns of password typing, there are a number of studies that focus on uncontrolled environments with dynamic text [2]. These studies, limited by the capabilities of physical keyboards, tend to gather information about typing latencies, cadences, or error rates. Some special keyboards can also provide pressure information, though this is not common in consumer-grade products. With our application, we leverage the additional data gathering power of a touch screen keyboard and can extend beyond features measurable on physical keyboards.

2.2   Mobile Phone Keypress Dynamics

Mobile phones have been getting increased attention over the last few years as security threats develop and risks are further revealed. The access to additional data from their touchscreens defines a research environment with both added benefits (e.g. more data) and added challenges (e.g. greater mobility, more dynamic environments). A number of studies have addressed keypress dynamics on mobile phones, though many use similar feature sets as on desktops [11]. Some, however, including a quite successful one on PINs by Zahid et al., analyze additional features such as the difference in *digraph time* between adjacent and non-adjacent keys [18]. Our work builds on this existing work by focusing on the mobile keypress features not possible on traditional desktops.

2.3   Mobile Phone Side-Channel Inference

Another growing area of research is the ability to leverage the other sensors on mobile phones (notably accelerometers and gyroscopes) to infer keypresses without direct access to keypress data. By measuring the changes in orientation [3], accelerometer readings [13,3], and/or gyroscopes [3], applications with very few special privileges [15] can provide attackers insight into passwords or PINs. Applications posing as games or with other innocuous guises could tap into these sensor channels in the background and infer keypresses. We have internally discussed, though not examined, how a gaming application could generate its own training data through in-game menus. While we focus on the direct analysis of touches, we leverage this area of research to guide the processing of our own orientation data.

2.4   Other Features Used to Aid Authentication

The many sensors and input methods of mobile devices may be used to develop other micro-behavior metrics for authentication. Work on using accelerometer patterns to detect anomalous behavior was done by Zhu et. al. to success in their application *SenSec* [20]. Use of higher-level patterns from call /SMS frequency, ratios of known to unknown numbers, GPS locations and browsing history have been studied by Shi et.al [17]. Additionally, swiping patterns can also be used to differentiate between people, as shown to be a very accurate predictor in *Touchalytics* [6].

3   Microbehavior Modeling of Soft Keyboard Interaction

3.1   Soft Keyboard Interaction

Soft keyboards are a relatively new form of *input method editor* (IME). Many smartphones ship with no physical keyboard, instead opting for keyboards controlled by the touchscreen (e.g. Figure 2). An image of a keyboard appears on screen and users tap the keys they would like to send. Challenges arise, however, because of the lack of physical feedback from buttons. Improper estimates of finger tap locations due to the small keys getting completely covered by fingers in addition to finger drift due to the smooth surface make these keyboards sometimes less appealing to use. However, many of these disadvantages help enable researchers to track these touch patterns over time to build a user profile. We took advantage of these features to build an trial *input method editor* (IME) to gather example user data. This application (implementing a custom KeyboardView for raw touchscreen access) records absolute pointer positioning and size/ pressure data for each finger or stylus. On most Android phones, there can be up to 4 or 5 touchscreen events per keypress, giving us an abundance of data with which to work.

3.2   User Keypress Variations

While typing, users have a variety of different typing rhythms and the physiological traits of their hands, joints and fingertips ensure that no two users type exactly alike. Alongside traditional desktop-like features such as experience level and posture, soft-keyboard typing seems to be influenced by hand size, finger length, fingertip size, muscle development, posture and position, one-handed or two-handed typing, orientation of the phone, user tiredness, coldness of fingers, focus of the user (mobile users are often partially engaged in other activities), and whether the user is walking, standing, sitting, lying down, or riding in a car, bus or subway. Additional influences are size/shape of the phone, screen, and external phone cases. Combined with technology literacy and familiarity with the typing application, real-world analysis of mobile keypress dynamics reveals itself as a significant challenge. We have considered these influencing factors and analyzed the available features on Android phones and have designed a feature set (Section 3.3) to match appropriately.

3.3   Feature Selection

After analyzing the prior research on keyboards as well as the smartphone-specific information described above, we developed our set of features to capture and analyze. These will be used to help train our model and be will analyzed for patterns between users. Later in the paper are a few visualizations of how these features can vary between users.

Location pressed on key is our primary micro-behavior metric and is recorded per key as an ordered pair $(X_{\text{offset}}, Y_{\text{offset}})$, expressed from that key's center.

Length of press from finger down to finger lift, a traditional metric, has much greater variation on mobile phones, but does improve model performance.

A user's *force of press* or *pressure* is available as a unitless value between 0 and 1 on many Android devices [16]. This allows for tracking of metrics such as distributions of *maximum touch pressure*, but is complicated by inconsistent scales between device models.

Similarly, the user's *size of touched area* is also available as a unitless value between 0 and 1 [16].

We can also analyze variability in *size* and *pressure* information within a single keypress. This allows analysis of *pressure and size dynamics* for the user.

Another feature, *drift*, records how much the user's finger moves between pressing down and lifting up and at what angle they slid.

Additionally, with easily available sensor data from accelerometers and gyroscopes, information about *orientation* (where the phone faces while held) could help improve comparisons and anomaly detection. This proved to be challenging to correlate between handsets, but the addition of a calibration session could enable successful consideration of this feature.

4   Application Considerations

4.1   Data Privacy and Security

By collecting so much data about each touch event on the keyboard, we are able to compare a wide variety of features between users and develop an improved model for user authentication. However, much of this information is highly sensitive or confidential. We cannot expect users to willingly use a keylogger on their personal devices and we certainly do not want to expose scores and scores of key sequences in the unfortunate event of server compromise. Given that we do comparisons key-by-key, it was necessary to find an obfuscation strategy that allows us to know which key was pressed, but cannot let someone find out *when* it was pressed. Thus, we remove timestamp information from the keypresses and order them by a cryptographically secure random number generator (Java's SecureRandom class) so that the original sequences are not reorder-able. This, combined with block-level encryption and large-batch HTTPS transfers to our server help protect user data while allowing us access to the information we need.

4.2   Power Consumption

Mobile devices are highly sensitive to power consumption considerations. Users expect that applications not only improve their mobile experience, but do so with limited impact on battery life [7]. It was observed from our users that the soft keyboard application was consuming less than 4 percent of the phone's battery life. For most, it did not even show up in the listing (alongside power hogs like Maps, Music). Further analysis of current draw is needed, but power consumption is markedly low. This will likely increase, however, once the behavioral model computation is done directly on the handset.

4.3   Development Concerns and Programming Challenges

While developing and testing an Android keyboard, a variety of challenges presented themselves:

- Multiple fingers need to be tracked independently. Android represents multi-touch gestures in combined Objects, but fingers in the same gesture must be recorded separately using independent identifiers.
- Phones have different size screens; press locations and offsets need to be scaled.
- The Android operating system has depreciated the high-level construct 'Orientation' as of API level 8, and correlating phone orientation information is very challenging between devices.
- When users intend to press a key—for example 'k'—and accidentally press 'j', we pick up misleading data points about where they tend to press on the 'j' key and miss out on a valuable data point about 'k'. Almost all keys have outliers of this type due to the occlusion of the actual touch location by the rest of the finger [8]. We monitor for users' corrections and modify the 'intended key' appropriately. This enables us to collect typical press information even upon mistakes, and we can analyze which keys are frequently mistakenly pressed.

5   Experimental Design

5.1   User Recruitment

A short recruitment drive resulted in a group of 13 trial users. The users were mostly technology literate students, as well as a few professors. To ensure there were a sufficient number of test users and to encourage natural typing behaviors, our application was designed to closely mirror the features of other android keyboards. We feel that spending time on the user experience side of application development was a worthwhile investment for increased user retention and positive reactions to the typing environment. If users have to spend a long time adjusting to the new system, their early data can be misleading or even counterproductive when developing a training model.

5.2   Data Collection

A three week long collection period resulted the a group of 13 active users contributing a total of roughly 86,000 keypresses (with highly variable contributions from each user) and about 430,000 touch data points. This gives some indication about how much data can be collected in a short period of time, especially when gathering keypress information in all contexts, not just from passwords or controlled phrases.

5.3   Training System Design

When designing learning algorithms, it is very important to ensure good training practices are followed [12]. Model training, validation and testing are important parts of the process and should be considered carefully. When analyzing, user data is split into five sections, the first four randomly sampled from the first two weeks of collection. The final set of testing data is from at least 3 days after the rest (to test in user environments independent from training data). Our results are generated from the 'final testing data.'

1. Training data for primary generative or discriminant models (50% $\simeq$ 3000 keypresses from user, 2000 from each of 3 other random users)
2. Cross validation for primary model (15%)
3. Testing data for model and training data for key-frequency scaling (10%)
4. Cross-validation for key-frequency scaling (10%)
5. Final testing data (15%)

6   Modeling Micro-behavior of Users' Keyboard Interaction

6.1   Discriminant Model

We developed two models for comparison testing between users—each suited for different environments. The method of analysis we used for the results in this paper is offline supervised learning trained with data from other users. While not as scalable as a purely generative version, this has some additional advantages— better non-authorized user recognition, better battery life by reducing on-phone computation, and more securely stored behavioral data (on server rather than directly on phone) [19]. This technique trains small neural networks for each key, using samples of other users' behavior as 'non-authorized user' training examples [5]. A high-level diagram explaining this technique can be seen in Figure 3 and the following paragraph contains a detailed explanation.

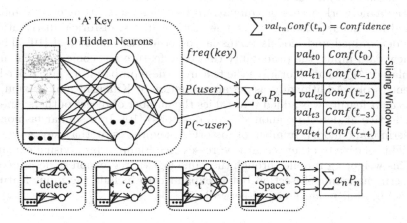

Fig. 3. A high-level diagram of how the discriminant algorithm is designed. Per-key neural networks generate confidence scores weighted against training size. These are aggregated into a combined score for a 5-key sliding window to generate likelihood of non-authorized user.

This model leverages the multi-user data collection environment and takes advantage of the high number of training keypresses. While more computationally expensive, this facilitates much higher recognition rates and fewer errors. Each key with a reasonable amount of training data (we set threshold at 15 keypresses) is trained with its own two-layer, feed-forward neural network. Scaled conjugate gradient back-propagation is the learning method [5]. We used 10 neurons for the one hidden layer to ensure there is sufficient power in the analysis. The performance function is the *mean squared error*, but another performance function checks after training to ensure the network is not ill-fitted. This may ask networks to retrain if they settle in poor local minima (e.g. classifying everything as the regular user). The output from these neural networks are then weighted by how many keypresses were used to train that key. The recent confidence scores are averaged using a simple mean and this is compared against a threshold. The threshold (and the per-key weighting) is set by using a regularized logistic regression algorithm [5]. The cost function for the algorithm is shown in Equation 1. To improve scalability and to allow for non-networked computation, this model will later be replaced with a single-user generative model (described below).

$$\min_\theta \frac{1}{m} \left[\sum_{i=1}^m y^{(i)} \left(-\log h_\theta(x^{(i)}) \right) + (1 - y^{(i)}) \left(-\log(1 - h_\theta(x^{(i)})) \right) \right] + \frac{\lambda}{2m} \sum_{j=1}^n \theta_j^2 \tag{1}$$

6.2   Generative Model

Our intention is to further develop our generative model that can detect anomalies without network access or comparison to other users. A generative model is needed for this approach. For a single user's features, historical distributions can be determined and models (Gaussian or otherwise) developed [10]. Then, upon new data input, the probability that each feature has come from the user is calculated. Aggregated for all of the features, these probabilities give a per-key confidence score. Additionally, as per an evaluation by Killourhy and Maxion, an *outlier count* feature was added that tallies the number of recent outliers (shown to be effective at detecting anomalies on desktops) [10]. In a similar fashion to the discriminant model, number of historical keypresses at that key serves as the weight relative to other recent keypresses. See Figure 4 for a visual explanation. This weighting is done through the same logistic regression as described in the 'discriminant model' section but is expanded to include the input features processed by that model's neural network [5].

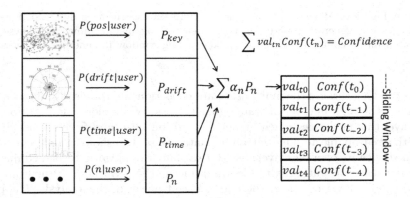

Fig. 4. A high-level diagram of how the generative algorithm is designed. It calculates feature probabilities individually, aggregates them to a confidence score for a single key press and uses a 5-key sliding window to generate likelihood of non-authorized user.

6.3   Feature Distributions

Described below are a few of the key metrics we analyzed for aptness of discrimination. The visualizations are generated from similarly-sized samples representing a variety of users and have been selected to be representative of typical variation of micro-behavior. Note again that we do not have contextual information such as movement speed, time of day, or number of hands typing, so this data is not filtered in that way.

Variability in Keypress Location was predicted to be the best differentiator between users, and it turned out to be correct. Figure 5 displays how there are particular patterns that develop for users on specific keys. 'User 1' is almost always in the bottom right, while 'User 2' is usually right around the vertical center of the key but with wide horizontal variability. Observe also that there are two area of concentration for 'User 2.' Based on some contextual knowledge about that user's behavior we found that the left concentration is from the left finger, while the right concentration is from the right finger. Figure 6 compares 5 different users' press locations on a single key, holding 'User 1' constant for reference.

With the key press location data, we applied a *bivariate Gaussian distribution* for each key. The formula for bivariate covariance is in Equation 2 [5].

$$cov = \frac{1}{n} \sum_{i=1}^{n} (w_i - \bar{w})(w_i - \bar{w})', \qquad (2)$$

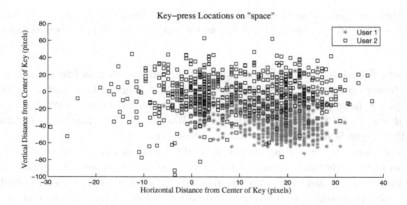

Fig. 5. Two-User Comparison of Keypress Locations on 'spacebar'. Observe how users tend to clump, and how 'User 2' presses in seemingly distinct areas with their left thumb versus right thumb.

Keypress Length, a common metric of authentication on desktops, turned out to be ineffective at discriminating users on mobile devices. While experienced desktop users tend to type faster than inexperienced ones [2], mobile users type in a much wider range of circumstances and at a much wider range of rates. Keypress length does, however, divide users into three general categories: fast, medium, and slow typers. If a user is very consistent, a deviation could reveal an unauthorized user.

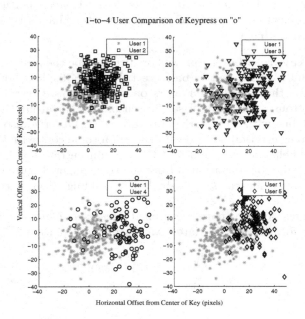

Fig. 6. Quad-comparison of Keypress Locations on 'o'. 'User 1' and the axes are static. This shows how different users have (sometimes widely) varying spreads and centers.

Drift was found to have different angle distributions depending on the user. Due to touchscreen noise, drift is only counted if a finger's last contact is more than 4 pixels from point of first contact. The numerical cutoff is referred to as the *drift threshold*. See Figure 7 for a visualization of drift angle distributions where the origin is normalized location of first contact.

The data for *drift* is by no means normally distributed, but tends to clump into a number of distinct areas for particular users. By grouping angles into a finite number of buckets (akin to the rose histograms below), we can calculate the historical probability of a particular drift direction against which to compare new data. Our formula for such analysis is below:

$$P(drift|user;\theta) = \alpha_{drift} * P(anyDrift|user) * P(\theta|user) \qquad (3)$$

Pressure, Size and Orientation revealed themselves to be rather challenging to manage features. For an individual user it is possible to measure the average and max *pressure* of the finger. It is, however, very challenging to correlate this data between users on different styles of handset; different screen technologies report pressure using different scales.

Additionally, the *size* of a user's finger on the screen is frequently not possible to compare between different phone styles (but can be analyzed for anomalies

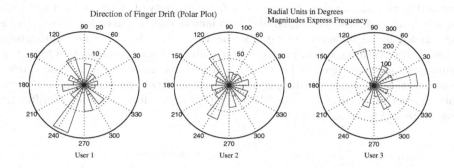

Fig. 7. Comparison of finger *drifts* between users. The center of each circle is the normalized location where the user first pressed down. The angles describe which direction the user drifted (but not how far). The ray lengths are the frequency of drifts in that direction.

for one user). The size is a unit-less value and can vary widely from device to device. Further research on multiple users using identical handsets is required.

Orientation suffers from a similar problem, though it should be possible to ask testing users for a calibration session upon installation. This may allow regularization between devices.

7   User Identification Results

7.1   Success and Error Metrics

When evaluating the success of a model or a process, it is important to define the metrics used. Our primary objective is to identify 'non-authorized users' quickly, accurately, and repeatably. This is essential in creating a functional authentication system. Our other main objective is to minimize how often the primary user is flagged as another user—an inconvenience. For these metrics we define *Detection Rate* as the frequency of successfully detecting 'non-authorized users', *False Rejection Rate* (FAR) as the frequency of flagging the primary user as 'non-authorized' and the *False Acceptance Rate* (FAR) as the frequency of failing to flag a 'non-authorized user' as such [12].

7.2   Attack Detection

Our discriminant algorithm trained on multiple users performed well in testing, detecting a median of 67.7% of simulated 'non-authorized users' within 5 keypresses. Our False Acceptance Rate (FAR) was 32.3% and we had a False Rejection Rate (FRR) of only 4.6%. For longer input sessions of 15 keypresses, our detection rate rose to 86.0% with a FAR of 14.0% and a FRR of only 2.2%. Models were trained with 3000 keypresses from the 'primary user' and 2000 from each of 3 other users. It was then tested against 550 'primary user' keypresses and 500 'non-authorized user' keypresses from a variety of other users. A few keypresses from each user were ignored due to lack of training data for those keys (a potential concern for analyzing symbol-heavy passwords). The 'non-authorized users' in the testing sets were not used for training data. The test data from the primary trainee was from at least 3 days after the training data to ensure independent (though not assuredly distinct) environments. The performance matrix and receiver operating characteristics (ROC) curves (for a number of different users) are in Figure 8.

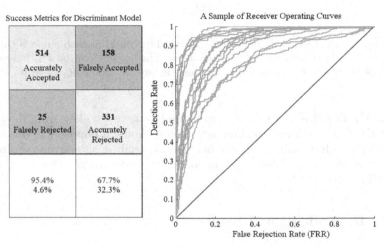

Fig. 8. Testing performance and receiver operating characteristics for discriminant model. 67.7% of simulated 'non-authorized users' were caught within a 5 keypress sliding window with a False Acceptance Rate of 32.3% and a False Rejection Rate of only 4.6%. The ROC curves represent a subset of all tests indicating variability of detection rates between users.

As seen in the ROC curves (a subset of all tests), there is a sizable spread to the recognition rates between users. This needs to be further explored, however it indicates that some users are easier to tell apart than others. Running a model trained on 'User 1' with two different sets of example 'non-authorized users' can generate very different detection rates.

Our results do suffer from a significant hole, however. Because we strip timestamp information from the data before logging, we cannot recreate exact strings to use as testing data. We counter this as best we can by creating each test string with data from a single log file (which typically contain only a few minutes of typing data). Further testing needs to be done on data known to be in ordered strings, however actual keylogging will only be acceptable in more limited environments.

8   Discussion and Next Steps

The next step of this research is to develop an on-device analysis tool that enables a live, learning model of users' behavior and the ability to flag suspicious activity (preferably without requiring network access). This could enable rapid recognition of suspicious activity without network lag, and also improve scalability without requiring additional server resources. The computational load would likely fairly substantial, but because it could be run only while the user is typing, it should not burden the phone's resting battery life.

Additional studies will be necessary to better understand a user's typing dynamics over time and in variable situations. Additional contextual information about phone usage could be used to improve accuracy and the robustness of the algorithm. Moreover, testing environments where users are using unfamiliar phones for the first time will enable direct comparison between unauthorized and primary users and may better reflect attack scenarios.

Collaboration between research groups can also be a highly fertile ground for future work. The groups working on user interface interaction characterization or side-channel keypress inference could be excellent teammates combining expertise on touch information and motion sensor readings. Also, groups looking into the trend towards swipe-based keyboards could leverage some of these techniques to develop similar models. Perhaps individual users' swiping gestures are also unique enough for micro-behavior authentication.

With this micro-behavior information and potential for improved phone security, these kinds of applications should be of great interest to businesses trying to improve "Bring Your Own Device" security policies. A stipulation of private phone usage could be a requirement to use a behavioral-modeling keyboard. Company provided phones could also integrate these features into a semi-customized OS that could analyze any user-level input method.

8.1   Deploying Behavioral Modeling to Secured Mobile Devices

After examining a variety of Android operating system functions and features, it became clear that there are a few security challenges the system still faces. Were behavior-modeling keyboards to be integrated into a public or private Android distribution, our team recommends a few enhancements that could improve device security:

- Weaken the potential for side-channel attacks by disabling sensors while entering text into password fields. This could substantially reduce the chance of reconstructing strings via accelerometer or gyroscope data.
- Require use of the default Android keyboard (or a manufacturer-vetted application) during password or sensitive text entry. Risk from malicious keyboards is likely to grow in the future and users may not carefully read privacy policies or permissions for their applications [15].

9   Conclusion and Future Work

Protecting user devices in mobile, dynamic environments is of essential importance in the academic, business, and personal worlds. We have taken a dramatic step towards developing *passive keyboard authentication* on smartphones. We demonstrated that using these micro-behavior features, we can *passively detect* that a mobile device is being used by a 'non-authorized user' within 5 keypresses 67.7% of the time. This comes with a False Acceptance Rate of 32.3% and a False Rejection Rate of only 4.6%. For longer input sessions of 15 keypresses, our detection rate rose to 86.0% with a False Acceptance Rate of 14.0% and a False Rejection Rate of only 2.2%.

Our long-term objective is to integrate a fully developed *KeySens* application with our team's larger, more inclusive sensor suite, *SenSec*, to provide multi-dimensional pattern recognition features [20]. Accelerometers, gyroscopes, awareness of opened applications, and other such features can help demonstrate the feasibility of an always-aware authentication structure. This larger project also has a technique for completely blocking access to applications and requesting an active authentication if the *confidence score* drops too low. We hope that our work will inspire further research into this subject. Passwords and PINs alone cannot protect mobile users. By deploying them in conjunction with micro-behavior metrics and other authentication techniques, mobile devices can become an ever-safer place in the computing world.

Acknowledgments. This work is supported in part by CyLab at Carnegie Mellon under grants from the Northrop Grumman Cybersecurity Research Consortium and by Cisco under the research award for "Privacy Preserved Personal Big Data Analytics through Fog Computing".

References

1. Banerjee, S.P., Woodard, D.L.: Biometric authentication and identification using keystroke dynamics: A survey. Journal of Pattern Recognition Research (2012)
2. Bergadano, F., Gunetti, D., Picardi, C.: User authentication through keystroke dynamics. ACM Trans. Inf. Syst. Secur. 5(4), 367–397 (2002)
3. Cai, L., Chen, H.: On the practicality of motion based keystroke inference attack. In: Katzenbeisser, S., Weippl, E., Camp, L.J., Volkamer, M., Reiter, M., Zhang, X. (eds.) Trust 2012. LNCS, vol. 7344, pp. 273–290. Springer, Heidelberg (2012)
4. Cherifi, F., Hemery, B., Giot, R., Pasquet, M., Rosenberger, C.: Performance evaluation of behavioral biometric systems. In: Behavioral Biometrics for Human Identification: Intelligent Applications, pp. 57–74. IGI Global (2010)
5. Duda, R.O., Hart, P.E., Stork, D.G.: Multi-layer neural networks. In: Pattern Classification, 2nd edn., vol. 2. John Wiley and Sons, Inc. (2001)
6. Frank, M., Biedert, R., Ma, E., Martinovic, I., Song, D.: Touchalytics: On the applicability of touchscreen input as a behavioral biometric for continuous authentication. IEEE Transactions on Information Forensics and Security 8(1), 136–148 (2013)

7. Gordon, D., Czerny, J., Beigl, M.: Activity recognition for creatures of habit. In: Personal and Ubiquitous Computing, pp. 1–17 (2013)
8. Holleis, P., Huhtala, J., Häkkilä, J.: Studying applications for touch-enabled mobile phone keypads. In: Proceedings of the 2nd International Conference on Tangible and Embedded Interaction, TEI 2008, pp. 15–18. ACM, New York (2008)
9. Jain, A., Hong, L., Pankanti, S.: Biometric identification. Commun. ACM 43(2), 90–98 (2000)
10. Killourhy, K.S., Maxion, R.A.: Comparing anomaly-detection algorithms for keystroke dynamics. In: IEEE/IFIP International Conference on Dependable Systems Networks, DSN 2009, pp. 125–134 (2009)
11. Maiorana, E., Campisi, P., González-Carballo, N., Neri, A.: Keystroke dynamics authentication for mobile phones. In: Proceedings of the 2011 ACM Symposium on Applied Computing, SAC 2011, pp. 21–26. ACM, New York (2011)
12. International Standards Organization. Biometric performance testing and reporting (2006)
13. Owusu, E., Han, J., Das, S., Perrig, A., Zhang, J.: Accessory: password inference using accelerometers on smartphones. In: Proceedings of the Twelfth Workshop on Mobile Computing Systems & Applications, HotMobile 2012, pp. 9:1–9:6. ACM, New York (2012)
14. Peacock, A., Ke, X., Wilkerson, M.: Typing patterns: a key to user identification. IEEE Security Privacy 2(5), 40–47 (2004)
15. Android Open Source Project. Android security overview
16. Android Open Source Project. Touch devices
17. Shi, E., Niu, Y., Jakobsson, M., Chow, R.: Implicit authentication through learning user behavior. In: Burmester, M., Tsudik, G., Magliveras, S., Ilić, I. (eds.) ISC 2010. LNCS, vol. 6531, pp. 99–113. Springer, Heidelberg (2011)
18. Zahid, S., Shahzad, M., Khayam, S.A., Farooq, M.: Keystroke-based user identification on smart phones. In: Kirda, E., Jha, S., Balzarotti, D. (eds.) RAID 2009. LNCS, vol. 5758, pp. 224–243. Springer, Heidelberg (2009)
19. Zhu, J., Hu, H., Hu, S., Wu, P., Zhang, J.Y.: Mobile behaviometrics: Models and applications. In: Proceedings of the Second IEEE/CIC International Conference on Communications in China (ICCC), Xi'An, China, August 12-14 (2013)
20. Zhu, J., Wu, P., Wang, X., Perrig, A., Hong, J., Zhang, J.Y.: Sensec: Mobile application security through passive sensing. In: Proceedings of International Conference on Computing, Networking and Communications (ICNC 2013), San Diego, CA, USA, January 28-31 (2013)

A Study of Graphical Password for Mobile Devices

Xiaoyuan Suo

Department of Math and Computer Science,
Webster University,
Saint Louis, MO, USA
xiaoyuansuo51@webtser.edu

Abstract. The objective of this project is to conduct a comprehensive research into the usability; design and security of graphical password on touch screen devices. We address the design limitation of touch screen devices and possible solutions. We also propose a simple graphical password scheme designed specifically for touch screen devices. Further, expert reviews and usability studies were used to explore user interactions in order to gain a more complete understanding on the potentials to improve the graphical password design for touch screen mobile devices.

Keywords: Graphical password, iPad/iPhone app, Mobile app design, Mobile.

1   Introduction

Mobile device, especially touch screen interface designs have attracted rising attention in recent years; devices such as ATM (automated teller machines), ticket machine, PDA (personal digital assistant), have been widely used in various occasions. Lately, touch screen devices are technologically becoming more accurate, usable and popular in any size; such as smart phones, or Apple's iPad, iPhone, and iPod touch [1] etc. Media report estimates that touch screen devices will account for more than 80 percent of mobile sales in North America by 2013[2].

Graphical passwords have been proposed as a possible alternative to text-based schemes, motivated partially by psychological studies [3] that show human can remember pictures better than text. Graphical password techniques include recall-based click password (e.g. imposing background image so user can click on various locations on the image), and recognize-based selection password (e.g. selecting images or icons from an image pool). In particular, recall-based click passwords have received much more attention in recent years[4]. However, very little studies have been done on graphical password on touch screen mobile devices.

In this work, we propose a novel graphical password scheme designed specifically for touch screen devices. Since touch screen devices dominate the mobile world, this project has the potential to influence design of mobile user experiences. The project is built on iOS platform using Objective C, and deployed as an iPad/iPhone application. This application is designed for research purposes only. To our knowledge, this is the first attempt in studying graphical password design scheme on touch screen devices.

G. Memmi and U. Blanke (Eds.): MobiCASE 2013, LNICST 130, pp. 202–214, 2014.

This study directly concerns user experiences and effective designs of touch screen applications.

Further, expert reviews and usability studies were used to explore user interactions in order to gain a more complete understanding on the following:

a. *Approaches to overcome limitations of a touch screen computer for graphical password designs.*
   Touch screens have special limitations such as: user's finger, hand and arm can obscure part of the screen; and the human finger as a pointing device has very low "resolution". It is also difficult to point at targets that are smaller than the users' finger width.

b. *The relationship between user password choices and the complexity of the background image.*
   The complexity of an image is defined as a combinational quantitative measure of the number of objects presented, the number of major colors, and the familiarity of the image to users and other factors. Careful selected background images can enhance effective graphical password design. The study highlights the vulnerability of click based graphical passwords. As a result, we discuss several graphical password attacking methods based on the choice of pictures. This study aims to achieve better balance between security and usability of click based graphical passwords through better choices of background images.

c. *The relationship between background image choice and successful authentication rate.*
   Successful rate, in this case, is defined as the number of successful authentications versus the number of trials within a critical time frame.

d. *The relationship between tolerance rate and successful rate.*
   The tolerance rate is defined as a number of pixels permitted to be selected around the original selection. A properly selected tolerance rate has direct impact on user experiences.

e. *Security concerns of using graphical password for touch screen devices*
   Although graphical password theoretically provides a large amount of password space, usability studies showed the number of "usable clicks" are significantly less.

f. *Assess the future of graphical password for touch screen devices.*
   This process involves preliminary assessment of potential for using graphical password on touch screen devices.

2   Touch Screen Mobile Device Design Limitations

One difficulty for interface design on mobile devices is lack of screen space caused by their small size [5]. Small displays and multiple inputs, especially with the presence of a figure, require users to register click-based password with pinpoint accuracy.

2.1   Screen Precision

The Touch-Screen device size and the Touch-Screen's effective area affect the Touch-Screen keyboard design. The device sizes can be small, medium, or large.

Small Touch-Screen devices[6], such as mobile and smart phones, Personal Digital Assistants (PDAs), and handheld computers, have a smaller Touch-Screen area and smaller onscreen objects. Finger use has become more popular in the research community since Apple's iPhone and iPod touch were released. In the recent years, researchers started to examine text entry specifically for tabletop displays [7].

The work by Parhi et al. [6]is presented to determine optimal target sizes for one-handed thumb use of mobile handheld devices equipped with a touch screen using a two phase study. The study primarily focused on small sized screen. Phase 1 of this study is intended to determine size recommendation for widgets used for single-target tasks, such as activating buttons, radio buttons and checkboxes; and phase 2 is trying to evaluate required key sizes for widgets used for text or numeric entry. The study concluded that no key size smaller than 9.6mm would be recommended for serial tapping tasks, such as data or numeric entry. A 9.2 mm target size for discrete tasks would be sufficiently large for one-handed thumb use on touch screen devices.

Investigations by Sears, A., et al. [8] showed the effect keyboard size has on typing speed and error rates for touch screen keyboards using the lift-off strategy. A cursor appeared when users touched the screen and a key was selected when they lifted their finger from the screen. Four keyboard sizes were investigated ranging from 24.6 cm to 6.8 cm wide. Results indicated novice users can type approximately 10 words per minute on smallest keyboard and 20 words per minute on the largest. Experienced users improved to 21 words per minute on smallest keyboard and 32 words per minute.

Work by Colle and Hiszem [9] estimates the smallest key size that would not degrade performance or user satisfaction. The results showed participants entry times were longer and errors were higher for smaller key sizes, but no significant differences were found between key sizes of 20-25mm. participants also preferred 20 mm keys to smaller keys, and they were indifferent between 20 and 25 mm keys. The work concludes a key size of 20 mm was found to be sufficiently large for land-on key entry. [9]

Three experiments conducted by Lee and Zhai focused on the operation of soft buttons (either using a stylus or fingers). The study showed button size affects performance, particularly when buttons are smaller than 10 mm. Styli can more accurately handle smaller buttons and they depend less on synthetic feedback than fingers do, but they can be lost easily and require an acquisition step that bare fingers do not. The two types of touch sensors explored, capacitive and resistive, afford very different behavior but only subtle performance difference. The first can be operated by fingers with very sensitive response, but is more error prone. [10]

Work by Brewster [5] describes a small pilot study and two formal experiments that investigate the usability of sonically-enhanced buttons of different sizes. An experimental interface was created that ran on a 3Com Palm III mobile computer and used a simple calculator-style interface to enter data. The buttons of the calculator were changed in size between 4x4, 8x8 and 16x16 pixels and used a range of different types of sound from basic to complex. Results showed that sounds significantly improved usability for both standard and small button sizes – more data could be entered with sonically-enhanced buttons and subjective workload reduced.

More sophisticated sounds that presented more information about the state of the buttons were shown to be more effective than the standard Palm III sounds. The results showed that if sound was added to buttons then they could be reduced in size from 16x16 to 8x8 pixels without much loss in quantitative performance. This reduction in size, however, caused a significant increase in subjective workload. Results also showed that when a mobile device was used in more realistic situation (whilst walking outside) usability was significantly reduced (with increased workload and less data entered) than when used in a usability laboratory. These studies show that sound can be beneficial for usability and that care must be taken to do testing in realistic environments to get a good measure of mobile device usability.

2.2   Techniques to Improve Screen Input Precision

When using a touch screen device, the user's finger, hand and arm can obscure part of the screen. Also, the human finger as a pointing device has very low "resolution". These limitations have been realized and tackled before--mostly notably by Sears, Shneiderman and colleagues [8, 11]. Their basic technique, called *Take-Off*, provides a cursor above the user's fingertip with a fixed offset when touching the screen. The user drags the cursor to a desired target and lifts the finger (takes off) to select the target objects. They achieved considerable success with this technique for targets between finger size and 4 pixels. Instead of using a bare finger, in some cases the user may use a stylus (pen) to interact with touch screens. A stylus is a much "sharper" pointer than a fingertip, but its resolution may still not be as good as a mouse cursor.

Work by Diller [12] studied various techniques to improve input areas of touch screen mobile devices; in this work, multiple approaches and studies were discussed. While these studies were limited to relatively large targets, Garwin and Levine reported single pixel accuracy when using a laser scanned touch screen. Selection time and error rate data were not reported. [13]

The goal of our work is to introduce a graphical password design for touch-screen devices and provide a study on the usability of such an application design. We hope to provide fellow researchers and practitioners in the field with a more complete guidance to achieve more usable touch screen device designs. Our work differs from this work by having a more comprehensive discussion and classification of techniques to increase accuracy of touch screen devices.

In addition to analyzing properties of tabletop displays and summarizing existing text entry methods for tabletop use; Work by Go et al. [14] also proposed a new keyboard design. In addition to the new design, the work primarily discussed touch screen keyboard use for finger typing; the analysis is from five aspects: screen size, touch screen keyboard types, number of keys, typing devices, and technique. Our work will focus more on the precision of Touch-Screen input.

Many researchers have shown the benefits of tactile feedback for touch screen widgets in all metrics: performance, usability and user experience [15-22]. Koskinen et. al, [22] showed people perceive some tactile feedbacks more pleasant than others when virtual buttons are pressed with fingers on a touch screen.

3   A Novel Scheme of Graphical Password on Touch Screen Mobile Device

The architecture of our novel graphical password scheme is shown in figure 1. The flow chart is based on two main logic paths, namely, registration and authentication. Users are given a database of images to select from; the images are categorized into different sections to improve user experiences.

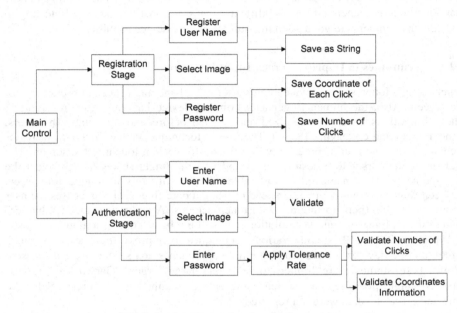

Fig. 1. Registration and authentication process

In the screenshot shown in figure 2, two categories are shown: personal images and natural images. The user is also given the choice of importing images from the personal collections.

During the registration stage, user is required to enter a user name and select an image first. The size of each image is adjusted to fit into the screen. After the image is loaded onto the screen, user will be asked to click on various places on the image. The sequence of clicks, with an X and Y coordinates, is recorded and saved along with the user name and choice of image into our database.

During the authentication stage, user will first be asked to enter a user name and select their registered image. Unless the user name and the choice of images match those in the database, the authentication will fail. When the image is loaded, user will be allowed to tap the image to authenticate. During this process, user will be allowed to select a tolerance rate, which means they can tap within a circle of pixels rather than the specific pixel they pre-selected.

Fig. 2. Screen shot of graphical password on iPad

4   Analysis and Lessons Learned from User Studies

In usability experiments conducted with a group of 25 users recruited from information technology or IT education related fields, the successful authentication rate of our scheme is more than 80%.

4.1   Click Recognition

We encourage each user to register at least 5 different clicks to increase security measures of a particular graphical password. Each click has a few asscociated values, namely, tolerance rate and coordinate.

In figure 4, the 5 dots represent 5 different clicks. The three authentication-clicks, A, A_2 and A_f represents two accepted authentications and one failure authentication respectively. It is quite obvious that $A_2(x_{a2}, y_{a2})$ belongs to the tolerance region of P2. However, $A(x_a, y_a)$ could potentially belong to either P1 or P2. The calculation is done using the logic shown in the figure below. In this particular case, since $D_1 < D_2$, $A(x_a, y_a)$ is a match to pre-registered click point-P_1.

$$D_1 = \sqrt{(x_1 - x_a)^2 + (y_1 - y_a)^2}$$
$$D_2 = \sqrt{(x_2 - x_a)^2 + (y_2 - y_a)^2}$$

$$if\ (D_1 > D_2)||(D_1 < T_1)$$
$$P_2$$
$$else$$
$$P_1$$

Fig. 3. Method to determine the authentication, when a particular authentication click falls into both regions

$A_f(x_f, y_f)$ is a false click in this case, since it's not within the tolerance region of either pre-registered click.

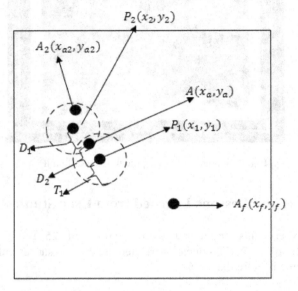

Fig. 4. P1 and P2 are the pre-registered clicks. $A_2(x_{a2}, y_{a2})$, $A(x_a, y_a)$ and $A_f(x_f, y_f)$ are the authentication clicks. D values represent the distance between two clicks. The dashed circular regions represent the tolerance regions. T1 represents the radius of the circular tolerance region.

4.2   The Choice of Tolerance Rate

The tolerance rate is defined as a number of pixels permitted to be selected around the original selection. A properly selected tolerance rate has direct impact on user experiences. The bigger the tolerance rate, the easier the user task is. At the same time, a bigger tolerance rate permits a bigger chance of educated guess. To balance security and usability, it is noted that a better tolerance rate is essential. After a brief user study, we found a tolerance rate bigger than 30 pixels is preferred among all users. When the tolerance rate is set below 30 pixels, the failure rate significantly increases. The following figure demonstrates how different tolerance rate affect the authentication failure rate.

Fig. 5. As the tolerance rate increases, the percentage of successes also increases

4.3   Effective Password Space Analysis

In this section, we introduce a term "Effective Password Space". In a touch pad or similar electronic devices that rely on finger touches or a hand-held tool for input, effective password space should be smaller than the touch pad screen size. Touch screens have special limitations such as: user's finger, hand and arm can obscure part of the screen; and the human finger as a pointing device has very low "resolution". It is also difficult to point at targets that are smaller than the users' finger width. It is generally assumed that touch input cannot be accurate because of the fat finger problem, i.e., the softness of the fingertip combined with the occlusion of the target by the finger [12]. In the experiment conducted; we required user to register 5 non-overlapping points as their graphical password.

Studies have shown using a stylus pen or computer aided input device would potentially achieve an ideal accuracy of 1 pixels square [14], but the usability of such an approach remains a question. In particular, selection time and error rate data were not reported under this scheme and this mechanism was reported to be impractical to carry out in regular users' daily life.

It also should be noted that "tolerance rate" is also a key factor in determination of effective password space. As shown from the previous section, a tolerance area should be set to accommodate the usability of the system. In the equation below,

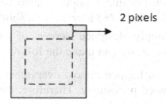

Fig. 6. Total effective password space for a touch screen, assuming the pressing area is 4 pixels square

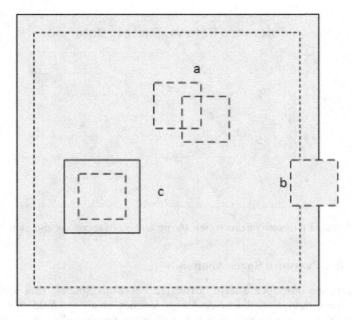

Fig. 7. Different touches on a touchpad

password space or the number of possible clicks can be defined in two possibilities (where n and m are the length and width of a particular screen in number of pixels):

$$password\ space = \begin{cases} 1, & if\ n \leq 4\ or\ m \leq 4 \\ (n-4)*(m-4), & if\ n > 4\ or\ m > 4 \end{cases}$$

There are typically three different cases for user touches, the first case, as shown in the figure above (a), two touches are overlapped. This is an illegal case of selection, since the overlapped region can belong to either touch. The second case (b) is very unlikely to happen, since part of the touch area would be outside of the touch screen. As a result, we conclude that the effective password space would be the inner dashed region, in another word, the difference of the actual touch screen size and the 2 pixels width side along each side. (c) is a legal registration in this case; the solid lines represents tolerance regions.

In the case of iPad, which became a popular hand-held touch pad device since April 2010, the screen size is $1024 \times 768\ pixels$. In a short experiment we conducted with users, we chose a simply designed screen of 16 rows and 12 columns, representing a total of 192 pixels; we can make the following calculations:

1. The first figure press can happen almost everywhere on the screen, except the edge areas as we discussed previously. Therefore, the possibility is 140—minus the edge pixels.
2. To calculate the second finger press possibility, we wrote a very simple program to statistically calculate the overall-possibility based on the first press's location.

As we mentioned before, first press has 140 possibilities. After measuring 140 different possibilities, the possibility of second press is close to 131 possible locations in average.

3. The third finger press is relatively harder to calculate. There should be four different types finger presses in general. The likelihood of each finger press is similar. After a brief calculation, we found 122 possible areas for the third finger press in average (as shown in figure 6).

4. When the similar rules applied, 113 possible areas are found for the fourth finger press. And 104 possible areas are found for the fifth finger press.

5. In total, we had a possibility of $140 \times 131 \times 122 \times 113 \times 104$ password space—fairly large, but not sufficiently large enough to prevent brutal force search. After all, 2.6×10^{10} is still a finite number that can be cracked by brutal force attack.

In fact, applications for touch screen devices all suffer "fat-finger" problem. We performed an experiment with our users on a 850×650 screen with simple white background, and no assistance from any commercial software. We then measured the pixel size of 41 sparsely distributed finger presses made by our users. The average size was 67.9 pixels; the smallest pixel size was 6 and the largest was 213; with most sizes found between 10 and 100.

While these studies were limited to relatively large targets, In an extreme case, where user can achieve the minimal figure pressing area of 4 pixels square, the effective password space has been significantly reduced, although not dramatically. In the average case of user selecting 5 different regions as their graphical password, none of the 5 regions should have overlap. Studies have shown using a stylus pen or computer aided input device would potentially achieve an ideal accuracy of 1 pixels square [13], but the usability of such approach remains to be a question. In particular, Selection time and error rate data were not reported under this scheme, other than the fact this mechanism is impractical to carry out in regular users' daily life. It also should be noted that "tolerance rate" is also a key factor in determination of effective password space. Typically, a tolerance area should be set to accommodate the usability of the system, when tolerance rates are too high, users end up with less effective password space, and vice versa.

With all factors discussed, effective graphical password space for touch screen devices is indeed very small.

4.4   Background Image Selection vs. User Experiences

The complexity of an image is defined as a combinational quantitative measure of the number of objects presented, the number of major colors, and the familiarity of the image to users and other factors. Careful selected background images can enhance effective graphical password design. The study highlights the vulnerability of click based graphical passwords. As a result, we discuss several graphical password attacking methods based on the choice of pictures. This study aims to achieve better balance between security and usability of click based graphical passwords through better choices of background images. Successful rate, in this case, is defined as the number of successful authentications versus the number of trials within a critical time frame.

Users were given the option of using their personal pictures for background. In the presence of a background image, it is arguable if the password space will remain its complete full-size. Users do have significant preference when it comes to different background images. In another word, background images reduce password space; yet regular users cannot live without background images. [23]

Complexity of the background image directly affects the usability of the graphical password. Some of the factors that define the image complexity are listed below:

1. Colors: We cannot always provide the user with meaningful pictures. When the graphical password is generated in a semi-automatic fashion, color can play a practical role.

2. Objects: Objects in the image are another. Face recognition [24] is one type of graphical password that uses objects as its main theme. Depend on the size of the object and the proportions the object occupancy compared to the entire image, user may only able to focus on one or a very limited number of objects at a time.

3. Location and Shapes: There can be two types of shapes in a graphical password images: the shape of the objects in an image, or the shape formatted by patterns of clicks.

4.5   Security Concerns

Relatively little study of usability has been done for graphical passwords. In addition, as Cranor, et al.[25] noted, little work has been done to study the security of graphical passwords as well as possible attacking methods. In fact, some recent studies have shown that there are in fact unintentional patterns in user created graphical passwords. In reality, security and usability[23, 26]of graphical passwords are often at odds with each other, but both factors are critical to all authentication systems.

Chiasson et, al [27] found out that click-based passwords follow distinct patterns; and patterns occurs independently of the background image. Our brief user study showed user passwords do not always fall into patterns; click patterns actually occur only when the complexity of an image is higher than the tolerance. In fact, user studies proved patterns occur much less frequently than the other factors we mentioned above.

Some other [28-31] work suggested hot-spots occurs in click-based password. The hot-spot analysis work by Julie Thorpe [31] suggested that by using an entirely automated attack based on image processing techniques, 36% of user passwords within 2^{31} guesses (or 12% within 2^{16} guesses) can be broken in one instance, and 20% within 2^{33} guesses (or 10% within 2^{18} guesses) can be broken in a second instance. We believe semi-automatic methods with the help from human will enhance the attack.

5   Conclusion

Expert review of the system revealed graphical password for mobile touch screen devices to be effective and promising. During the debriefing following the experiment, experts proposed improving graphical targets through a variety of design innovations that may be avenues for future research. Expert reviews and usability experiments indicate graphical passwords have potentials to work well with touch screen devices.

Through experimental examination of touch sizes, tolerance areas and recall basked passwords, our scheme produced successful authentication rates of greater than 80%. This study contributes additional data to the field of graphical password research.

References

1. Apple, http://www.apple.com
2. Gartner, Gartner Says Touchscreen Mobile Device Sales Will Grow 97 Percent in 2010 (2010), http://www.gartner.com/it/page.jsp?id=1313415
3. Shepard, R.N.: Recognition memory for words, sentences, and pictures. Journal of Verbal Learning and Verbal Behavior, 156–163 (1967)
4. Wiedenbeck, S., et al.: PassPoints: Design and longitudinal evaluation of a graphical password system. International Journal of Human Computer Studies (to appear)
5. Brewster, S.: Overcoming the Lack of Screen Space on Mobile Computers. Personal and Ubiquitous Computing 6(3) (2002)
6. Parhi, P., Karlson, A., Bederson, B.: Target Size Study for One-Handed Thumb Use on Small Touchscreen Devices. In: MobileHCI 2006, Helsinki, Finland (2006)
7. Hinrichs, U., et al.: Examination of Text-Entry Methods for Tabletop Displays in Horizontal Interactive Human-Computer Systems. In: Second Annual IEEE International Workshop on TABLETOP 2007, Newport, RI, pp. 105–112 (2007)
8. Sears, A., et al.: Investigating Touchscreen Typing: The effect of keyboard size on typing speed. Behaviour & Information Technology 12, 17 (1992)
9. Colle, H., Hiszem, K.: Standing at a kiosk: Effects of key size and spacing on touch screen numeric keypad performance and user preference. Ergonomics 47(13), 17 (2004)
10. Lee, S., Zhai, S.: The Performance of Touch Screen Soft Buttons. In: CHI 2009, Boston, MA (2009)
11. Sears, A.: Improving Touchscreen Keyboards: Design issues and a comparison with other devices. Interacting with Computers 3(3), 253 (1991)
12. Diller, F.: Target Practice: Current Efforts to Improve Input Areas on Touchscreen Mobile Devices (2010)
13. Garwin, R.L., Levine, J.L.: Light-sensitive pen to substitute for finger in laser-scanned touch screen. IBM Technical Disclosure Bulletin 32(3B), 11 (1989)
14. Go, K., Endo, Y.: Touchscreen Software Keyboard for Finger Typing. Advances in Human-Computer Interaction (2008)
15. Poupyrev, I., Maruyama, S.: Tactile interfaces for small touch screens. In: 16th Annual ACM Symposium on User Interface Software and Technology, New York, NY (2003)
16. Lee, J.C., et al.: Haptic pen: a tactile feedback stylus for touch screens. In: 17th Annual ACM Symposium on User Interface Software and Technology (2004)

17. Fukumoto, M., Sugimura, T.: Active click: tactile feedback for touch panels. In: CHI 2001 Extended Abstracts on Human Factors in Computing (2001)
18. Nashel, A., Razzaque, S.: Tactile virtual buttons for mobile devices. In: CHI 2003 Extended Abstracts on Human Factors in Computing Systems (2003)
19. Brewster, S., Chohan, F., Brown, L.: Tactile feedback for mobile interactions. In: SIGCHI Conference on Human Factors in Computing Systems (2007)
20. Hoggan, E., Brewster, S.A., Johnston, J.: Investigating the effectiveness of tactile feedback for mobile touchscreens. In: Annual SIGCHI Conference on Human Factors in Computing Systems (2008)
21. Poupyrev, I., Maruyama, S., Rekimoto, J.: Ambient touch: designing tactile interfaces for handheld devices. In: 15th Annual ACM Symposium on User Interface Software and Technology (2002)
22. Koskinen, E., Kaaresoja, T., Laitinen, P.: Feel-good touch: finding the most pleasant tactile feedback for a mobile touch screen button. In: 10th International Conference on Multimodal Interfaces (2008)
23. Suo, X., Zhu, Y., Owen, G.S.: The Impact of Image Choices on the Usability and Security of Click Based Graphical Passwords. In: Bebis, G., et al. (eds.) ISVC 2009, Part II. LNCS, vol. 5876, pp. 889–898. Springer, Heidelberg (2009)
24. Davis, D., Monrose, F., Reiter, M.K.: On user choice in graphical password schemes. In: Proceedings of the 13th Usenix Security Symposium, San Diego, CA (2004)
25. Cranor, L., Garfinkel, S.: Secure or Usable? Security & Privacy 2(5), 2 (2004)
26. Suo, X., Zhu, Y., Owen, G.S.: Graphical Password: A Survey. In: Proceedings of Annual Computer Security Applications Conference (ACSAC), Tucson, Arizona. IEEE (2005)
27. Chiasson, S., et al.: User interface design affects security: Patterns in click-based graphical passwords (2008)
28. Chiasson, S., et al.: A Second Look at the Usability of Click-based Graphical Passwords. In: SOUPS (2007)
29. Dirik, A.E., Menon, N., Birget, J.C.: Modeling user choice in the PassPoints graphical password scheme. In: SOUPS. ACM (2007)
30. Gołofit, K.: Click Passwords Under Investigation. In: Biskup, J., López, J. (eds.) ESORICS 2007. LNCS, vol. 4734, pp. 343–358. Springer, Heidelberg (2007)
31. Thorpe, J., van Oorschot, P.C.: Human-Seeded Attacks and Exploiting Hot-Spots in Graphical Passwords. In: 16th USENIX Security Symposium, Boston, MA (2007)

A Cloudlet-Based Proximal Discovery Service for Machine-to-Machine Applications*

Jonas Michel and Christine Julien

Department of Electrical & Computer Engineering,
The University of Texas at Austin,
Austin, Texas USA
{jonasrmichel,c.julien}@mail.utexas.edu

Abstract. Many of today's applications attempt to connect mobile users with resources available in their immediate surroundings. Existing approaches for discovering available resources are either *centralized*, providing a single point of lookup somewhere in the cloud or *ad hoc*, requiring mobile devices to directly connect to other nearby devices. In this paper, we explore an approach based on *cloudlets*, marrying these two approaches to reflect both the proximity requirements of the applications and the dynamic nature of the resources. We present the design and implementation of a cloudlet-based proximal discovery service, solving key technical challenges along the way. We then use real world data traces to demonstrate, evaluate, and benchmark our service and compare it to a completely centralized approach. We find that, in supporting highly localized queries, our service outperforms the centralized approach without significantly affecting the quality of the discovery results.

Keywords: location-based discovery, pervasive computing.

1 Introduction

Pervasive computing demands the ability to discover locally available resources, whether data shared by nearby users or digital capabilities in the surroundings. More specifically, applications require a location-based discovery service that, when provided a user's or device's location, can "look up" nearby (digital) resources. In this paper, we focus specifically on the need to discover resources relevant in a particular user's space and time; we are interested in finding digital resources that are available in the user's *here and now*. Existing approaches fall into one of two general categories: (*i*) *centralized indexing* approaches that provide (at least abstractly) a single point of lookup for location-based discovery or (*ii*) *local broadcast* approaches that rely on ad hoc discovery among peers.

The dynamics of pervasive computing environments make the approaches from mobile ad hoc networks less desirable simply due to the high degree of churn in

---

* This work was funded, in part, by the National Science Foundation, Grant #CNS-0844850 and a Google Research Award. The views and conclusions herein are those of the authors and do not necessarily reflect the views of the sponsoring agencies.

G. Memmi and U. Blanke (Eds.): MobiCASE 2013, LNICST 130, pp. 215–232, 2014.

information. These dynamics force continuous updates to the distributed structures that overlay the mobile ad hoc network to support persistent discovery. On the other hand, as the density of available smart devices (both carried by users and embedded in environments) increases, completely centralized approaches fail to scale. The obvious next step is to take the best of both approaches, distributing the centralized index in a way that is reflective of both the proximity requirements and dynamic nature of location-based discovery. This is precisely the strategy employed by distributed spatial indexing (e.g., Peer-Tree [6] and P2PR-Tree [21]) in which the universe is decomposed into a hierarchy of regions; each node in a peer-to-peer (P2P) network is responsible for managing data concerning a region in the distributed index. These approaches assume that nodes are capable of arranging themselves in a connected network topology using ad hoc wireless communication [6] or a global addressing scheme [21]. We make no such assumptions—indeed, supporting the formation of such a P2P network is a motivating scenario of our work.

Our location-based discovery service creates *cloudlets* that are responsible for maintaining knowledge about the digital resources available in specific regions of space. A cloudlet is a trusted computing resource with good Internet connectivity that is available for use by physically nearby mobile devices over a wireless LAN [33]. Essentially, a cloudlet has the same responsibilities as the cloud—it hosts a service that performs the significant computation required by a mobile application while enabling the mobile device to act as a thin client with respect to the service. Cloudlets differ from the cloud in that they are inherently within close physical proximity to the mobile devices that utilize their resources, which reduces network latency and jitter and mitigates peak bandwidth demands [33]. Consequently, cloudlets service fewer users and keep data close to where it originates. Satyanarayanan et al. envision cloudlets to satisfy the requirements necessary to transform many areas of human activity through classes of mobile computing that "seamlessly augment users' cognitive abilities via compute-intensive capabilities" (e.g., speech recognition, natural language processing, computer vision, augmented reality, planning, decision making, etc.).

We leverage cloudlets to implement proximal discovery for pervasive computing applications that operate in densely populated and highly mobile physical spaces. A cloudlet-based approach for co-located peer discovery becomes seriously advantageous, perhaps even necessary, when applications need to operate in spaces with hundreds of thousands of devices per square mile (e.g., as in the Internet of Things [1]). Consider the following scenario on a university campus:

It's the first week of the semester and construction efforts on several university buildings are behind schedule, requiring paths and building entrances be temporarily blocked off as necessary by construction crews. In an effort help students navigate campus and discover nearby friends, interest groups, and special first-week events amongst these sporadic closures, the university has deployed a mobile application that leverages the campus' cloudlet infrastructure. The app enables student users to advertise themselves, their location, and student-run events. Additionally, special privileges have been given to construction teams' foremen who may indicate pathways and building entrances as "closed" or "open" via the mobile app. As students and construction foremen move about campus, their devices periodically push this information to the cloudlet responsible for the region of the campus they are in via the university's wireless network. Ultimately, this changing and location-dependent information is displayed on the app's "live" campus map that dynamically updates as fresh data is received from nearby cloudlets.

One could also envision such an application to be used to deliver location-dependent messages. For example, if a student wished to form an impromptu study group, she could employ the cloudlet service to alert nearby classmates of her availability and location. Alternatively, the university may wish to use the application to deliver location-dependent emergency alerts or requests for ground-level information (e.g., pictures of a particular crowded area as described in [32]) if, for example, there were a dangerous suspect or a missing person.

A cloudlet-based proximal discovery service performs the same duties as would a location-based service that may exist in the cloud—the service provides extra knowledge about a user's physical surroundings. However, by harnessing a cloudlet infrastructure, data is kept geographically close to where it will most likely be relevant, rather than in a distant cloud under a third party's administration. Moreover, each cloudlet only serves tens to hundreds of users who experience crisp interaction with the cloudlet service due to cloudlets' physical proximity and one-hop network latency. Our example scenario also teases out a key technical challenge: as users move, they migrate between *administrative regions*, the physical regions managed by cloudlets. Devices that are on the *fringe* of two bordering administrative regions may fail to discover other devices beyond the region's boundary, though they may be physically nearby. Some means of synchronization between bordering cloudlets is therefore necessary.

We present the architecture, implementation, and API for a cloudlet-based proximal discovery service that leverages a physically dispersed infrastructure of cloudlets, each of which provides the service for a specific geographic region. The distributed nature of a cloudlet infrastructure mitigates the congestion and resource contention of a centralized cloud-based mechanism. Moreover, the physical and logical proximity of cloudlets to the clients they serve results in low one-hop network latency. These factors combined provide the support required by mobile pervasive applications targeting densely populated physical spaces. A key technical challenge in the design of a cloudlet-based proximal discovery service is the synchronization of information at the boundaries of bordering or overlapping cloudlet administrative regions. As users and devices move around, they inevitably migrate between cloudlets' administrative regions. An application running on a device within the fringe of one of these ambiguous spaces may request information that exists *beyond* the administrative boundary of its respective cloudlet's administrative region, though the geographic relevance of that information may be physically close. We evaluate our service's performance in terms of the system-level *cost* and the *quality* with which it performs proximal neighbor discovery under various bordering cloudlet synchronization strategies.

2   Related Work

Existing location-dependent resource discovery approaches can generally be classified into two categories: centralized methods, which rely on a single index to resolve spatial queries, and distributed methods, which can further be decomposed into infrastructure-dependent and infrastructure*less* (i.e., ad hoc) approaches.

Centralized Location-Dependent Discovery. Geographic information systems (GIS) have emerged over the last few decades out of advancements in both database management systems (DBMS) and positioning and tracking systems (e.g., GPS) (see [26] for an excellent survey of this work) and are now an industry standard. A GIS is a collection of software geared at efficiently performing a wide range of operations over geographic data, for example, resolving spatial queries, generating maps, detecting geographic patterns over time, etc. [11]. GIS extensions exist for most modern DBMS and are the enabling technology for location-based services (LBS), which integrate a mobile device's location with other (spatially-dependent) information [34].

Google Latitude[1], Foursquare[2], Facebook Places[3], and Follow Me [38] are cloud-based examples of LBS that enable users to share their location with friends. The NearMe wireless proximity server [17] compares clients' Wi-Fi fingerprints (observed access points and signal strengths) to compute their relative proximity. MoCA (Mobile Collaboration Architecture) [29] is a client-server middleware for developing and deploying context-aware applications; MoCA supports mobility by monitoring a mobile client's location and switching to the application proxy (an intermediary between an mobile client and the application server that exists at the edge of a wired network) closest to the user. Similarly, Hydra [31] facilitates mobile pervasive application development by providing mobile agents that follow a user about a pervasive environment and construct a virtual machine that meets a user's current needs based on her location, tasks, number of co-located people, etc.

These approaches employ a single point of lookup to store participants' locations and resolve queries for location-based resources. Ypodimatopoulos and Lippman point out that any system that centralizes user location information by definition compromises user privacy [38], which can have potentially dangerous implications (e.g., burglary[4] and personal information inference [10]). For this reason their Follow Me indoor location sharing service is intended to be implemented at the per-building level instead of at a global level. We further argue that a completely centralized approach fails to meet the requirements of pervasive applications that demand low latency and target densely populated physical spaces where hundreds of thousands of devices may be carried by mobile users (e.g., Body Area Networks [3]) and embedded in the environment (e.g., the Internet of Things [1] and Web of Things [12]). These types of applications are more aptly supported by computing resources that are physically near participating devices and do not

---

[1] http://latitude.google.com
[2] http://foursquare.com
[3] http://facebook.com/about/location
[4] http://pleaserobme.com

rely on a (potentially distant) single globally known resource to manage devices' location information. This flavor of approach both reduces network latency and keeps location availability as local as possible.

Distributed Location-Dependent Discovery. The efficient discovery of "nearby" peers is an active area of interest in peer-to-peer (P2P) applications, where nodes interact directly with one another in a decentralized and localized fashion. Zero Configuration Networking (zeroconf)[5] and the serverless messaging extensions of the Extensible Messaging and Presence Protocol[6] (XMPP) both enable automatic discovery of available services on a local area network (LAN). Friends Radar [19] uses XMPP messaging to support P2P location sharing. Likewise, Virtual Cloud [15] employs XMPP messages to facilitate forming on-demand mobile clouds comprising co-located mobile devices. While zeroconf discovery over a wide-area network (WAN) is possible, it requires advanced setup at each client. Our proximal discovery service makes no assumptions about the *type* of network clients are a part of, simply that they are reachable.

Still other P2P applications maintain network overlays and routing tables to leverage *logical* locality. pSense [35] enables discovery of virtually visible peers in position-based massively multiplayer online games (MMOGs) through localized multicast; this eliminates the need to propagate players' location updates to a global resource. Proximal peer discovery could be implemented on top of a decentralized routing and location infrastructure like Tapestry [39] or Chord [36]. These approaches could certainly be applied in scenarios where *physical* locality was the citizen of interest. However, overlay and routing table based approaches require knowledge of at least one peer already in the network who may act as an entrance point for the new peer. In the implementation we present here, we require advanced knowledge of cloudlets and their administrative regions. However, one could envision cloudlet resources existing at the edge of a wired network infrastructure (e.g., in physically dispersed wireless access points) [32], and a device would implicitly interact with the cloudlet resource hosted on the Wi-Fi access point it was currently connected to.

Purely ad hoc approaches are *inherently* localized in both space and time due to the attenuation of radio signals as they propagate. FlashLinQ [37] is a telecommunication technology that enables long-range (approximately two mile) P2P discovery and operates in a licensed 5MHz spectrum. Other existing pieces of work use short range communication to localize (and co-localize) mobile users. Virtual Compass [2], for example, constructs a two dimensional graph of nearby devices via periodic (Wi-Fi or Bluetooth) signal strength measurements. Clearly, ad hoc strategies are advantageous in densely populated spaces as they eliminate the need for a bottleneck centralized resource and keep device interaction entirely local. Nevertheless, the maintenance of accurate routing tables, network overlays, and distributed data structures becomes expensive in scenarios that exhibit heavy churn in formation and high degrees of node mobility.

---

[5] http://zeroconf.org

[6] http://xmpp.orgextensions/xep-0174.html

Distributed Spatial Indexes. Our work aims to combine characteristics from both extremes: we desire the reliability and simplicity of centralized LBS systems and the scalability of entirely distributed approaches. We adopt a similar approach to that of distributed spatial indexing techniques [6, 21], which leverage the hierarchical nature of a spatial index structure (e.g., an R-Tree [13]) to strategically distribute portions of its hierarchy among networked peers. Rather than distribute portions of a holistic data structure, our proximal discovery service distributes independent computing resources that each employ their own spatial index. Moreover, our discovery service is designed under the assumption that pervasive applications likely require localized device interaction; we dictate that a computing resource monitoring device location information for a spatial region be physically near or within that region. Therefore our discovery service is able to keep location data about proximal peers as local as possible.

3   Architecture and Implementation

Under the assumption that cloudlets will be deployed within an existing Internet infrastructure [33], we implement our proximal discovery service as a Web service intended to be hosted on a cloudlet computing resource and made available through a RESTful API over HTTP. Very generally, the REST (REpresentational State Transfer) style [8] is a design technique for implementing remote procedure calls over the Web. Typically, in REST architectures, clients initiate requests to servers, which process the requests and return a response. Unlike WS-* integration techniques (e.g., SOAP, WSDL, the WS-* stack) that focus on *functions* and use HTTP merely as a transport-level protocol for application-level functionality, REST's requests and responses focus on the transfer of *resources* and use HTTP constructs directly as an application-level protocol[7]. In other words, "RESTful" Web services adopt a *data*-centric (rather than an *operation*-centric) model where "everything" is treated as a resource accessible strictly via HTTP operations (GET, PUT, POST, DELETE).

A RESTful architecture is an ideal candidate for any cloudlet-based Web service for two reasons. First, REST has become a standardized design technique and is the basis for most Web 2.0 services (e.g., those provided by Google, Twitter, Facebook, Amazon, etc.). Therefore, a RESTful cloudlet-based service can seamlessly integrate into existing Internet infrastructures. Second, since REST integrates application-level functionality directly with HTTP, it does not require additional higher level constructs or middleware. REST's lightweight nature makes it ideal for resource-constrained pervasive computing devices [12]. In the particular case of our proximal discovery service, it is natural to translate our scenario's notion of nearby *devices* to that of the REST concept of *resources*.

The Proximal Discovery Service. Our proximal discovery service's architecture is shown in Fig. 1. The service has two components that reside on a cloudlet:

---

[7] See [24] for a thorough comparison of WS-* and REST.

a spatial index to keep track of resources' locations and a REST API that enables remote storage and retrieval of these resources via an Internet connection. A "resource" is anything that a particular application wishes to associate with a geographic location—e.g., a user's mobile device, a sensor embedded in the environment, a location-dependent message, or a mobile software agent that migrates between machines. We implement the spatial index using a PostgreSQL[8] database with PostGIS[9] geospatial database extensions. PostGIS employs an R-Tree [13] to intelligently index and efficiently query geospatial data. Our service's REST API is implemented in Node.js[10], which is a particularly good fit for our use case because of its small footprint and ability to efficiently handle many simultaneous connections and requests.

Our service exposes a minimalist REST API with the following resource "routes." We aim solely to facilitate discovery of physically nearby resources, leaving other application-specific functions to applications themselves.

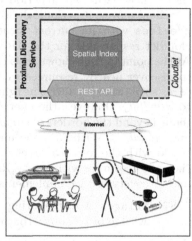

POST /devices A client (mobile device, embedded sensor, software agent) issues this request to an instance of the discovery service to create or update the resource representing the client on the cloudlet.

GET /neighbors A client issues this request to query a cloudlet for resources within its vicinity. We parameterize the request with a *range* to limit the query's geographic search space. An application could further impose additional application-specific parameters. Upon receiving this request, the cloudlet responds with a list of resources whose locations are believed to be within the request's range of the client.

Fig. 1. The Proximal Discovery Service's Architecture. Dashed arrows are **POST /devices** requests; the solid arrow is a **GET /neighbors** request.

Our approach only provides an advantage over a centralized cloud-based LBS when many independent instances are distributed across a geographic region, where each instance assumes responsibility for a particular sub-region. However, important challenges arise when clients physically move between these sub-regions or issue queries that cross the boundaries of these sub-regions.

Distributed Cloudlet Synchronization. Our proximal discovery service supports pervasive computing applications in densely populated physical spaces. To fully utilize the potential of a cloudlet infrastructure and support large numbers of anticipated clients, many instances of our service must be deployed in a geographic region, with each instance responsible for a particular sub-region. These

---

[8] http://postgresql.org
[9] http://postgis.net
[10] http://nodejs.org

spaces are highly mobile—people and their devices move and inevitably migrate between adjacent cloudlet-administered sub-regions; our proximal discovery service must address the distributed synchronization of cloudlets governing these adjacent sub-regions.

Consider the scenario in Fig. 2. A space is decomposed into nine *administrative regions* (AR). One cloudlet exists in each AR and is responsible for responding to cloudlet-bound requests for that region. The solid dot represents a mobile client that has traveled along the dashed path over a period of time. As the client moves, it periodically issues a POST /devices with its current location to the cloudlet responsible for the AR it occupies. At the point in time shown, this client wishes to discover nearby resources within a range of r, so it issues a GET /neighbors query to $cloudlet_1$. However, the query's range extends beyond the borders of $cloudlet_1$'s AR and into those of $cloudlet_0$, $cloudlet_3$, and $cloudlet_4$. Without some means of synchronization, $cloudlet_1$ can only respond with the four resources in the shaded region of the query's target space (i.e., the resources within its AR). To facilitate this synchronization, our proximal discovery service implements a third resource route:

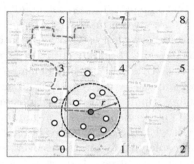

Fig. 2. A query for resources within a range of r from a mobile client

POST /fringes A neighboring cloudlet issues this request to communicate knowledge of resources that exist at or near the border of an adjacent AR.

To both capture and quantify "at or near the border," we introduce the concept of a *fringe*, illustrated in Fig. 3. A fringe is a sliver of space of width δ on the interior of an AR's border. For simplicity, the ARs shown in Fig. 3(a) are rectangular, and therefore the computed fringes are also rectangular. In

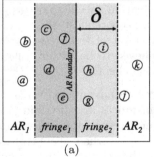 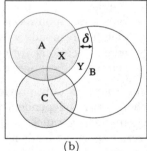

Fig. 3. Computing administrative region fringes

actuality, ARs can be of any shape and even overlapping. AR_i's fringe with AR_j consists simply of any point within AR_i that is within a specified distance (δ) of AR_j. Consider the more complex pair of ARs in Fig. 3(b). AR_A overlaps AR_B; any resource within the area marked X can report to either AR_A or AR_B (or both of them). The fringe that AR_B computes to create a digest for AR_A contains all of the resources it knows about located in Y *and* all of the resources it knows about located in X (because they may not have also reported their locations to A). Fringes can also overlap; consider the adjacency of AR_B and AR_C; the fringe of AR_B with respect to AR_C (not depicted) will include not only their overlapping area but also a sliver adjacent to this area that also overlaps Y.

Periodically, our service computes each of its fringes' *digest*, or a snapshot of the fringe's resources, which it sends to the appropriate adjacent cloudlet via a POST /fringes. In Fig. 3(a), for example, $cloudlet_1$ computes AR_1's fringe digest to be (c, d, e, f), which it POSTs to $cloudlet_2$.

Our service entails three variable deployment parameters, each which must be tuned for a particular application's needs:

μ The number of administrative regions (and correspondingly, cloudlets) that a geographic region is decomposed into.
δ The width of administrative regions' fringes.
T The interval of time between fringe digest computations.

A particular combination of parameters, represented by the tuple (μ, δ, T), is a *synchronization strategy*. In Section 5 we evaluate our service's performance under various synchronization strategies in terms of the *quality* with which proximal discovery queries are satisfied and the system-level *cost* of the strategy.

Operating Assumptions. We assume clients can localize themselves and have a labeled map of cloudlets and their ARs. Localization may be too expensive a task for severely resource constrained devices (e.g., battery operated sensors); however, lightweight localization methods are currently a very active area of research [2, 4, 20, 25]. Alternatively, resource-constrained devices could communicate with cloudlets via less resource-constrained *gateways* [12]. We also assume that cloudlets are aware of neighboring cloudlets; in our implementation, clients and cloudlets each possess a copy of the same labeled map.

4   Application Examples

We next provide some concrete examples of mobile and pervasive machine-to-machine (M2M) applications that are enabled by our proximal discovery service, how they can be built with our service, and the inherent advantages of doing so.

Location Based Services. Perhaps the most obvious application of our service is for the types of LBS discussed earlier (e.g., location-based social networking services, location sharing services, friend finders, and spatial crowdsourcing [16]). Using our cloudlet-based service for localized discovery, such services could target small and heavily crowded regions (e.g., music festivals, parades, theme parks, university campuses, etc.) much more efficiently. Instead of shipping application requests to a (physically and logically) distant central cloud index, requests *and* users' location information would be localized to the geographic areas where they are inherently relevant, providing low-latency responses, lighter server-side loads, and privacy gains through the distributed cloudlets [38].

P2P Network Overlays and Routing. In Section 2 we discussed the fact that using a P2P routing and location infrastructure like Tapestry [39] or Chord [36] to implement proximal resource discovery requires new network participants to have advanced knowledge of at least one peer already in the P2P overlay. This crucial discovery step could be performed with our proximal discovery service, where the resource of interest is any peer already in the overlay. The use of a cloudlet infrastructure, in this case, encourages and facilitates P2P interaction between devices that are *physically* near one another. Peer physical proximity is not a requirement for these systems but can be advantageous if the P2P overlay exists to store spatio-temporal events [40].

Mobile Ad Hoc and Opportunistic Networks. Our proximal discovery service could also be used to construct *virtual* mobile ad hoc network (MANETs) and opportunistic networks. Beyond the ability to implement MANET-style routing algorithms without a separate dedicated radio interface, virtualization of MANETs has added security benefits [14]. Virtual MANETs could be used to form on-demand mobile clouds [30], execute geographic routing [5], implement location-based publish-subscribe [7], or enable wireless sensor network (WSN) query-access mechanisms [9, 18, 22] across smartphones. The realization of cloudlet-based virtual MANETs for mobile computing could conceivably lead to a renaissance of techniques formerly developed for MANETs and WSNs.

5   Evaluation

We next benchmark the performance of our service in terms of its system-level cost and the quality with which the service performs proximal resource discovery under various combinations of (μ, δ, T) (number of administrative regions, fringe width, fringe digest computation period), in an effort to guide application developers in tuning our service's parameters to meet application requirements. We simulate mobile clients using two real-world and one simulated mobility trace data sets (Table 1). Our framework is implemented in Python.

We decompose a square geographic region into μ administrative regions (ARs), assign each AR one instance of our discovery service, and generate a labeled map of these regions and their ARs; the clients and the μ service instances each receive a copy of this map. Each simulated client moves about the region and

Table 1. Mobility Trace Data Sets

Data Set	Geographic Region	Description
UT-Real	$640m^2$ UT Austin campus	24 hours of location information from 18 users of a mobile application deployed on the UT Austin campus in June 2013
UT-Sim	$640m^2$ UT Austin campus	6 hours of simulated location information for 200 nodes generated using MobiSim [23] and Levy-walk [28] mobility
Cabspotting [27]	$10km^2$ downtown San Francisco	6 hours of location information for ~500 taxi cabs in downtown San Francisco, USA

issues a `POST /devices` with its current location at most once per minute to the cloudlet-hosted service responsible for the AR it occupies. Every T seconds, each of the μ instances of the discovery service computes the digest[11] for each of its fringes. The service instance then issues a `POST /fringes` containing the digest to the respective neighboring service instance. During each simulation, we perform periodic proximal resource discovery queries (i.e., cloudlet-bound `GET /neighbors` requests): at 10 randomly chosen simulation times we randomly select 25 simulated clients[12] and issue three queries ($r =$["near", "medium", "far"])[13]. For each data set, we also generate an *Oracle*, which is effectively a central (cloud) server to which every client posts its location once per minute.

Table 2 shows our evaluation parameters; in cases where we explored multiple values, the value in parentheses is the default. We first evaluate the *quality* of our service in terms of the mean number of *false positives* (resources *in* a cloudlet result and *not in* the corresponding *Oracle* result) and *false negatives* (resources *not in* a cloudlet result, but *in* the corresponding *Oracle* result) produced per query under various synchronization strategies. In both cases, we normalize the false positives and false negatives to the size of the *Oracle* result set. That is, a value of 0.1 for a normalized false negative score indicates that for every 10 items in the *Oracle* result, there was one result missing from the cloudlet result.

Table 2. Evaluation Parameters

Parameter	Value(s)
μ: number of cloudlets	$4, 9, 16, (25), 36, 49, 64, 81, 100$
δ: fringe width (fraction of width of an AR)	$\frac{1}{10}, \frac{1}{9}, \frac{1}{8}, \frac{1}{7}, \frac{1}{6}, (\frac{1}{5}), \frac{1}{4}, \frac{1}{3}, \frac{1}{2}$
T: digest update period (in seconds)	$60, 300, (900), 1800, 3600, 7200, 18000$
t: client location update period (in seconds)	60^{14}
u: location update size (in bytes)	80

Fig. 4 shows the false negative and false positive rates for varying the number of cloudlets for the *UT-Real* and *Cabspotting* traces; we omit the results for *UT-Sim* as they are very similar to the results for *Cabspotting*. Two observations are relatively consistent across all data sets. First, the errors show a slight upward trend as the number of cloudlets increases. As the cell sizes decrease, queries are increasingly likely to rely on the digest from neighboring cloudlets for correct information, and this information is more out of date than the local cloudlet's information. Second, the false positive and false negative rates for "near" queries are significantly better than for "medium" or "far." This demonstrates (and begins to benchmark) that the cloudlet-based approach is more suited for highly

---

[11] To prevent "stale" resources, we restrict digests to contain only resources that issued a `POST /devices` within the last T seconds (i.e., since the last fringe digest).

[12] Only 18 clients were available in the *UT-Real* data set.

[13] We define the ["near", "medium", "far"] ranges as $(25m, 50m, 75m)$ for the *UT-Real* and *UT-Sim* data sets and $(100m, 500m, 1000m)$ for the *Cabspotting* data set.

[14] The client update period was set to exactly 60 seconds for *UT-Sim*. For *UT-Real* and *Cabspotting*, the period was determined by the data set but was close 60 seconds.

localized search and is not as well suited to searching for information that is located further afield. Consider a query in the *UT-Real* when μ is 64, where each cloudlet is responsible for a 10 x $10m^2$ area. A "medium" query, looking for resources within $50m$, may match resources that are not even located in an adjacent administrative region and will be impossible to find using our service.

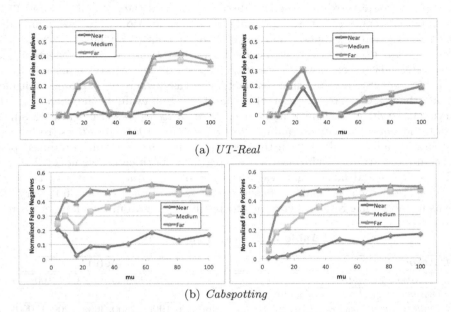

(a) *UT-Real*

(b) *Cabspotting*

Fig. 4. Impact of varying the number of cloudlets

Fig. 4(a) also shows an interplay between the behavior of real users and the definition of cloudlets. For μ values of 36 and 49, the upward trend of the error rates is violated. The reason can be identified by examining the location traces of the users, shown in Fig. 5. In the case of $\mu = 36$, the common areas

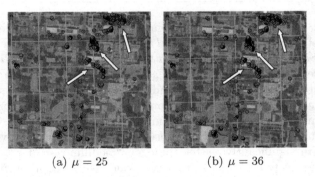

(a) $\mu = 25$ (b) $\mu = 36$

Fig. 5. A "poor" choice of μ may split clusters

where users cluster (in this case, three buildings on the university campus) happen to lie entirely within single administrative regions. In the case of $\mu = 25$, these clusters cross the boundaries of administrative regions. Users' queries therefore also often cross these boundaries, meaning that they increasingly rely on digests for correct query resolution. The conclusion from this observation is that defining administrative regions should account for user mobility patterns and should not create artificial boundaries to separate users within natural congregation areas.

We next examine the impact of varying the fringe width. Fig. 6 shows the false positive and false negative rates for the *UT-Real* and *Cabspotting* traces; we again omit the results for *UT-Sim*, which are again very similar to the results for *Cabspotting*. Except within the (small) *UT-Real* data set, there is little relationship between changing δ and false positives and false negatives. These figures again show the significant difference in quality for "near," "medium," and "far" queries. While the error (as measured by the false positive or false positive rate) is routinely below 10% for "near" queries, it grows up to nearly 50% for "far" queries. This again demonstrates that the cloudlet based approach is particularly suited to very local queries of the immediate surroundings.

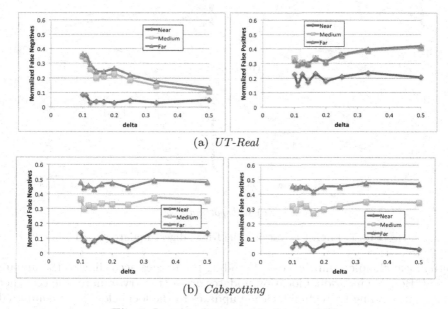

(a) *UT-Real*

(b) *Cabspotting*

Fig. 6. Impact of varying the fringe width

Finally, we examine the quality of our cloudlet based discovery service with respect to the update interval for fringe digests in Fig. 7. As T increases up to 50 minutes, quality degrades substantially. In the limit, the false positive rates also decrease; this is a result of the fact that the digests are simply not updated well, so they do not contain extra (irrelevant) information. However, we can also discern that it is acceptable for the update interval to be larger than the frequency with which the clients update their own cloudlets; specifically, any setting of T under 900 seconds has only a marginal impact on false negatives.

We also benchmark the system-level *cost* of a synchronization strategy in terms of the mean overhead (in KB) for sending both individual location updates

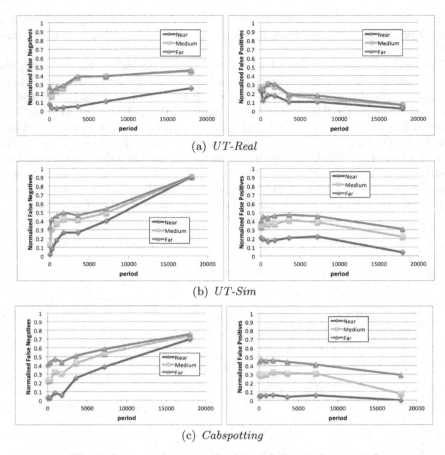

(a) *UT-Real*

(b) *UT-Sim*

(c) *Cabspotting*

Fig. 7. Impact of varying the fringe digest update period

to the local cloudlet and the cost of sending the fringes according to the update period. Because individual location updates are sent every minute, the cost, per minute, of sending individual location updates to the local cloudlet is computed as: $n \times 80\text{B} \times 1 \text{ hop} \times \frac{1\text{KB}}{1024\text{B}}$, where n is the number of clients sending location updates, and 80 bytes is the size of a client location update (from Table 2). We assume that each client is located within one network hop of the cloudlet server. We compute the cost of sending the digests between cloudlet servers as:

$$4(\mu + \sqrt{\mu}) \times \overline{size_{digest}}\text{B} \times 1 \text{ hop} \times \frac{1\text{KB}}{1024\text{B}}$$

where $4(\mu + \sqrt{\mu})$ is the number of fringes in our square region and $\overline{size_{digest}}$ is measured during execution. We assume a single network hop between adjacent cloudlet servers. The total cost for the cloudlet approach is the sum of these two values. We compare this to the system-level cost of the centralized approach, computed as: $n \times 80\text{B} \times h \text{ hop} \times \frac{1\text{KB}}{1024\text{B}}$, where the only cost is sending the clients' individual updates to the central server. In the following results, we used the

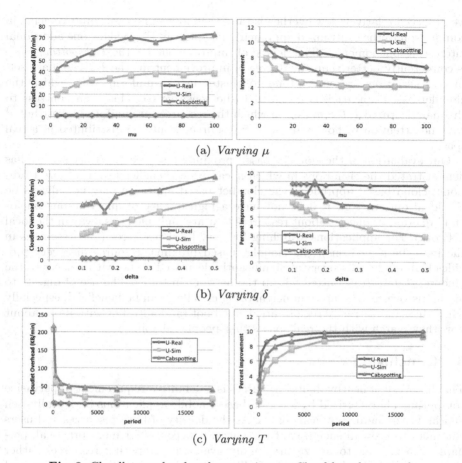

(a) *Varying μ*

(b) *Varying δ*

(c) *Varying T*

Fig. 8. Cloudlet overhead and comparison to Cloud based approach

(conservative) assumption of 10 hops to the central server[15]. Fig. 8 shows the results, which include both the absolute values of the overhead (measured in KB/min) for the cloudlet based approach and the improvement of the cloudlet based approach over the centralized approach.

Overhead increases with both increasing μ and increasing δ. As μ increases, there are more digests to be sent because there are more fringes. Note, though, that the overhead increases relatively slowly for increasing μ. Overhead increases with δ simply because, as the fringe size increases, there are more resources within the fringe, so the size of the digest grows. Interestingly, the overhead falls off rapidly with increasing T; for all values of T greater than 60 seconds,

---
[15] The value of 10 hops is significantly below the values we measured using `traceroute`s to common cloud servers, which were routinely above 15 hops. The number of network hops is not the only (or necessarily "best") measure of cost, but it gives a reasonable measure of the relative costs of these two approaches.

we observed relatively low overheads (and therefore significant improvements in comparison to the centralized approach). The plots in Fig. 8 show one additional interesting phenomenon. The degree of improvement for the *Cabspotting* trace is consistently better than the degree of improvement for the *UT-Sim* data set. In real situations, resources tend to cluster in non-uniform ways, which the cloudlet-based approach is designed to be sensitive to. This is in contrast to the manufactured *UT-Sim* case in which the resources are uniformly distributed with no attention to how real users or resources would be distributed in a real space.

Our evaluation of the cloudlet based proximal resource discovery service has demonstrated the situations in which it can prove beneficial over a more traditional cloud based approach. The cloudlet based approach may not always be the ideal option (e.g., it does not have a high quality of query resolution for "far" queries, or queries about resources that are multiple hops away in the local network). For applications searching for very local resources (i.e., resources in the immediate environs), the cloudlet based proximal resource discovery provides high quality discovery at significantly decreased costs (with respect to the amount of data transmitted within the network in total). The use of digests to aid in discovering resources in neighboring cloudlets can be beneficial, especially when the administrative regions are defined not randomly, but with input about how they match with the real spaces that people inhabit.

6 Conclusion

The discovery of nearby digital resources is a definitive requirement of pervasive computing, characterized by location-based mobile applications in digitally-rich and highly dynamic physical spaces. As the density of both resources and users continues to grow in such operating spaces, it becomes far more practical, perhaps even crucial, to utilize proximally available computing resources rather than a distant cloud resource to facilitate the discovery of nearby users and resources. In this paper, we presented the design and implementation of a distributed location-based discovery service based on physically dispersed *cloudlets*, which provide the service for well-defined physical regions. Our approach takes advantage of the inherent proximity of clients, cloudlets, and relevant resources. We explored various deployment settings of our service and demonstrated that a cloudlet-based approach requires significantly less in-network traffic than a centralized cloud-based approach while still providing good "look-up" query quality. Our evaluation focused on cloudlets that were responsible for rectangular regions; our implementation does presuppose a particular shape of a cloudlet's administrative region (AR)—our service could operate over cloudlets with ARs of arbitrary shapes that even overlap. Immediately, we envision that our proximal discovery service could be used to supplement existing location-based discovery services and P2P overlay approaches in heavily populated small physical spaces. More generally, and more importantly, our service enables the realization of *virtual* MANETs, the full-scale creation of which could lead to a revival of interest in a whole body of MANET and WSN resource management techniques.

References

[1] Atzori, L., Iera, A., Morabito, G.: The internet of things: A survey. Computer Net. 54(15), 2787–2805 (2010)

[2] Banerjee, N., Agarwal, S., Bahl, P., Chandra, R., Wolman, A., Corner, M.: Virtual compass: Relative positioning to sense mobile social interactions. In: Floréen, P., Krüger, A., Spasojevic, M. (eds.) Pervasive 2010. LNCS, vol. 6030, pp. 1–21. Springer, Heidelberg (2010)

[3] Chen, M., Gonzalez, S., Vasilakos, A., Cao, H., Leung, V.: Body area networks: A survey. Mobile Net. and App. 16(2), 171–193 (2011)

[4] Constandache, I., Bao, X., Azizyan, M., Choudhury, R.R.: Did you see Bob?: human localization using mobile phones. In: Proc. of MobiCom (2010)

[5] Das, S., Pucha, H., Hu, Y.: Performance comparison of scalable location services for geographic ad hoc routing. In: Proc. of INFOCOM (2005)

[6] Demirbas, M., Ferhatosmanoglu, H.: Peer-to-peer spatial queries in sensor networks. In: Proc. of P2P (2003)

[7] Fiege, L., Gärtner, F.C., Kasten, O., Zeidler, A.: Supporting mobility in content-based publish/subscribe middleware. In: Endler, M., Schmidt, D.C. (eds.) Middleware 2003. LNCS, vol. 2672, pp. 103–122. Springer, Heidelberg (2003)

[8] Fielding, R.T., Taylor, R.N.: Principled design of the modern web architecture. ACM Trans. Internet Technol. 2(2), 115–150 (2002)

[9] Galpin, I., Brenninkmeijer, C., Gray, A., Jabeen, F., Fernandes, A., Paton, N.: Snee: a query processor for wireless sensor networks. Dist. and Parallel Databases 29, 31–85 (2011)

[10] Gambs, S., Killijian, M.-O., del Prado Cortez, M.N.: Show me how you move and I will tell you who you are. In: Proc. of SPRINGL (2010)

[11] Goodchild, M.: Research Methods in Geography, 3rd edn., pp. 376–391. Wiley-Blackwell (2010)

[12] Guinard, D., Vlad, T.: Towards the web of things: web mashups for embedded devices. In: Proc. of WWW (2009)

[13] Guttman, A.: R-trees: a dynamic index structure for spatial searching. In: Proc. of SIGMOD (1984)

[14] Huang, D., Zhang, X., Kang, M., Luo, J.: MobiCloud: Building secure cloud framework for mobile computing and communication. In: Proc. of SOSE (2010)

[15] Huerta-Canepa, G., Lee, D.: A virtual cloud computing provider for mobile devices. In: Proc. of MCS (2010)

[16] Kazemi, L., Shahabi, C.: Geocrowd: enabling query answering with spatial crowdsourcing. In: Proc. of SIGSPATIAL (2012)

[17] Krumm, J., Hinckley, K.: The NearMe wireless proximity server. In: Mynatt, E.D., Siio, I. (eds.) UbiComp 2004. LNCS, vol. 3205, pp. 283–300. Springer, Heidelberg (2004)

[18] Madden, S., Franklin, M., Hellerstein, J., Hong, W.: The design of an acquisitional query processor for sensor networks. In: Proc. of SIGMOD (2003)

[19] Mayrhofer, R., Holzmann, C., Koprivec, R.: Friends Radar: Towards a private P2P location sharing platform. In: Moreno-Díaz, R., Pichler, F., Quesada-Arencibia, A. (eds.) EUROCAST 2011, Part II. LNCS, vol. 6928, pp. 527–535. Springer, Heidelberg (2012)

[20] Minami, M., Fukuju, Y., Hirasawa, K., Yokoyama, S., Mizumachi, M., Morikawa, H., Aoyama, T.: DOLPHIN: A practical approach for implementing a fully distributed indoor ultrasonic positioning system. In: Mynatt, E.D., Siio, I. (eds.) UbiComp 2004. LNCS, vol. 3205, pp. 347–365. Springer, Heidelberg (2004)

[21] Mondal, A., Lifu, Y., Kitsuregawa, M.: P2PR-Tree: An R-Tree-based spatial index for peer-to-peer environments. In: Proc. of EDBT Workshops (2005)

[22] Mottola, L., Picco, G.: Programming wireless sensor networks with logical neighborhoods. In: Proc. of InterSense (2006)

[23] Mousavi, S.M., Rabiee, H., Moshref, M., Dabirmoghaddam, A.: MobiSim: A framework for simulation of mobility models in mobile ad-hoc networks. In: Proc. of WIMOB (2007)

[24] Pautasso, C., Zimmermann, O., Leymann, F.: Restful web services vs. "big" web services: making the right architectural decision. In: Proc. of WWW (2008)

[25] Peng, C., Shen, G., Zhang, Y., Li, Y., Tan, K.: BeepBeep: a high accuracy acoustic ranging system using cots mobile devices. In: Proc. of SenSys (2007)

[26] Peuquet, D.: Making space for time: Issues in space-time data representation. GeoInform. 5, 11–32 (2001)

[27] Piorkowski, M., Sarafijanovic-Djukic, N., Grossglauser, M.: CRAWDAD data set epfl/mobility (v. 2009-02-24) (2009), Downloaded from http://crawdad.cs.dartmouth.edu/epfl/mobility

[28] Rhee, I., Shin, M., Hong, S., Lee, K., Kim, S.J., Chong, S.: On the levy-walk nature of human mobility. IEEE/ACM Trans. Netw. 19(3), 630–643 (2011)

[29] Sacramento, V., Endler, M., Rubinsztejn, H., Lima, L., Goncalves, K., Nascimento, F., Bueno, G.: Moca: A middleware for developing collaborative applications for mobile users. IEEE Dist. Sys. Online 5(10), 1–14 (2004)

[30] Samimi, F.A., McKinley, P.K., Sadjadi, S.M.: Mobile service clouds: A self-managing infrastructure for autonomic mobile computing services. In: Keller, A., Martin-Flatin, J.-P. (eds.) SelfMan 2006. LNCS, vol. 3996, pp. 130–141. Springer, Heidelberg (2006)

[31] Satoh, I.: Dynamic deployment of pervasive services. In: Proc. of ICPS (2005)

[32] Satyanarayanan, M.: Mobile computing: the next decade. SIGMOBILE Mob. Comput. Commun. Rev. 15(2), 2–10 (2011)

[33] Satyanarayanan, M., Bahl, P., Caceres, R., Davies, N.: The case for vm-based cloudlets in mobile computing. IEEE Pervasive Computing 8(4), 14–23 (2009)

[34] Schiller, J., Voisard, A.: Location-Based Services. Morgan Kaufmann (2004)

[35] Schmieg, A., Stieler, M., Jeckel, S., Kabus, P., Kemme, B., Buchmann, A.: pSense: Maintaining a dynamic localized peer-to-peer structure for position based multicast in games. In: Proc. of P2P (2008)

[36] Stoica, I., Morris, R., Karger, D., Kaashoek, M.F., Balakrishnan, H.: Chord: A scalable peer-to-peer lookup service for internet applications. In: Proc. of SIGCOMM (2001)

[37] Wu, X., Tavildar, S., Shakkottai, S., Richardson, T., Li, J., Laroia, R., Jovicic, A.: FlashLinQ: A synchronous distributed scheduler for peer-to-peer ad hoc networks. In: Proc. of Allerton (2010)

[38] Ypodimatopoulos, P., Lippman, A.: Follow me: a web-based, location-sharing architecture for large, indoor environments. In: Proc. of WWW (2010)

[39] Zhao, B.Y., Kubiatowicz, J.D., Joseph, A.D.: Tapestry: An infrastructure for fault-tolerant wide-area location and routing. Technical report, University of California at Berkeley, Berkeley, CA, USA (2001)

[40] Ziotopoulos, A., de Veciana, G.: P2P network for storage and query of a spatio-temporal flow of events. In: Proc. of PerCom Workshops (2011)

LOX Framework: Designing Human Computation Games to Update Street Views

Jongin Lee[1], John Kim[1,2], and Kwan Hong Lee[3,4]

[1] KAIST, Div. of Web Science and Technology, Korea
[2] KAIST, Dept. of Computer Science, Korea
[3] Redstar Ventures, USA
[4] POSTECH, Korea
{jongin.lee,jjk12}@kaist.ac.kr, kwantify@postech.edu

Abstract. Although the Web has abundant information, it does not necessarily contain the latest, most recently updated information. In particular, interactive map websites and the accompanying street view applications often have outdated information because street views change constantly and are very costly to update. In this work, we propose the LOX (Labeling and O/X) framework – a scalable human computation framework that discovers the latest updates of street views through mobile games. The challenge in this work is providing an interface to identify the differences between the latest street view and the outdated street view images. The LOX framework addresses this problem through three mobile games – a compatibility ESP (cESP) Game, a Drag&Drop Labeling Game and an O/X Game. The cESP and Labeling Games encourage users to identify new updates on outdated street view images while the O/X Game increases the precision of the differences identified by the users between the existing street view images and the latest street view. We conducted several user studies to assess the design and usability of the game. The collected data allowed us to assess the performance of utilizing human computation games to update new information while providing us guidance on how to design user interfaces and workflows to increase the quality of the data. The games provide an opportunity for significant cost savings to the service providers by providing an inexpensive method to determine which street views need to be updated.

Keywords: crowdsourcing, human computation, game with a purpose.

1 Introduction

Information that is available on the Web is constantly changing and, in many cases, does not accurately reflect the most current information in the real world. Mapping sites such as Google Maps have such limitations. In addition to simply providing street information and directions, the mapping sites provide different points of interests (POIs), restaurants, stores, reviews and street views. However, the information constantly changes (e.g. a restaurant might close and be replaced with a different store) and keeping the street view up-to-date by an organization

G. Memmi and U. Blanke (Eds.): MobiCASE 2013, LNICST 130, pp. 233–251, 2014.
© Institute for Computer Sciences, Social Informatics and Telecommunications Engineering 2014

can be extremely costly. Therefore, a grass roots manner that involves crowd sourcing is a very attractive approach to find updates and maintain the latest real world information.

The street views provide a panoramic view of a particular location from the perspective of someone walking along the street. It provides a close-up view of the area so that users can more easily identify their destination or discover the appearance of an area. Capturing and updating street view images require a vehicle equipped with specialized omniview cameras to drive around the streets. Based on the images collected, a panoramic view of the street is created. Since this is time consuming and costly[1], it is not realistic to always have the most recently updated view of the particular location. For example, in Google Street View, some street views from London are very recent as they are from 2012, but other major cities in the world are much older. The images from Paris were captured in 2008, Seoul in 2009, and New York City and San Francisco in 2011.

One Internet service provider in Korea (Daum) has a very similar service (called "Road View") and they provide information on the date that the current and prior road view images were obtained[1]. Based on this information, it can be known that some views near major cities are updated approximately every six months while other locations are updated every year or two. An example of how a street view changed over a period of two years is shown in Figure 1 for a major city within Korea. It is clear that some information (e.g. TGI Fridays) remains the same while other parts of the image (highlighted in the yellow square) have consistently changed during this time.

June 2009   October 2010   October 2011

Fig. 1. An example of how a street view has changed over time

Because of this limitation of maps and street views, Google provides a Map Maker service[2] that allows individuals to submit changes to the current map information, including identifying new streets, new stores, new restaurants, etc. Once update requests are submitted, it requires another "expert" to verify and validate the request. However, this service is very labor-intensive and the process is not scalable and increases the difficulty in providing numerous updates. On the OpenStreetMap[3], map information is allowed to be modified by lots of contributors and seems to effectively maintain the latest map data. However, this service is limited to the traditional top-down view of the maps and does not

---

[1] It is estimated that Google spends $1-2 billion per year on street view to take photos all over the world. However, the cost will be much higher if Google Street View attempts to provide higher coverage as many cities outside of the US do not have street views available.

include the street views. With the wide spread use of smart phones and tablets, people are spending more time on their mobile devices and using them to navigate and find destinations. The value of grassroots community contribution is demonstrated by recent acquisition of Waze[4] by Google. Waze mobile application has shown great utility of community edited routes and maps – particularly to deal with traffic, constructions, potholes, and police radars. In our work, we enhance such capability by helping map service providers find updates or "differences" in the street views more easily through human computation games on mobile devices.

In this work, we attempt to identify the outdated information in the street view through a human computation game framework called LOX (Labeling Game and O/X Game) that is designed for users to identify differences between a stored image from existing street view database and the corresponding view in the current real world. The game is based on similar principles to the "Hidden Catch" game, which presents two images where the user has to identify their subtle differences (Figure 2(a)). This type of game is very straightforward and depending on the subtlety of the differences, the difficulty of the game increases or decreases. If necessary, the computer can easily solve this problem by comparing the images. However, if one of the reference images is not available (e.g. Figure 2(b)), then the Hidden Catch game cannot be completed by a computer. In this work, the LOX framework was inspired by similar principles to those in the Hidden Catch game, i.e. leveraging the user's familiarity of the street views in order to identify the differences and to obtain the updated information. In order to achieve this, the LOX framework consists of multiple games: an ESP game, a "labeling" game and a simple O/X game.

(a) (b)

Fig. 2. An example of (a) the Hidden Catch game and (b) our LOX game with an unknown image

2   Related Work

LOX Game follows the principles of game with a purpose (GWAP) [5] to facilitate finding of updates in street views of the physical world using a mobile game. Visual recognition and labeling has been a prominent activity for many human-computation researches. By providing the physical context to inform and fix the outdated online data is novel due to the wide availability of smart phones and street views at your fingertips. This addresses issues on what kind of scale and performance are needed for such human computation to be effective in reducing the effort to promptly collect data on these updates. There have been many research and commercial efforts on crowdsourcing through mobile phones. TxtEagle, deployed in Kenya, used SMS text messages to provide tasks like audio transcription, local language translation and market research[6]. MobileWorks provided OCR tasks that people in developing countries can play to earn wages anytime, anywhere. These applications show how these tasks can be accomplished on the mobile phone in a user friendly manner while contributing to the daily wages of people at the bottom of the pyramid[7].

As mobile phones have become more powerful computing and networked devices with sophisticated sensors and rich user interfaces, tracking peoples mobility behaviors, mapping out activity of urban cities, providing reviews, recommendations, and real time feedback on events happening in geographical locations have become mainstream[8][9][10]. Mobile phones have allowed people to participate in environmental participatory sensing such as spotting birds and their migration patterns or plants and their budding seasons[11], and bus arrival times that can be changed or updated in real time[12]. The projects have shown how widely deployed mobile phones and peoples contributions can provide the latest data in a very distributed manner and make the data collection more efficient than any centralized manner. LOX game attempts to engage general public through a mobile local game, utilizing their memory or physical presence at particular locations to capture latest changes on the street view data. Such labeling would allow street view creators to more efficiently gather new locations that need updated images.

3   Obtaining the "Unknown" Image

Following the principle of the Hidden Catch game, the biggest challenge in our LOX framework is to obtain the "unknown" image that corresponds to the latest street view image to identify the differences. With the growth of mobile devices with cameras, there are many street images available on the web and Google uses these images to shows streams of pictures when a particular location is searched on their map service. However, despite the availability of many of these images, it is very challenging to create a framework to discover the latest updates on POI's based on these images because these pictures can be taken on different dates, resolutions, directions and angles. In addition, comparing street view images with individual pictures taken from different perspectives make the comparison a huge computational challenge making it not trivial to find images that contain any recently updated information.

Thus, to identify the updated spots in the "unknown" image for the game, there are two different possible sources for the unknown image.

1. Physical Image : The most ideal image is the "physical" image – i.e., if the user is physically present at the location of the street view, the unknown image is provided in front of the users and the street view (from the service

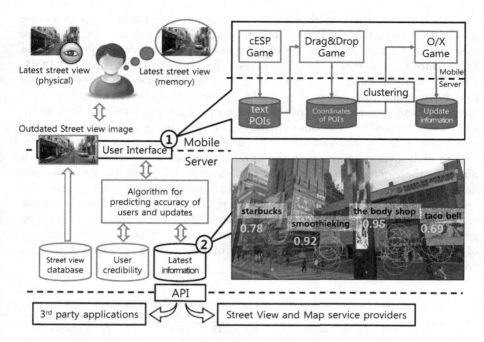

Fig. 3. High-level block diagram of the LOX framework

provider) can be directly compared against the physical image. Since we intend the game to be played on mobile devices, the game can leverage the GPS location information. For example, if a user is waiting for a friend at an intersection in a downtown district, the user can play the game to help discover latest updates needed in the street view images.

2. Memory Image : People are often very familiar with different street views – especially in areas around work, school, home, hangout places and perhaps places on their commute route [13]. Based on the user's familiarity with a given region, the "memory image" can be leveraged to play the LOX game and help identify the differences.

In this work, we focus on using the "physical" image within the LOX framework and we leave using the memory image to future work.

4   LOX Framework

A high-level block diagram of the LOX framework is shown in Figure 3. The goal of the LOX framework is not only to obtain the latest information but also to identify the *differences* with the existing street view images. The LOX framework consists of three games - the compatibility ESP (cESP) game, the Drag&Drop Labeling game and the O/X game. The purpose of the cESP game is to obtain text of new POIs for a given location. The Drag&Drop game uses information from Google Places to get coordinates of existing POI's. It also uses the text collected from the cESP game to augment with potential new POI's since Google Places does not necessarily have the latest, updated POI's. The information collected from these two games provides the potential latest POI information and where they might be located. However, we still need to identify whether certain parts of street view image are outdated. To provide the *differences* (difference between existing street view image and the latest actual street image), we introduced the O/X game.

The high level description of the LOX framework is described in Figure 3. Since the three games are independent of each other, the games do not necessarily have to be played by the same player. For quality control, cESP game uses 'output agreement[14]' while both the Drag&Drop game and the O/X game compares the data to the data in the database, which enable players to play our game individually. 'Database agreement' is introduced to measure the credibility of the users and accept the contributions of the users in proportion to their credibility scores.

Table 1. Comparison of different games within the LOX framework

	cESP Game	Drag&Drop Game	O/X Game
Players	2 players	1 player	1 player
Summary	POI text collection	POI location identification	image processing
Genre	compatibility game	driving game	speed game
Quality control	output agreement	database agreement	database agreement
Input	street view images	street view images, POI's	street view images, locations of POI's, POI's
Output	latest POI's (text)	locations of POI's	differences between outdated and latest

4.1 Compatibility ESP (cESP) Game

The compatibility ESP (cESP) Game is a mobile version of the ESP Game [14] and the screen snapshot of cESP Game is shown in Figure 4. The original ESP game was designed to leverage human computation to label images by pairing up two random players and collecting labels that describe a given image. In our cESP game, the goals are still the same – have two players enter the same text to obtain "labels" for the features in the image. However, the labels are not describing the image (as in the original ESP game) but the collected labels from the cESP game are names and categories that identify the different POIs (e.g., Starbucks, T.G.I. Friday, etc.). In addition, a key difference with the ESP game is that instead of having two random players, we have two players that know each other play the game at the same time and leverage the simple "compatibility game" principle. The compatibility game [15], which is offered as a board game

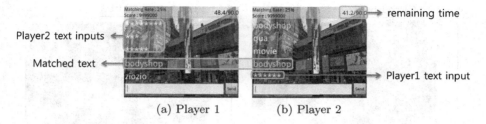

Player2 text inputs

Matched text

remaining time

Player1 text input

(a) Player 1   (b) Player 2

Fig. 4. An example of two-player compatibility ESP (cESP) Game

but also played on- or off-line, attempts to evaluate how much compatibility exists between two people by how similar their answers are to different questions. We use this entertainment aspect to motivate the users to play the cESP game.

In our cESP, each player is shown a street view image and is assumed to be present nearby the street view physically. The two mobile players are connected to each other through bluetooth and each player enters any text that represent the POI's or signs one sees in the image. The labels typed by each player appears on the screen and the labels typed by the other player is also shown but as strings of "***". Once a label matches a label entered by the partner, the label is highlighted to signal "compatibility". The compatibility score depends on the number of matches and the sequential order of matches. Similar to the ESP games, we use the matched labels to update our database and they are used as inputs to the Drag&Drop Game.

4.2 Drag&Drop Game

The goal of the Drag&Drop game is to identify whether a label[2] exist or not in the latest or "current" street view and identify their locations on the street view images. The Drag&Drop game leverages 1) the intuitive concept of drag and drop which is a popular gesture in touch user interfaces [16](i.e., a given label should be dragged and dropped at the right coordinate to map the label based on the current world) and 2) the driving game. To provide similar experience as a driving game, the street view "moves" toward the destination and the route is shown on the map located at the upper right corner of the screen (Figure 5(a)). For a given street view image, labels drop down the left side of the screen and while they fall, the player has several options:

1. Select and drag: The user selects or grabs the falling label and drags it over the street view to identify within the limited time (Figure 5(b))
2. Touch and delete: If the user determines that the given label is not available in the given street view, the user can touch the falling label and it will be marked for deletion.

---

[2] Labels can be different categories of POIs (e.g., coffee store) as well as particular names of the POIs (e.g., Starbucks).

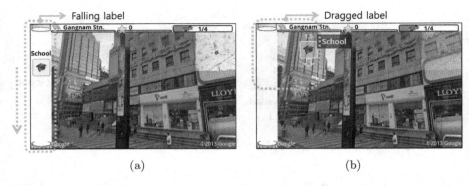

(a)   (b)

Fig. 5. The user interface of a falling a label(a) and a dragged label(b) in the Drag&Drop Game. The fingertip is touching the screen right below the arrow pointing down underneath the label in (b).

Fig. 6. Examples of different label categories used in the Drag&Drop game

3. Do nothing: If the user is uncertain about the label, the user can simply let the label fall through to the bottom.

The basic user interface is shown in Figure 5(a). At the top, the location name of the place of street view image, game score and the progress bar are shown. Top-down map with the current location and the destination is shown at the upper right corner. This map becomes transparent when a player touches any area on the screen. Two types of labels are introduced in the game: a category label (as shown in Figure 6) and a 'text' label where the 'text' is obtained from the cESP game.

Designing the User Interface. The user interface of the Drag&Drop Game evolved for better interaction with players based on feedbacks and observations from several early user studies. There were 5 significant updates from the first iteration of the user interface:

1. The concept of falling labels was introduced to enforce players to drag the labels to the right location in a limited time. Left column area for the falling labels replaced the remaining time bar which had occupied the top area of the screen and increased the available device screen area.
2. In the initial driving method street view image changed into the next image abruptly after finishing marking of given labels. Although several parts of the street view image overlapped and changed into the next street view

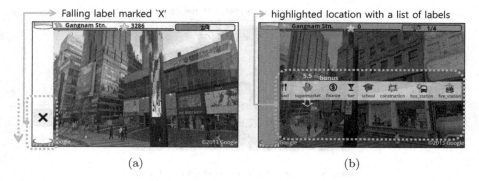

Fig. 7. Falling label is marked as 'X' (a) when the label is touched and marked for deletion. For the bonus, when the label is dragged and dropped, several labels pop up like (b) and wait for user's selection.

image, players pointed out that they could not feel moving forward and even indicated that the images did not seem to be related to each other. Thus, for better driving experience, animation was used to transition from one street view image to the next street view image.

3. The labels were designed with an arrow that points down to where the users are touching the screen. Otherwise the players cannot recognize the feature on the image because it becomes hidden by the label icon.
4. To give feedback on the coordinates specified by the players, a star icon was shown at the coordinate of the label after dropping the icon.
5. Because some players tend to drag a label into the hole on the left bottom of the device screen (i.e., they want to cancel or delete a label while dragging the label), later version of the game allowed this action.

Bonus Label. After an initial implementation of the game, one problem was the lack of "proper" labels – e.g., the user knows that a new convenience store exists at a given location but a convenience store label does not drop. This can be frustrating to the user but also problematic for the game itself since it prevents us from obtaining valuable information. To allow this (while keeping the game simple), we introduce a bonus label as shown in Figure 7. When this bonus label appears, the user can drag and drop it to any location where the user feels a new feature exists. After the bonus label is dragged and dropped, as (b) in Figure 7 a list of different labels pop up so that the user can select an appropriate label.

4.3   O/X Game

The information collected from the Drag&Drop game provides latest street view information but does not provide the differences between the latest street view image and the street view image from the service provider. The difference information can be very useful to the service providers – for example, the information can be useful

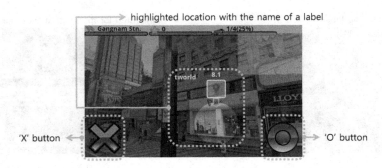

Fig. 8. User interface for the O/X Game

as a guidance to identify regions where the street views need to be re-captured. As a result, some form of image processing is necessary to identify the differences.

To provide the image processing, we leverage a simple O/X Game. The O/X game is based on the same principle as O/X quiz (or True/False quiz). In traditional O/X (or True/False quiz), the user is provided with a statement and is required to respond either with TRUE ('O') or FALSE('X'). The interface for the O/X Game is shown in Figure 8. Similar to the Drag&Drop game, the user is also shown a street view but instead of a falling label, the user is provided with a label and an arrow pointing to a given location. To focus on the region of interest, the image is shaded aside from the region in the circle and the arrow. At the bottom of the screen, there are two buttons – an 'O' button and an 'X' button. Based on the shown image, the user is asked to select the 'O' (if the label correctly identifies the feature of interest) or the 'X' otherwise. Thus, an 'X' output from the O/X Game is interpreted as a "difference" in the street view or POIs that have changed. Unlike the cESP game and the Drag&Drop game, which either requires familiarity with the street view or locally being present at the location, this game does not require any familiarity with the region. It works simply based on both the shown labels and the street view image to identify whether the label matches the shown feature on street view image.

5   Algorithm

There are two significant challenges in the LOX framework: 1) can the user selection be trusted? (i.e., user credibility) and 2) how accurate are the labels that are currently in the database? (i.e., label accuracy). These two scores are inter-related as an input from a more credible user will increase the label score while an input from a less credible user will not significantly impact the label accuracy score. In this section, we discuss how these two components are determined and their impact on overall performance of LOX framework.

5.1   User Credibility

The *user_credibility* has a value between 0 and 1 and shows the degree of a user's right prediction based on current database($label\_score_n$). The user who

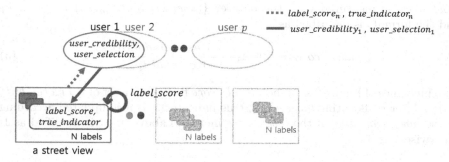

Fig. 9. Relationship between *user_credibility* and *label_score*

performs better on the prediction has a higher *user_credibility*. Given N labels in a street view image, a participant's *user_credibility* is measured with the dataset $\{(label\_score_n, s_n, t_n),\ n = 1, ..., N\}$ where $t_n \in \{1, 0\}, s_n \in \{1, 0\}$. s^n and t^n are shorthand for *user_selection* and *true_indicator* respectively. Each label has a confidence variable(*label_score*) and its corresponding tentative true indicator(t)(e.g.,if a *label_score* is higher than 0.5 then t is 1; otherwise, t is 0). User's selection(s) is decision between 'true' and 'false' about a label. The formula is described as :

$$user\_credibility = \frac{\sum_n \mathbb{I}[s_n = t_n] score(label\_score_n, t_n)}{\sum_n score(label\_score_n, t_n)} \quad (1)$$

$$score(label\_score, t) = \begin{cases} label\_score, & \text{if } t = 1 \\ 1 - label\_score, & \text{if } t = 0 \end{cases} \quad (2)$$

The function *score* is introduced to deal with both true and false *label_score* fairly. Each player is encouraged to predict each label's t_n by selecting s_n in the LOX games. Therefore, the more a player matches the pair of t_n and s_n, the higher *user_credibiltiy* the player gets. Green dotted line of Figure 9 shows how *user_credibility* flows in the over game.

5.2   Label Scores

The *label_score* has a value between 0 and 1, with a value closer to 0 representing a label that is likely to be false while a label with a value closer to 1 representing label that is likely to be true. The *label_score* changes based on the players' selection(s) and the player's *user_credibility*. Thus, every time *user_credibility* and user selection(s) are added, *label_score* increases or decreases by the amount represented by *user_credibility* (An example from the user study is shown later in Figure 12).

Given p users for a label, the *label_score* is the ratio of the sum of a group of *user_crediblity* whose selection is 1 to the sum of a group of *user_credibility* whose selection is 0 or 1 (i.e., How many players regard the label as 1). Then, the *label_score* is measured with the dataset $\{(user\_credibility_n, s_n), n = 1, ..., p\}$ and the formula is described as :

$$label\_score = \frac{\sum_n \mathbb{I}[s_n = 1]user\_credibility_n}{\sum_n user\_credibility_n} \tag{3}$$

Two blue lines of Figure 9 show how *label_score* flows with a set of *user_crediblity* and *s*. After reallocating *label_score*, true indicator(*t*) is also updated according to the *label_score* (e.g.,if the *label_score* increases above 0.5, *t* is modified as 1; otherwise, *t* is 0).

Initializing Label Scores. The *label_score* of the Drag&Drop and the O/X game need to be initialized. In the Drag&Drop game, the score of category label (as shown in Figure 6) is relatively determined by the frequency of the extracted information from Google Places API (e.g., extracted multiple category of POIs can be used as strong signal of existence of the 'category'). The POIs which do not change frequently can be used strong signal of existence (e.g., right part in Figure 6). Another type of label in Drag&Drop game is *text* label which are the output from the cESP game. The *label_score* of the type is relatively initialized based on the frequency of the matched numbers. In the O/X game, the score of labels from the Drag&Drop game is initialized as '0.5'. as it is difficult to determine if a label (or POI) has changed or not. As a result, we also introduce *random* labels whose location is randomly selected. The random labels' *label_score* is initialized as a low value (0.3) to represent it is very likely to be a wrong label.

5.3   Identifying Location and Number of POI's

A simple clusting algorithm is needed to identifying location and the number of POI's captured. Common k-means algorithm could not be used since it needs the parameter *k* known ahead of time. Instead, DBSCAN [17] algorithm was used because of two reasons : 1) it does not need to specify the number of clusters and 2) some noises are not selected during the clustering. Because the algorithm is density-based clustering, two parameters are required : ε (eps) and the minimum number of points required to from a cluster(minPts). ε (eps) can be easily decided by the size of touched finger point and the minPts is configured as '1'(i.e., we assume that some positions where at least two people agreed on are accepted). Figure 10(a) shows the raw coordinates from players and Figure 10(b) is their clustered result by DBSCAN. Although the cinema account for the several floors of the building, the final result shows the centroid of the building.

5.4   Cheating and Filtering Noise

In any human computation game, cheating needs to be addressed. In this section, we describe different methods in LOX framework that help identify such behavior.

(a) raw coordinates of labels   (b) clustered coordinates by DBSCAN

Fig. 10. Example of result of clustered positions by DBSCAN

cESP Game. Players of the cESP Game can input text that is not related to street view. However, the output of cESP is not the final results but input to the Drag&Drop gaem and thus, this process can help filter out some of the noise in the input. Global count of each word is maintained to prevent group of players from typing same word. In addition, some players might type the same texts cooperatively but unlike the original ESP game, this does not necessarily degrade quality of the text collected.

Drag&Drop Game. Players of the Drag&Drop game can drag or delete labels randomly. To prevent this, *user_credibility* is used to measure the credibility or accuracy of the player's selection based on the current database. The input or selection from players with low *user_credibitliy* will have small impact on the database. One observation that we made from the user study was that players who have higher *user_credibility* took relatively short time (i.e., milliseconds) in determining 'X' or 'drag and drop' – most likely because the player was confident in the decision. This information can likely be incorporated into the user's credibility.

O/X Game. Players of the O/X Game can select 'O' or 'X' randomly. To minimize this impact on the database, we introduce random false labels – i.e., labels with very high probability that it should be 'X'. In addition, for some labels, we introduce the same label twice within the same game to determine if there is an agreement in the player's response. These approach helps to properly calculate the credibility of the player.

6   User Study

To evaluate the feasibility and performance of LOX framework, we performed a user study near Gangnam subway station[3] in Korea for 5 days. To access the "real" street view, participants were randomly recruited at two coffee shops that had windows facing the streets. Participants played one of the LOX games and

---

[3] We choose Gangnam subway station because it is one of the most popular places where people hang out during the day in Korea.

then filled out survey for feedback and demographic information. The purpose of the game was not explained to the participants. Total of 4 street view images dated 2009 were obtained from the Google Street View image API and used in the study. Android mobile device (Samsung Galaxy Note) was used for the user study. 62 participants participated in the user study (Table 2) – with 42 participants for the cESP and Drag&Drop game in the Gangnam area and 20 participants who were not familiar with the given street view images played the O/X game.

Table 2. Demographic information of participants within the LOX framework

	cESP Game	Drag&Drop Game	O/X Game
# of Participants	20	22	20
Woman(%)	11(55%)	11(50%)	1(5%)
Man(%)	9(45%)	11(50%)	19(95%)
Age group($20 < age \leq 30$)	19	22	20
Age group($30 < age$)	1	0	0

6.1   LOX Framework User Study Results

The result of the cESP game is shown in Figure 11 and shows the number of typed words from each player, and the number of words matched. The matched texts of POI were used as input to the Drag&Drop game.

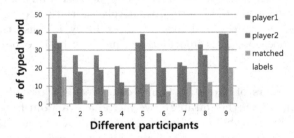

Fig. 11. Different matched numbers in the cESP game

From the Drag&Drop game, 132 labels from four street view images were collected. 56 labels whose score was above 0.6 are assumed to be true and the clustered labels are passed to the O/X game. Results from Drag&Drop game are shown in Figure 12(a). Labels which did not change such as 'McDonald's' – which correspond to labels that were available in the street view database – converged very quickly to a value of 1. In addition, some of the other obvious labels ('fire station'), which did not exist in the street view database image, converged quickly to a value of 0. As for the other labels, the scores fluctuated.

Some results of O/X game are shown in Figure 12(b). Scores of the different labels mostly converge as more participants (x-axis) played the game. The results

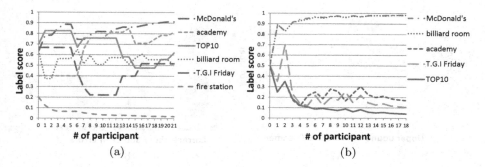

Fig. 12. Score of different labels and how they evolved in (a) Drag&Drop Game and (b) O/X Game (TOP10 is clothing store.)

show that for two labels, the scores converges to score of 1 which identifies that they are 'O' or labels that have not changed and shown on current street view database image. For the other three labels, they converge to a score closer to 0 signify that they are 'X' or "differences" and information that is not available from the service provider street view database image.

6.2   Result Validation

We evaluated the accuracy of the labels that were collected by manually verifying the new POIs. An example comparing the labels obtained from LOX with a manual picture taken from the same location is shown in Figure 14. We focus the analysis on the 20 labels that are the outputs of O/X game with a score higher than 0.5. The precision shows correctly identified new labels – i.e., for example, 9/19 precision refers to 19 labels were identified through the LOX framework but 9 were manually verified to be correct new POIs (i.e., 10 labels were incorrectly identified.) The score reflects the confidence of the new labels that we obtain. As the results show in Figure 13(a), if we only consider labels with very high scores (i.e., scores higher than 0.95), the accuracy is over 80% but if we consider all labels with score of higher than 0.7, the accuracy drops to approximately 60%. Thus, by maintaining a high threshold, the accuracy of the label obtained from LOX can be much more accurate.

To understand the "errors" or the incorrect labels, we analyzed the false labels and classified the source of errors into one of the following three categories(Figure 13(b)), based on the data collected.

1. Since the street view image is often captured from a car, some obstacles (e.g. street light, trees, or people) can hide some part of the street view image and make it difficult to identify some POIs. This error type mostly occurred in the O/X Game.
2. Another source of error was difficulty in identifying the exact location of the POIs. For example, a theatre was located in a building, occupying several

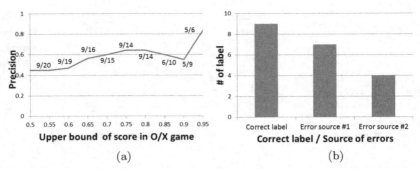

Fig. 13. The final result according to the upper bound of score(a) and the types of the final results of labels(b)

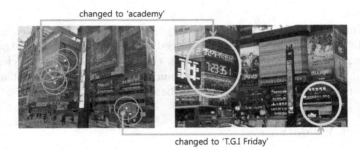

Fig. 14. Example of new labels(English academy and T.G.I Friday) in the game(left) and their corresponding real locations in the real street view(right)

floors but some participants were confused where to drag the labels to. This error type occurred mostly in the Drag&Drop game.

3. After manual analysis, we found the off-line cluster algorithm also caused some errors (but the number of errors was relatively small, compared to the other two error types.)

6.3   Survey

We did a post user-study survey to capture the demographic information, their experience with given street view images, experience with mobile games, evaluation of how fun or was user interface, and some feedback on games. Almost all participants had experience playing mobile games – more than 80% of participants played mobile games twice a month.

The survey on the user interface and entertainment of the different games within the LOX framework are shown in Figure 15. Although the purpose of the game was not explained, approximately 30% of the participants agreed that they want to play the game again for entertainment purpose. Overall, all the games were shown to have easy user interface. It was interesting to note that the O/X game had the simplest user interface but not necessarily the most interesting game, according to the survey.

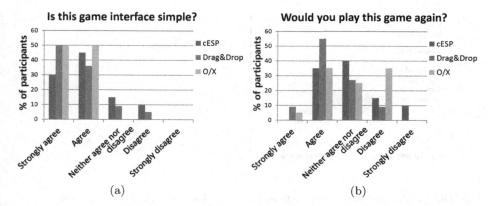

Fig. 15. Survey results on (a) LOX user interface and (b) entertainment aspect of the game

Feedback. In terms of additional feedback, some of the participants found the games interesting since it involved "real" street views, compared with most other mobile games. The two player game approach also appealed to some participants. In addition, perhaps a significant contribution of this game came from a participant who commented "I become more aware of the street POIs after playing the game." This initial interest in game can provide additional motivation to play the game again in the future.

6.4 Potential Applications

In this section, we describe how the outputs of LOX framework (either the output of the Drag&Drop game or the output of the O/X game) can be used. The analyzed output of LOX can be provided through an API for use by 3rd party application and an example is shown in Figure 16(a). RESTful API is a web API design model that is relatively simple and scalable [18] and we provide a RESTful API so that applications and service providers can make use of LOX data. Figure 16(a) example shows how the output of LOX framework can be presented – which include providing the information and location of the latest POIs. For each POI, the "score" determines the confidence of the new POI. And other API interface can provide additional street view information.

The output from LOX can also be leveraged by map service providers to identify how much the street view has changed. An example of such output is shown in Figure 16(b) where the higher intensity identifies regions with larger amount of changes or *differences*. The amount of change is calculated as a fraction of the POIs that have changed. The service providers can use this information to determine which regions need to have the street views updated. In addition, we expect the outputs of LOX can be leveraged for other purpose. For example, demographic information obtained from LOX games can be used for marketing purposes and while the latest city information can also be leveraged by city or urban planners.

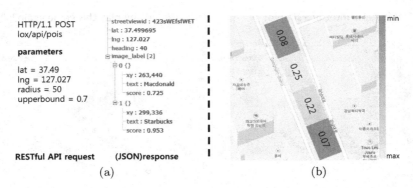

Fig. 16. (a) Request and response from REST API and (b) the heatmap showing the amount of changes

7   Conclusion

In this work, we proposed the LOX framework that consists of human computation games to provide updates to point of interests (POIs) on the street view maps. The LOX framework consists of different games that are used to help provide the text for the latest POIs, identify their locations on the street view maps, and finally help identify how much they differ from the existing street view maps. Based on the user studies, we were able to collect new information on the latest POIs while identifying the amount of differences with the current street view images provided by the service providers. Although the main purpose of the LOX framework was to provide updated information to the often outdated street view information, there are many other applications that can make use of the output of the LOX framework – with applications ranging from marketing to city/urban planning. We plan on exploring these opportunities as part of future work.

Acknowledgement. This research was supported in part by the SW Computing R&D Program of KEIT (2013, No.10041313, UX-oriented Mobile SW Platform).

References

1. Daum road view, http://map.daum.net/
2. Google map maker (2013), http://www.google.com/mapmaker
3. Openstreetmap, http://www.openstreetmap.org/
4. Waze mobile application, http://www.waze.com
5. von Ahn, L., Dabbish, L.: Designing games with a purpose. Commun. ACM 51(8), 58–67 (2008)
6. Eagle, N.: txteagle: Mobile crowdsourcing. In: Aykin, N. (ed.) IDGD 2009. LNCS, vol. 5623, pp. 447–456. Springer, Heidelberg (2009)

7. Narula, P., Gutheim, P., Rolnitzky, D., Kulkarni, A., Hartmann, B.: Mobileworks: A mobile crowdsourcing platform for workers at the bottom of the pyramid. In: AAAI 2011 Workshops, vol. WS-11-11 (2011)
8. Kanhere, S.S.: Participatory sensing: Crowdsourcing data from mobile smartphones in urban spaces. In: Hota, C., Srimani, P.K. (eds.) ICDCIT 2013. LNCS, vol. 7753, pp. 19–26. Springer, Heidelberg (2013)
9. Lane, N., Miluzzo, E., Lu, H., Peebles, D., Choudhury, T., Campbell, A.: A survey of mobile phone sensing. IEEE Communications Magazine 48(9), 140–150 (2010)
10. Celino, I., Cerizza, D., Contessa, S., Corubolo, M., Dell'Aglio, D., Valle, E., Fumeo, S.: A social and location-based game with a purpose to crowdsource your urban data. In: PASSAT 2012, pp. 910–913 (2012)
11. Budburst mobile project, http://networkednaturalist.org/budburstmobile/
12. Zimmerman, J., Tomasic, A., Garrod, C., Yoo, D., Hiruncharoenvate, C., Aziz, R., Thiruvengadam, N.R., Huang, Y., Steinfeld, A.: Field trial of tiramisu: crowdsourcing bus arrival times to spur co-design. In: CHI 2011, pp. 1677–1686 (2011)
13. Quercia, D., Pesce, J.P., Almeida, V., Crowcroft, J.: Psychological maps 2.0: a web engagement enterprise starting in london. In: WWW 2013, pp. 1065–1076 (2013)
14. von Ahn, L., Dabbish, L.: Labeling images with a computer game. In: CHI 2004, pp. 319–326 (2004)
15. Lawrence, E.C.: Compatibility game, [US Patent 5,681,046] (October 28, 1997)
16. Shneiderman, B.: Designing for fun: how can we design user interfaces to be more fun? Interactions 11(5), 48–50 (2004)
17. Sander, J., Ester, M., Kriegel, H.-P., Xu, X.: Density-based clustering in spatial databases. Data Mining and Knowledge Discovery 2(2), 169–194 (1998)
18. Böck, H.: Restful web services. In: The Definitive Guide to NetBeans^{TM} Platform 7, pp. 345–352 (2011)

Chill-Out: Relaxation Training through Respiratory Biofeedback in a Mobile Casual Game

Avinash Parnandi[1], Beena Ahmed[2], Eva Shipp[3], and Ricardo Gutierrez-Osuna[1]

[1] Department of Computer Science and Engineering, Texas A&M University, USA
[2] Department of Electrical and Computer Engineering, Texas A&M University, Qatar
[3] School of Rural and Public Health, Texas A&M Health Science Center, USA
{parnandi,rgutier}@tamu.edu, beena.ahmed@qatar.tamu.edu,
eshipp@srph.tamhsc.edu

Abstract. We present Chill-Out, an adaptive biofeedback game that teaches relaxation skills by monitoring the breathing rate of the player. The game uses a positive feedback loop that penalizes fast breathing by means of a proportional-derivative control law: rapid (and/or increasing) breathing rates increase game difficulty and reduce the final score of the game. We evaluated Chill-Out against a conventional non-biofeedback game and traditional relaxation based on deep breathing. Measurements of breathing rate, electrodermal activity, and heart rate variability show that playing Chill-Out leads to lower arousal during a subsequent task designed to induce stress.

1   Introduction

The World Health Organization has deemed job stress a global epidemic [1]. Job stress can have serious health consequences; it contributes to the obesity epidemic worldwide [2] and promotes a host chronic diseases, specifically cardiovascular disease –the leading cause of death in the developed world [1]. Stress can also have a profoundly negative effect on mental health, an under-acknowledged growing health problem around the world. Thus, reducing job stress could help reduce a number of negative health outcomes, increase the quality of life for workers, and result in an economic benefit for employers, e.g., increased worker productivity, reduced healthcare costs; as an example, workplace stress has been estimated to cost $150-300 billion to the US economy alone [3].

A number of techniques have been developed to help individuals self-regulate the impact of stress, including various forms of meditation, deep breathing and biofeedback [4]. Deep or diaphragmatic breathing (DB) is among the easiest and most intuitive evidenced-based methods for reducing stress [5]. Essentially, DB addresses the autonomic nervous system imbalance that arises following exposure to a stressor and activation of the sympathetic nervous system. As DB recruits the parasympathetic nervous system, action of the sympathetic nervous system becomes inhibited leading to a calmer, more relaxed state [6]. Many of the stress management programs delivered in workplace settings demonstrate that DB substantially reduces the

G. Memmi and U. Blanke (Eds.): MobiCASE 2013, LNICST 130, pp. 252–260, 2014.

symptoms of stress [4]. Biofeedback techniques are also used frequently as components of worksite stress management programs. Biofeedback allows patients to see changes in their physiology (e.g., skin conductance, heart rate) while they perform relaxation exercises, and can be effective, provided that the patient adheres to the training regime. Although beneficial, however, these traditional programs may not be sustainable since they require prolonged and substantial commitments of time and other resources from both workers and employers [7]. In addition, these techniques teach subjects to regulate their stress response in a quiet, relaxed environment; a skill that may not transfer to stressful, high-stakes scenarios, where it is really needed [8].

Thus, there is a need for treatment techniques that are inherently engaging and that promote relaxation in the presence of stressors. Video games appear ideally suited for this purpose: they are tremendously popular (53% of adults age 18 and older play video games, both men and women [9]), and are very effective at manipulating arousal levels [10, 11]. Early research showed that even short and "easy" deep relaxation exercises could positively impact workers' cardiac autonomic function [12]. Consequently, relaxation exercises embedded in a videogame and played frequently for a few minutes each session may allow workers to achieve sustained health benefits while also maintaining their productivity over the long term. As a step towards our goal of relaxation training, we present Chill-Out, a novel method that combines biofeedback and adaptive games. Our approach combines an open-source casual game (Frozen Bubble) with a proportional-derivative positive feedback controller [13] that modulates game difficulty to reward slow breathing patterns and penalize high or increasing breathing rates. We compared the approach against a non-adaptive game and deep breathing (DB). We hypothesized that Chill-Out would lead to (1) better transfer of DB skills, (2) a reduction in physiological arousal, and (3) improved performance, all measured during a subsequent stress-inducing task.

2   Methods

We use concepts from classical control theory to model the process of adapting the videogame in response to the player's breathing rate. Illustrated in Fig. 1(a), a control loop consists of (i) the plant we wish to control, (ii) a sensor that measures the plant's output, and (iii) a controller that seeks to minimize the difference between the desired and actual output. When applied to game adaptation, the plant becomes the player, whose breathing rate we seek to regulate, the feedback loop consists of a respiratory sensor, and the controller is an algorithm that modulates the game's difficulty accordingly –see Fig. 1(b).

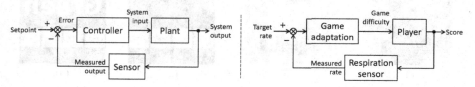

Fig. 1. Block diagram of (a) a classical feedback control system, and (b) our adaptive physiological game

In this work, we use a positive feedback control law where states of non-relaxation, which we define as those with breathing rates higher than 6 breaths per minute (brpm) and increasing $(BR > 6 \wedge \Delta BR > 0)$, are penalized by increasing the game difficulty; breathing rates lower than 6 brpm are not penalized. We use a proportional derivative (PD) control law to adapt the game:

$$d(t) = K_p\, \epsilon(t) + K_d\, d\epsilon(t)/dt \tag{1}$$

$$\epsilon(t) = \begin{cases} b(t) - b_0 & (b(t) > b_0) \wedge \big(b(t) > b(t-1)\big) \\ 0 & otherwise \end{cases} \tag{2}$$

where $d(t)$ is the game's difficulty level, and $\epsilon(t)$ is the error in the current breathing rate $b(t)$ relative to the desired rate $b_0 = 6$. The term K_p is a proportional gain that causes the game difficulty to increase when the respiratory rate is higher than the desired value. Likewise, the term K_d is a derivative gain that adjusts the game difficulty based on the rate of change in respiration; adding a derivative term reduces overshoot and helps stabilize the process. Our implementation uses $K_p = 0.5$ and $K_d = 1$, values that were determined empirically.

2.1   Integration with a Casual Game

Selection of a suitable game genre is critical because it is the activity through which players learn to regulate their breathing rate. A few genres (e.g., first-person shooter) are unsuited due to their violent content and their possible connection with aggressive behavior. A few other genres require long time commitment (e.g. role playing, strategy), which makes them best suited for a specialized segment of the population, such as hardcore players [14]. A few of the remaining genres (e.g., quiz, board games) also lack the dynamic content that would be required to develop adaptive gameplay. The ideal game for physiological training belongs to what have been described as casual games: *"games developed for the general public,... appeal to people of all ages, gender and nationalities, ... are fun and easy to play, ... and are usually played for a short period of time, from 5 to 20 minutes"* [15].

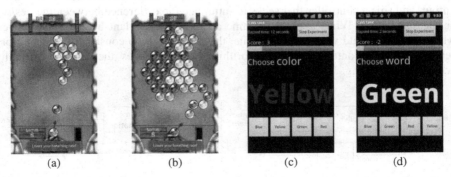

(a)	(b)	(c)	(d)

Fig. 2. (a-b). Screenshots of the Frozen Bubble game. (c-d) Screenshots of the modified Stroop CWT used as pre- and post-tasks.

Based on these considerations we adopted Frozen Bubble, a very popular casual game that is also available through a GNU General Public License. Fig. 2 shows a screenshot of the game; the user controls a small cannon that shoots bubbles of different colors into a playing area. The objective of the game is to eliminate all the hanging bubbles before the ceiling collapses; to do so, the player has to group three or more bubbles of the same color, which causes them to collapse. Frozen Bubble provides a few parameters that are amenable to adaptation, such as auto-shooting rate, how fast the ceiling drops, or angular rate and lag of the cannon. Out of these, we chose the auto-shooting frequency as the game difficulty to be adapted, i.e., parameter $d(t)$ in equation (1), as it demands immediate action from the player. As the breathing rate crosses the threshold $(BR > 6 \wedge \Delta BR > 0)$, the auto-shooting frequency increases making it harder to play the game. Hence to make progress on the game, the user must maintain a slow and sustained breathing pattern.

3   Experiments

We validated the approach using an experimental protocol with three phases. During the first phase (pre-task), participants performed a modified Stroop color word test (CWT[1]) for 4 minutes. During the second phase (treatment), participants were randomly assigned into one of three groups, a group that played the biofeedback game (GBF), a baseline group that performed deep breathing (DB[2]), and a control group that played the original Frozen Bubble game without adaptation or respiratory feedback (game only - GO[3]). Following our prior work [11], the duration of the treatment was 8 minutes for the three groups. During the final phase (post-test), participants repeated the CWT for an additional 4 minutes. Prior to the experiments the participants were asked to relax for 5 minutes. We adopted this between-subjects experimental design to avoid ordering effect due to learning or fatigue. Nine participants, (7 male 2 female; age range 22-33 years) participated in the study. Participants reported that they were in good health; none reported excessive drinking

---

[1] The CWT is widely used in psychophysiology to increase arousal. In the conventional CWT, participants are shown one of four words (red, blue, green, and yellow) displayed in different ink color, and are asked to choose the ink color of the displayed word; see fig 2(c). To make the task more challenging, our implementation switched between asking for the ink color or the text of the word –see fig 2(d), and also switched between two modes (congruent and incongruent) every 30 s. In congruent mode, the concept and the ink color were the same, e.g., the word "red" in red ink. In incongruent mode, the concept and ink color were different, e.g., word "blue" in red ink. During pre-test, the stimulus was displayed for 1 sec, and the participant had 3 sec to respond; the response time was reduced to 2.5 sec during post-test to ensure the task remained challenging despite any learning effects from the pre-test.

[2] Participants in the DB condition were asked to follow an audio pacing signal that guided them to breathe at a rate of 6 brpm. None of the participants received prior training in DB.

[3] The game difficulty level in the GO condition was the lowest level (i.e., easiest) in the GBF condition, which GBF participants could only achieve under slow and sustained breathing.

or smoking habits. We received approval from the Institutional Review Board (IRB) prior to the study and consent from individual participant before the session.

We used a Google Nexus-1 smartphone running Android 2.3.6 for the game, pre- and post- CWT, and guided DB. To compare the effectiveness of the adaptive game in managing stress levels, we extracted two physiological measures that are commonly used as indicators of autonomic activity: heart rate variability (HRV) and electrodermal activity (EDA) [16]. When used in combination, these two measures provide a robust index of arousal: changes in EDA and HRV are generally in opposite direction with increasing task demands (e.g. EDA increases while HRV decreases), so simultaneous increases (or decrements) in both variables can be dismissed as noise or motion artifacts [17].

We extracted HRV from a Bioharness BT sensor (Zephyr Tech.), which also provided the respiratory signal for game adaptation. BR and ΔBR were updated every second. Our measure of HRV was the root mean square of successive differences (RMSSD) in R-R intervals (sampled at 18 Hz), computed over a 30-second window [16]. We monitored EDA with a FlexComp Infinity encoder (Thought Technology Ltd.) at 32 Hz. Disposable AgCl electrodes were placed at the palmar and hypothenar eminences of the player's non-dominant hand; from this, we extracted the number of skin conductance responses (phasic response) over a 30-second window using a peak detection algorithm with a threshold of 1 mS.

4   Results

Skill Transfer. We compared the three treatments (GBF, GO, and DB) by their ability to transfer the relaxation skill. For this purpose, we analyzed the respiratory signal during pre and post-tests. Fig. 3(a) shows the power spectrum density (PSD) of the breathing waveform for the 9 subjects (light blue: pre-test; dark red: post-test). For subjects in the GBF condition, there is a marked difference in the respiratory PSD before and after game play: the pre-task breathing spectra is broad and shifted towards high breathing rates, whereas the post-task breathing spectra is narrowband and centered on 0.1Hz (6 brpm), the breathing rate rewarded during gameplay. In contrast, the respiratory PSD for subjects in the DB does not show a significant difference before and after treatment, suggesting that the DB skill did not transfer; notice how subject #5 maintained a low respiratory rate during the entire experimental session, which suggests that none of the treatments could have been of much direct benefit. Finally, subjects in the GO condition displayed a high breathing rate pre- and post-test, showing that playing a casual game alone[3] does not encourage a relaxing respiratory behavior.

Similar conclusions can be extracted by analyzing the breathing rate in the time domain over the duration of the experiment –see Fig. 3(b). Subjects in the GBF condition lower their breathing rate during the treatment phase from its initial high value at pre-test and, more importantly, maintain that slow breathing rate during post-test, an indication that the deep breathing skill transferred successfully. Subjects in the DB condition also lower their breathing rate while performing the treatment but,

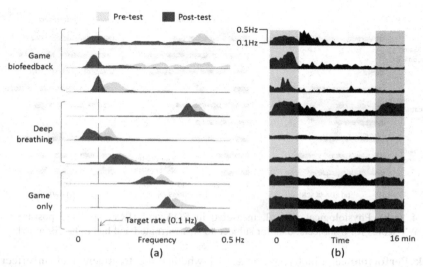

Fig. 3. (a). Power spectral density of the breathing signal during pre-test (light blue) and post-test (dark red); each row represents a participant. (b) Evolution of the breathing rate during the experiments (0.1Hz and 0.5Hz correspond to 6 brpm and 30 brpm, respectively).

unlike GBF subjects, revert during post-test to the high breathing rate shown at pre-test; this is particularly noticeable for subject #4. Finally, the breathing rate for subjects in the GO condition does not change significantly over the duration of the experiment, and never reaches the deep breathing zone.

Physiological Arousal. We also analyzed the subjects' arousal levels, as measured by EDA and HRV. It is important to note that these indirect measures were collected for monitoring purposes and were not used for biofeedback in any way. EDA results for all subjects in the experiments are shown in Fig. 4(a). For subjects in the GBF condition, there is sharp decrease in EDA when going from pre-test to post-test, which indicates that playing the biofeedback game led to a significant reduction in arousal at post-test. In contrast, only 2/3rd of the subjects in the DB and GO conditions had a decrease in EDA, and the remaining 1/3rd experienced an increase in EDA. A 1-way ANOVA of the difference in EDA between pre-test and post-test with treatment (GBF, GO, and DB) as the factor shows statistically significant differences among the three protocols ($p = 0.02$).

Fig. 4(b) shows the average HRV computed over the duration of the pre-test and post-test segments. HRV increased significantly for subjects in the GBF condition, corroborating results from EDA that indicate lower arousal after completion of the biofeedback game. Two of the subjects in the DB condition also had higher HRV post-test, but the increase is not as marked. HRV for subjects in the GO condition remained largely unaltered. A 1-way ANOVA on the HRV difference between pre-test and post-test with the three treatments as factors also shows a statistically significant difference ($p = 0.01$).

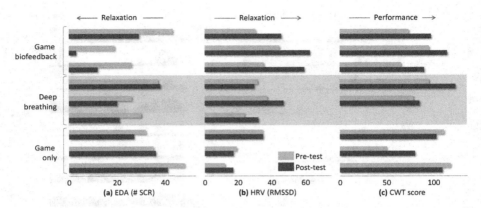

Fig. 4. (a-b). Physiological arousal, measured in EDA and HRV, pre- and post-treatment. (c) CWT scores for 8 subjects; data for subject #6 was corrupted and had to be discarded.

Task Performance. Finally, we analyzed whether the treatment had an effect on performance, measured as the difference in CWT scores between pre-test and post-test. Results are shown in Fig. 4(c) for 8 subjects. Subjects in the GBF and DB conditions had higher CWT scores in the post task, whereas subjects in the GO condition had mixed results. In this case, a 1-way ANOVA shows that the differences among treatments were not statistically significant ($p = 0.40$).

5   Discussion

We have proposed a new strategy for teaching relaxation skills that leverages the broad appeal of casual games. The approach consists of monitoring physiological signals during gameplay, and adapting the game in a way that encourages relaxing behaviors. To test the feasibility of this approach we have developed Chill-Out, a biofeedback game for smartphones that adapts in response to respiratory rate to reward sustained slow breathing. We tested Chill-Out against traditional deep breathing and a non-adaptive non-biofeedback version of the game. Our results show that Chill-Out is more effective than either alternative in transferring deep breathing skills to a subsequent stress-inducing task, and it also leads to significantly lower arousal, as measured by electrodermal activity and heart rate variability.

Chill-Out teaches relaxation techniques while performing a task (i.e. a game) that is designed to increase the user's arousal level [10]. And herein lies the main difference with traditional relaxation training, which encourage practice in quiet settings that do not reflect the environments we encounter in daily life. As a result, our method may lead to better transfer of relaxation skills to other stressful tasks, as demonstrated in our study. This hypothesis is also supported by prior research on stress exposure training in military settings [18], which shows that (for many tasks) normal training procedures do not improve performance when the task is later to be performed under stress.

Future work will test the method with other physiological measures (e.g. HRV, EDA, EEG) as the feedback signal. Additional work is needed to test whether the learning effects observed in our study carry over to subsequent days; longer and repeated training periods beyond the 8-minute treatment in our protocol will likely promote lasting effects. We believe, however, that long-term behavioral changes are not necessary for our approach to be of practical benefit in the workplace; as shown by our study, a single session of Chill-Out leads to reductions in arousal and shows ways in which the practice could be of use in work settings for short-term relief.

Acknowledgments. This publication was made possible by NPRP grant # 5-678-2-282 from the Qatar National Research Fund (a member of Qatar Foundation). The statements made herein are solely the responsibility of the authors. We are grateful to Christopher Blanchard, James Burian, Mary Thompson, Kim Truong, and Youngpyo Son for early work on implementing Chill-Out.

References

1. DeVries, M.W., Wilkerson, B.: Stress, work and mental health: a global perspective. Acta Neuropsychiatr. 15(1), 44–53 (2003)
2. Dallman, M.F.: Stress-induced obesity and the emotional nervous system. Trends Endocrinol. Metabol. 21(3), 159–165 (2010)
3. Leiter, M.P., Maslach, C.: Banishing burnout: six strategies for improving your relationship with work, 1st edn., ix, 193 p. Jossey-Bass, San Francisco (2005)
4. Richardson, K.M., Rothstein, H.R.: Effects of occupational stress management intervention programs: A meta-analysis. J. Occup. Health Psychol. 13(1), 69 (2008)
5. Varvogli, L., Darviri, C.: Stress Management Techniques: evidence-based procedures that reduce stress and promote health. Health Sci. J. 5(2), 74–89 (2011)
6. Jerath, R., et al.: Physiology of long pranayamic breathing: neural respiratory elements provide a mechanism that explains how slow deep breathing shifts the autonomic nervous system. Med. Hypotheses 67(3), 566–571 (2006)
7. Henriques, G., et al.: Exploring the effectiveness of a computer-based heart rate variability biofeedback program in reducing anxiety in college students. Appl. Psychophys. Biof. 36(2), 101–112 (2011)
8. Driskell, J.E., Johnston, J.H.: Stress exposure training. In: Making Decisions Under Stress: Implications for Individual and Team Training, pp. 191–217 (1998)
9. Williams, D., et al.: The virtual census: representations of gender, race and age in video games. New Media & Society 11(5), 815–834 (2009)
10. Bailey, K., West, R., Anderson, C.A.: The influence of video games on social, cognitive, and affective information processing. In: Handbook Social Neurosci., pp. 1001–1014 (2011)
11. Parnandi, A., Son, Y., Gutierrez-Osuna, R.: A control-theoretic approach to adaptive physiological games. In: Intl Conf. Affect Comput. & Intellig. Interact. (2013)
12. Toivanen, H., et al.: Impact of regular relaxation training on the cardiac autonomic nervous system of hospital cleaners and bank employees. Scand. J. Work Environ. Health, 319–325 (1993)
13. Kuo, B.C., Golnaraghi, M.F.: Automatic Control Systems, vol. 4. John Wiley & Sons, New York (2003)

14. Gackenbach, J., Bown, J.: Mindfulness and Video Game Play: A Preliminary Inquiry. Mindfulness 2, 114–122 (2011)
15. http://www.casualgamesassociation.org (cited November 21, 2011)
16. Cacioppo, J.T., Tassinary, L.G., Berntson, G.: Handbook of Psychophysiology. Cambridge University Press (2007)
17. Boucsein, W., Haarmann, A., Schaefer, F.: Combining skin conductance and heart rate variability for adaptive automation during simulated IFR flight. In: Harris, D. (ed.) HCII 2007 and EPCE 2007. LNCS (LNAI), vol. 4562, pp. 639–647. Springer, Heidelberg (2007)
18. Cannon-Bowers, J.A., Salas, E.E.: Making decisions under stress: Implications for individual and team training. American Psychological Association (1998)

Using Low-Power Sensors to Enhance Interaction on Wristwatches and Bracelets

Simon T. Perrault and Eric Lecolinet

Telecom ParisTech - CNRS LTCI UMR 5141,
46 rue Barrault, Paris, France
firstname.lastname@mines-telecom.fr

Abstract. In the last few years, new interactive wristwatches are available on the market. Despite their impressive hardware capacities, the interaction on such devices remains rather limited. We propose a cheap and low power consuming way to enhance interaction on a wristwatch but adding position sensors on the watchband. We then present a MP3 player application as a proof of concept for our prototype.

Keywords: input, digital jewelry, wristwatch, bracelet, interaction, low-power, potentiometer.

1 Introduction

After decades of miniaturization race, mobile computing is reaching a new step with the emergence of small mobile devices such as digital jewelry [3]. Interactive wristwatches, in particular, have gained an increased attention from researchers and companies. In the last two years, mature commercial products arrived, such as the "I'm Watch"[1] or the Sony Watch[2]. The hardware capacities of these devices are really

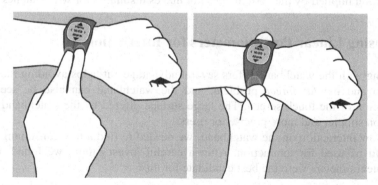

Fig. 1. Interaction on the watchband that prevents screen occlusion and offers a large interaction surface for precise interaction

---

[1] http://www.imsmart.com/en
[2] http://www.sonymobile.com/global-en/products/accessories/smartwatch-2-sw2/

G. Memmi and U. Blanke (Eds.): MobiCASE 2013, LNICST 130, pp. 261–264, 2014.

impressive, but since 2001 and the IBM Linux Watch [4], interaction with wristwatches did not evolve and remains rather limited: interaction relies solely on small touch screens.

These small touch screens suffer from two main problems in terms of interaction: screen occlusion and *fat finger* problem [5]. When interacting on a touch screen, the user will place his finger directly on the screen, hiding anything displayed under. Also, since the surface of the finger is quite large compared to the surface of the screen, it becomes harder to acquire small targets on such devices (the *fat finger* problem). A solution would be to add additional sensors on the wristwatch, but that would lead to an increase of power consumption on a device where power is a critical and rare resource.

To solve the two interaction problems presented, we propose to add low power consuming potentiometers on the watchband of a wristwatch to take advantage of a large surface that was previously not used for interaction. We then present how a MP3 player can be controlled using simple gestures on the watchband.

2   Related Work

The usual approach to avoid the screen occlusion and the fat finger problem on small devices is to interact around the device and not directly on the screen. To the best of our knowledge, no previous work suggested the use of watchband for interaction.

Abracadabra [2] allows the user to point around the device by using a magnetometer. It allows for precise input and does not consume a lot of power (around 0.15 mA for the additional magnetometer). However, this technique requires the use of a magnet that can be lost or bothersome to wear.

Other techniques, such as Butler's SideSight [1] use proximity sensors to track finger positions around the device for mid-air pointing, but the additional power consumption implied by the system does not makes it suitable for wristwatches.

3   Using Linear Potentiometers for Interaction

Interacting with the watchband offers several advantages: it helps avoiding the screen occlusion and the *fat finger* problem, and the watchband can also be seen as a prolongation of the touch screen. The large surface offered by the watchband makes interaction simpler and more precise for users.

To allow interaction on the watchband, we needed to find a low consuming sensor that could be used for interaction. After a careful investigation, we found out that linear potentiometers were the best candidate for this.

3.1   Hardware

We designed our first watchband prototype using a 2-cm wide watchband composed of four resistive potentiometers: two of them were positioned on the internal part of the band (below the screen) and the two others on the external part of the band.

The potentiometers consist of 5-cm long thin bands flexible enough to be used on the watchband without getting damaged. Each potentiometer is a variable resistor (100 Ω to 10kΩ) with low variability (less than 1%). They are all connected to an Arduino Fio board, that provides a 3.3V input and to an additional 100 kΩ resistor. It requires only 0.03 mA/potentiometer.

The microcontroller detects up to 1024 different positions on the potentiometer (around 200 positions/cm). The hardware prototype is presented on the Fig. 2. With this implementation, pseudo "multi touch" interaction is possible: two different contacts can be sensed on each part of the band.

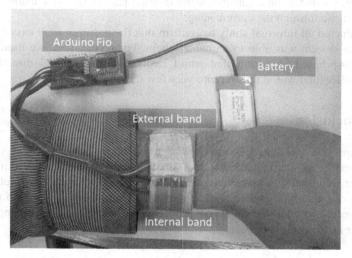

Fig. 2. Hardware prototype of the augmented wristband

3.2   Advantages of the Technology

While capacitive technology was an possibility, we chose the resistive technology for the following reasons:

1. It requires less power to be operated (0.03 mA/sensor).
2. The pressure needed to activate them helps preventing accidental activation.
3. The potentiometers can also be hidden under an opaque layer that would make the sensors totally invisible and would thus not alter the aesthetics of the device, and could be integrated on any commercial product to integrate.

4   MP3 Player Application

We want our system to be simple to use. Yet, it has to provide a rich interaction that could allow the user to command any application without having to directly interact on the touch screen. We thus designed a simple gesture vocabulary based on pointing or sliding the finger on the watchband.

First, we found that a nice resting position for users is to grab their wrist by putting their thumb on the internal part of the band, and their index and middle fingers on the external part of the band. Then, by simply tapping with one finger on the corresponding band, it is possible to simply input three different commands: by tapping with the thumb, it would trigger the "Play/Pause" command, by tapping with the index, it would be "Previous Song", and "Next Song" with the middle finger.

For volume control, users would first grab their wrist with the thumb and the index finger (one on the internal part, other on the external one) and simply slide them.

Our software also allows navigating inside a song: in that case, users simply put both their index and middle fingers on the internal part of the watchband and slides them to navigate through the current song.

We conducted an informal study to confirm that the gestures were easy to perform and that our system was able to recognize them. For recognition, we used a simple state machine based algorithm that could easily be implemented directly on the microcontroller (and would thus require very few CPU power).

5   Conclusion

In this paper we presented a novel way to enhance interaction on interactive wristwatches. In the particular context of small mobile devices, battery life is quite critical. Our solution relies on resistive technology that does not require a lot of power to operate, can also be invisible and prevents two well known interaction problems: the screen occlusion and the fat finger problem. We also presented an implemented MP3 player as a proof of concept.

References

1. Butler, A., Izadi, S., Hodges, S.: SideSight: multi-"touch" interaction around small devices. In: Proc. UIST 2008, pp. 201–204. ACM, New York (2008)
2. Harrison, C., Hudson, S.E.: Abracadabra: wireless, high-precision, and unpowered finger input for very small mobile devices. In: Proc. UIST 2009, pp. 121–124. ACM (2009)
3. Miner, C.S.: Pushing functionality into even smaller devices. Communications of the ACM 44(3), 72–73 (2001)
4. Narayanaswami, C., Kamijoh, N., Raghunath, M.T., et al.: IBM's Linux watch, the challenge of miniaturization. IEEE Computer 35(1), 33–41 (2002)
5. Roudaut, A., Huot, S., Lecolinet, E.: TapTap and MagStick: Improving One-Handed Target Acquisition on Small Touch-screens. In: Proc. AVI 2008, pp. 146–153. ACM (2008)

Towards Unsupervised Remote Therapy
for Individuals with Aphasia

Conor Higgins, Aine Kearns, Conor Ryan, Mikael Fernstrom, and Sue Franklin

University of Limerick, Limerick, Ireland
conor.higgins@ul.ie

Abstract. This paper discusses the use of evolutionary algorithms in mobile computing in order to provide individuals with aphasia a means of self-guided and unsupervised speech and language therapy. Traditional speech and language therapy approaches necessitate significant time commitments and are resource intensive. By harnessing evolutionary computation, therapy sessions can be generated, which consider the best practices of a speech and language professional whilst factoring in the abilities and idiosyncrasies of the user. The primary goal of this research is the provision of a self-directed rehabilitative application targeted at aphasic individuals with writing difficulties (particularly dysgraphia).

Keywords: evolutionary computation, therapy, speech and language therapy, genetic algorithm, aphasia, dysgraphia.

1   Introduction

Aphasia can be defined as a degradation of the ability to comprehend or convey language in a coherent manner. Aphasia is most commonly associated with and caused by cerebrovascular accidents (CVA's), better known as 'strokes', though it can be caused by various injuries, which result in damage to the brain. Aphasia can affect an individual in terms of their spelling, reading, writing, articulation, recognition and expression of words or sentences. Dysgraphia is an issue commonly associated with aphasic individuals, whereby they experience difficulties in writing, most often with handwriting, but often in terms of their coherence. Individuals with dysgraphia tend to omit or substitute letters, whilst their handwriting exhibits frequent stylistic inconsistencies and functional issues, such as a lack of speed and composure. While numerous therapies exist which seek to rehabilitate individuals with aphasia, they often demand a significant time commitment from both a person with aphasia (PWA) and a speech and language therapist (SLT), not to mention family members and carers. Traditional forms of therapy are considered to be resource-intensive and as such it may not be possible for a PWA to participate in clinical therapy consistently. With this in mind, a mobile application has been developed, which harnesses artificial intelligence in order to enable self-guided continuous therapy.

G. Memmi and U. Blanke (Eds.): MobiCASE 2013, LNICST 130, pp. 265–268, 2014.

2   Related Work

2.1   Technology and Aphasia

van de Sandt-Koenderman (2011) [1] discussed the role of computer technology in aphasia rehabilitation, presenting the benefits and complexities associated with such technologies for PWA's. Greig et al. (2008) [2] presented the barriers and facilitators to mobile technology for aphasic individuals, claiming the physical attributes of modern mobile devices as being highly responsible for the alienation of users with aphasia. Katz (2010) [3] defined technologies related to aphasia by their intended usage, grouping them by the following; Alternative and Augmentative Communication (AAC), Computer-Assisted Treatment (CAT) and Computer-only Treatment (COT). Cherney & Halper (2008) [4] demonstrated the potential for computers to be used unassisted by aphasic patients with noticeable benefits. The authors employed a novel script training computer application in order to rehabilitate individuals with aphasia and concomitant cognitive deficits.

2.2   Traditional Therapy Forms

The work of Marshall et al. (1990) [5], Nettleton & Lesser (1991) [6] and Boyle & Coelho (1995) [7] among others targeted the reactivation and rehabilitation of aphasic patients word retrieval, employing semantic and or phonological approaches. Maher et al. (1998) [8] and Francis et al. (2001) [9] adopted reactivation and relearning approaches respectively to therapies focused on reading. As well as word retrieval/production and reading, a number of authors ([11] - [10]) have investigated the rehabilitation of writing using methods including writing to dictation, anagrams, participant cueing, etc. While the above have proven to be successful in their own regard, clinical therapy often necessitates a substantial and intense time commitment on the behalf of all associated individuals, whilst requiring the individual to be in close proximity to either a therapist or clinic. The developed system features a prompting framework, influenced by both Anagram and Copy Treatment (ACT) and Copy and Recall Treatment (CART). Beeson (1999) [12] chose both ACT and CART, whereby the studys participants were tasked with arranging anagrams and repeated word copying with and without professional assistance. Beeson et al. (2002) [10] demonstrated the potential for ACT and CART in rehabilitating individuals with aphasia and concomitant writing deficits.

3   Implementation

A mobile application has been developed, which enables PWA's to facilitate their own continuous therapy sessions. The application features a word identification task, presenting users with a target image and requiring them to identify and spell the associated word correctly. Throughout the application's use, the user is supported via a cyclically presented cueing hierarchy. This hierarchy consists of semantic prompts (an easily understood sentence with the target word omitted/occluded), semantic prompts with the target word's initial grapheme presented and finally an interactive anagram. Therapy sessions are generated for users via a genetic algorithm (GA), assessing words based on criteria such as length, spelling regularity and frequency, whilst maintaining categorical similarity and significance and gradual increases in complexity.

The GA is solely responsible for selecting words for sessions, which are in-keeping with the user's capabilities. The GA chooses groups of words from the system's vocabulary, which consists of a sample of 1000 words, taken from WordNet [13]. WordNet is a vast lexical database, which not only offers a strong dictionary of indexed terms, but also provides valuable information for determining the difficulty of each individual term. WordNet arranges words in sets of cognitive synonyms known as synsets, as well as linking these synsets to one another conceptually. The GA leverages these conceptual linkages in order to select terms, which are categorically similar to one another, allowing the application to cater sessions to the interests of the individual. Words are represented by images selected from ImageNet, an image-based dataset, based on WordNet's hierarchy.

The GA first generates a large collection of potential sessions (the initial population). Each individual is analysed and assigned a fitness value via the GA's fitness function. Through roulette wheel selection and the application of genetic operators (mutation and crossover), fitter offspring are continually produced until a viable solution is found. Words are assessed based on word length, spelling regularity, frequency, imageability, presence of homophones and presence of embedded words. Viable individuals should generally place an emphasis on low word length, high frequency and high imageability, while secondary goals include the avoidance of homonyms, irregularly spelt words and the presence of embedded words. These criteria are subject to flexible weightings when being evaluated by the fitness function.

4   Future Work

Future evaluations of the GA's performance have been designed and will be implemented in the coming period. An early evaluation has already been carried out, which assessed the GA's ability to gauge the perceived spelling difficulty of words, in comparison to the expectation of SLT practitioners and SLT students. During this study, sessions were deliberately generated with a diverse level of difficulty among the individual terms and presented to the participants. The purpose of the study was to collate feedback related to the overall ability of the GA to define perceived difficulty. While the participants largely agreed with the choices made by the GA, some individuals cited issues with the initial weightings, specifically related to the weighting associated with spelling regularity.

5   Conclusion

A mobile application has been presented, which seeks to enable self-guided therapy for individuals with aphasia, particularly those with writing deficits. The application features a genetic algorithm, which generates sessions catered to the idiosyncrasies of individual users. The GA first and foremost assesses the perceived spelling difficulty of words, whilst placing an emphasis on maintaining enough categorical similarity so that sessions are in keeping with the interests of the user. The application features a cueing hierarchy influenced by traditional ACT and CART approaches to speech and language therapy. Further experiments have been planned and designed which will rigorously test the GA's ability to continuously provide suitable therapy sessions for individuals with aphasia, whilst adapting to the capabilities and interests of the individual in question.

References

1. van de Sandt-Koenderman, W.M.E.: Aphasia rehabilitation and the role of computer technology: Can we keep up with modern times? Int. J. Speech Lang. Pathol. 13, 21–27 (2011)
2. Greig, C.-A., Harper, R., Hirst, T., Howe, T., Davidson, B.: Barriers and Facilitators to Mobile Phone Use for People with Aphasia. Topics in Stroke Rehabilitation 15, 307–324 (2008)
3. Katz, R.C.: Computers in the treatment of chronic aphasia. Semin. Speech Lang. 31, 34–41 (2010)
4. Cherney, L., Halper, A.: Novel Technology for Treating Individuals with Aphasia and Concomitant Cognitive Deficits. Topics in Stroke Rehabilitation 15, 542–554 (2008)
5. Marshall, J., Pound, C., White-thomson, M., Pring, T.: The use of picture/word matching tasks to assist word retrieval in aphasic patients. Aphasiology 4, 167–184 (1990)
6. Nettleton, J., Lesser, R.: Therapy for naming difficulties in aphasia: Application of a cognitive neuropsychological model. Journal of Neurolinguistics 6, 139–157 (1991)
7. Boyle, M., Coehlo, C.A.: Application of Semantic Feature Analysis as a Treatment for Aphasic Dysnomia, http://aphasiology.pitt.edu/archive/00000227/
8. Maher, L.M., Clayton, M.C., Barrett, A.M., Schober-Peterson, D., Gonzalez Rothi, L.J.: Rehabilitation of a case of pure alexia: exploiting residual abilities. J. Int. Neuropsychol. Soc. 4, 636–647 (1998)
9. Francis, R.D., Riddoch, M.J., Humphreys, G.W.: Treating agnosic alexia complicated by additional impairments. Neuropsychological Rehabiltation 11, 113–145 (2001)
10. Beeson, P.M., Hirsch, F.M., Rewega, M.A.: Successful single-word writing treatment: Experimental analyses of four cases. Aphasiology 16, 473–491 (2002)
11. Luzzatti, C., Colombo, C., Frustaci, M., Vitolo, F.: Rehabilitation of spelling along the sub-word-level routine. Neuropsychological Rehabilitation 10, 249–278 (2000)
12. Beeson, P.M.: Treating acquired writing impairment: strengthening graphemic representations. Aphasiology 13, 767–785 (1999)
13. Princeton University "About WordNet." WordNet, Princeton University (2010), http://wordnet.princeton.edu

Empowering Mobile Users: Create Your Own Mobile Application for Data Collection in the Cloud

Arlindo F. da Conceição[1], Jimmy V. Sánchez[1], Alvaro H. Mamani-Aliaga[1],
Bruno G. dos Santos[1], Matheus F. Mendonça[1], Dario Vieira[2],
and Vladimir Rocha[3]

[1] Institute of Science and Technology (ICT)
Federal University of São Paulo (UNIFESP)
Rua Talim 330, São José dos Campos-SP, Brazil
http://maritaca.unifesp.br
arlindo.conceicao@unifesp.br

[2] Ecole d'ingénieurs en informatique et technologies du numérique (Efrei)
30-32 avenue de la République
94 800 Villejuif, Paris, France
dario.vieira@efrei.fr

[3] Institute of Mathematics and Statistics (IME)
University of São Paulo (USP)
São Paulo-SP, Brazil
vmoreira@ime.usp.br

Abstract. This paper presents a cloud infrastructure that allows users to create mobile applications to collect and visualize data. The system offers simple and intuitive interfaces to create Apps, without the need for any programming skill to develop them. The platform allows the collection of conventional data, such as numbers and text, and also non-conventional data, such as multimedia files, location information, barcodes, etc. The collected data can be shared among users on a social network, allowing Apps to extract intelligence from the collected data. The system is based on free software and can be accessed at the following address: http://maritaca.unifesp.br.

Keywords: Mobile Data Collection, Mobile Devices, Cloud Computing, User Empowerment, Collective Intelligence, Mobile Social Networks.

1 Introduction

The mobile communication market has evolved fast. This evolution is mainly characterized by three factors: reduced smartphone prices, launch of mobile devices with high processing capability, and emergence of new technologies for the development of Mobile Applications (Apps). These factors have created appropriate conditions for the large-scale usage of Mobile Applications.

However, despite the advances in hardware and software, the creation of mobile applications continues to demand programming efforts and involvement of

G. Memmi and U. Blanke (Eds.): MobiCASE 2013, LNICST 130, pp. 269–272, 2014.
© Institute for Computer Sciences, Social Informatics and Telecommunications Engineering 2014

programmers and IT professionals. In our opinion, this is the main limitation to wider usage of mobile solutions and applications, since most companies have no resources (money or/and programmers) to develop these mobile applications. The same constraint applies to the end users, they cannot pay for the development of customized applications.

We believe that success in the Mobile Market is related to the capacity of delivery applications that can deliver exactly what the user needs. To do this, it is necessary to allow the user to create and customize their own mobile applications. We refer to this concept as **User Empowerment**. To evaluate the concept of User Empowerment (UE) we have developed an infrastructure for Mobile Data Collection [3]; we call it Maritaca[1]. The project is open source and was designed to be highly scalable. The tool is available at `http://maritaca.unifesp.br`. The source code can be found at `http://sourceforge.net/p/maritaca`.

2   Maritaca Project: System Architecture

The Maritaca project was developed as a cloud application [1]. The data collected using Android devices are stored in the cloud and can be visualized using standard web browsers. Furthermore, the whole process of data collection can be done without programming skills. The main components are:

- **Application Server**: the server side uses the application server *JBoss* to host the services and web components. All the server side, except for some test scripts, were implemented in Java using *Spring*. All web services were implemented based on the *RESTFul* approach.
- **Form Editor**: this is an independent Web application, written using HTML5 and Ajax. It allows the quick and intuitive development of questionnaires by implementing drag-and-drop interfaces. As a result this component generates a questionnaire descriptor, which is persisted in XML format.
- **Mobile component**: this is an Android application that interprets the XML file (questionnaire descriptor) and generates the interfaces automatically. In fact, the mobile component is an engine, based on the design pattern Interpreter [5].
- **Cassandra Data Server**: component used for scalable storage of information. It is based on the paradigm *NoSQL* [6].
- **Hadoop file system**: distributed file system [8] used to store non structured data, such as Apps and multimedia files.
- **Solr Engine**: distributed search engine [7] used to enable searching of Apps. Each App has a description; we used Solr to index the keywords of this description, so that it is possible to search for specific Apps.

In addition to provide for the collection of usual data, such as texts and numbers, the solution also allows collection of unusual data, such as multimedia (audio, video and images) [2], geolocation [4], drawings, barcodes, etc.

---

[1] MARitaca Is a Tool to creAte Cellular phone Applications.

In summary, the questionnaire can include questions such as: *What is your current location? Take a picture! Record audio!*

The implementation of new types of data captured can be easily performed. To do this, simply extend the class *Question* and make the appropriate changes to the XML parser.

2.1 Automatic Generation of Apps

Every time a form is saved in the Form Editor, the system generates a new Android App (executable APK file format) and stores it in the Hadoop distributed file system.

3 Creating an App for Data Collection

The system allows users to build applications for data collection, which can be installed onto any compatible mobile device that runs Android 2.2, or above. To use it, the user needs to authenticate their identity in the login interface. This can be done in two ways: (*i*) using the username and password registered in the system (*ii*) or with OpenID standard. After authentication, the user can visualize the interface for forms management. The interface is automatically rendered in the mobile device.

On the mobile device, the application allows data to be collected using user-friendly interfaces. Data is stored on the mobile device before being transferred to the server. To carry out the data collection, it is not necessary to be connected to the Internet.

The data collection process can be performed many times and it is not necessary to be connected to the Internet. After the data has been collected, the user can connect to the Internet and send the answers to the server, where the data can be visualized.

Currently, the supported types are: text, numeric (simple, double precision and money), date, multiple choice (*radio button and combo box*), multiple selection (*check box*), picture, audio, video, geolocation, barcode, percentage (*slider control*) and draw. New types of question can be easily implemented due to the system design.

Currently, the system allows the creation of three types of forms: private, public and shared.

4 How Can Maritaca Help to Empowering the Mobile Users?

The user can create and modify their own app for data collection. For example, a salesman can coordinate a customer's orders, students can share pictures of a party, and parents can visualize where their children are. There are no costs and no need for programming skills. In addition, the user can define three models of data sharing and create social networks for specific interests. By combining these features is possible to create effective mobile applications, without cost. That is what was defined as Mobile User Empowerment.

5 Conclusion

This work has explored the concept of user empowerment, which gives the user the power to create, modify and use mobile applications. The project offers tools to collect, share and analyze data, allowing users total customization of software requirements using simple interfaces, without needing knowledge of programming languages or IT infrastructure.

In addition, the work describes a system architecture and its cloud implementation that can be used by any software company needing a Mobile Data Collection solution. The architecture has been developed to cover most mobile applications based in questionnaires, storing both conventional (number, text, etc) and non-conventional data (video, pictures).

In the coming years, predictions point to the increasing usage of mobile devices and the necessity to personalize apps by users with no software development expertise. With Maritaca, we try to solve this necessity by giving power to users.

References

1. Armbrust, M., Fox, A., Griffith, R., Joseph, A.D., Katz, R., Konwinski, A., Lee, G., Patterson, D., Rabkin, A., Stoica, I., et al.: A view of cloud computing. Communications of the ACM 53(4), 50–58 (2010)
2. da Conceição, A.F., Pereira, R.L., Rezende, J.V.P., Silva, B.N.M., Correia, R.J.P., Domingues, H.H., Kon, R., Kon, F.: Projeto Borboleta: Ferramentas Móveis e Multimídia para Atenção Básica Domiciliar. In: Congresso Brasileiro de Informática em Saúde. Artigo curto (2008)
3. da Conceiç o, A.F., Sánchez, J.V., Barabasz, T., Mamani-Aliaga, A.H., dos Santos, B.G., Mendonç a, M.F.: Open architecture for mobile data collection using cloud computing. In: International Workshop on Mobile Cloud Computing: Data, Management & Security (mCloud). In conjunction with 14th IEEE International Conference on Mobile Data Management (IEEE MDM), Milan, Italy (2013)
4. El-Rabbany, A.: Introduction to GPS: The Global Positioning System. Artech House Publishers (2002)
5. Gamma, E., Helm, R., Johnson, R., Vlissides, J.: Design Patterns. Addison-Wesley Professional (1994)
6. Hewitt, E.: Cassandra: the definitive guide. O'Reilly Media, Incorporated (2010)
7. Smiley, D., Pugh, E.: Solr 1. 4 Enterprise Search Server: Enhance Your Search with Faceted Navigation, Result Highlighting, Fuzzy Queries, Ranked Scoring, and More. Packt Publishing (2009)
8. White, T.: Hadoop: The definitive guide. O'Reilly Media (2012)

Design and Evaluation of a Medication Application for People with Parkinson's Disease

Ana Correia de Barros[1], João Cevada[1], Àngels Bayés[2], Sheila Alcaine[2], and Berta Mestre[2]

[1] Fraunhofer Portugal AICOS,
R. Alfredo Allen 455, 4200-135 Porto, Portugal
{ana.barros,joao.cevada}@fraunhofer.pt
[2] Centro Médico Teknon, Unitat de Parkinson i Trastorns del Moviment,
Bonanova 26, 08022 Barcelona, Spain
11741abr@comb.cat

Abstract. Smartphones may allow disease self-management, which is relevant for people with Parkinson's Disease (PD) in need of frequent medication adjustments. Yet, there is little data on the interaction of people with PD with smartphones. We describe the processes of the design and usability evaluation of a smartphone medication application for PD. Results show that participants with PD were generally able to successfully interact with the tailored user interfaces (UI), and grasp navigation and organization principles designed into the application. The paper lists issues for UI improvement and further testing.

Keywords: Smartphone, Usability tests, Parkinson's disease, Gestures.

1   Introduction

Parkinson's Disease (PD) requires frequent medication adjustments, for which medication intake tracking may be useful. Smartphones offer a possibility to act as a mobile medication reminder and manager; however, it is possible that motor and non-motor symptoms of PD [1] affect the way in which people with PD interact with a smartphone. There are reports of solutions targeting people with PD [2] and medication management [3]. However, usability tests with such smartphone applications have not, to our knowledge, been reported in the literature.

This paper briefly presents the process and choices in the design of a medication application specifically tailored to PD—which is part of a larger personal health system for PD management, REMPARK[1]—followed by the results on usability tests with people with PD.

---

[1] http://rempark.cetpd.upc.edu/

G. Memmi and U. Blanke (Eds.): MobiCASE 2013, LNICST 130, pp. 273–276, 2014.
© Institute for Computer Sciences, Social Informatics and Telecommunications Engineering 2014

2   Design and Evaluation

The medication application offers 4 main functionalities through its main menu: Medication list, Intake schedule, Missed intakes and Intake history (Fig. 1). The design options were structured after existing guidelines for older adults, specific PD studies, and user requirements that were gathered in different iterations: interviews with medical doctors, interviews with people with PD and focus groups composed of people with PD and their informal caregivers who provided input on the use cases, layouts, navigation or graphic elements. The application allows adding reminders to the intake hours and to record medication intake, postpone it or to skip it. PD-related medication is fed through the REMPARK server, therefore saving the user from having to input all the data (minimizing effort and chance for error), but users may also add extra medication. A set of patterns was designed, with dimensions previously optimized for PD, combining guidelines for displays for older adults [4] (as PD is more prevalent amongst seniors) and insights from primary and secondary users. These patterns were used throughout the entire application in different combinations, so as to ease the learning curve. Even though literature suggests in breath navigation [5], a trade-off was made when it came to text edit/input: these actions have their own screen so as to avoid confusing the users with keyboard animations and focus users' attention on the task at hand. When navigating in-depth, the user can always rely on the back button which shows on every screen at the same place and which also acts to prevent error when users tap the back button in the course of an unfinished task.

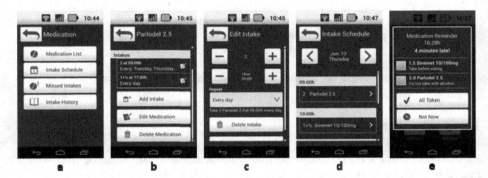

Fig. 1. Medication application sample screens

Usability tests were designed to assess ease of touch interaction, accuracy, and navigation. These were not meant to test the entire application's mechanics, as this is but one of many applications on the REMPARK project. Furthermore, the use of identical patterns throughout the applications eliminates the need to test everything in each application. The usability tests sessions were conducted at Teknon Parkinson's Unit, from where participants were recruited. Participants were brought to a quiet room, apart from distracting stimuli, and tests were led by one researcher. The sample was composed of 12 participants, 7 male and 5 female, with ages ranging from 48 to 80 (average: 71.2, SD 9.3). The exclusion criterion was the presence of dementia.

All participants signed an informed consent prior to test onset. The medication application was running on Android in a Samsung Galaxy Nexus with a 4.65'' AMOLED display. Tests were recorded in video. Tactile interaction with the touch screen was also recorded for later analysis.

Errors in tasks were considered to be low, generally recoverable and non-severe. Task performance, as shown in Table 1, was high across tasks.

Table 1. Task performance, number of errors and time (E=Errors; TP=Task Performance)

	Interact with medication reminder (2 sub-tasks)		Check medication schedule (2 sub-tasks)		Check & edit medication details (6 sub-tasks)		Check missed intakes (1 sub-tasks)	
Participant	E	TP	E	TP	E	TP	E	TP
1	0	Yes	0	Yes	1	Yes	0	Yes
2	1	Yes	1	Yes	3	No	2	No
3	0	Yes	1	Yes	1	Yes	0	Yes
4	1	No	2	Yes	3	Yes	2	No
6	-	-	0	Yes	0	Yes	1	Yes
7	-	-	1	Yes	1	Yes	0	Yes
8	0	Yes	1	Yes	2	Yes	0	Yes
9	1	Yes	0	Yes	0	Yes	0	Yes
10	-	-	1	Yes	2	Yes	1	Yes
11	0	Yes	0	Yes	1	Yes	0	Yes
12	0	Yes	0	Yes	1	Yes	0	Yes

Despite large tapping areas for all buttons (the wide buttons were 10.5cm high and the square shaped buttons had 14.0cm sides) some participants with less than good accuracy still had problems tapping them. Either in menu or list buttons, participants generally aimed at the icon, which may induce errors if icons are placed too close to button borders. We observed some particularities regarding taps on the user interface (UI) back button: participants generally tapped to the right side of the button and the interaction was often not a tap, but a swipe gesture from right to left (Fig. 2).

Fig. 2. Tactile interaction with menu (left), back button (middle) and list elements (right)

The back button concept was already known to the majority of participants: 66% had a smartphone and most of the times used the native back button. Nevertheless, the remaining also quickly grasped the concept and quickly learned how to use it, either by themselves or after a hint from the facilitator. Participants were also generally able to: 1) use a navigation widget with arrows to go back and forth on consecutive days (Fig. 1d); 2) understand and use pickers to change hours (Fig. 1c); 3) read and understand the list of intakes (Fig. 1d) and missed intakes; 4) find and navigate through medication schedules (Fig. 1b); 5) understand how to edit a medication/intake; and 6) understand and interact with a medication reminder pop-up (Fig. 1e). In the last item some participants were not very accurate in tapping the checkboxes, nor did some understand that they were required to tap "Taken" for confirmation (as soon as one checkbox is ticked, the label on the button changes from "All taken" to "Taken").

3   Discussion and Conclusion

Users were able to make sense out of the structure and content, understand groups and categories and understand how to edit. One challenge was the tap interaction with buttons: in future iterations, icons should be displaced farther away from the edge of the clickable area. Despite interaction issues, the success rates of task accomplishment and the reduced number of errors suggest a general positive assessment, and that the elements' dimension seems appropriate for the interaction of PwP with smartphone UIs. Even though 66% of participants owned a smartphone, none used a medication management application. There were two participants who used sound alarms to remember to take medication, but which did not do any digital tracking of medication intake. Even with this low familiarity with medication management applications, users were able to grasp the main concepts and the errors being recorded were not considered to be severe or blocking task performance, thus suggesting that people with PD would indeed be generally able to use this medication application.

Acknowledgments. REMPARK is carried under the 7th Framework Programme for Research and Technological Development (FP7) and financed by the European Commission (REMPARK ICT-287677).

References

1. Fahn, S.: Description of Parkinson's disease as a clinical syndrome. Ann. N. Y. Acad. Sci. 991, 1–14 (2003)
2. Memedi, M., Westin, J., Nyholm, D., Dougherty, M., Groth, T.: A web application for follow-up of results from a mobile device test battery for Parkinson's disease patients. Biomedicine 104(2), 219–226 (2011)
3. Krishna, S., Boren, S.A., Balas, E.A.: Healthcare via cell phones: A systematic review. Telemedicine and e-health 15(3), 231–240 (2009)
4. Pak, R., McLaughlin, A.: Designing displays for older adults. CRC Press, Boca Raton (2011)
5. Parush, A., Yuviler-Gavish, N.: Web navigation structured in cellular phones: The depth/breadth trade-off issue. Int. J. Hum-Comput. St. 60(5-6), 753–770 (2004)

A Mobile Environmental Air Quality Information System as a Support for m-Health

Elena Mitreska, Danco Davcev, and Kosta Mitreski

Faculty of Computer Science and Engineering – Skopje, University "Ss. Cyril
and Methodius" – Skopje
elenamitreska@gmail.com,
{danco.davcev,kosta.mitreski}@finki.ukim.mk

Abstract. Considering mobile device limitations, such as storage, computing power and bandwidth, we propose a mobile cloud computing in order to provide the necessary resources and for delivery of any multimedia data like maps, alarms or messages to the mobile user devices.

The main contribution of this paper is the scalability of our mCloud-based pollution monitoring system. The system can be extended to the entire territory of the country and it integrates all sensor pollution data with patient databases. By using mobile technologies, users/patients receive alerts concerning the air quality levels through user-friendly messages.

Keywords: Air Quality Index, Cloud Computing, m-Health, Lung Disease, Prevention, Alerts.

1   Introduction

In this paper, as a part of our e-Health system, we focus on patients with lung diseases. The database of radiological images is used as a ground level for diagnostics and cloud computing is used to connect this system with data from the Airpointer system. The Airpointer system gathers raw data through various sensors for which GIS technology can be used to make visualization from the air pollution parameters.

In the sections that follow, we present several related works that depict some important topics concerning our system (Section 2). Afterwards, the Architecture of the Air Quality Monitoring System is presented (Section 3). The experimental results present the outcome of the different systems and their interaction (Section 4). Section 5 concludes the paper and presents some possible future upgrades of the system.

2   Related Work

Many authors (see [1] for example) try to find various ways to measure air pollution, to increase public awareness and eventually to prevent medical conditions that are in direct correlation with this environmental problem.

G. Memmi and U. Blanke (Eds.): MobiCASE 2013, LNICST 130, pp. 277–281, 2014.

The framework in [4] uses location-based technologies such as GPS/GSM modules, wireless sensor networks and mobile device technology to enable real-time patient monitoring and communication through alerts for potential environmental dangers to prevent asthma patients more accurately and develop care plans for the patients.

Throughout the world, patient data including their pictures are already stored in clouds. One solution uses the cloud to store patients data, gathered from the sensors attached to existing medical equipment that are interconnected to exchange service for later processing by expert system and fast data delivery to medical staff [7].

Another solution provides patient images in a cloud to save storage capacity, to promote energy savings and to use less paper and film for printing reports. Moreover, data would be accessed independently, using adequate security measures [8].

In [3], the cloud computing (CC) paradigm and WSN are used for the data process ability and as a service model. In the framework, the data from WSN are efficiently utilized and managed, depending on which, information services are well provided to the users.

A similar air pollution monitoring system with GIS modeling is used in the work where Nanotechnology Based Solid State Gas Sensors are used to detect pollution levels in some industrialized areas in Thailand [2].

Our system uses mobile technologies to spread more rapidly and provide the system with greater flexibility and urgency, since it deals with patients known to have a lung disease. Patients receive alerts with air quality levels through user-friendly messages. The web service providing the alerts is in mCloud. An Airpointer [5] that contains various sensors that measure air pollution parameters is connected to the mCloud where GIS technology is used to visualize this gathered data.

3   Architecture of the Air Quality Monitoring System

The main components of our Air Quality Monitoring System are shown on Fig.1. All pollution measurement data are provided by the Airpointer and other sensor stations and transmitted to the pollution database (PDB) in the mCloud. The patient database containing lung radiology images and other patient data is also located in the mCloud. Users connect to the mCloud through mobile devices like smart phones, tablets etc. By using mobile technologies, these patients receive alerts for the air quality levels given from the web service.

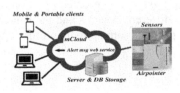

Fig. 1. Architecture of the Air Quality Monitoring System

The pollution data is continuously renewed, approximately in real time. Publishing of this data is regulated every hour. The six steps procedure of the Air Quality Monitoring System is presented in Table 1.

Table 1. Six steps of the Air Quality Monitoring System

Steps	Actions
1	Acquisition of data from the measurement stations.
2	Pollution data are enriched with spatial coordinates (using Python PL) for every measuring point.
3	Building GIS layers from PDB with the use of interpolation module (IDW from ESRI software).
4	Presentation of layers on the map for each parameter.
5	Visualization by different colors of the parameters concentration as a new layer over a map of the city of Skopje.
6	Sending of messages for air quality levels in Skopje to alert mobile users in categories with lung diseases.

As a result of the above procedure, the visualized pollution state can be presented as shown on Fig. 2.

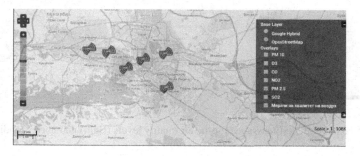

Fig. 2. The position of the sensors and visualized pollution state of the city of Skopje (http://www.skopjefinki.ekoinformatika.mk)

One concrete parameter rarely determines the current air pollution. Usually, it is the combination of parameters and their density, calculated with a formula [6] that retrieves the "Air Quality Index-AQI" for a given area (the measurement point).

Finally, as has been mentioned before, we keep the patient database with the corresponding lung radiological images in the mCloud.

4   Experiment Results

The alert output messages to the users (patients) involved in the category with lung diseases, depending of the AQI range are presented on Table 2.

Table 2. Alert outputs according to the AQI

Alert (Low to High)	AQI Range	Output Message
1	0-50	No risk.
2	51-100	Low risk for health sensitive people.
3	101-150	Medium risk for children and people with lung problems.
4	151-200	High risk for children and people with lung problems. Medium risk for the rest.
5	201-300	Very high risk for children and people with lung problems. High risk for the rest.
6	301+	Extremely high risk for everyone.

AQI (Air Quality Index) calculated from these pollution parameters is used as a basis for the following web pollution service:
{ "EcoMethodResult":"Time; AQI_all_avg1\u000a2013-07-13 22:17:00; 58,44 \u00a0" }

On Fig.4 the results of the above Web pollution service is shown, as well as the Android mobile application where patients receive alert messages.

Fig. 3. Screenshot of alert messages for the air quality levels (right) and corresponding links

5   Conclusion

Future improvements and upgrades of the system would be to directly connect the tracking system to the m-Health Radiology Consultation and Alerting System. We plan to extend this system on the entire territory of the country and to all lung diseases patient especially asthma patients as a service connected to the Ministry of Health.

References

1. Lee, K., Murray, D., Goodfield, D., Anda, M.: Experiences and Issues for Environmental Engineering Sensor Network Deployments. In: 6th IEEE International Conference on Digital Ecosystems Technologies (DEST), pp. 1–6 (2012) E-ISBN: 978-1-4673-1701-6
2. Pummakarnchana, O., Tripathi, N., Dutta, J.: Air pollution monitoring and gis modeling: a new use of nanotechnology based solid state gas sensors. Science and Technology of Advanced Materials, 251–255 (2005)

3. Pengfei Y., Yuxing P., Hang G.: Providing Information Services for Wireless Sensor Networks through Cloud Computing. In: IEEE Computing Conference (2012)
4. Wan, D.B., Shayma, A., Sada, N., Cheng, C.L.: A mobile Data Analysis Framework for Environmental Health Decision Support. In: IEEE Ninth International Conference on Information Technology - New Generation, pp. 155–161 (2012)
5. Airpointer by Recordum,
   http://www.recordum.com/index.php?gr_id=104&k_id=750
6. AQI-brochure, http://www.epa.gov/airnow/aqi_brochure_08-09.pdf
7. Rolim, O.C., Luiz Koch, F., Becker Westphall, C., Werner, J., Fracalossi, A., Schmitt Salvador, G.: A Cloud Computing Solution for Patient's Data Collection in Health Care Institutions. In: Second International Conference on eHealth, Telemedicine, and Social Medicine (2010)
8. Ferraro de Souza, R., Becker Westphall, C., dos Santos, D.R., Westphall, C.M.: A Review of PACS on Cloud for Archiving Secure Medical Images. International Journal of Privacy and Health Information Management (IJPHIM) 1(1), 10 pages (2013)

A Privacy-Preserving Contactless Transport Service for NFC Smartphones

Ghada Arfaoui[1,4], Sébastien Gambs[2], Patrick Lacharme[3],
Jean-Francois Lalande[4,2], Roch Lescuyer[5,*], and Jean-Claude Paillès[3]

[1] Orange Labs, Caen, France
ghada.arfaoui@orange.com
[2] SUPELEC/Inria/CNRS/Université de Rennes 1, IRISA (UMR 6074)
sebastien.gambs@irisa.fr
[3] Laboratoire GREYC (Unicaen, Ensicaen, CNRS), UMR 6072, F-14032 Caen
patrick.lacharme@ensicaen.fr,
jean-claude.pailles@unicaen.fr
[4] ENSI de Bourges, Univ. Orléans, LIFO, EA 4022, F-18020, Bourges, France
jean-francois.lalande@ensi-bourges.fr
[5] Morpho, F-92130, Issy-Les-Moulineaux, France
roch.lescuyer@morpho.com

Abstract. The development of NFC-enabled smartphones has paved the way to new applications such as mobile payment (m-payment) and mobile ticketing (m-ticketing). However, often the privacy of users of such services is either not taken into account or based on simple pseudonyms, which does not offer strong privacy properties such as the unlinkability of transactions and minimal information leakage. In this paper, we introduce a lightweight privacy-preserving contactless transport service that uses the SIM card as a secure element. Our implementation of this service uses a group signature protocol in which costly cryptographic operations are delegated to the mobile phone.

1 Introduction

The design of a secure and private mobile transport service is one of the most challenging application for NFC-enabled device. In particular, this service requires a proof of the customer's identity and of the validity of his attributes in relation with the product. In transport systems, these attributes are controlled by the service provider and stored on the user's smartphone. Thus, the user's personal data are exposed to any type of surveillance from the service provider.

In this paper, we introduce an architecture in which the user's identity can be dematerialized in a secure element, in our case, the SIM card. More precisely, we propose a privacy-preserving identity management system for transport service, whose security is based on the combination of a secure element embedded in the smartphone together with the use of a privacy enhancing cryptographic protocol.

---

* This work was done while the fifth author was at Ensicaen, Caen, France.

G. Memmi and U. Blanke (Eds.): MobiCASE 2013, LNICST 130, pp. 282–285, 2014.
© Institute for Computer Sciences, Social Informatics and Telecommunications Engineering 2014

2   M-Ticketing Solutions for Transportation

CALYPSO is a standard describing contactless transactions between a smart card and a reader that is used in transport applications [1]. This standard has been developed by a European consortium composed of transportation operators such as the Belgium STIB and the French RATP. For instance in France, the Navigo pass is based on the Calypso standard. This standard specifies all details of transactions related to e-ticketing for transport service ranging from the purchase of the tickets to their uses. Unfortunately, this standard does not propose any technical solution for protecting the privacy of users.

The German FRDB has proposed the service Touch and Travel (T&T), a mobile ticketing service [2] since 2008. The user must first subscribe to the service by showing his identity along with his bank account. Afterwards, he gets a user number and a PIN allowing him to use the T&T application. To travel from a station A to a station B, a user must start the T&T application upon departure by using either a touchpoint if available in the station or a GPS location or a location based on network cell. Arriving to the station B, the user must indicate the end of his trip. When controlled, the T&T application generates and displays a QR code to prove that the payment for the trip is proceeding normally. However, a recent study [2] has shown that T&T does not respect the privacy requirements as the application T&T stores the list of all recent trips in a centralized database.

Recently, it has been proposed an identity verification ticketing scheme that is embedded in a trusted execution environment [3]. This solution complies with a major functional requirement: carrying out an identity verification transaction should require less than 300 milliseconds (ms). In subsequent papers [4,5], the same authors have investigated how to report evidences of the trip even if no connectivity is available and how to implement post-payment of m-tickets. However, the authors acknowledge that their solution does not comply with anonymity and unlinkability properties.

3   Embedding Cryptographic Algorithms for Privacy

A full description of the cryptographic protocols deployed in our solution is out of the scope of this paper. However, we want to highlight that designing and implementing such a technology in a mobile phone is a challenging task. In particular, using complex cryptographic signatures are not well-suited in our context because we want to deliver anonymous credentials using a SIM card that has low computing resources. Thereafter, we sketch some problems that we had to address as well as the approaches chosen to overcome them.

Restricted Resources. 2A SIM card is not powerful enough to compute group signatures or DAA. Indeed, existing schemes rely on computationally costly algebraic tools, like pairings, that are currently not available in chips like the SIM cards. Moreover, the validation of an m-ticket should not take more than 300 ms, including the interaction between devices, which strengthens the difficulty.

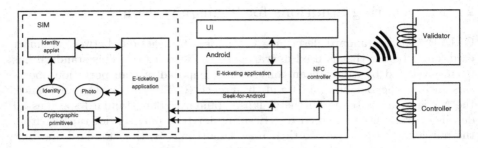

Fig. 1. Architecture of our m-ticketing application

Revocation Issues. In practice, full untraceability might be dangerous and we must address the revocation issue. For example, a manager may want to revoke a user that has lost his SIM card. Moreover, with unconditional anonymity, it becomes impossible to blacklist a SIM card that has been stolen or compromised.

In order to deal with the computational constraints, we built a cryptographic protocol that is working jointly between the SIM card and the smartphone. It is based on a group signature in which time-consuming cryptographic operations are delegated to the mobile phone. Regarding the revocation concerns, we combine the partial unlinkability property of DAA mechanisms with the blacklisting of users on the verifier side. In a DAA, signatures are linkable only if they share the same basename, a specific value included in all signatures. In our case, each basename stands for a period of time. Therefore using the same smartphone multiple times will be detected by the validation device because the SIM used the same basename multiple times. Similarly, if a cloned SIM card is deployed, the system is able to detect that the same SIM card is used several times during the same period of time. In addition to this detection, blacklists on the validation device side allow to reject some SIM cards.

4 Architecture

The proposed architecture for our m-ticketing application relies on a SIM card and an Android operating system that includes the Seek-for-Android patch as shown in Figure 1. The m-ticketing application, which is stored directly inside the SIM card, can access to the proof of personal attributes and can communicate with the NFC controller, while the application located on the smartphone memory manages the interactions with the user.

During the product registration, the m-ticketing application establishes a secure channel between the SIM card and the remote server. During this operation, the unforgeability property of the m-ticket is ensured.

During the m-ticket validation or during the travel control, a secure channel is also first established between the SIM card and the acceptance device. Afterwards, this device determines if the current m-ticket is correct, with respect to the proof of personal attributes possessed by the user as well as with respect to the validity zones and the validity period. To realize this, the device sends a challenge and power up the NFC controller of the smartphone. Then, the SIM card returns a proof of personal information linked to the challenge in a zero-knowledge manner (*i.e*, without revealing in clear the corresponding information) using a group signature, thus achieving the data minimization principle.

Being able to realize this operation in a limited time is a challenging implementation issue. Currently, our prototype succeeds in validating the product in less than 300 ms including 150 ms that are dedicated to the communication overhead of the NFC technology. To obtain such performances, some parts of our validation protocol are delegated and precomputed by the smartphone and the final operations are done into the SIM card.

Certain types of m-ticket must incorporate a photo-ID for visual control by transport company agents of a ticket issued to a single traveler. Our solution is simple and yet provides a fair amount of privacy: the photo ID is shown on the traveler smartphone display, and a specific mechanism enforces its authenticity, based on a random mark inserted by the SIM card (which is trusted) onto the photo-ID, and verifiable by the agent.

5   Conclusion

In this paper, we have focused on the security and privacy aspects related to m-ticketing applications. More specifically, we have designed a privacy-preserving architecture for an m-ticketing application and developed a demonstrator of this application[1]. The security of the solution relies on the use of the SIM card as a secure element that enables to use anonymous, unlinkable and revocable m-tickets. The efficiency of the implementation is achieved by delegating the non-critical operations to the smartphone.

References

1. Calypso Networks Association: Calypso handbook v1.1 (2010)
2. Pirker, M., Slamanig, D.: A framework for privacy-preserving mobile payment on security enhanced arm trustzone platforms. In: 2012 IEEE 11th International Conference on Trust, Security and Privacy in Computing and Communications (Trust-Com), pp. 1155–1160 (2012)
3. Tamrakar, S., Ekberg, J.E., Asokan, N.: Identity verification schemes for public transport ticketing with NFC phones. In: Sixth ACM Workshop on Scalable Trusted Computing, STC 2011, pp. 37–48. ACM, New York (2011)
4. Tamrakar, S., Ekberg, J.-E.: Tapping and Tripping with NFC. In: Huth, M., Asokan, N., Čapkun, S., Flechais, I., Coles-Kemp, L. (eds.) TRUST 2013. LNCS, vol. 7904, pp. 115–132. Springer, Heidelberg (2013)
5. Ekberg, J.-E., Tamrakar, S.: Mass transit ticketing with NFC mobile phones. In: Chen, L., Yung, M., Zhu, L. (eds.) INTRUST 2011. LNCS, vol. 7222, pp. 48–65. Springer, Heidelberg (2012)

---

[1] This work has been supported by the ANR-11-INS-0013 LYRICS Project.

iOS Application for Guiding Visually Impaired People at the University of Alicante

Alejandro Zaragoza[1], Javier Ortiz[1], Juan José Galiana-Merino[1], and Irene Sentana[2]

[1] Department of Physics, System Engineering and Signal Theory
[2] Department of Graphical Expression and Cartography.
University of Alicante, Spain
duke.alex87@gmail.com,
{javier.ortiz,jj.galiana,irene.sentana}@ua.es

Abstract. This paper shows the development of an iOS application to guide visual disabled people at the University of Alicante by voice indications. The user interface has a bigger visual typography and a bigger contact buttons area. Moreover, the application provides voice indications when the user touches any of the elements in the interface.

Keywords: Mobile application, Visual disabled people, Voice messages, iOS.

1   Introduction

This paper shows an application to guide people with visual disability at the University of Alicante. This application has been developed for mobile devices, specifically for iOS [1, 2].

General applications oriented to visual disabled people area available. J. Roig [3] has developed "OnTheBus", which is an application to guide blind people by by voice (only Android operating system). Sergio Macetti [4] presents "ZebraLocalicer", which is an application to find crosswalks in cities for blind people. Related to voice guidance, we can find "WalkyTalky" [5]. Google also has another application called "Intersection Explorer" [6]. Moreover, we find "Kapten for Smartphone" [7], a GPS navigation app with a fully vocal and accessible user interface.

Paper is organized as follows: Section 2 deals with the methodology and procedure carried out. In Section 3 we report the experimental results of the algorithm. Finally, in Section 4 we show the main conclusions.

2   Development of the Application

2.1   Resources

The development of the new application has been possible by means a variety of tools that Apple provides for developing applications in iOS. We have employed Xcode [8]. Also, we have used the universities license provided by Apple, known as iOS Developer University Program (Licensed to the University of Alicante). We use the other app of the University of Alicante (iUA) to access the buildings data. [9].

G. Memmi and U. Blanke (Eds.): MobiCASE 2013, LNICST 130, pp. 286–289, 2014.

2.2   User Interface and Map Controller

The application provides two functionalities: first, a guide to go to any particular building along the Campus and on the other hand, an audio database with a brief description of the different buildings around the user. Thus, the interface presents two different tabs.

The main element of the application is the map view controller [10] since it's in charge to control, at any time, the position of the user and the direction towards which the phone device is pointing, to generate the proper indication in each situation: go straight, turn right, turn left, turn around.

Our controller also checks the position where we are, in order to adapt the view of the map to the characteristics of each function, showing only the position of the building where we want to go, or all the other buildings around us. This controller changes the message with vocal indications according to each situation whenever the user touches on the map view.

Once the application knows where the user is pointing, it generates a message through a set of conditional blocks (Fig. 1). The emitted message by the app has two indications for guiding the user: go "forward / back" and turn "left / right".

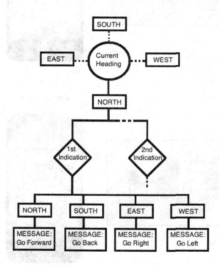

Fig. 1. Conditional blocks for generating voice message in "OrientatUA". If the user is taking a wrong route, the app corrects him. The user can check if he is on the right track at any time just by touching on the screen.

3   Results

Table 1 shows the data used by our application to generate voice messages along the route. In this example, the route begins at the campus entry and goes until the Science building of the University of Alicante. Fig. 2 shows four indications of the route that the user should follow.

Table 1. Data for generating voice messages in "OrientatUA"

Positions	Latitude	Longitude	Pos_Lat	Pos_Long	Dist_A – Dist B (m)
Building	38.3872	-0.5134	--------	--------	--------
Position #1	38.3865	-0.5113	NORTH	WEST	300 – 300
Position #2	38.3863	-0.5124	NORTH	WEST	200 – 150
Position #3	38.3870	-0.5128	NORTH	WEST	100 – 100
Position #4	38.3872	-0.5136	NORTH	EAST	50 - 20

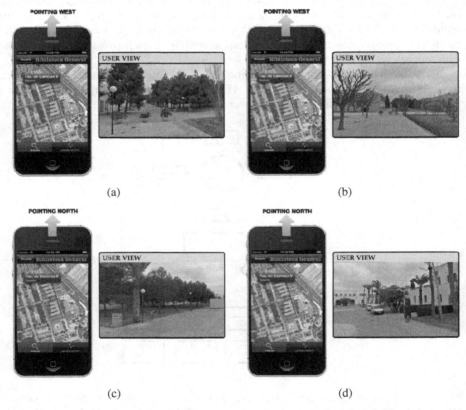

Fig. 2. App running. Steps to locate the Science building (University of Alicante)
Voice messages:

(a) Voice message, Position# 1: "The building you are looking for is about three hundred meters to the forward direction and about three hundred meters to the right".

(b) Voice message, Position# 2: "The building you are looking for is about three hundred meters to the right and about one hundred meters to the forward direction".

(c) Voice message, Position #3: "The building you are looking for is about one hundred meters to the left and about one hundred meters to the forward direction".

(d) Voice message, Position #4: "The building you are looking for is on your right."

4   Conclusions

In this paper we have shown an application to guide visual disabled people at the University of Alicante. The application works properly and provides the right indications in every moment for all the buildings of the Campus, with an accuracy of 100%. The application can be easily updated to new facilities by just updating the database with the new information about the position of the buildings. Currently, we are implementing the application "OrientaUA" for Android OS devices.

For future development, we would like to adapt this application to the iPad device, and including the voice messages information about the estimated time to reach any destination, based on the speed at which the user walks. Moreover, a new tab with language selection will be also included.

References

1. Teng, C., Helps, R.: Mobile Application Development: Essentials New Directions for IT. In: Proc. International Conference on Information Technology, Las Vegas, US (2010)
2. LeMoyne, R., Mastroniani, T., Cozza, M., Coroian, C.: Implementation of an Iphone for characterizing Parkinson's disease tremor through a wireless accelerometer application. In: Proc. 32nd International Conference of the IEEE EMBS, Buenos Aires (2010)
3. Roig, J.: OnTheBus, http://onthebus-project.com
4. Macetti, S.: ZebraLocalicer, http://homes.di.unimi.it/~mascetti/Sergio_Mascetti_home_page/Research_files/CameraReady.pdf
5. Eyes-Free Project by Google, WalkyTalky, http://play.google.com/store/apps/details?id=com.googlecode.eyesfree.walkytalky&hl=es
6. Google Inc. Intersection Explorer, http://play.google.com/store/apps/details?id=com.google.android.marvin.intersectionexplorer&hl=es
7. KapSys. Kapten for iPhone, http://apsys.com/fr/produits/kapten-for-iphone
8. Apple. Xcode, http://developer.apple.com/xcode
9. University of Alicante. iUA App., http://itunes.apple.com/es/app/iua/id416776674?mt=8
10. Stelte, B., Hochstatter, I.: iHagMon – Network Monitoring on the Iphone. In: Proc. Third International Conference on Next Generation Mobile Applications, Services and Technologies (2009)

Phone Call Translator System in Real-Time

Yoko Iimura*, Yu Kojo, Masahiro Oota, and Shinya Tachimoto

NTT DOCOMO, INC.,
3-6 Hikarinooka, Yokosuka-shi, Kanagawa, 239-8536, Japan
{iimuray,kojou,ootamas,shinya.tachimoto.yw}@nttdocomo.co.jp

Abstract. Recently, various kinds of automatic translator services have become available. Most of them are provided as a client-server model. We developed a phone call translator service, which enables people speaking different languages to communicate with each other over the phone. In this paper, we present the system architecture of the service and describes how the system works.

Keywords: translation, phone, mobile application.

1 Introduction

In recent years, an automatic translation function has been provided as various software applications and web services. Most of them are offered in one-to-one setting between the user and the server and designed to indirectly support communication between different languages..

The telephone provides communication services, which have the following features:

· Natural communication experience by talking to the other person while listening to his/her voice
· Real-time communication

These conventional features of the telephone, however, make it difficult for a general telephone translation service as described above to be applied effectively to the telephone; because via the existing telephone system it is hard to achieve smooth communication between persons speaking different languages and maintain a real-time conversation at one time. To address such difficulty, we developed an automatic phone call translator system. In this paper, we describe how to implement the phone call translator system.

2 Service Overview

The phone call translator system automatically converts what the user says in Japanese into another language (English, Chinese or Korean) and vice versa.

---

* Corresponding author.

G. Memmi and U. Blanke (Eds.): MobiCASE 2013, LNICST 130, pp. 290–293, 2014.

The system provides translations both in screen texts and voice readouts in a synthesized voice.

Using the conventional phone lines and functions, the system allows users to hear each other's voice as they converse over the phone. This gives users a face-to-face like natural communication experience that the telephone especially can provide. In addition, the system allows users to use basic functions of the automatic translator service with anyone who can be reached by phone.

In order to enhance the convenience of the translator service, we provide a translation application (hereinafter called the translation app) operable for Android OS 2.2 or later. Figure1 shows some images of the translation app when using the service. Fusion of telecom (phone) and web (app) makes it possible for users to visually as well as aurally confirm their operation details, results of voice recognition and translation and manipulate them on the translation app. All of these capabilities offer a new style of communication.

The translation function, however, is not intended to be applied to all conversations on the phone; the function is turned on and off by the user operation. The function to start/stop the translation function is offered in two ways: one works with the translation app and the other works with the button on the phone for the user who does not use the translation app.

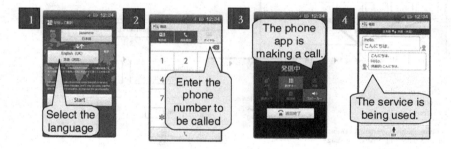

Fig. 1. User interface up to service usage

3   Overall Sequence

The phone call translator service is provided through a translator system that operates as a B2BUA. To activate the translator service, the user dials the special number "138" and the translation language code (2 digits) before the other party's phone number. When the special number "138" is dialed, a SIP_INVITE signal is sent to the translator system. Upon receiving the SIP_INVITE signal, the translator system calls the other party if the system determines that the user may be connected to the other party based on their service and user conditions. When the called party answers the call, the U-Plane connection is established. Then the basic function of this service is available. When using the translation app, the app makes a call instead of the user. The user just selects the language and the party to be called according to the navigation of the app. The translator system sends a push signal to every UE to activate the translation app and connects the packet network communication from the app with the established session over the phone line. The translation app receives the results of voice recognition and translation of phone conversations via the packet communication and displays them on the screen.

4   System Configuration

We are building a network infrastructure designed to provide value added services. The infrastructure is called the Service Enabler Network (SEN), which implements AS (Application Servers) of the IMS （IP Multimedia Subsystem） infrastructure [1]. The SEN infrastructure consists of an array of different functional components and service scenarios. The policy of this infrastructure is to provide services timely by combining necessary components only through the development of service scenarios.

The phone call translator system is implemented as an AS on the SEN infrastructure stated above.

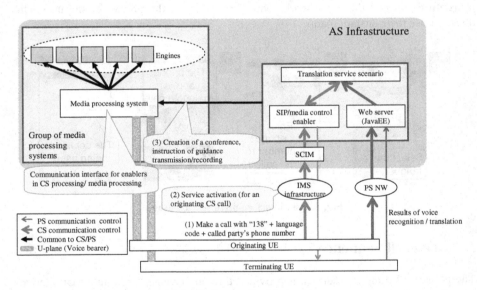

Fig. 2. System Architecture

When the user's device initiates a voice call, dialing the special number "138," the IMS infrastructure recognizes it as the service number of the phone call translator service and connects the call to the SCIM (Service Capability Interaction Manager)[2] (Figure2 (2)). When the SCIM determines that the service does not conflict with other services, it connects the voice call to the phone call translator service scenario. The scenario generates a conference in the media processing system based on the INVITE signal from the SCIM. Then it activates a conference service to be joined by the calling and called parties as participants and draws the voice call into the media processing system. When the call starts, the scenario instructs the media processing system to send guidance to tell the start of recording and start recording the voice call (Figure 2 (3)). The media processing system records voice data and sends the guidance based on the request from the service scenario.

Each component of enablers necessary for translating speech over the phone is called an engine. For example," voice recognition engine", "Voice synthesis engine"," Translation engine" are implemented for the phone call translator service. Any gaps of engine interfaces are absorbed by the media processing system to abstract the media processing instructions from the scenario. This enables the use of the same service scenario for different engine products. It also makes it possible to select the most accurate product for each function and language and use them in combination. In addition, the system will allow us to replace an engine by more advanced one without affecting the service scenario when such need arises in the future.

5   Service Evaluation

The phone call translator service has achieved a certain level of close-to-real-time performance in its usage in Japan: for example, in case of spoken words of about 8.3 seconds in Japanese, the results of voice recognition and translation were displayed on the translation app screen about 1 second after the speech; the replay of the translated speech in a synthesized voice was started from the phone line almost at the same time.

When the service was used in areas with longer packet transmission delays, however, there were certain timing gaps between the speech of the words over the phone line and the display of the results on the screen.

6   Conclusion

In this paper, we have presented how to implement a new phone call translator system that provides new additional value for communication, enabling interactions between the phone line and the packet network.

To be able to utilize this translator system in more diverse scenes, it is essential to improve the accuracy of technical components for both voice recognition and machine translation. To this end, our future work should focus on extracting unknown words that the current engine cannot recognize from the actual translation data and list them in dictionaries as well as adopting timely words as necessary.

References

1. 3GPP TS23.228
2. 3GPP TS23.002

An Approach for Using Mobile Devices in Industrial Safety-Critical Embedded Systems

Ashraf Armoush[1], Dominik Franke[2], Igor Kalkov[2], and Stefan Kowalewski[2]

[1] An-Najah National University
armoush@najah.edu
[2] Embedded Software Laboratory, RWTH Aachen University
Ahornstr. 55, D52074 Aachen, Germany
{franke,kalkov,kowalewski}@embedded.rwth-aachen.de

Abstract. With the booming mobile market and increasing capability of mobile devices, mobile platforms like Android emerge from end-user to industrial application areas. This paper sketches an approach to implement industrial safety-critical embedded systems with fail-safe state on the mobile platform Android. The approach consists of safety-critical software design patterns, a real-time extension to the Android platform and fail-safe application life cycle management.

Keywords: safety-critical, fail-safe, patterns, real-time, life cycle, Android.

1 Introduction

Safety-critical systems are those systems or applications in which failure can lead to serious injury, loss of life, significant property damage, or damage to the environment [3]. The industrial safety-critical embedded systems should be carefully designed with the help of the well-established and common design techniques to fulfill the real-time and safety requirements.

While smartphones and tablets are classified as embedded devices, they serve as the key computing and communication choice for other embedded devices. Modern smartphones contain a wide variety of networking technologies and a set of powerful embedded sensors, such as GPS, accelerometer, gyroscope, compass, and camera. The availability of these capabilities and technologies has opened new applications across a wide variety of domains, and allow them to become an attractive and complementary choice for safety-critical embedded systems. However, their operating systems must be modified and extended to support the reliability and real-time requirements for safety-critical systems.

Fail-safe state in safety-critical system is a state which, in the event of failure, can be identified as being safe without risk. In many design methods, a safety function should be executed in the case of failure to reach a fail-safe state. For smartphones, the application life cycle should be carefully studied and investigated to find the best way to integrate the required safety function.

G. Memmi and U. Blanke (Eds.): MobiCASE 2013, LNICST 130, pp. 294–297, 2014.

2   Applying Safety Patterns on Mobile Platforms

The design of safety-critical embedded systems is considered to be a complex process to fulfill two types of requirements: functional and non-functional requirements. The first part includes the function to be performed, while the non-functional requirements involve the attributes of a system as it performs its job. They include a set of requirements like high reliability and safety, availability, low cost and small size. While the influence of these requirements varies from one domain to another, all safety-critical systems must guarantee an acceptable level of safety. The concept of design patterns, which introduces an abstract representation for how to solve general design problems have been widely used in hardware and software. In the field of safety-critical embedded systems, a collection of common design methods has been presented in a previous work as a catalogue of safety pattern [1].

2.1   Mobile Application Life Cycle and Safety Function

Android schedules its applications and services on application level using states and state transitions. The states and state transitions are often called *life cycles*. Depending of the state an application or service is in, it has access to certain resources (RAM, CPU, ...). For instance, if an Android application is in the state *running* it has access to all resources of the device. If the application is shut down or killed, it has no access to any resources.

Safety-critical system with fail-safe state can be executed on Android as services or applications. In previous work on application and service life cycles, we analyzed which would be the best way to prevent a service from being shut down and how to make sure that an application executes specified actions before being shut down. If a system with fail-safe state is executed on Android as a service, the service should be bound to an Android application and display an icon in the Android notification bar. Both actions increase the priority of the service from, as it is displaying information (in the notification bar or in the bound application), which immediately contribute to the user experience [4].

If a system with fail-safe state is executed on Android as an application, the application life cycle callback methods should be used to trigger fail-safe actions in case of application state changes [5]. As on Android usually only one single application can be active at a time, applications often change their states. An application being responsible for the fail-safe state system can act and react best, if it is in the state *running*. If it changes its state, it might not be able to execute fail-safe actions any more. From our previous work on Android application life cycles, we know that during regular operation a running Android application always calls the life cycle callback method *onPause()*. This method should be used in safety-critical applications to trigger appropriate fail-safe actions.

2.2   Real-Time Requirements and Real-Time Extension

Most safety-critical embedded systems have real-time requirements, as they must react on specific conditions within predefined time intervals. The integration of smartphones in safety-critical environments urges for modifications and extensions of available platforms to support applications with real-time requirements.

RTAndroid is a modified version of the Android 2.2 platform extended with a real-time capable scheduler, which reduces maximal scheduling latencies for real-time applications from over a second to just a few milliseconds [6]. The approach uses the RT_PREEMPT patch to equip Android's Linux kernel with basic real-time support, but additionally allows reliable priority-based process scheduling for background services and a non-blocking automatic memory management. Furthermore, RTAndroid is fully backward compatible to already existing Android components and applications. New features and real-time components can be used in the standard Android manner, e.g. simply by extending introduced classes like a real-time service.

Fail-safe state systems can be executed on RTAndroid using reliable background services. Instantiating a new service based on the new ServiceRT class in RTAndroid prevents the corresponding process from being shut down or killed by the system. Thus, safety-critical applications can be executed in real-time prioritized Linux processes with non-blocking, concurring garbage collector. In this case, the application stays responsive and precise scheduling guarantees bounded reaction times to upcoming events, such that a fail-safe state can be entered.

3   Example Pattern

Chemical process control is considered as one of common examples for real-time and safety-critical system with multiple inputs and outputs. Let us have a small experimental reactor to perform a specific chemical reaction. It is clear that such an application includes a set of measured values like temperature, pressure, gas concentration and many others. Any failure in such system could lead to critical situation. The Monitor-Actuator Pattern [2] is suitable for this case due to the low availability requirement and the existing fail-safe state. As shown in Fig.1, the pattern consists of two heterogeneous channels that run independently: The main actuation channel can be a microcontroller that reads the measured values from input sensors and provides a check on the input data and the system itself to ensure the correct processing of the desired operations. The Monitoring channel is used to improve the safety of the system by providing a continuous monitoring for the actuation channel. It takes the information from the set point source and the actuator sensors and compares it with the provided set points to detect possible faults in the actuation channel. In the case of improper operation, it forces the actuation channel to enter the fail-safe state. The monitoring channel should be independent from the actuation channel, so Android device is selected in our approach to perform this task. The heterogeneous redundancy in the two channels reduces the possible concurrent failure. Finally, the real-time extension and the life cycle assessment ensure the real-time requirement for this application and the proper time to call the safety function to enter the fail-safe state.

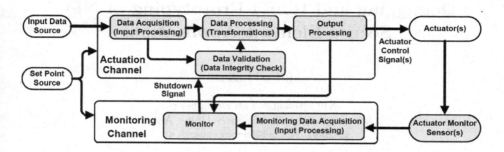

Fig. 1. The Monitor-Actuator Pattern

4   Conclusion

The design of safety-critical embedded systems requires the integration of common design methods with the recent advances in information technologies. In this paper we presented a conceptual approach to implement safety-critical systems with fail-safe state on Android devices by using appropriate safety design patterns. Moreover, a real-time extension and a corresponding life cycle management have been used for Android to ensure the non-functional requirements in the developed application. As shown in the example, the proposed approach is more suitable for the cases with low availability and clear fail-safe sate.

This work was supported by the UMIC Research Centre, RWTH Aachen University, Germany.

References

1. Armoush, A.: Design patterns for safety-critical embedded systems. PhD thesis, RWTH Aachen University (2010)
2. Douglass, B.P.: Real-time design patterns: robust scalable architecture for real-time systems. Addison-Wesley Professional (2003)
3. Dunn, W.R.: Designing safety-critical computer systems. Computer 36(11), 40–46 (2003)
4. Franke, D., Elsemann, C., Weise, C., Kowalewski, S.: Reverse Engineering of Mobile Application Lifecycles. In: Proc. 18th Working Conference on Reverse Engineering (WCRE 2011), pp. 283–292. IEEE (2011)
5. Franke, D., Kowalewski, S., Weise, C., Prakobkosol, N.: Testing Conformance of Lifecycle-Dependent Properties of Mobile Applications. In: Proc. 5th International Conference on Software Testing, Verification and Validation (ICST 2012), pp. 241–250. IEEE (2012)
6. Kalkov, I., Franke, D., Schommer, J.F., Kowalewski, S.: A Real-time Extension to the Android Platform. In: Proceedings of the 10th International Workshop on Java Technologies for Real-time and Embedded Systems (JTRES 2012), pp. 105–114 (2012)

Debugging and Rapid Prototyping of NFC Secure Element Applications

Michael Roland

NFC Research Lab Hagenberg
University of Applied Sciences Upper Austria
michael.roland@fh-hagenberg.at

Abstract. The ecosystem behind secure elements is complex and prevents average developers from creating secure element applications. In this paper we introduce concepts to overcome these issues. We develop two scenarios for open platforms emulating a secure element for the Android platform. Such an open emulator can be used for debugging and rapid prototyping of secure element applications. Moreover, by trading the secure element's security and trust for openness, such a platform can be used as a replacement for the secure element for long-term testing and for showcasing of applications.

Keywords: Near Field Communication, Secure Element, Java Card, Rapid prototyping, Debugging, Testing.

1 Introduction

Since Google added support for Near Field Communication (NFC) technology to their Android operating system and to their Nexus devices in 2010, the number of smart phones equipped with NFC functionality is rapidly increasing. This growing availability also boosts many developers' interest in developing NFC applications. Particularly card emulation is an often demanded feature. Card emulation is the ability of an NFC device to interact with existing contactless smartcard reader infrastructures. Therefore, an NFC-enabled smart phone in card emulation mode could replace smartcards in payment, access control, identification and ticketing applications. Especially payment use-cases and their potential for generating high revenues boost the developers' demand for NFC card emulation [8].

The central component of card emulation is the secure element. The secure element is a smartcard microchip that is embedded (fixed or removable) into the NFC device. This chip is a tamper proof hardware platform that provides highly secure storage and a trusted execution environment. Modern secure elements (just like many other modern smartcards) contain a Java Card run-time environment. Thus, developers can create applications independent of the actual secure element hardware using Java Card's subset of the Java programming language.

G. Memmi and U. Blanke (Eds.): MobiCASE 2013, LNICST 130, pp. 298–313, 2014.

While the secure element's high levels of security and trust are important requirements for many application scenarios, they also form an enormous obstacle for many developers [8]: The secure element ecosystem is complex and has several different players. Secure elements are usually controlled by their issuer (e.g. the handset manufacturer for an embedded secure element in a mobile phone or the mobile network operator for a UICC-based secure element). Issuers often delegate the management of their secure elements and the applications on them to a trusted service manager (TSM). The trusted service managers act as connectors between providers of secure element applications and the secure elements of a large number of users.

Besides acting as a connector, a TSM will typically also act as a filter: To maintain the security and the trusted state of the secure element, a TSM has to assure the quality and the security of applications deployed to the secure element. Thus, secure element applications will most likely have to undergo some form of (costly) security certification. Moreover, the available space on a secure element is very limited. Therefore, the TSM has to choose which applications to deploy to a particular secure element. This may result in a high cost for application developers and service providers to deploy their applications to secure elements. It may even cause applications that compete with services provided by a secure element's owner or by large service providers to be blocked completely from some secure elements (cf. [1, 2]). Currently, many secure element issuers do not even provide development access to their secure elements for average developers.

Therefore, the barriers towards getting an application into a secure element (even for development purposes) are very high. Nevertheless, developers seek simple ways to develop and test their applications (Java Card applets) for secure elements. An ideal debugging and prototyping environment would permit the applets to be tested in-place with other application components while allowing source-level debugging of the applets' code.

In the context of the secure element in an NFC-enabled smart phone, in-place debugging would mean that the secure element (Java Card) would be emulated in software. This emulator would then be accessible to apps through regular secure element APIs, as well as to external smartcard readers, through the contactless NFC interface. Besides source-level debugging, such a scenario would also provide an environment for rapid prototyping of secure element applications without access to an actual secure element. I.e. the emulator could be used as a drop-in replacement for a secure element that provides the same functionality while trading security for openness. Thus, on the one hand, this environment would not provide the high level of security of a smartcard chip, but, on the other hand, would be open to all developers.

In this paper, we describe the conceptual design of such an open secure element development environment for Android devices. We show how such a secure element emulator could be integrated in both, an actual Android smart phone and an Android device emulator.

2   Java Card

Java Card technology is a subset of the Java programming language combined with a run-time environment that is optimized for tiny embedded devices like smartcards [12]. The run-time environment consists of a Java Card virtual machine (as defined in [13]), a Java Card specific API and Java Card specific security features. In this paper, we refer to Java Card version 2.2.2. While this version is used in many current secure elements, it is not the most recent Java Card version. Our decision is based on the fact that – while Java Card version 3.0 is fully specified since 2009 – it is still unclear when commercial products (particularly secure elements) based on that new and enhanced version of Java Card will hit the mass market.

2.1   Language and API

Java Card has been optimized for tiny embedded devices with limited memory and processing power. Therefore, many features of Java are unavailable in Java Card to assure that applications have a small footprint that matches the constrained resources of a smartcard. For instance, Java Card only supports the primitive data types *boolean, byte, short* and optionally *int*. The types *char, float, double, long* and the wrapper classes for primitive data types are not supported. Moreover, some language constructs like enumerated types, enhanced *for*-loops for array iteration or variable-length argument lists do not exist in the Java Card language. As a result of the constrained smartcard environment and the command-response interaction with smartcards, Java Card does not offer multi-threading capabilities. Furthermore, most of the core API classes of the Java language are unsupported. Specifically, only classes related to exceptions and the class *Object*, as a common root for the class hierarchy, are available.

Besides these limitations, the Java Card run-time environment provides an API with smartcard-specific classes. This API comprises of classes related to the interaction with the Java Card run-time environment, the structure and operation of Java Card applications and the processing of ISO/IEC 7816-4 smartcard commands (application protocol data units, APDUs). Moreover, the API contains classes related to smartcard-specific security functionality (e.g. management of PIN codes and cryptographic keys, encryption, decryption, and computation of checksums, cryptographic hashes and digital signatures based on various algorithms). Additionally, the Java Card API contains further (partly optional) helper classes for smartcard-related tasks.

2.2   Virtual Machine

The Java Card virtual machine is the execution environment for the Java Card run-time environment and for all Java Card applications. In comparison to other Java virtual machines, the Java Card virtual machine runs throughout a smartcard's lifetime. The virtual machine and all applications persist across power-cycles. This is possible because the code and data memory is backed by persistent storage technologies. Protection against data corruption due to unexpected power-cycles is achieved with an atomic transaction mechanism.

2.3 Security

Besides the different life-cycle, another major difference between Java and Java Card is the security architecture. Java Card has been designed for security critical applications. Particularly, Java Card introduces a strict separation between the contexts of installed applications. Thus, applications cannot access each other's objects (data) without being granted explicit permissions. It has to be noted, though, that the strict firewall between application contexts seems to be weakened by the lack of an on-card byte code verifier on many platforms (cf. [3, 6]) and, therefore, often relies on a trusted installation process including security evaluation of applications prior to their deployment. This issue also complicates developers' and service providers' access to the secure element.

2.4 Applications and Life-Cycle

The main entry point of a Java Card application is an applet (i.e. an instance of a class that extends the *Applet* class). An applet implements the central interface to the Java Card run-time environment that is used to control the application's life-cycle. The applet's *install* method is invoked to create and initialize an applet instance. After installation, applet instances remain in a suspended state until they are explicitly selected through a smartcard command. During selection, the applet instance's *select* method is invoked to prepare the applet for further processing. Once an applet is selected, all further smartcard commands are forwarded to that applet instance by triggering its *process* method. Upon selection of another applet instance, the current applet instance's *deselect* method is invoked and the applet instance returns into suspended state. Similar to the virtual machine, Java Card applets execute forever (or until they are explicitly uninstalled). However, applet instances return to the suspended state upon power loss or reset.

3 Java Card Simulators

Several Java Card simulators exist which allow simulation and testing of Java Card applets without real smartcard hardware. These simulators and simulation environments can be divided into three different categories:

1. reference implementations of the Java Card virtual machine and the Java Card run-time environment,
2. smartcard simulators provided by manufacturers for their smartcard products, and
3. general-purpose Java Card simulators that operate on top of Java virtual machines.

Sun's (now Oracle's) Java Card reference implementation is an example for the first category. Regarding debugging and simulation capabilities, this type of simulation environment is comparable to a regular smartcard. It processes compiled Java Card applications and interacts through smartcard commands. For instance, the Java Card reference implementation integrates with Java ME's secure element API. However, it does not offer source-level debugging capabilities of Java Card applications.

An example for the second category are G&D's Java Card Simulation Suite and Gemalto's Simulation Suite. These smartcard manufacturers provide their custom Java Card simulation environments that simulate their specific smartcard architectures and can be used to debug Java Card application prior to deployment to real cards.

The Java Card Workstation Development Environment (JCWDE) and the open-source jCardSim are examples for the third category. These simulators emulate the Java Card run-time environment on top of a standard Java virtual machine. Thus, instead of compiling Java Card applications to Java Card byte code, they are compiled to Java byte code. Both simulators offer source-level debugging for applets based on standard Java debugging tools. However, both implementations lack some features of a full Java Card run-time environment. While the JCWDE provides integration with Java ME's secure element API and direct interaction through APDU scripts, jCardSim offers support for APDU scripts and an interface to the Java Smart Card IO API.

4   Towards a Secure Element Emulator

The available simulators provide a good starting point for developing Java Card applications. However, especially with current NFC-enabled smart phones, developers would be interested in more advanced debugging mechanisms. An ideal debugging environment would offer the following capabilities:

1. a complete (or as much complete as possible) Java Card run-time environment,
2. source-level debugging capabilities, and
3. in-place testing and debugging together with other application components.

In the context of the secure element in an NFC-enabled smart phone, for instance, in-place debugging would mean that the secure element emulator (Java Card emulator) is accessible to apps through regular secure element APIs, as well as to external smartcard readers through a contactless NFC interface.

In such a scenario, Java Card applications can be tested and debugged while they are communicating with apps on the smart phone or while they are communicating with external smartcard reader devices over the contactless interface. Source-level debugging capabilities can come handy at this stage to trace the execution path through the Java Card application during actual communication. Emulating the Java Card run-time environment on top of a regular Java virtual machine permits using standard Java debugging tools. In comparison, creating a custom Java Card virtual machine would also require to create custom debugging tools that interact with that VM.

Besides source-level debugging capabilities, such a scenario would also provide another advantage: A Java Card emulator that can be used as a drop-in replacement for a secure element in a smart phone would provide an environment for rapid prototyping of secure element applications without access to an actual secure element. Thus, developers and service providers would have an open tool to showcase their secure element applications bypassing the need for a real secure element. While the emulator would operate at a much lower security level (no dedicated smartcard hardware, no protections by a Java Card virtual machine, etc.), it would be an open platform that provides comparable functionality to a regular secure element and that is available to all developers without the restrictions of the complicated and closed ecosystem of a regular secure element chip.

5   Implementing a Secure Element Emulator for Android

We chose Android as the target platform for the secure element emulator. The main reasons for this decision are:

1. Android is an open-source system. This provides a detailed insight into system's internal structures and even makes modification on the system level fairly simple.
2. Android uses a Java-based run-time environment. This is a good starting point for Java Card emulation.
3. An Android implementation of the Open Mobile API, a standardized secure element API, exists. Though this API has not been integrated in main-line Android, manufacturers already integrated it in many NFC-enabled Android devices.
4. Android has a large market share and, consequently, many requests for card emulation capabilities and secure element access focus on the Android platform.

Our vision is that the secure element emulator would integrate into an Android device the same way as any other secure element. Therefore, Java Card applets running in the emulator should be accessible by apps on the mobile device through the secure element API as well as by external smartcard readers through card emulation. As a result, the emulator would become an open drop-in replacement for a secure element for testing, debugging, prototyping and showcasing purposes. The openness would, however, come at the price of less (or no) security.

We developed two scenarios for integrating such an open environment into Android:

1. integration of the secure element emulator with the Android emulator and
2. integration of the secure element emulator with an actual Android device.

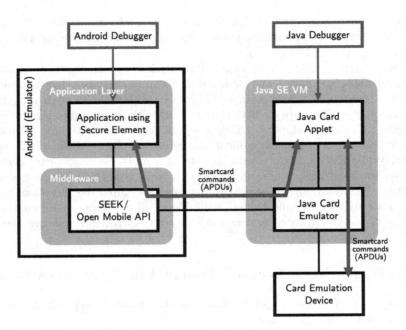

Fig. 1. Java Card emulator attached to the Android platform emulator

5.1   Integration into the Android Emulator

Fig. 1 shows our scenario for integrating the secure element (Java Card) emulator with the Android emulator. We chose a split approach, where the secure element emulator runs separately from the Android emulator. The Java Card emulator and the Java Card run-time environment operate on top of a standard Java SE virtual machine. Therefore, standard Java debugging tools can be used to debug Java Card applets that run inside this environment. Moreover, the separation makes the secure element emulator independent of the Android emulator's life-cycle (e.g. restarts of the emulator, etc.)

Our secure element emulator has two interfaces: One is connected to the Android emulator so that apps can access the emulated secure element and the other is connected to a card emulation device.

In order to connect our open environment to the Android emulator, it listens on a TCP socket for smartcard commands. On the Android side, Android's Open Mobile API-based secure element API (cf. [11]) is extended with a terminal interface that connects to our emulator using a TCP/IP socket. This approach is used by existing secure element simulators (e.g. Java Card reference implementation and JCWDE) too. Thus, if we use the same communication protocol over the TCP socket, we can maintain compatibility to these simulators as well as to the tools that use them.

The second interface connects the emulator to card emulation hardware (e.g. an NFC reader, like the ACR122U, in software card emulation mode). Consequently,

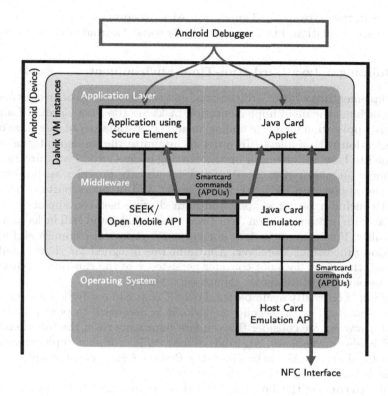

Fig. 2. Java Card emulator integrated into an Android device

external smartcard readers can communicate with Java Card applets running inside the emulator.

5.2 Integration into an Android Device

Fig. 2 shows our scenario for embedding the Java Card emulator into an Android device. In this scenario, the Java Card emulator and the Java Card run-time environment operate on top of the Dalvik virtual machine (Android's version of a Java virtual machine). Therefore, Android's Java debugging tools can be used to debug Java Card applets that run inside this environment. Besides debugging, this scenario can also be used to showcase applications that would normally require a secure element. These applications could use our Java Card emulator platform as an open prototyping environment.

Similar to the scenario with the Android emulator, our secure element emulator has two interfaces: One is connected to Android's secure element API so that apps can access the emulated secure element. In this scenario, the Java Card emulator is directly connected to the Open Mobile API through a terminal interface without the need for a TCP/IP connection. The second interface is connected to the software card emulation API (sometimes also called "soft-SE" or "host card emulation") that is available for some Android devices (cf. [8,14]).

5.3 Building a Java Card Run-Time Environment

When implementing a Java Card run-time environment on top of an existing Java virtual machine, the main implementation tasks are the Java Card API and the Java Card application life-cycle management (i.e. installation of, selection of and communication with applets). In order to minimize the implementation effort, we decided to base our emulator on the existing open-source Java Card run-time environment simulator jCardSim[1]. jCardSim already provides an implementation of the application life-cycle management and of many parts of the Java Card API including cryptography and data sharing between applets [4]. However, jCardSim is based only on Java Card version 2.2.1 and still lacks some core functionality. For instance it does not yet support logical channels and atomic transaction processing. Moreover, jCardSim was designed for short simulation cycles and, therefore, does not consider persistence of the run-time environment and the application state across simulation sessions.

jCardSim is currently available for Java SE so it can easily be integrated into the first scenario. For the second scenario, it is necessary to port jCardSim to Android. However, we consider this a minor issue as most of the functionality of Java SE is also available on Android. Moreover, jCardSim's implementation of the Java Card crypto API is based on the Bouncy Castle cryptography API, an API that is included into the Android system.

In order to connect the Java Card run-time environment to the outside world, jCardSim provides an interface that permits registration ("installation") of Java Card applications and dispatching of commands to the registered Java Card applet instances. This interface could be used to attach our emulator environment to Android's secure element API and to the card emulation hardware.

5.4 Integration with the Open Mobile API

In order to access the secure element emulator from Android apps, it needs to be integrated with a secure element API. Main-line Android currently has no standardized secure element API, though it contains a proprietary, undocumented API to access the embedded secure element on some Android devices. However, many device manufacturers added the SEEK-for-Android[2] framework to their Android distributions in order to expose a secure element API on their devices.

SEEK-for-Android is an implementation of the standardized Open Mobile API [11]. Fig. 3 gives an overview of the architecture of this API. The API consists of a transport API that permits APDU-based access to secure elements as well as a service API that provides a higher abstraction level for access to secure element applications. The Open Mobile API can be used for any type of

---

[1] http://jcardsim.org/

[2] http://code.google.com/p/seek-for-android/

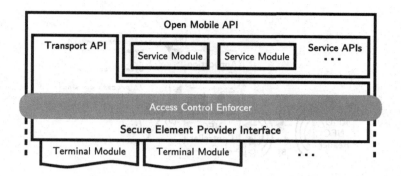

Fig. 3. Architecture of the Open Mobile API [11]

secure element. For each secure element it needs a terminal module that acts as an interface layer between the API and the actual secure element.

A terminal module is a Java class within the namespace *org.simalliance.open-mobileapi.service.terminals* that implements an interface consisting of several methods (cf. [10]):

1. `public byte[] getAtr()`
   This method returns the secure element's answer-to-reset (ATR). Our implementation could return a generic ATR like '3B 85 01 4A 43 45 4D 55 D0' that indicates the smartcard protocol T=1 and contains the historical bytes "JCEMU".

2. `public String getName()`
   This method returns the secure element's name (e.g. "JCEMU: JavaCard-Emulator")

3. `public boolean isCardPresent()`
   This method indicates if the secure element is currently available and, therefore, must return `true` for our implementation.

4. `public void internalConnect()`
   This method establishes a connection to our emulator and is used for any initialization that should take place before any communication with the secure element. In the Android emulator scenario, this method can be used to establish the TCP socket to the secure element emulator.

5. `public void internalDisconnect()`
   This method closes an open connection to our emulator and is used for cleanup that should take place after all communication with the secure element. In the Android emulator scenario, this method can be used to close the TCP socket to the secure element emulator.

6. `public byte[] internalTransmit(byte[] command)`
   This method is used to pass smartcard commands (APDUs) to the terminal module and, thus, to our emulator. The resulting responses are returned to the calling application.

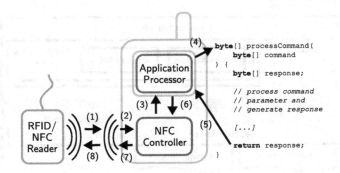

Fig. 4. Communication flow of software card emulation in a mobile phone [8]

7. `public int internalOpenLogicalChannel()`
   This method is used to open a new logical channel to the secure element
   selecting the logical channel's default applet. The method returns the new
   logical channel's number.
8. `public int internalOpenLogicalChannel(byte[] aid)`
   This method is used to open a new logical channel to the secure element
   selecting the applet that matches the given AID. The method returns the
   new logical channel's number.
9. `public void internalCloseLogicalChannel(int iChannel)`
   This method is used to close a given logical channel.
10. `public byte[] getSelectResponse()`
    This method is used to receive the last response to an applet selection (that
    was either performed through `internalTransmit` or `internalOpenLogic-
    alChannel`).

5.5   Support for Software Card Emulation

The concept of software card emulation was first brought to mobile phones by
BlackBerry (formerly RIM) in their BlackBerry 7 platform [7]. The idea is that
the NFC controller acts as a contactless card and forwards all received smartcard
commands to an app on the application processor. In turn, responses generated
by the app are returned over the contactless interface. Fig. 4 shows the flow of
communication in a software card emulation scenario.

Therefore, our secure element emulator would first register for software card
emulation with the NFC controller chip. Then, the emulator would receive all
smartcard commands received by external smartcard readers and forward them
to the Java Card applets for processing. Finally, the response generated within
the Java Card environment would be returned through the NFC chip to the
smartcard reader.

Using Dedicated Card Emulation Hardware. An example for a device that could be used for card emulation is the ACS ACR 122U NFC reader. It contains NXP's PN532 NFC controller chip. This reader device can be connected to a Java application through the Java Smart Card IO API using PC/SC. Commands for the PN532 that are used to activate card emulation mode and to exchange data during card emulation are wrapped in PC/SC APDU commands.

An explanation on how to put the PN532 NFC chip into card emulation mode is given in [9]. First, the PN532 has to be set up for ISO/IEC 14443 Type A at 106 kbps:

```
PN532.WriteRegister(
    CIU_TxMode,
    TxCRCEn | TxSpeed = 106 kbps | TxFraming = ISO/IEC 14443A);
PN532.WriteRegister(
    CIU_RxMode,
    RxCRCEn | RxSpeed = 106 kbps | RxFraming = ISO/IEC 14443A);
PN532.WriteRegister(CIU_TxAuto, InitialRFOn);
```

Then, the PN532 has to be initialized to PICC (proximity integrated circuit card) mode:

```
PN532.SetParameters(fISO14443-4_PICC | fAutomaticRATS);
PN532.TgInitAsTarget(
    PICCOnly | PassiveOnly,
    MifareParams = { SENS_RES = { 0x00, 0x04 } |
                     NFCID1t = { 0x76, 0x82, 0x4F } |
                     SEL_RES = 0x20 },
    FelicaParams = { 0x00, ..., 0x00 },
    NFCID3t = { 0x00, ..., 0x00 },
    GeneralBytes = { },
    HistoricalBytes = { 0x4A, 0x43, 0x45, 0x4D, 0x55 });
```

Finally, the card emulator listens for commands received on the contactless interface, passes them to the Java Card emulator and sends the responses back over the contactless interface:

```
while (emulating) {
    byte[] command = PN532.TgGetData();
    byte[] response = JCEmulator.process(command);
    PN532.TgSetData(response);
}
```

Using Android. On Android, software card emulation is currently only available in version 9.1 and later of the CyanogenMod aftermarket firmware for Android devices. Elenkov [5] explains how to use software card emulation in apps on the CyanogenMod platform. The basic idea is to register for detection of either an ISO 14443 Type A (IsoPcdA) or Type B (IsoPcdB) smartcard reader:

```
PendingIntent pi = activity.createPendingResult(
    1, new Intent(), 0);
nfcAdapter.enableForegroundDispatch(
    activity, pi,
    new IntentFilter[]{
        new IntentFilter(NfcAdapter.ACTION_TECH_DISCOVERED)
    },
    new String[][]{
        new String[]{ "android.nfc.tech.IsoPcdA" }
    });
```

As soon as a smartcard reader connects to the emulated card, the app gets triggered and can communicate with the smartcard reader. Thus, commands can be received from the smartcard reader and can be passed to the Java Card emulator. In turn, responses from the Java Card emulator can be sent back to the smartcard reader:

```
IsoPcdA isoPcd = IsoPcdA.get(tag);

isoPcd.connect();
byte[] response = new byte[]{ (byte)0x90, (byte)0x00 }

while (emulating) {
    byte[] command = isoPcd.transceive(response);
    response = JCEmulator.process(command);
}

isoPcd.close();
```

6   Developing a First Prototype

Fig. 5 shows the architecture of our first prototype of the secure element emulator platform. Instead of separating the emulator from the apps that access it, both, the app and the emulator environment are combined into one app. The emulator platform consists of a minimal implementation of the Java Card API and the run-time environment. We used an existing Java Card applet of a payment application that we previously used on a Java Card smartcard. We designed our Java Card API and run-time environment implementation so that the applet could be run without any modifications. We added a user interface that communicates with the applet by invoking the emulator environment. Moreover, the user interface allows to switch to external card emulation, where CyanogenMod's software card emulation mode API is used to communicate with the emulated applet.

Our applet worked as expected, both when communicating with the app and when communicating through software card emulation. We were able to do source-level debugging and to single-step through the applet's source code.

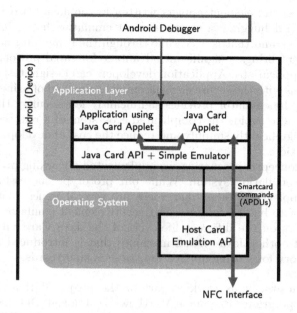

Fig. 5. First prototype for Java Card emulation on Android

However, during implementing and testing of our prototype we found several issues that need to be addressed in future research:

1. We were not able to implement Java Card's atomic transaction mechanism using the available set of APIs on the Android platform. This was not an issue for most transactions, as these transactions would be completed even after the emulated card was torn from the card reader's RF field. The reason is that while an actual smartcard stops all processing and clears its RAM upon power-loss, the emulator platform continues and finishes applet execution. However, we could not implement the case when a Java Card applet tries to intentionally roll-back a transaction. Therefore, a method to roll-back an application's state to a defined boundary is necessary.
2. When our application process (including the emulation environment) is terminated, the state of the Java Card applets is lost. Therefore, as soon as the app starts again, the Java Card applets start from the beginning of their life-cycle. However, for long-term testing and prototyping, the secure element emulator needs to maintain its state beyond application process lifetime and particularly across reboots of the Android device. Therefore, a method to extract and restore application state has to be implemented.

7   Conclusion

In this paper, we showed two scenarios for integrating a secure element emulator into the Android platform. Such a secure element emulator can be used to test and debug secure element applets written in the Java Card language. Besides source-level debugging, a secure element emulator that is integrated into an Android device and that is accessible through the same interfaces as a regular secure element brings a significant advantage for rapid prototyping and for showcasing of applications. Application developers can design, test and even use their applications with the secure element emulator instead of using a real secure element. While the emulator provides significantly less security than a real secure element, it also avoids the complicated ecosystem of a real secure element. Thus, it could significantly simplify and reduce the cost of development of secure element applications.

Besides our conceptual scenarios, we implemented a working prototype of the secure element emulation system. While our prototype successfully emulated a Java Card applet, we found that there are several issues that need to be resolved in order to build a fully working secure element emulator. These issues particularly focus on the different life-cycle of the Java Card virtual machine in comparison to other Java virtual machines that is introduced by the use of persistent memory for storing application state on smartcards.

Acknowledgments. This work is part of the project "High Speed RFID" within the EU program "Regionale Wettbewerbsfähigkeit OÖ 2007–2013 (Regio 13)" funded by the European regional development fund (ERDF) and the Province of Upper Austria (Land Oberösterreich).

Moreover, this work has been carried out in cooperation with "u'smile", the Josef Ressel Center for User-Friendly Secure Mobile Environments, funded by the Christian Doppler Gesellschaft, A1 Telekom Austria AG, Drei-Banken-EDV GmbH, LG Nexera Business Solutions AG, and NXP Semiconductors Austria GmbH.

References

1. Balaban, D.: Telcos Close Ranks as Google Threat Looms. NFC Times Blog (July 2011),
   http://www.nfctimes.com/blog/dan-balaban/
   telcos-close-ranks-google-threat-looms
2. Balaban, D.: With Launch of Google Wallet, the Wallet War Begins. NFC Times Blog (June 2011),
   http://www.nfctimes.com/blog/dan-balaban/
   launch-google-wallet-wallet-war-begins
3. Barbu, G., Giraud, C., Guerin, V.: Embedded Eavesdropping on Java Card. In: Gritzalis, D., Furnell, S., Theoharidou, M. (eds.) SEC 2012. IFIP AICT, vol. 376, pp. 37–48. Springer, Heidelberg (2012)
4. Dudarev, M.: jCardSim – Java Card is simple! Presentation at JavaOne Russia (April 2013), http://jcardsim.org/sites/default/files/CON1160.pdf
5. Elenkov, N.: Emulating a PKI smart card with CyanogenMod 9.1. Android Explorations (October 2012),
   http://nelenkov.blogspot.com/2012/10/
   emulating-pki-smart-card-with-cm91.html

6. Mostowski, W., Poll, E.: Malicious Code on Java Card Smartcards: Attacks and Countermeasures. In: Grimaud, G., Standaert, F.-X. (eds.) CARDIS 2008. LNCS, vol. 5189, pp. 1–16. Springer, Heidelberg (2008)
7. RIM: Blackberry API 7.0.0: Package net.rim.device.api.io.nfc.emulation (2011), http://www.blackberry.com/developers/docs/7.0.0api/ net/rim/device/api/io/nfc/emulation/package-summary.html
8. Roland, M.: Software Card Emulation in NFC-enabled Mobile Phones: Great Advantage or Security Nightmare? In: 4th International Workshop on Security and Privacy in Spontaneous Interaction and Mobile Phone Use, Newcastle, UK (June 2012), http://www.medien.ifi.lmu.de/iwssi2012/ papers/iwssi-spmu2012-roland.pdf
9. Roland, M.: Security Issues in Mobile NFC Devices. Ph.D. thesis, Johannes Kepler University Linz, Department of Computational Perception (January 2013)
10. SEEK for Android: AddonTerminal: How to create an Addon Terminal (May 2012), http://code.google.com/p/seek-for-android/wiki/AddonTerminal
11. SIMalliance: Open Mobile API specification (June 2012)
12. Sun Microsystems, Inc.: Java Card Platform: Runtime Environment Specification, Version 2.2.2 (March 2006)
13. Sun Microsystems, Inc.: Java Card Platform: Virtual Machine Specification, Version 2.2.2 (March 2006)
14. Yeager, D.: Added NFC Reader support for two new tag types: ISO PCD type A and ISO PCD type B. Patches to the CyanogenMod aftermarket-firmware for Android devices (January 2012), https://github.com/CyanogenMod/android_packages_apps_Nfc/ commit/d41edfd794d4d0fedd91d561114308f0d5f83878

Enhancing the Restaurant Dining Experience with an NFC-Enabled Mobile User Interface

Diego Argueta[1], Yu-Ta Lu[1], Jing Ma[1], Diego Rodriguez[1], Yuan-Hung Yang[1], Thomas Phan[2], and Won Jeon[2]

[1] Stanford University, Stanford CA, USA
[2] Samsung Research America - Silicon Valley, San Jose CA, USA

Abstract. We provide a field study of a smartphone application and server-side software for improving the on-premises restaurant experience. To increase customer engagement, the smartphone client uses Near-Field Communication (NFC) to bootstrap the communication with the server and to localize customers to specific tables. The application further provides a complete end-to-end experience by allowing users to select food items, read micro-reviews of dishes, submit their order, and be alerted when the food is ready. We deployed our prototype system in a cafe-style restaurant in the dining commons of Stanford University and observed that the system was able to successfully streamline and enhance the dining experience for both customers and restaurant staff.

1 Introduction

The ubiquity of smartphones running mobile operating systems such as Android, iOS, and others has grown tremendously with smartphone global unit sales reaching 1.7 billion in 2012 [8]. This growth in hardware sales has co-occurred with the growth in mobile applications for business, gaming, and other domains. However, one area that has not been fully explored is the use of the smartphone in an on-premises retail business environment as an assistive platform to augment the customer experience.

In this paper we provide a work-in-progress field study of *in situ* smartphone usage in a restaurant dining scenario where the smartphone serves as an extension of the interface between customers and the restaurant's operational staff. We developed NapkiNotes, an Android smartphone application that interacts with a restaurant-side server. The application allows users to select dishes from a menu (thereby eliminating or reducing the need for paper-based physical menus), filter food selection based on ingredient preferences, look at high-granularity reviews of individual dishes, submit the order, and be alerted when the food is ready.

A key component of the system is the use of Near-Field Communication (NFC) [16] to bootstrap the communication between an NFC-enabled smartphone and the server by having the customer tap the smartphone against a restaurant-provided NFC tag affixed to dining tables. We encoded each tag with a unique (restaurant, table) tuple that uniquely identifies the location of the tag, thereby allowing the restaurant staff to find the user. Further, NFC improved

G. Memmi and U. Blanke (Eds.): MobiCASE 2013, LNICST 130, pp. 314–321, 2014.
© Institute for Computer Sciences, Social Informatics and Telecommunications Engineering 2014

the user experience by allowing a tap-to-start gesture that is easier to perform than other start-up methods such as taking a picture of a QR code.

We deployed our prototype in a cafe-style restaurant in the student dining commons of Stanford University and observed that the system was able to successfully streamline and enhance the dining experience for both the customers and the restaurant staff. In particular, customers found that NapkiNotes made ordering the food more convenient, while results suggested that the system helped reduce the restaurant's operational effort.

This paper is organized as follows: We discuss related work in Section 2, describe our system in Section 3, show field study results in Section 4, and conclude in Section 5.

2   Related Work

Our work focuses on a smartphone-based interface between users and a physical business, a topic explored by several companies. Foursquare [7] is a social smartphone application that allows users to "check in" at a store, thereby gaining social credibility points. Unlike Foursquare, our NapkiNotes focuses on improving the on-premises restaurant experience rather than just establishing user geo-presence. Yelp [22] has a mobile application that allows consumers to write reviews of businesses; NapkiNotes lets users write reviews of specific food dishes. Services like OpenTable [17] and SeatMe [18] provide smartphone-based restaurant table reservation for customers but not in-restaurant ordering.

Prior research has also looked at smartphone usage in physical stores. Mobile advertising [3,11,5] and mobile recommendation agents [15,12,13] look to facilitate an immediate, on-site purchase. NapkiNotes instead targets a more involved, ordered flow; unlike advertising where user interaction is potentially disconnected from subsequent in-store activities, the food selection and delivery process in a restaurant is sequentially connected, making this field study relevant to domains where time spent between the customer and the business is elongated.

To implement our tap-to-start feature, we used NFC, a low-power, short-range wireless technology used for contactless communication similar to RFID [21]. In many countries, NFC is already used for mobile ticketing and point-of-sale payment. In the USA at the time of this writing, Google is building out a mobile wallet for Android phones [9]. NFC has also been used in research scenarios, including device-spanning applications [6], automotive vehicles [19], tourism [2], sales management [10], and health care [14].

NFC has also recently been used in limited dining scenarios. Cityvox deployed NFC tags at the windows of restaurants, allowing users to tap the tag and be directed to a Web site to read and write reviews [20]. In our work, NFC is affixed to individual restaurant tables to identify the user's seat, and our application allows users to order their meal. The CustomerIn concept [4] suggests per-table NFC localization but does not consider end-to-end meal ordering.

3   Design and Implementation

3.1   Overview

The NapkiNotes application addresses an important user need: improving the restaurant experience. For example, consider a scenario where a user is visiting an unfamiliar restaurant. The user sits down at the table, reads the menu, and then becomes daunted because there are too many unknown food item choices. Additionally, ordering food and requesting service can be frustrating at high-traffic restaurants where the waiters are busy, resulting in users flailing their hands in attempts to draw the attention of the staff. Therefore, we wanted to create an application that aims to make the restaurant experience more enjoyable.

The NapkiNotes system follows a client-server model. Users are required to download and install the NapkiNotes Android application onto their smartphone in order to access the restaurant functionality. Although a Web-based application was feasible, we chose to implement an Android application to more tightly control the user interface and to leverage the NFC feature. In our work we used a Samsung Nexus S smartphone running Android.

Upon visiting the restaurant and finding an NFC tag at a table, the user can tap his or her smartphone against the tag, which launches the application through Android's Intent application-dispatch system and bootstraps subsequent communication between the application and server over 802.11 Wi-Fi or 3G/4G. (We note, though, that throughout our experiments, the users accessed the network through Wi-Fi since the phones were not equipped with a 3G/4G SIM card.) When the user submits a food order, the information is sent to a restaurant server over HTTP with a custom application-layer payload and protocol. The restaurant can then prepare and serve the food to the customer.

3.2   Customer-Side Client Application

Our prototype's customer-facing features and interface derived from extensive usability tests and interviews involving seventeen Stanford undergraduate and graduate students. Screenshots are shown in Figure 1. The application provides:

- Tap-to-start: The user taps an NFC-enabled smartphone against NFC tags on the restaurant table to initiate communication with the server. Each NFC tag at a table contains, among other pieces of data, a unique restaurant identifier and a unique table identifier. The restaurant-side server is intended to provide online service to multiple restaurants, so this combination allows the tapping smartphone to be localized to a specific table.
- Setting preferences and filters: Preferences for select ingredients and meats can be set, thereby filtering the display of dishes. This capability allows customers with dietary restrictions to narrow down dishes.
- Menu browsing and food ordering: The user can view the available dishes, including full descriptions and pictures, and place an order.
- Reading and writing micro-reviews of dishes: Each dish can be reviewed and given a one-to-five star rating along with a pithy opinion.

Fig. 1. Screenshots from the NapkiNotes smartphone application. Left: Users can browse through food on the restaurant's menu. Note that preferred items are highlighted. Center: Micro-reviews of individual dishes can be read and written. Right: Users can submit orders and then await notification of availability.

- Interaction between customer and staff: In fast-food restaurants, the staff can signal to the user's smartphone when the food is ready, and in more formal restaurants, the user can signal the restaurant for service by the waiter.

In our prototype we used the NFC capability provided by the Nexus S smartphone and the Android NFC API to read NFC NDEF messages stored on MIFARE tags. Data containing restaurant and table information was written beforehand onto the tag running tag-writing Android software. For use in the restaurant, we used NFC as an initiator to invoke the application and to bootstrap subsequent Wi-Fi or cellular communication between the application and the server. This initiation can be performed by the user with a convenient tap between the phone and the tag. Android's NFC API provides two modes of activation: intent dispatch, where an application is invoked by the runtime system, or foreground dispatch, where a foreground activity is required. In our system we used intent dispatching.

3.3 Restaurant-Side Server

We implemented a prototype design where multiple restaurants can be provisioned through one server, with the restaurant instances being branches of the same corporate family or separate entities. The NapkiNotes Android application communicates with the server through NapkiNotes Data Transfer (NNDX), a custom protocol that defines data types and handshaking with the data payload delivered in an HTTP POST message. The restaurant's system management interface is Web-based for ease of accessibility and use, comprising three major parts: the order monitor, the service request monitor, and the menu editor.

The **order monitor** is the most important part of the server. The NNDX server receives orders from the clients and places keys with an order number into the current session's entry, where the monitor finds them, reads the keys with its order information, and displays them to the staff. The **service request monitor** is a webpage table that shows service requests coming in from their respective tables. The **menu editor** allows menu entries to be entered into the restaurant database, including item name, description, prices, and so on.

4   Field Trial Evaluation and Results

To test NapkiNotes we deployed our system at The Dish At Stern, a fast-food eatery on the Stanford University campus that is open to the public but primarily serves undergraduate and graduate students. Typical fare includes made-to-order pizzas, sandwiches, and paninis. A patron waits in line to place an order and then returns to a table to await the completion of the food, which is vocally called out by a member of the staff.

We initially set up our server-side database with the restaurant's dish inventory using the menu editor system described earlier. Once the data input was finished, we invited random customers, all of whom were students, on a weekend day to use NapkiNotes with our phones. As mentioned before, we used the Samsung Nexus S smartphone running Android with WiFi connectivity.

This section discusses the results of the field trial and projects our findings for the domain of on-premises mobile applications in general.

4.1   Time to Complete Order Submission

One of the primary benefits of NapkiNotes is that the user can order food while at a table without having to wait in line. On average, customers took less than two minutes to look through the menu items on the application and then place an order. We contrast that with the amount of time a customer must wait in line at a cafe or restaurant that does not have a service like NapkiNotes.

Table 1. Empirical measurements of customer waiting times at restaurants around the Bay Area, all taken on the same day. Duration times are stated as minutes:seconds. Durations were measured for each customer from entrance to exit from the queue.

Eatery	Location	Time of day	Mean queue duration	Median	Max
In-N-Out Burger	San Francisco	10:00 AM	2:18	2:12	3:02
Subway Sandwiches	Stanford	1:00 PM	11:46	10:21	16:53
Pho Vi Hoa Restaurant	Mountain View	7:00 PM	8:56	11:46	12:34

For completeness we found other eateries in the Bay Area that had a similar serving style to The Dish At Stern and took empirical measurements there, as shown in Table 1. Depending on the time of day, customers can potentially wait in line for over ten minutes. The last two eateries had only one cashier at the time, exacerbating the wait times. We noted that some people chose to depart the eatery immediately when seeing how long the line was in front of them. A system like NapkiNotes can alleviate this queuing time to place an order by allowing the customer to perform the ordering action on the premises with the convenience of his or her own smartphone.

4.2   User Satisfaction

Among the customers who used NapkiNotes, 16 elected to fill out a paper-based questionnaire to evaluate our system, where feedback scaled from 1 to 5 (highest). Table 2 shows user satisfaction results for the system's features, Table 3 shows user satisfaction with the Android application's interface, and Table 4 shows user interest in future deployment to other restaurants and cafes. In general, users were satisfied with the system, with all features scoring above 4.0 except for the user interface for selecting food preferences, which we explain below.

Table 2. User satisfaction results for overall NapkiNotes usage

Feature	Rating
Tap-to-start using NFC	4.69
Viewing the menu	4.35
Ordering food	4.62
Read/write dish reviews	4.27
Food-ready notification	4.50

Table 3. User satisfaction results for the NapkiNotes smartphone user interface

User interface	Rating
Application start	4.65
Menu	4.54
Menu item details	4.15
Ordering food	4.54
Food-ready notification	4.46
Setting user preferences	3.92

Table 4. User interest results for NapkiNotes future deployment to other restaurants and cafes in the future

Future deployment focus	Rating
Viewing the menu	4.62
Ordering food	4.15
Reading per-dish review	4.23
Food-ready notification	4.85

In addition to the ratings, users wrote their opinions on the features and interface. The results of these comments and the ratings are summarized below.

Tap-to-Start: The use of NFC to allow users to initiate the application by tapping on an NFC tag was found to be the most useful feature. NFC receives much of the popular press' attention in the USA for its potential to replace credit cards in point-of-sale payments [1], but we have found that using it as a bootstrapping mechanism for subsequent communication is already very valuable because the tapping motion for the customer is easy to understand and quick to perform. Its use can replace taking photos of QR codes, which is not as intuitive as tapping and requires more user interaction in aiming a camera.

Customization of Orders and User Preferences: From the questionnaire comments and the low rating on "setting user preferences," it was seen that the customers were disappointed in the application's inability to capture customization of food orders, which prevented them from ordering something not on the menu or making special requests on a specific dish, such as no pickles on a burger. Furthermore, we did not implement a means to allow the user to inquire about vegetarian variations, such as replacing beef with tofu. The root cause of this problem is that communicating such details over the smartphone is not as efficient as having a verbal exchange with human staff. Although we can potentially add a text field to allow users to specify food customization, some customers already mentioned that, in general, working with the virtual keyboard on the smartphone was difficult.

Ordering via the Smartphone Rather than via Interactive Human Discourse: Some customers enjoyed the experience of casually browsing through the detailed information presented on the smartphone because it let them look through the items at their own pace. Others mentioned that it was impersonal because one would then not get to know the restaurant staff members.

More Information for Display: In general, the customers wanted more information displayed in the application, not less, in order to let them make informed food-selection decisions. Suggestions included adding information to denote vegetarian dishes and nutrition facts.

4.3   Restaurant Staff Feedback

The management responded positively to the system and stated that they were interested in using the system further. In general, they were appreciative of the interface, the restaurant-side order management system, and the benefit of customers submitting orders directly, bypassing the service staff. Importantly, they were enthusiastic about the use of NFC that allowed customers to become more quickly engaged with the menu and ordering system while also providing immediate localization of these customers to specific tables. The management further wanted to expand upon the system to collect statistical information on the number of customers using NapkiNotes and to have access to the history of orders and service requests in order to improve their service. Long-term benefits for the restaurant would be faster throughput of customer order processing and improved customer satisfaction, resulting in more customer visits and purchases.

5   Conclusion

We provided an initial evaluation of our in-progress work on NapkiNotes, an NFC-enabled smartphone application and server-side system that looks to improve the on-premises restaurant experience by streamlining the interaction between the customer and staff. Our field study of a real-world deployment at a Stanford campus eatery shows that users responded positively to the system. In general, our findings reveal the potential for using mobile user handhelds as a replacement for paper-based informational content as well as an assistive communicative channel between customers and staff in a physical store location. In the future, we look to improve the server-side software by running on a provisioned, secure service.

References

1. Bilton, N.: The Technology Behind Making Mobile Payments a Reality, NY Times Bits blog (March 21, 2011)
2. Borrego-Jaraba, F., Luque Ruiz, I., Gómez-Nieto, M.Á.: NFC Solution for the Development of Smart Scenarios Supporting Tourism Applications and Surfing in Urban Environmentss. In: García-Pedrajas, N., Herrera, F., Fyfe, C., Benítez, J.M., Ali, M. (eds.) IEA/AIE 2010, Part III. LNCS, vol. 6098, pp. 229–238. Springer, Heidelberg (2010)
3. Cheng, H.-T., Sun, F.-T., Buthpitiya, S.: SensOrchestra: Collaborative Symbolic Location Recognition for Context-Based Mobile Advertising. In: Gris, M., Yang, G. (eds.) MobiCASE 2010. LNICST, vol. 76, pp. 195–210. Springer, Heidelberg (2012)
4. CustomerIn website, http://www.customerin.com
5. Dhar, S., Varshney, U.: Challenges and business models for mobile location-based services and advertising. Communications of the ACM 54(5) (May 2011)
6. Dodson, B., Lam, M.S.: Micro-interactions with NFC-enabled mobile phones. In: Zhang, J.Y., Wilkiewicz, J., Nahapetian, A. (eds.) MobiCASE 2011. LNICST, vol. 95, pp. 118–136. Springer, Heidelberg (2012)
7. Foursquare website, http://www.foursquare.com
8. Gartner press release (February 13, 2013), www.gartner.com/newsroom/id/2335616
9. Google Wallet website, www.google.com/wallet/
10. Karpischek, S., Michahelles, F., Resatsch, F., Fleisch, E.: Mobile Sales Assistant - An NFC-Based Product Information System for Retailers. In: Proc. of the Intl. Workshop on NFC (2009)
11. Kim, B., Ha, J.-Y., Lee, S., Kang, S., Lee, Y., Rhee, Y., Nachman, L., Song, J.: AdNext: A Visit-Pattern-Aware Mobile Advertising System for Urban Commercial Complexes. In: Proc. of ACM HotMobile (2011)
12. Kowatsch, T., Maas, W.: In-store consumer behavior: how mobile recommendation agents influence usage intentions, product purchases, and store preferences. Computers in Human Behavior 26(4) (July 2010)
13. Lee, Y., Benbasat, I.: "Interaction design for mobile product recommendation agents: Supporting users' decisions in retail stores. ACM Transactions on Computer-Human Interaction 17(4) (December 2010)
14. Marcus, A., Davidzon, G., Law, D., Verma, N., Fletcher, R., Khan, A., Sarmenta, L.: Using NFC-Enabled Mobile Phones for Public Health in Developing Countries. In: Proc. of the Intl. Workshop on NFC (2009)
15. Miller, B., Albert, I., Lam, S., Konstan, J., Riedl, J.: MobiLens Unplugged: Experiences with an Occasionally Connected Recommender System. In: Proc. of the Intl. Conf. on Intelligent User Interfaces (2003)
16. NFC Forum website, www.nfc-forum.org
17. OpenTable website, www.opentable.com
18. SeatMe website, www.seatme.com
19. Steffen, R., Preissinger, J., Schollermann, T., Muller, A., Schnabel, I.: Near Field Communication (NFC) in an Automotive Environment. In: Proc. of the Intl. Workshop on NFC (2010)
20. Swedberg, C.: NFC RFID System Lets French Restaurant-goers Access Reviews On-Site, www.rfidjournal.com/articles/view?10172
21. Want, R.: An introduction to RFID technology. IEEE Pervasive Computing 5(1) (January-March 2006)
22. Yelp website, www.yelp.com

Securing NFC Mobile Services with Cloud of Secure Elements (CoSE)

Pascal Urien[1] and Selwyn Piramuthu[2]

[1] Telecom ParisTech, UMR 5141,
23 Avenue d'Italie, 75013, France
[2] Information Systems and Operations Management,
University of Florida, Gainesville, FL 32611-7169, USA
pascal.urien@telecom-paristech.fr, selwyn@ufl.edu

Abstract. The availability of NFC smartphones has facilitated the development of a large number of related applications. Some of these NFC applications necessitate communication with other systems, which may not necessarily be secure, through communication channels and mechanisms that may be open to vulnerabilities. Security is therefore paramount to the success of these NFC mobile services. While Peer-to-Peer (P2P) communication mode is common in mobile NFC applications, it is vulnerable to security-related issues that arise from the use of untrusted devices for storage and to process applications. We propose the concept of a Cloud of Secure Elements (CoSE) where the secure services are hosted by servers rather than by smartphone Secure Elements. We discuss the use of CoSE for mobile payments. We also illustrate how an NFC smartphone may be efficiently used as a bridge between an NFC reader and an Internet server of secure microcontroller that hosts EMV applications.

Keywords: Cloud of Secure Elements, Secure Element, NFC, Security, Mobile Services.

1 Introduction

As the number of applications of smartphones with NFC increases, there is a concomitant need to secure these phones against vulnerabilities that arise from each additional application. Moreover, several applications together can expose the smartphone to new security weaknesses. We propose a new concept that we call the "Cloud of Secure Element" (CoSE) for securing NFC smartphones from vulnerabilities that are associated with the use of their Secure Elements or smartcards.

A smartcard is a tamper resistant micro-controller [1] whose security is enforced by multiple software and hardware countermeasures. It was invented in the 1980s to facilitate electronic payment in situations where both the merchant and the buyer were not connected. The BO' smartcard, used in France by the end of the 20th century generated cryptogram (based on a 3xDES algorithm), realizing the payment proof, and backed up every night via modem connections. Today's electronic payment technology deals with EMV [2] smartcards, that still generate cryptograms (based on

G. Memmi and U. Blanke (Eds.): MobiCASE 2013, LNICST 130, pp. 322–331, 2014.

the 3xDES algorithm) but in a context in which the merchant is connected while the buyer is offline. About 1.5 billion EMV bank cards are scheduled to be in service during 2013 [3]. Apart from the payment market, secure microcontrollers are used for access control purposes such as those that are used in transportation tickets or electronic keys.

Over the last several years, the EMV standard has supported contactless technology [4], named Near Field Communication (NFC [5]) based on inductive coupling at 13,56 Mhz. Furthermore, about one million NFC-enabled smartphones are manufactured every week; NFC modems are logically connected to a secure micro-controller (such as SIM modules) hosted EMV payment applications, and therefore able to perform payment transactions.

Because smartphones are more and more connected to the Internet, it becomes possible to remotely use secure microcontrollers by establishing a logical relay hosted in the mobile, between the NFC links (with a working distances of a few centimeters) and an Internet server hosting secure microcontrollers.

Relay techniques have been discussed in many research publications since 2005 [6][7][8]. Since relay techniques have the potential to create security threats, various countermeasures to such relay attacks have been studied, for example, based on signal round-trip measurements and evaluations [9].

We propose CoSE for mobile smartphones and illustrate this concept, using a platform that we developed using commercially available devices, for payment purposes. We illustrate how a mobile smartphone can be efficiently used as a bridge between a NFC reader and an Internet server of secure microcontroller hosting EMV applications. We also show how an (EMV) application may be downloaded and activated in the server and thereafter remotely used from the phone.

The rest of the paper is organized as follows: Since its introduction, NFC-enabled smartphones have been used in a wide variety of disparate applications. We discuss a select few NFC-enabled mobile smartphone applications in Section 2. NFC P2P applications constitute a majority among different available means. However, researchers and practitioners have identified several vulnerabilities in NFC P2P systems. We discuss some security issues associated with mobile NFC P2P applications in Section 3. We then present and briefly discuss the essentials of CoSE in Section 4. We conclude the paper with perspectives and future directions in Section 5.

2   NFC-Enabled Mobile Applications

With the availability of NFC-enabled mobile phones, both researchers and practitioners have been interested in exploring possible applications of these devices. NFC-enabled smartphones, for example, allows for automating processes (e.g., retail transactions, where these mobile phones provide secure interface between payment systems and retail systems).

Several researchers have considered the use of mobile phones with NFC for pervasive healthcare applications. For example, Sidén et al. [10] study tele-healthcare and assisted living where NFC-enabled mobile phones (Google Nexus S) interact with

RFID tags connected to appropriate sensors to automatically relay information such as the presence of new blood inside a bandaged wound, urine saturation in adult diaper, among others. Hancke and Opperman [11] consider remote monitoring and control systems using NFC and develop an interface that can be used with sensors (e.g., heart rate monitor). While Hancke and Opperman only develop an interface, Morak et al. [12] develop a prototype hardware platform for NFC-supported Bluetooth communication for acquisition and transmission of blood pressure and ECG. They use an analog ECG front-end and an off-the-shelf blood pressure monitor as sensors.

González et al. [13] propose and develop prototypes for the use of mobile phones with NFC and an NFC-phone-based interactive panel for learning environments through touching note, touching cabinet, and touching campus. These are used respectively for communication between teachers and students, increase ease of location of items in a cabinet, and interaction of students and campus buildings whereby the student can easily obtain information on a campus building that is in close physical proximity.

NFC-enabled mobile phones are also used for ticket payments. For example, Widmann et al. [14] discuss seamless integration of electronic ticketing system for public transportation using NFC mobile phones whereby the amount charged is computed based on entry and exit points registered when the NFC-enabled mobile phones are tapped at these points (check-in/check-out principle). They also discuss some issues or constraints with such use of NFC-enabled mobile phones for ticketing applications. For example, they lament the shortage of mobile phones that support card emulation mode and inaccessible secure elements due to issues with trusted service management.

Chaumette et al. [15] discuss the pros and cons of offline and online NFC-enabled mobile phone-based event-ticketing system in terms of user experience, security, economical aspects, reliability and speed of use. The online system requires the existence of Secure Element that stores and retrieves the static ticket identifier in the user's mobile device. In such an online system, no dynamic information (e.g., ticket) is stored in the mobile phone. The static ticket identifier is verified for successful user authorization by the back-end system that processes all dynamic information. The offline system, on the other hand, stores a copy of the ticket in digital format in the mobile phone and this ticket is transferred to the ticket verifier for successful authorization. Based on their evaluation, they find that both online and offline systems offer similar advantages, with a slight edge for the offline system in terms of speed of use and the online system providing a slight edge in terms of user experience.

There is an extensive set of literature on mobile payments using NFC-enabled mobile phones. For example, Mainetti et al. [16] observe the blocking of Secure Elements in mobile devices by smartphone and OS manufacturers and propose a peer-to-peer (P2P)-based framework for Android mobile phones that bypasses the need for special hardware. Monteiro et al. [17] also consider P2P mobile payment systems. Urien and Piramuthu ([18],[19]) present a suite of authentication protocols for NFC-based P2P retail store transaction processing. However, there are some issues in NFC P2P that need to be addressed. We discuss some of these in the next section.

3   Security of P2P Mobile NFC

Several vulnerabilities of P2P mobile NFC security have been identified over the past few years. These vulnerabilities range from relay attacks (e.g., [7]), eavesdropping attacks that are based on the weakness of applications that run in NFC, Denial of Service (DoS) attacks through saturation with communication requests when an on/off switch is not present, message modification attacks, implementation attacks (e.g., [20]), and attacks that are instantiated when the user loses the NFC device.

For example, Miller [20] performed fuzzing test and showed that (with high-level fuzzing) vulnerabilities in parsing of incoming message could be used to open a malicious web page, open an application, image, video, contacts, or documents without any interaction from the user. With a Nokia Meego, he initiated Bluetooth pairing, which allows for access of this device from farther away. Miller also showed that it is possible to take complete control of a mobile phone through NFC, resulting in stolen photos, contacts, as well as the use of this phone to send messages and make phone calls.

Although relay attacks are difficult to prevent using cryptography, this is an active area and we believe that there is some progress in this general area (e.g., [21])

Since NFC is a gateway to all associated devices, this too opens up opportunities for attacks from resourceful adversaries. For example, through fuzzing Mulliner [22] found a vulnerability in the processing of NDEF record payload length. He also discovered a means to spoof smart poster URI by inserting space, tab and newline characters into the title record. He observes that a man-in-the-middle attack can be easily mounted using a web-based proxy. He also created a proof-of-concept NFC worm, through the PushRegistry to intercept all URI NDEF messages, which is activated when a smart poster tag is read. A similar attack was illustrated at the 2012 RSA conference (e.g., [23]) with the modification of the NFC tag on a smart poster that resulted in the smartphone browser to open a phishing site. A variant of this attack was shown by [24] that allows an attacker to automatically execute USSD codes without the user's permission which could cause serious damage such as permanent kill of the SIM card, remote wipe, among others.

4   Cloud of Secure Elements

The experimental Cloud of Secure Elements platform comprises four elements.

- A service kiosk. It is a personal computer equipped with a contactless smartcard reader that is used to establish an NFC session in accordance with the reader/writer card-emulation paradigm. A free software (an EMV explorer tool) drives the reader and parses the content of a contactless EMV bank card
- A mobile. The smartphone is an NFC-enabled device (Nexus S), which supports the card emulation NFC mode. It runs a mobile application that establishes a logical relay between the kiosk and a remote grid of secure elements.

- A grid of secure elements (GoSE). It is a server (manufactured by [25]) that handles hundreds of smartcards. These secure microcontrollers host various trusted software, such as EMV payment applications.
- An administration console. It is a TCP/IP client that remotely manages the content of the smartcards hosted by the GoSE, thanks to protocols compliant with the Global Platform [26] standards

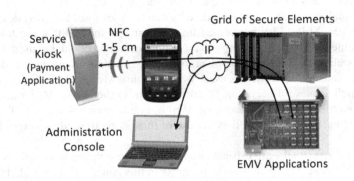

Fig. 1. A prototype of Cloud of Secure Elements

4.1 The Service Kiosk

The service kiosk is instantiated by a laptop equipped with a contactless smartcard reader. A free EMV explorer tool is used in order to parse and display the content of EMV NFC cards. This software works with physical PVC cards. It also transparently works with a mobile connected to the Grid of Secure Elements.

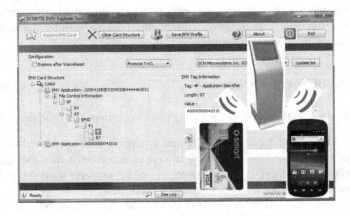

Fig. 2. The NFC service Kiosk

4.2   The Mobile

The platform works with an android smartphone (Nexus S), running the Gingerbread operating system. We use a software patch released by [27] providing software card emulation. It defines a new class, named "android.nfc.tech.IsoPcdA" that implements three procedures (connect, isConnected, and transceiver), similar to those available for the legacy android.nfc.tech.NfcA class.

A proxy application establishes a logical relay between the service kiosk and the GoSE. It is connected to the remote grid server, identified by its IP address and port number. Upon connection, it sends a hello-message, acknowledged by the server whose response packet may contain a request to setup a secure channel. This optional feature was not activated by the experimental platform.

When the mobile is tapped against the kiosk reader, a NFC link is established between the two devices. The kiosk (i.e. the EMV explorer tool) transmits ISO7816 [28] requests thereafter relayed by the proxy to a smartcard plugged in the GoSE, which returns ISO7816 responses.

Because this model of mobile supports NFC payment facilities (for example the Google Wallet), the service kiosk is generally not aware of the relay operations. However, counter measures based on round-trip time evaluations could possibly detect unusual computing latency when communication time dominates computing time by at least a few factors of magnitude, and is induced by heavy network traffic.

4.3   The Grid of Secure Elements

A Secure Element (SE) is a secure microcontroller, equipped with host interfaces such as ISO7816, SPI or I2C. The security is enforced by multiple logical and hardware countermeasures. Usually it runs a Java Virtual Machine (JVM) and therefore it is able to execute small applications (whose size is about a few 10KB) written in Java. The popular form factor for SE is smartcards, of which about 6 billion were produced in 2012 [3], for use in SIMs, bank cards, or passports.

Command	Topic
CONTENT	Return the list of used slots
USE	Select a slot
FREE	Release a slot
RESET	Reset a Secure Element
APDU	Send an ISO7816 request and get a response

Fig. 3. Summary of the SIM array commands

The grid of smartcards is a TCP/IP server that hosts a set of secure microcontrollers. Thanks to a dedicated Grid-Protocol, software running in these tamper-resistant devices may be handled from anywhere at any time.

Our server consists of a mother rack (SIM Array [25]) that manages up to 13 daughter boards, equipped with at most 32 smartcards. A single server holds a maximum of 416 SEs. Each SIM Array is connected to the Internet and has an IP address and manages a TCP server. An ASCII-oriented protocol, whose main commands are listed by figure 3, provides the functionalities needed for the grid inventory and the routing of ISO7816 commands toward a smartcard plugged in the server and identified by a number. Each SE is identified by its plugged slot number.

4.4   The Administration Console

During the grid lifecycle, it is required to download or remove applications in smartcards. The Global Platform committee [26] manages a set of standards to provide these services that include downloading applications, activation and deletion (see figure 4).

Commands	Topic
SELECT	Activate an embedded application. The Issuer Security Domain (ISD) is the application in charge of GP operations
INITIALIZE UPDATE	Initialize mutual authentication with ISD
EXTERNAL AUTHENTICATE	Ends mutual authentication with ISD
DELETE	Delete a package or an application
INSTALL	Allocate memory before package loading or instantiate an application
LOAD	Load a package

Fig. 4. Summary of the GP commands

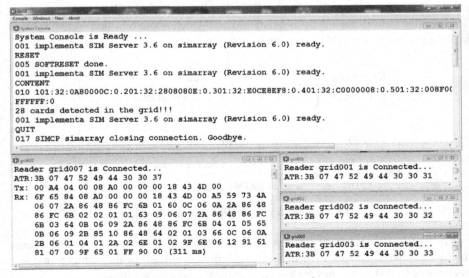

Fig. 5. The administration console

GPShell [24] is an open software running over the PC/SC API. It is a script interpreter that supports the main GP (version 2.0 and 2.1.1) facilities, illustrated by figure 5, and used to load, instantiate, delete, and list embedded applications in smartcards. The GPShell tool has been modified thanks to a logical bridge between PC/SC and the grid protocol. The administration console enables remote download, activate and delete embedded applications in secure micro-controllers. In the demonstration it is used for downloading or removing EMV software in the SIM array.

5   Perspectives and Future Works

This paper demonstrates that the Cloud of Secure Elements concept may work in the current technological landscape. Existing devices, such as NFC EMV cards, can be virtualized and readily migrated from consumer pockets towards the cloud.

NFC communications are not secure in terms of information privacy and integrity. As an illustration we are currently designing for NFC P2P a secure stack (named LLCPS [30]) based on the well-known TLS protocol.

Obviously there are no standards for data exchanges with the CoSE, both for service and management purposes. Furthermore the security of such sessions is a very sensitive topic. In a recent paper [31] we made a tentative list of issues that need to be solved in order to build and use secure cloud of secure elements. A first protocol (Remote APDU Call Secure – RACS) has been recently proposed in [34] in order to fulfill these requirements.

The CoSE technology could be used in the cloud, in order to provide a high trust environment, relying on tamper-resistant devices such as smartcards. This would offer an alternative to technologies based on Virtual HSM (Hardware Secure Module) described in [32].

European projects, like SecFuNet (Security for the Future Internet [33]), work toward this general direction.

References

[1] Jurgensen, T.M., et al.: Smart Cards: The Developer's Toolkit. Prentice Hall PTR (2002) ISBN 0130937304
[2] https://www.emvco.com/
[3] http://www.eurosmart.com/publications.html
[4] MasterCard® PayPass™, M/Chip, Acquirer Implementation Requirements, v.1-A4 6/06
[5] ISO/IEC 18092, Information technology - Telecommunications and information exchange between systems - Near Field Communication - Interface and Protocol (NFCIP-1) (April 2004)
[6] Hancke, G.: A Practical Relay Attack on ISO 14443 Proximity Cards (January 2005)
[7] Francis, L., Hancke, G., Mayes, K., Markantonakis, K.: Practical NFC peer-to-peer relay attack using mobile phones. In: Ors Yalcin, S.B. (ed.) RFIDSec 2010. LNCS, vol. 6370, pp. 35–49. Springer, Heidelberg (2010)

[8] Roland, M.: Applying recent secure element relay attack scenarios to the real world: Google Wallet Relay Attack, technical report (August 2012)

[9] Reid, J., et al.: Detecting Relay Attacks with Timing-Based Protocols. In: Proceedings of the 2nd ACM Symposium on Information, Computer and Communications Security (2007)

[10] Sidén, J., Skerved, V., Gao, J., Forsström, S., Nilsson, H.-E., Kanter, T., Gulliksson, M.: Home Care with NFC Sensors and a Smart Phone. In: Proceedings of the 4th International Symposium on Applied Sciences in Biomedical and Communication Technologies (ISABEL), vol. 150, pp. 1–5 (2011)

[11] Hancke, G.P., Opperman, C.: A Generic NFC-enabled Measurement System for Remote Monitoring and Control of Client-side Equipment. In: Proceedings of the Third IEEE International Workshop on Near Field Communication, pp. 44–49 (2011)

[12] Morak, J., Kumpusch, H., Hayn, D., Modre-Osprian, R., Schreier, G.: Design and Evaluation of a Telemonitoring Concept Based on NFC-Enabled Mobile Phones and Sensor Devices. IEEE Transactions on Information Technology in Medicine 16(1), 17–23 (2012)

[13] González, G.R., Organero, M.M., Kloos, C.D.: Early Infrastructure of an Internet of Things in Spaces for Learning. In: Proceedings of the Eighth IEEE International Conference on Advanced Learning Technologies (ICALT), pp. 381–383 (2008)

[14] Widmann, R., Gruenberger, S., Stadlmann, B., Langer, J.: System Integration of NFC Ticketing into an Existing Public Transport Infrastructure. In: Proceedings of the 4th International Workshop on Near Field Communication, pp. 13–18 (2012)

[15] Chaumette, S., Dubernet, D., Ouoba, J., Siira, E., Tuikka, T.: Architecture and Comparison of Two Different User-Centric NFC-Enabled Event Ticketing Approaches. In: Balandin, S., Koucheryavy, Y., Hu, H. (eds.) NEW2AN 2011 and ruSMART 2011. LNCS, vol. 6869, pp. 165–177. Springer, Heidelberg (2011)

[16] Mainetti, L., Patrono, L., Vergallo, R.: IDA-Pay: An Innovative Micro-Payment System Based on NFC Technology for Android Mobile Devices. In: Proceedings of the 20th IEEE International Conference on Software, Telecommunications and Computer Networks (SoftCOM), pp. 1–6 (2012)

[17] Monteiro, D.M., Rodrigues, J.J.P.C., Lloret, J., Sendra, S.: A Hybrid NFC–Bluetooth Secure Protocol for Credit Transfer among Mobile Phones. In: Security and Communication Networks (2013), doi:10.1002/sec.732

[18] Urien, P., Piramuthu, S.: Framework and Authentication Protocols for Smartphone, NFC, and RFID in Retail Transactions. In: Proceedings of the 8th IEEE International Conference on Intelligent Sensors, Sensor Networks and Information Processing (ISSNIP), pp. 77–82 (2013)

[19] Urien, P., Piramuthu, S.: LLCPS and SISO: A TLS-Based Framework with RFID for NFC P2P Retail Transaction Processing. In: Proceedings of IEEE International Conference on RFID, pp. 152–159 (2013)

[20] Miller, C.: Don't Stand So Close to Me: An Analysis of the NFC Attack Surface (July 25, 2012),
http://www.blackhat.com/usa/bh-us-12-briefings.html#miller

[21] Urien, P., Piramuthu, S.: Identity-Based Authentication to Address Relay Attacks in Temperature Sensor-enabled Smartcards. In: Proceedings of the European Conference on Smart Objects, Systems and Technologies (Smart SysTech), Erlangen/Nuremberg (2013)

[22] Mulliner, C.: Vulnerability Analysis and Attacks on NFC-enabled Mobile Phones. In: Fourth International Conference on Availability, Reliability and Security (ARES), pp. 695–700 (2009)

[23] Ries, U.: "Phishing via NFC," The H Security (March 2, 2012),
      http://www.webcitation.org/6BzrM8Qmp
[24] Borgaonkar, R.: USSD/Android Dailer vulnerability (June 2012),
      http://www.webcitation.org/6DW71H3uK
[25] http://www.implementa.com/products/sim-array
[26] http://www.globalplatform.org/
[27] Lee, E.: NFC Hacking: The Easy Way, DEFCON 20 (July 2012)
[28] ISO 7816, Cards Identification - Integrated Circuit Cards with Contacts
[29] http://sourceforge.net/p/globalplatform/wiki/GPShell/
[30] Urien, P.: LLCPS: A New Security Framework Based on TLS For NFC P2P Applications
      in the Internet of Things, IEEE CCNC 2013 (January 2013)
[31] Urien, P., Piramuthu, S.: Towards a Secure Cloud of Secure Elements Concepts and
      Experiments with NFC Mobiles. In Proceeding of the CTS 2013 Conference (May 2013)
[32] AWS CloudHSM Getting Started Guide, Kindle Edition, Amazon WEB Services (2013)
[33] SECFUNET, a research project funded by the European Commission's Framework
      Programme 7 and CNPq, the Brazilian National Council for Technological and Scientific
      Development, http://www.secfunet.eu
[34] IETF Draft, Remote APDU Call Secure (RACS), draft-urien-core-racs-00 (August. 2013)

Author Index

Adagale, Amul   1
Ahmed, Beena   252
Alcaine, Sheila   273
Arfaoui, Ghada   282
Argueta, Diego   314
Armoush, Ashraf   294

Banova, Vassilena   19
Bayés, Àngels   273
Beigl, Michael   140
Bertin, Emmanuel   33
Bessho, Masahiro   54

Cevada, João   273
Chihani, Bachir   33
Collange, Denis   33
Conchon, Emmanuel   166
Correia de Barros, Ana   273
Crespi, Noël   33

da Conceição, Arlindo F.   269
Davcev, Danco   277
Dorfmeister, Florian   122
dos Santos, Bruno G.   269
Draffin, Benjamin   184

Faily, Shamal   47
Falk, Tiago H.   33
Fernstrom, Mikael   265
Franke, Dominik   294
Franklin, Sue   265
Frauen, Sven   140

Galiana-Merino, Juan José   286
Gambs, Sébastien   282
Gordon, Dawud   140
Greenspun, Joseph   98
Guilbourd, Roman   90
Gustarini, Mattia   72
Gutierrez-Osuna, Ricardo   252

Hamze, Mohamad   166
Harrison, Rachel   47
Heggen, Scott   1
Higgins, Conor   265
Homann, Marcus   19

Iacob, Claudia   47
Iimura, Yoko   290

Jeon, Won   314
Julien, Christine   215

Kalkov, Igor   294
Kearns, Áine   265
Kim, Jee-Eun   54
Kim, John   233
Kojo, Yu   290
Koshizuka, Noboru   54
Kowalewski, Stefan   294
Krcmar, Helmut   19

Lacharme, Patrick   282
Lalande, Jean-Francois   282
Lecolinet, Eric   261
Lee, Jongin   233
Lee, Kwan Hong   233
Lescuyer, Roch   282
Lu, Yu-Ta   314

Ma, Jing   314
Maier, Marco   122
Mamani-Aliaga, Alvaro H.   269
Mendonça, Matheus F.   269
Mestre, Berta   273
Michel, Jonas   215
Mitreska, Elena   277
Mitreski, Kosta   277

Oelbermann, Paul   19
Oota, Masahiro   290
Ortiz, Javier   286

Paillès, Jean-Claude   282
Parnandi, Avinash   252
Payton, Jamie   1
Perrault, Simon T.   261
Peyrard, Fabrice   166
Phan, Thomas   104, 314
Piramuthu, Selwyn   322
Pister, Kristofer S.J.   98

Rocha, Vladimir   269
Rodriguez, Diego   314

Rojas, Raul   90
Roland, Michael   298
Ryan, Conor   265

Sakamura, Ken   54
Sánchez, Jimmy V.   269
Sentana, Irene   286
Shipp, Eva   252
Suo, Xiaoyuan   202

Tachimoto, Shinya   290
Tsiourti, Christiana   158

Urien, Pascal   322
ur Rehman Laghari, Khalil   33

Vieira, Dario   269

Wac, Katarzyna   72, 158
Wittges, Holger   19

Yang, Yuan-Hung   314

Zaragoza, Alejandro   286
Zhang, Joy   184
Zhu, Jiang   184